GREEN
Office Buildings
A Practical Guide to Development

Editor
Anne B. Frej

Primary Authors
William D. Browning
Patrick Curran
Anne B. Frej
Gregory H. Kats
Ann Moline
Ron Nyren
Kalvin Platt
Jenifer Seal
Leanne Tobias
Rod Wille

 **Urban Land Institute**

About ULI–the Urban Land Institute

ULI–the Urban Land Institute is a nonprofit education and research institute that is supported by its members. Its mission is to provide responsible leadership in the use of land in order to enhance the total environment.

ULI sponsors education programs and forums to encourage an open international exchange of ideas and sharing of experiences; initiates research that anticipates emerging land use trends and issues and proposes creative solutions based on that research; provides advisory services; and publishes a wide variety of materials to disseminate information on land use and development. Established in 1936, the Institute today has more than 26,000 members and associates from more than 80 countries representing the entire spectrum of the land use and development disciplines.

Richard M. Rosan
President

Project Staff

Rachelle L. Levitt
Executive Vice President, Policy and Practice
Publisher

Gayle Berens
Vice President, Real Estate Development Practice

Anne B. Frej
Office/Industrial Development
 Consultant
Project Director

Alexa Bach
Associate, Policy and Practice

Nancy H. Stewart
Director, Book Program

Barbara M. Fishel/Editech
Sandra F. Chizinsky
Manuscript Editors

David James Rose
Associate Editor

Betsy VanBuskirk
Art Director

Byron Holly
Senior Designer
Book Design/Layout

Diann Stanley-Austin
Director, Publishing Operations

Karrie Underwood
Administrative Manager

Recommended bibliographic listing

Frej, Anne B., editor. *Green Office Buildings: A Practical Guide to Development.* Washington, D.C.: ULI–the Urban Land Institute, 2005.

ULI Catalog Number: G13
International Standard Book Number: 978-0-87420-937-2
Library of Congress Control Number: 2005904468

Copyright 2005 by ULI–the Urban Land Institute
1025 Thomas Jefferson Street, N.W.
Suite 500 West
Washington, D.C. 20007-5201

Authors and Reviewers

Primary Authors

William Browning is a partner in Browning + Bannon LLC, a research and consulting firm focused on the development of green real estate projects and building products. He is a senior fellow of Rocky Mountain Institute, where he founded Green Development Services.

Patrick Curran, associate landscape architect with the SWA Group, focuses on urban wild land interfaces and the opportunities to use landscape as a means to solve contemporary infrastructure problems. He is a member of the American Society of Landscape Architects Sustainability Task Force and of the Society for Ecological Restoration, and he is a LEED-credited professional.

Anne B. Frej is a real estate market analyst and consultant to ULI–the Urban Land Institute. She has directed a variety of ULI publications on office and industrial development.

Gregory H. Kats is principal of Capital E, a national environmental and energy technology consulting firm, and the principal adviser in Green Communities, a five-year, $550 million initiative to build more than 8,500 environmentally healthy homes for low-income families. He formerly served as the director of financing for the Office of Energy and Renewable Energy at the U.S. Department of Energy.

Ann Moline is a business writer specializing in real estate and international economic development. She writes frequently on these topics for numerous national publications.

Ron Nyren is a Berkeley, California–based writing consultant who specializes in architecture and sustainable development issues, and is a frequent contributor to *Urban Land* magazine.

Kalvin Platt, chairman of the SWA Group, is a planner and architect with extensive experience in community and conservation planning and urban design. He is past vice chairman of the ULI Sustainable Development Council, a fellow of the American Institute of Architects, a member of the American Planning Association and the American Society of Landscape Architects, and former director of the Land Development Studio at the Harvard Graduate School of Design.

Jenifer Seal, principal, SeaCray Consulting, is a project manager with extensive experience in green development. She was formerly a principal at Rocky Mountain Institute where she directed green design consultation workshops and contributed to numerous publications, including *Green Development: Integrating Ecology and Real Estate* and its companion CD-ROM *Green Developments*.

Leanne Tobias is a commercial real estate expert with extensive experience in project development, investment acquisitions and sales, and property leasing and operations. She writes and speaks nationally on green real estate and sustainable development as a principal of Malachite LLC, and offers client-specific real estate consulting services as managing director of the Metis Group, a Washington, D.C., consulting company.

Rod Wille is senior vice president and national manager of sustainable construction for Turner Construction Company. He oversees the company's green resources and manages its Center of Excellence, which provides support to all 45 Turner Construction offices nationwide. Wille is a registered professional engineer and LEED-accredited professional.

Other Contributors

Christine Ervin
President
Ervin + Company
Portland, Oregon

Dan Heinfeld
President
LPA, Inc., LLC
Irvine, California

Jennifer Henry
LEED Program Manager for Neighborhood Developments
Blue Moon Urban Fellow
U.S. Green Building Council
Washington, D.C.

Alexis Karolides
Team Leader
Green Development Services
Rocky Mountain Institute
Snowmass, Colorado

Stuart Miner
Partner
Brownfield Partners, LLC
Denver, Colorado

Tim Martin
Partner
Drivers Jonas
London, England

Charles Lockwood
Writer
Topanga, California

Anita Molino
Principal
Bostonia Partners LLC
Boston, Massachusetts

Dan Winters
Founder
Evolution Partners
Washington, D.C.

Steve Zenker
Senior Managing Director
Valuation Advisory Services Practice
Cushman and Wakefield
Portland, Oregon

Reviewers
Anthony Bernheim
Principal, Green Design
SMWM Architects
San Francisco, California

Ann Cutner
Principal
IMA Design Group
Irvine, California

David Gottfried
Founder, U.S. and World Green Building Councils
President, WorldBuild
Berkeley, California

Donald Horn
Sustainable Design Program
Office of Applied Science
U.S. General Services Administration
Washington, D.C.

Kenneth Hubbard
Executive Vice President
Hines
New York, New York

Ronald M. Izumita
Chairman and Senior Principal
IMA Design
Irvine, California

Gwyn Jones
Marketing Manager
SmithGroup
Washington, D.C.

Libby Kavoulakis
Managing Member
The Metis Group
Washington, D.C.

Gregory Mella
Principal
SmithGroup
Washington, D.C.

Sheila Sheridan
Sheridan Associates
Plymouth, Massachusetts

Richard Tilghman
Senior Vice President
Pepper Construction
Chicago, Illinois

Mark Weintraub
Principal
Weintraub Associates
London, England

Alex Wilson
President
BuildingGreen, Inc.
Brattleboro, Vermont

Acknowledgments

In the several years between the initial conception of this book and its publication, the practice of "green" building has evolved considerably. Not only is the term more familiar to a wider audience, but also there are many more real-life examples to learn from. Significantly, it is no longer just government buildings or research laboratories or university facilities that are built with a concern for the environment. Today, there are more and more large-scale green offices. Often, these are built as corporate headquarters for companies with a mission of environmental responsibility, but increasingly, they are built on a speculative basis by developers who recognize that green buildings are good for the bottom line—as well as the environment.

Many thanks to the contributors of this book whose passion for green building motivated them to take the time from busy professional schedules to write chapters or review text or contribute information. Special gratitude goes to the chapter authors who gave generously of their knowledge. Thanks also to those who wrote feature boxes or shared information through interviews. In addition to the people listed here, there were many professionals who answered technical questions, pointed to further sources of information, and provided photographs. Anthony Bernheim of SMWM; Brian Lee of Skidmore, Owings & Merrill; Gregory Mella of SmithGroup; Lee Polisano of Kohn Pedersen Fox; Sandra Mendler of Hellmuth, Obata + Kassabaum; and Melissa Mizell and Nellie Reid of Gensler deserve thanks for their assistance with the chapter on design. Jennifer Fink from Gensler provided photos and project information. Dan Heinfeld of LPA, Inc., contributed several feature boxes as well as detailed information on two case studies in southern California. Much appreciation also goes to the review committee members who read chapter manuscripts and provided comments and clarifications that helped make the book more concise and more practical.

Rocky Mountain Institute (RMI) was an active collaborator in this project. Jenifer Seal (now Jenifer Seal Cramer) was instrumental in selecting case studies to be profiled and in researching and writing their descriptions, with assistance from Alexis Karolides. Both Jenifer and Bill Browning, formerly with RMI's green development services, contributed chapters and ideas on the direction the book should take in its early phases.

At ULI, recognition goes to Alexa Bach whose input ensured that all the pieces came together correctly. Thanks also to Rachelle Levitt for her encouragement and direction throughout the process, and to Gayle Berens whose insightful comments are always appreciated. The excellent editorial team put together and directed by Nancy Stewart included Barbara Fishel and Sandy Chizinsky, with David Rose providing strong assistance. Byron Holly created the book design and united all the parts under a rigorous deadline.

Finally, although it is impossible to name them, I wish to acknowledge the earlier generations of green building practitioners—the architects, builders, and others who were involved in various aspects of environmentally sustainable building before it had a name and a constituency as it does today.

Anne B. Frej
Project Director

Foreword

To be an environmentalist, it is essential to consider buildings—not only how they are constructed and furnished, but also where they are located and how they are accessed by the people who use them. The figures are sobering. By some estimates, buildings consume more than 40 percent of energy, 20 percent of landfills, 30 percent of water supplies, 20 percent of wood supplies and other limited resources. If we care about our future survival, then we must address the built environment.

Establishment of the U.S. Green Building Council in 1993 was a major step in recognizing the benefits of green buildings. This model is now under development all over the world, and the LEED certification program has become an international standard.

I used to think that the key to sustainability was to create more green buildings, particularly those recognized as the greenest by certification at the highest level, LEED Platinum. In an epiphany, however, I realized that buildings are really just a subset of life. In the bigger picture, the most important thing in life is life itself. I see life as the bull's-eye in the center of a series of concentric "value rings." The next ring around the core of our compass includes life-sustaining elements—fresh air, clean water, ample food, healthy soil, plentiful resources, and shelter. Once we have these essentials, we can aggregate to create communities, common systems, and methods of commerce and trade—the next ring. Products and services come next, and the outermost ring is luxury items. I believe almost all cultures would agree with these givens of value. Unfortunately, much of our economy today treats the outer ring as more important than life and the elements that sustain it.

How do our economy and the things we build contribute to value in society? We do not have to go far to learn that the ecological impact is devastating. Many of our products are damaging our environment and impacting the ability of society to sustain future life.

Most of us do not want to hear this grim message, and many of us in the developed world are shielded from the alarming issues of overpopulation and environmental degradation. These are enormous global trends, but they can easily be ignored when they do not visibly influence our day-to-day life. Yet recognition is growing that it is time for individuals, governments, and large corporations to treat our environment in a new way. Global corporate standards of environmental conduct and stewardship are growing, simultaneously with more available environmentally preferable products and a proliferation in green standards for buildings and products. These standards embrace the principles of life-cycle assessment—tracking the environmental impact of the full life of the things we make, from materials extraction to fabrication, shipping, installation, operation, and even disposal. Corporate stewardship goes even further, encompassing procurement, transportation policies, and employee equity. Most significant, the ultimate environmental performance of a product or company has started to affect not only its image but also its value and financial viability.

This book addresses the question of how to apply responsible environmental stewardship to our built environment, focusing on the places where many of us spend a huge proportion of our waking hours—the office. It provides a step-by-step guide to land planning, designing, constructing, and managing green buildings. It also provides useful background on the resources available from the federal government and from a multitude of recent books, periodicals, Web sites, and other sources.

Most of the focus in the real estate industry today is on how much green buildings cost; as Chapter 2 indicates, green buildings today typically cost no more than 2 percent more than a standard office building and often much less. But as pointed out in Chapter 7, income and valuation assessment is more appropriate than a narrow view of cost. High-performance green buildings can potentially increase a project's rate of return and improve its underlying property valuation in the marketplace. The case studies in Chapter 9 illustrate that through green building practices, it is possible to reduce energy costs and, at the same time, create market differentiation that can lead to increased rents, accelerated tenant lease-up periods, and lower vacancy rates. As illustrated here, creative property owners are now using green methods not only to design, construct, and manage their buildings but also to raise investor equity and lower the developer's out-of-pocket cash requirement. Green building can produce a higher internal rate of return for all parties. Banks and investors like Bank of America, PNC, and Goldman Sachs are already integrating green building principles into their own construction, and it is likely not long before these organizations will begin offering better loan terms, lower capitalization rates, and higher loan-to-value ratios for green buildings.

This book is an excellent starting point if you are new to the field of sustainable development, but it also provides the latest information and a multitude of examples that can be useful if you have been at it for a while. I sincerely hope that future editions will include your own personal green building case studies—depicting not only how you have enhanced your company's bottom line but also reduced your impact on the world's ecological footprint. My own experience in promoting green buildings changed my life. I found that the people I met along the way are fellow journeyers. They too want to integrate purpose and value into their lives, not just at home but also in their work.

Our time here is short. The key is to grasp hold and do the most with each day, each breath. As stewards of our family's future, it is important that we construct buildings that not only are functional but also are worthy of the life we have been given and able to stand up to an evaluation of our time here by future generations.

I wish you well in your life journey and encourage you to integrate sustainability into all that you do.

David Gottfried
President, WorldBuild
Founder, U.S. and World Green Building Councils

Contents

Glossary of Abbreviations

A&E–architecture and engineering
AIA–American Institute of Architects
ASHRAE–American Society of Heating, Refrigerating, and Air-Conditioning Engineers
ASTM–American Society for Testing and Materials
BAS–building automation system
BIDS–Building Investment Decision Support
BOMA–Building Owners and Managers Association
BOMI–Building Owners and Managers Institute
BREEAM–Building Research Establishment Environmental Assessment Method
CalPERS–California Public Employees' Retirement System
CBA–cost benefit analysis
C&D–construction and demolition
CFD–computational fluid dynamics
CMBS–commercial mortgage–backed security
DARPA–Defense Advanced Research Projects Agency
DCR–debt coverage ratio
DOE–(U.S.) Department of Energy
DSIRE–Database of State Incentives for Renewable Energy
EERE–Office of Energy Efficiency and Renewable Energy (DOE)
EMS–environmental management system
EPA–(U.S.) Environmental Protection Agency
EPAct–Energy Policy Act of 1992
EPP–environmentally preferable purchasing
ESPC–energy savings performance contract
FAR–floor/area ratio
FM–facilities management
FNS–Federal Network for Sustainability
GIS–geographic information system
GMP–guaranteed maximum price
GSA–(U.S.) General Services Administration
HVAC–heating, ventilation, and air conditioning
IAQ–indoor air quality
IEQ–indoor environmental quality

IFMA–International Facility Management Association
IPT–integrated product team
IRR–internal rate of return
ISDC–integrated sustainable design and constructability
ISO–International Organization for Standardization
LED–light-emitting diode
LEED–Leadership in Energy and Environmental Design
LTV–loan-to-value (ratio)
MEMS–microelectromechanical systems
MEPT–multi-employer property trust
NASA–(U.S.) National Aeronautics and Space Administration
NECPA–National Energy Conservation Policy Act
NEPA–National Environmental Policy Act of 1969
NOAA–(U.S.) National Oceanic and Atmospheric Administration
NPV–net present value
OFEE–(U.S.) Office of the Federal Environmental Executive
O&M–operations and maintenance
PBS–Public Buildings Service
PenRen–Pentagon Renovation Program
PUC–public utilities commission
PV–photovoltaic
PV–present value
RCRA–Resource Conservation and Recovery Act
R&D–research and development
RMI–Rocky Mountain Institute
SBS–sick building syndrome
SMUD–Sacramento Municipal Utility District
SPiRiT–sustainable project rating tool
T&D–transmission and distribution
TI–tenant improvement
UESC–utility energy-efficiency service contract
USDA–U.S. Department of Agriculture
USGBC–U.S. Green Building Council
VAV–variable air volume
VOC–volatile organic compound

chapter 1

Introduction

Introduction

Jenifer Seal,
William D. Browning,
and Anne B. Frej

In the last two decades, the green building movement made an enormous leap forward. Environmentally sustainable projects representing every sector of the real estate industry have been constructed around the world. Leading-edge developers, designers, and other professionals have generated volumes of information on these high-performance buildings: case studies documenting the lessons learned; green building criteria; standards and certification programs for buildings, products, and materials; technical manuals; and sophisticated modeling tools. Trade associations have formed around various green topics, and governments have created standards and implemented incentive programs. It is clear that the real estate industry is on the cusp of a tremendous change that will affect our places of work and daily life in the coming decades.

The JohnsonDiversey headquarters in Sturtevant, Wisconsin, was designed and built in the late 1990s before the advent of many green building systems and products that are available today. Even so, the project was completed ahead of schedule and under budget. Indoor air quality and natural daylighting are two of the building's notable features. JohnsonDiversey

Winston Churchill's comment that has been so widely quoted in years past rings true: "We shape our buildings, and afterwards our buildings shape us." Developers have an opportunity to direct change in a way that will benefit not only their investments but also society and the ecosystems of which we are all a part.

Just as developers in the decade after World War II largely defined the built environment that existed at the end of the 20th century, so too will today's developers make a major mark on society in the years to come. To quote the late Jim Rouse, one of the 20th century's visionary developers, "We are invited to correct the past, to build places that are productive for business and for the people who live there, places that are infused with nature and stimulating to man's creative sense of beauty—places that are in scale with people and so formed as to encourage and give strength to the real community [that] will enrich life; build character and personality; promote concern, friendship, brotherhood."[1]

What Is a Green Office Building?

Green buildings *are* different from conventional buildings. Attention to design and engineering detail and an emphasis on performance often combine to create a building that is better than the sum of its parts.

Unlike a conventional building development in which members of the development team work individually, the green design process requires a highly integrated approach involving all members of the development team—devel-

Eastgate in Harare, Zimbabwe, was designed to take advantage of its location in a tropical high-altitude climate with sunny days and cool nights. It features thick exterior walls, solar panels, precast concrete sunscreens, and a cost-saving ventilation system that takes advantage of the difference between daytime and nighttime temperatures to flush hot air out of the building through ducts and chimneys. Mick Pearce, Pearce McComish Architects

oper, project manager, architects, landscape architects, engineers, contractor, facility manager, and others. Experience has shown that this collaborative approach leads to solutions that might not have been possible in a traditional development process.

Higher upfront costs were often associated with the first generation of green buildings because of, among other factors, the more intensive design approach and the need to use new or untested technologies. In recent years, however, higher first costs for green offices are less common as project development team members gain valuable experience with green projects. Just a few years ago, green office buildings were considered "pioneering," and new technologies and materials often had to be created from scratch. Today's architects, engineers, and developers can benefit from the

lessons learned by their predecessors. They can also take advantage of a wide variety of now-mainstream products that have been developed to meet criteria for building sustainability and performance. For example, when the state of California constructed a building for the Department of Education in Sacramento in the 1990s, few furniture and carpet products met the strict emission standards. But with a $60 million contract at stake, manufacturers had the incentive to create sustainable products. Today, many members of the carpet industry are in the forefront of the change to sustainable products.

Any higher upfront costs for green building features are often offset by savings on equipment such as smaller heating, ventilation, and air-conditioning (HVAC) systems or reduced ductwork for air conditioning. As illustrated in Chapter 2, evidence is growing that considerable future savings can be associated with green buildings.

Currently, green offices are priced competitively with comparable conventional buildings. At the 624,000-square-foot (58,000-square-meter) Toyota Motor Sales North American Headquarters in Torrance, California, green features were "cost neutral"; that is, they did not affect the overall cost of the facility.

Green offices offer a wide variety of features that make them environmentally sustainable. Although no rigid definitions apply, certain certification systems such as LEED (Leadership in Energy and Environmental Design) and BREEAM (Building Research Establishment Environmental Assessment Method) used around the world offer guidelines and ways of measuring how sustainable a building is (see feature box). In broad terms, they share the following characteristics.

Respect for Their Environment and Setting

Whether located on a suburban greenfield site or in the middle of a dense downtown, green buildings respect their environment and setting—and often they enhance it. The PNC Firstside building located on a formerly underused brownfield site in central Pittsburgh has brought new life and activity to its surroundings. The Gewerbehof Prisma mixed-use development in Nuremberg, Germany, helped spur the revitalization of its inner-city neighborhood. Construction of the Tuthill Corporate Center in Burr Ridge, Illinois, included restoration of on-site wetlands and the native prairie landscape.

Efficient Use of Resources

Green buildings are designed and engineered to conserve materials and resources such as water and energy. Often, the results are striking. The Philip Merrill Environmental Center in Chesapeake, Maryland, uses 90 percent less water than a conventional office of the same size. The 37-story Bank One Corporate Center in downtown Chicago has achieved a 15 percent reduction in energy attributable to its innovative under-floor air delivery system. The Johnson-Diversey headquarters is estimated to save more than $100,000 per year as a result of lower energy consumption, and the California Department of Education Building in Sacramento is projected to save $400,000 annually in energy costs.

Green buildings are also constructed so as to minimize waste and promote recycling. During construction of the University of Texas School of Nursing and Student Community Center in Austin, Texas, more than three-quarters of the previous building on the site was reused or recycled. A focus on scaling down mechanical systems such as air conditioning is also common to green offices. By paying attention to building orientation, insulation, windows, and lighting, it is often possible to install smaller systems, resulting in lower construction costs and the possibility of reduced energy costs in the future.

Use of Environmentally Preferable Materials

The environmentally preferable materials used in green offices are chosen with a number of criteria in mind: sensitivity to the environment, durability, and energy use.

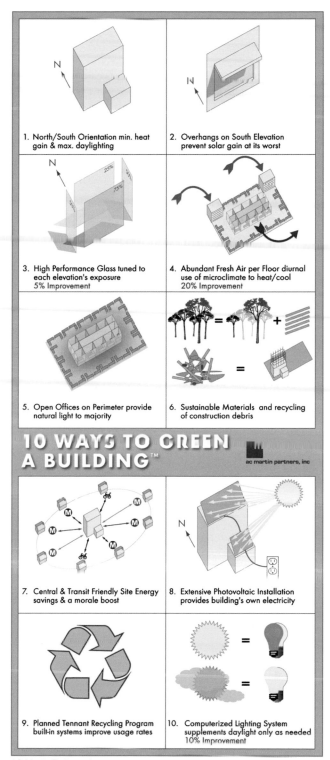

1. North/South Orientation min. heat gain & max. daylighting
2. Overhangs on South Elevation prevent solar gain at its worst
3. High Performance Glass tuned to each elevation's exposure 5% Improvement
4. Abundant Fresh Air per Floor diurnal use of microclimate to heat/cool 20% Improvement
5. Open Offices on Perimeter provide natural light to majority
6. Sustainable Materials and recycling of construction debris

10 WAYS TO GREEN A BUILDING™ ac martin partners, inc

7. Central & Transit Friendly Site Energy savings & a morale boost
8. Extensive Photovoltaic Installation provides building's own electricity
9. Planned Tennant Recycling Program built-in systems improve usage rates
10. Computerized Lighting System supplements daylight only as needed 10% Improvement

AC Martin Partners, Inc.

Measuring Sustainability: LEED®

Jennifer Henry

Measuring the level of sustainability is key to knowing the effectiveness of green design. The most respected and established independent measurement system in the United States is the LEED Green Building Rating System. Developed by the U.S. Green Building Council, a non-profit organization formed by building industry leaders to promote environmentally responsible buildings, the LEED system provides a voluntary consensus-based standard for high-performance sustainable buildings. LEED is transforming the marketplace by providing a catalyst, guidelines, and a system of recognition to promote integrated, whole-building design in the building industry.

At the core of the LEED rating system is building certification. The certification process has several steps, the first of which is to register the project, preferably during the early phases of design. Registration provides access to USGBC resources, including online tools. The next step is for the design team to document the project's sustainable measures to show that they have satisfied LEED's credit requirements.

LEED evaluates building performance in six categories: sustainable sites, water efficiency, energy and atmosphere, materials and resources, indoor environmental quality, and innovation and design. Each category includes a number of "credits" that a given project can aim to achieve. To be awarded a credit, projects must fulfill the specified requirements and submit the prescribed documentation associated with the credit. USGBC reviews completed building projects against the established LEED criteria and

recognizes their achievements at four levels—Certified, Silver, Gold, and Platinum—with each level of certification requiring a higher number of credits.

In the United States, LEED has quickly been accepted as the national standard for green building design, construction, and operations in new and existing commercial, institutional, and high-rise residential buildings. Each new LEED certification brings greater awareness of green building benefits and demonstrates the broad applicability of green building practices. As of September 2004, more than 1,500 public, private, and nonprofit building owners sought certification of their projects—from office buildings to schools and laboratories to restaurants—in all 50 states and in ten countries. Federal, state, and local government entities as well as private corporations are now formalizing their commitment to better building practices by requiring LEED certification for their buildings.

Analyzing the cost of LEED can be complex, but in most cases, going for certification pays off rapidly while it ensures optimal building performance. Any additional costs, including fees to register and certify the project, and the time necessary for the design team to prepare its application for certification are usually more than offset by numerous savings and benefits. LEED certification provides access to a number of USGBC resources, and, more important, it provides an objective measurement tool. LEED validates that designers and builders have achieved a certain level of performance and helps owners communicate the benefits to stakeholders with a nationally recognized

brand. As further recognition of their accomplishments, owners of LEED-certified buildings also qualify for a growing number of state and local incentives, including tax rebates and density bonuses. Many green building strategies safeguard not only the environment and occupants' health but also the bottom line. Green buildings have demonstrated savings in life-cycle operating costs as well as gains in employees' productivity, tenancy rates, retail sales, and student test performance.

LEED strives to achieve a balance between established practices and emerging concepts. As a result, market demand for new standards continues to drive the evolution of LEED; LEED Version 2.1 for new commercial construction was released in 2002, and USGBC member committees are working to update and adapt the rating criteria for LEED Version 2.2 and to develop other LEED rating systems for other market segments. Rating systems for ongoing building maintenance and operations (LEED for Existing Buildings) and tenant improvement projects (LEED for Commercial Interiors) were released in 2005. LEED for Core and Shell, for building owners who do not make decisions affecting tenants' space, is currently being piloted and will be launched soon, while LEED for Homes and LEED for Neighborhood Developments are under development and should be piloted soon.

As part of the LEED program, USGBC offers comprehensive resources and services to facilitate widespread adoption of green building practices and support building certification. As of September 2004, LEED workshops—introductory through advanced—held across North America have educated nearly 20,000 building professionals about LEED and sustainable design. The LEED Reference Guide, a complete sustainable design guide and user's manual for the rating system, describes the performance standards, documentation requirements, recommended strategies, and available resources for each credit in detail. The LEED Professional Accreditation program identifies individuals with green building expertise in the marketplace. LEED-Accredited Professionals have the knowledge of green building practices and principles and the familiarity with LEED requirements, resources, and the process needed to guide projects to certification. As of August 2004, the program had accredited nearly 17,000 professionals.

Although LEED offers many advantages, it is best not to use any rating system to drive the design process or to try to accumulate points in individual categories at the expense of an integrated approach that responds to the specific context and program. To this end, LEED workshops and training materials stress the importance of using an integrated design and build approach as early as possible when planning a new construction project. Using LEED as a checklist does not guarantee sustainable results; having a design team with experience in and a deep commitment to sustainable projects is essential.

For more information about using LEED to design, build, and operate buildings that are better for people, the planet, and the bottom line, visit www.leedbuilding.org or www.usgbc.org.

BREEAM (BRE Environmental Assessment Method)

Tim Martin

BREEAM is a well-established system developed by the Building Research Establishment (BRE) to assess the environmental performance of buildings. BRE is the United Kingdom's leading center of expertise on building construction and the environment and has been operating the BREEAM system for more than ten years. It has become the industry standard for sustainable design, representing the industry's best practices.

BREEAM assesses the performance of buildings in several areas:
- Overall management policy, commissioning, and procedure;
- Operational energy and carbon dioxide issues;
- Indoor and external issues affecting health and well-being;
- Air and water pollution;
- Transport-related carbon dioxide issues and location-related factors;
- Greenfield and brownfield issues;
- Ecological value of the site;
- Environmental implications of building materials, including life-cycle impacts; and
- Consumption and water efficiency.

Buildings are rated across these nine areas, and environmental weightings are applied to give a total score for the building. This score allows buildings to be classified on a scale of Pass, Good, Very Good, or Excellent. A BREEAM Certificate recording the building's environmental assessment can be used to promote the building and the organizations involved.

BREEAM gives designers, builders, and owners a quick, visible, and comprehensive benchmark for the industry to compare the sustainability and environmental performance of individual buildings. It allows parties involved in the development process, from planners to end users, to demonstrate the building's environmental credentials against established environmental standards, thus promoting environmental improvement industrywide.

Historically, BREEAM has had a strong association with office buildings, but assessment schemes for industrial units, supermarkets, and homes are growing in popularity. Specialized versions of BREEAM are used to assess other building types such as leisure centers and laboratories.

BREEAM is a voluntary scheme available for implementation on any of these types of building. The formal assessments are carried out by licensed assessors trained and licensed by BRE. BRE retains responsibility for the scheme, training for assessors, and quality assurance of the procedures.

For more information, see www.breeam.org

Jennifer Henry is LEED program manager for Neighborhood Developments, and Blue Moon Urban Fellow at USGBC.

Tim Martin is a partner at Drivers Jonas in London, England.

The headquarters of ING Bank (formerly known as NMB), completed in 1987, was one of the first large-scale green buildings in Europe. Rather than conventional air conditioning, it relies on a passive cooling system with backup absorption chiller—a feat for a building of this size. © William Browning, RMI

employees. Features such as ample natural lighting, opportunities for individual climate control, and materials that emit little or no toxic gas promote a healthier environment than typically found in conventional office buildings.

Focus on Flexibility and Adaptability

Flexible designs that look beyond the typical 20-year life cycle of an office building and include the possibility of future modifications are important factors that help save money and resources. For example, heating and air-conditioning systems that can use either natural gas or electricity take advantage of the lowest utility prices. Combined air-conditioning and natural ventilation systems can operate alternately, depending on cooling needs.

Ventilation systems used in green buildings often use cutting-edge solutions to ensure energy efficiency. At the Eastgate complex in Harare, Zimbabwe, the building's cooling system is modeled after African termite mounds, in which air is cooled below the earth and then drawn upward through chimneys, forcing hot air out. The Pier 1 building in San Francisco uses a heat exchanger that is cooled by water from the San Francisco Bay.

According to Environmental Building News, publisher of *GreenSpec Directory*, green products should meet at least one of six criteria:

■ Be made from salvaged, recycled, or agricultural waste content;

■ Conserve natural resources;

■ Reduce environmental impacts during construction, demolition, or renovation;

■ Save energy or water;

■ Contribute to a safe, healthy indoor environment; and

■ Avoid toxic or other emissions.

Provision of a Healthy and Comfortable Setting for Employees

Through attention to features that influence employees' comfort and health, green buildings are often recognized as promoting high morale and improved productivity among

Performance-Based Building Management and Monitoring

Green buildings benefit from the use of sophisticated computer modeling systems to determine optimal solutions for such features as building shape and orientation, mechanical and electrical systems, windows, and internal lighting. Analyses during the early design phases can help guide the design and engineering process and result in savings over the years. Many green buildings use systems that monitor and manage energy use. Equipment such as occupancy sensors that control internal lighting and window blinds controlled by automatic sun sensors help conserve energy and costs.

The Birth of Modern "Green Building"

In 1973, the environmental movement of the late 1960s and 1970s crashed headlong into the Arab oil embargo and America suddenly had an "energy crisis." The energy crisis was most noticeable in the way it affected transportation energy, but it also made an impression on the building industry; the notion that fossil fuels could indefinitely power large HVAC systems was suddenly challenged.

During the energy crisis, much more attention was paid to energy costs, and an early generation of "green" buildings was constructed. For example, Hines constructed several office buildings in Midland, Texas, with green features, including an orientation away from direct sun exposure, dual pane reflective glass, and energy-efficient interior lighting.

Environmentally friendly building construction and management had become part of the federal mandate as far back as 1969 (see Chapter 8). Although the definition of "environmentally friendly" or green development was still very much in its infancy, the National Environmental Policy Act of 1969 dictated that federal agencies incorporate such techniques.

For much of the private sector in the United States, though, the general environmental movement of the 1970s did not catch on immediately; in fact, it floundered well into the 1980s. As architect James Wines noted in *Green Architecture,* "exploitative politics of 'supply side' economics and its recklessly self-serving environmental policies" dominated social and political life,' and it took several environmental disasters in the late 1980s and early 1990s to bring resource issues back to center stage. As many people are now witnessing major environmental events on an annual (or more regular) basis, it is likely that how humans treat the world will remain at center stage.

The Confederation of Indian Industry–Godrej Green Business Centre in Hyderabad, India, was the first building outside the United States to receive the highest LEED Platinum rating by the U.S. Green Building Council. It combines advanced green technologies with traditional design and construction techniques. CII and Karan Grover

Lessons from the Energy Crisis

Christine Ervin

A little more than a decade ago, high-performance green buildings were as hard to define as they were to locate. There were no common standards, guidelines, or other tools needed to nurture an emerging market. There was no ENERGY STAR program, which would usher in a whole new way of marketing public/private partnerships to boost environmental and economic performance. There was no LEED green building rating system to put market-savvy tools in the hands of building teams eager to practice integrated building design.

All that has changed. Green building has emerged as one of the most powerful market transformations affecting the building industry in decades. But it might have been a different story without the energy crisis of the 1970s.

When OPEC imposed its oil embargo on the United States in October 1973, President Nixon called upon Americans to unite behind "Project Independence," a plan to free America from imported oil by 1980. In addition to driving less, citizens were urged to lower thermostats and cut unnecessary lighting. That pronouncement paved the way for major infusions of public and private dollars for energy research—including energy efficiency and renewable energy. In 1974, the Solar Energy Research Institute was formed. And in 1977, President Carter announced a national energy plan with major emphasis on conservation and renewable energy. Suddenly, "sustainable" energy became a promising field for architects, engineers, builders, manufacturers, scientists, and policy analysts.

We learned a good deal from that national emergency. Many of today's leaders in the green building movement started their careers in those heady days of the 1970s and early 1980s. Building energy codes and professional design standards quickly adopted new demands for energy efficiency. Entrepreneurs in the building industry produced new structures and technologies that cut energy use—sometimes by large margins. Such advances, coupled with economic structural changes, finally decoupled the connection between economic growth and consumption of energy. We were now producing more with less—the harbinger of good things to come.

Of course, many of the trials and errors expected with market innovations occurred, some of which were exacerbated by swings in policy and levels of financial investment. Early solar applications lacked the infrastructure to keep them operating well. Early fluorescent lights were unattractive and noisy. Too many new office buildings were drabber, darker, and draftier with a narrow focus on "tightening up" structures without corollary principles of integrated design. Slowly and surely, however, new products emerged, new techniques were advanced (sometimes old techniques were relearned), and architects demonstrated the beauty of green building. With the emergence of ENERGY STAR and LEED years later, new models of private/public partnerships and market-driven tools would transform the market.

How can we explain the success of green buildings today? Certainly, the phenomenon reflects the happy convergence of proven tools, technologies, expertise, and a ready market—all built over several decades and sparked initially by a national energy emergency. But in the end, the market thrives because farsighted businesses see boundless opportunities from enhancing the quality of life for building occupants and communities. As the real estate community asserts an even stronger leadership role, a whole new chapter about the evolution of green buildings will be written.

Christine Ervin was assistant secretary of energy from 1993 to 1997 and president and CEO of USGBC from 1999 to 2004.

A larger shift toward efficiency in buildings began in the early 1980s. Early efforts in energy modeling allowed designers to more accurately project how buildings would perform under a variety of conditions. In addition, technological advances led to the advent of more efficient products such as electronic ballasts, compact fluorescent lamps, and low-e coatings for windows. At this time, "green" building projects typically focused on a single issue, for the most part energy. Efficiency measures were typically tacked on, not fully integrated design concepts. In contrast, the Western Building in Pittsburgh, a partial double-skin design by Burt Hill Kosar Rittleman, and the Gregory Bateson State Office Building, a large daylit passive solar building designed by Sim van der Ryn and Peter Calthorpe for the state of California, are examples of pioneering projects with well-integrated design.

Concerns about indoor air quality began to emerge as buildings were more tightly sealed for efficient heating and cooling. The off-gassing of building materials such as carpets and glues and the 1990s movement against smoking in the United States helped bring this discussion to the fore. "Sick building syndrome" (SBS)—characterized by widely varying symptoms including dizziness, headaches, irritated eyes, nausea, throat irritation, and coughing—increasingly made headlines. Ironically, SBS was first highly publicized in the early 1990s after a large number of employees at the Environmental Protection Agency's (EPA's) newly remodeled building in Washington, D.C., became sick. Off-gassing from new carpeting, cleaning solutions, and glue was ultimately found to be the culprit.

Toward the end of the 1980s, the industry began to more comprehensively integrate the array of green building principles. Some of the first truly integrated green design projects included the interiors of the Natural Resources Defense Council and the Environmental Defense Fund buildings, both in New York City, and the NMB bank (now ING bank) in Amsterdam. The Audubon renovation project in New York City by the Croxton Collaborative was the most comprehensive integration project of the early 1990s. Closely tied to their missions, many of the first true green building office projects were spearheaded by organizations dedicated to environmental concerns.

A focus on green building in the trade organizations started in the energy subgroups. The first coalescence around environmentally responsible design happened in the American Institute of Architects (AIA) with the creation of the Committee on the Environment (COTE) in 1990, led by architect Robert Berkebile. With the thought that green building could benefit from a broader network than just architects, developer David Gottfried and attorney Michael Italiano in 1993 started the U.S. Green Building Council (USGBC) to formalize a cross-industry coalition on green building advocacy with representatives from the real estate development, engineering, design, manufacturing, and construction industries, environmental organizations, technical consultants, nongovernmental organizations, and the government. Once the organizational infrastructure across the various sectors of the industry was established, USGBC then set out to tackle the creation of a common definition of "green design" and a rating system that set standards for measuring it. Over several years with input from some of the burgeoning industry's leaders, the LEED green building rating system was born.

In 2003, USGBC celebrated its tenth anniversary, and by 2005, council membership grew to almost 6,000, with an operating budget of more than $20 million and a staff of 60. More than 60 chapters operate around the United States, and 13 countries use LEED as a certification tool. Gottfried founded the World Green Building Council in 1998 to expand the successful council model to other countries. The nonprofit federation of national green building councils now has nine members, including the United States, India, Canada, Mexico, Australia, Japan, Spain, Brazil, and Taiwan. In 2004, USGBC and the Ministry of Construction in China signed a memorandum of understanding to create the China Green Building Council.

The LEED rating system is realizing tremendous success, encompassing great diversity in building types, ownership, and geography. As of 2005, more than 200 million square feet (18.6 million square meters) of commercial space was registered with USGBC. These thousands of projects represent about 5 percent of the new construction market, according to USGBC. The misconception persists, however, that most LEED projects are operated by the government; in fact, more than half are undertaken by private companies and nonprofit organizations.

Bringing More Green to Bryant Park

New York City's Bryant Park, an oasis of green in midtown Manhattan, will welcome a new green building to the neighborhood. On August 2, 2004, Bank of America and the Durst Organization, a New York City–based real estate firm, broke ground for construction of the Bank of America Tower at One Bryant Park.

The 945-foot (290-meter) tower, directly across Sixth Avenue from the park, between 42nd and 43rd streets, is being billed as "the world's most environmentally responsible high-rise office building" and will seek Platinum certification under the U.S. Green Building Council's LEED program. The glass, steel, and aluminum skyscraper, to be constructed largely of recycled and recyclable building materials, will feature a wide range of sophisticated environmental technologies, including filtered under-floor displacement air ventilation, advanced double-wall technology, and translucent insulating glass in floor-to-ceiling windows. It also will include an on-site 4.6-megawatt cogeneration plant that will provide the building with clean, efficient energy.

The tower will reduce water requirements through use of a graywater system to capture and reuse all rain and wastewater and will feature planted roofs to help mediate the urban heat island effect. A thermal storage system will produce ice in the evenings to reduce the building's peak demand loads on the city's electrical grid, and daylight dimming and light-emitting diode lighting will reduce electricity use. Finally, carbon dioxide monitors will automatically introduce more fresh air into the building when necessary.

Designed by New York City–based Cook + Fox Architects, the tower will be 52 sto-ries tall and have 2.1 million square feet (195,000 square meters) of space, including six major securities trading floors ranging from 43,000 to 99,000 square feet (4,000 to 9,200 square meters). Bank of America will occupy roughly half the space. Also in the building will be the 50,000-square-foot (4,600-square-meter) restored and reconstructed Henry Miller Theater and 1 million square feet (93,000 square meters) of office space for other tenants.

Cook + Fox's design casts the building as a multifaceted crystalline structure featuring sculptural surfaces with folds and vertical lines that will be animated by the movement of the sun and the moon. The building will be transparent, with floor-to-ceiling windows and a clear glass curtain wall. In addition, the building's form will be sculpted to provide a south-facing surface to address its prominent relationship to Bryant Park and to permit views into and out of the structure.

The work will include preservation and restoration of the Georgian-style landmark facade of the Henry Miller Theater; the oval reception room, doors, and decorative plasterwork will be salvaged and incorporated into the new design. The goal is to create a state-of-the-art Broadway playhouse that captures the intimacy and proportions of the original 1918 Allen, Ingalls & Hoffman Theater.

In the public realm, the area around the tower will include widened sidewalks, street furniture, and an urban garden room at 43rd Street and Sixth Avenue that will serve as an extension of Bryant Park. The design also incorporates a new glass-enclosed subway entrance with wider stairs and an elevator at 42nd Street on the southeast corner of Sixth Avenue. An underground pedestrian

The 52-story One Bryant Park is designed with advanced double-wall technology and translucent insulating glass. © dbox studio for Cook + Fox Architects

walkway on the north side of 42nd Street will link the B, D, and F subway lines to the Times Square station, and a new mid-block subway entrance on 42nd Street will connect to the below-grade walkway.

The tower is scheduled to open in 2008.

Reprinted with permission from **Urban Land,** *September 2004, published by* **ULI–the Urban Land Institute.**

The London Bridge Tower, designed by Renzo Piano, includes 26 floors of office space as well as hotel, residential, retail, and restaurant uses. A ventilated double-skin facade reduces heat gain. Excess heat generated by the offices can be provided to the hotel and apartment uses above. Hayes Davidson and John MacLean

One of the landmark integrated green projects of the 1990s that incorporated LEED standards is the 250,000-square-foot (23,000-square-meter) office and laboratory for JohnsonDiversey's worldwide headquarters in Sturtevant, Wisconsin (see Chapter 9). Built on a fast-track schedule, the project was completed for 15 percent less than the average for U.S. offices and laboratory buildings and saved $4 million in capital costs. The building's architect, Bill O'Dell of HOK, commented that the initial goal-setting sessions and up-front interdisciplinary design approach were instrumental in the project's success. In 2003, the building was awarded the new LEED for Existing Buildings Gold rating.

In 1992, the ENERGY STAR program developed by the U.S. EPA came onto the scene. The program analyzes, tests, and rates the energy efficiency of 40 categories of products; it was extended in 1998 to include office buildings submitted for ENERGY STAR certification. To become certified, a building must be among the top 25 percent of all comparable buildings in the United States in terms of energy efficiency. The impact of this program for buildings alone has been enormous. Two thousand offices, schools, hospitals, and other kinds of nonresidential buildings covering about 400 million square feet (37.2 million square meters) had earned the ENERGY STAR label through 2004. By cutting energy use 40 percent on average, these buildings save an estimated $200 million in energy bills annually—or, in terms of greenhouse gases, the equivalent of removing emissions from 500,000 cars each year.

Throughout the 1990s, groups such as USGBC made great strides in taking green building to a sophisticated level and in articulating the reasons—beyond the moral argument—that the real estate industry should build green.

Now scores of green projects from every sector of real estate development with broad international representation have been built, including the University of Texas School of Nursing in Houston, the new communities of Stapleton in Denver and the former Athletes' Village for the 2000 Olympics in Sydney, the Beddington zero-energy development in London, the CII-Sohrabji Godrej green business center in Hyderabad, the David L. Lawrence Convention Center, and the Boston Park Plaza Hotel. Pushing the envelope are such prominent projects as Ford Motor Company's Rouge Plant, the Durst Organization's One Bryant Park, and Tishman Speyer's Goldman Sachs world headquarters in New York City.

Financial Benefits of Green Buildings: Summary of Findings (per Square Foot)

Category	20-Year NPV
Energy Value	$5.79
Emissions Value	$1.18
Water Value	$0.51
Waste Value (construction only)—1 year	$0.03
Commissioning O&M Value	$8.47
Productivity and Health Value (Certified and Silver)	$36.89
Productivity and Health Value (Gold and Platinum)	$55.33
Less Green Cost Premium	($4.00)
Total 20-year NPV (Certified and Silver)	**$50.00**
Total 20-year NPV (Gold)	**$65.00**

Source: Capital E analysis.

Why Build Green?

Real estate represents one-third of all global wealth; it largely defines our cities and rural areas. It is the physical manifestation of humankind's imprint on Earth, and it literally affects everyone.

Open space, farmland, wildlife habitat, and wetlands are disappearing at a rate of more than 2 million acres (810,000 hectares) every year in the United States—an area more than twice the size of Rhode Island. Many states have lost a huge percentage of their farms over the last 50 years. Connecticut, for example, had 22,240 farms in 1944 but just 3,500 by 1987—a decrease of 83 percent. Today, 50 acres (20 hectares) of farmland is converted to development every hour, and 70 percent of prime farmland is threatened by sprawl—234.5 million acres (95 million hectares) nationwide.[3]

Building green has numerous benefits. After interviewing hundreds of developers and design teams and surveying dozens of projects, Rocky Mountain Institute (RMI) documented those benefits:[4]

- Reduced capital and operating costs;
- Garnering free press and differentiating one's product in the market;
- Increased and faster absorption rates;
- Streamlined approval;
- Reduced liability risk;
- Improved health and productivity for employees;
- The ability to stay ahead of the curve on government and industry regulations;
- New business opportunities;
- Enhancing the community; and
- Satisfaction in doing the right thing.

In 2003, the U.S. Green Building Council, ULI–the Urban Land Institute, and the Real Estate Roundtable produced a booklet, "Making the Business Case for High Performance Green Buildings." As noted by Christine Ervin, president of USGBC at the time, the purpose of this document was to stimulate new thinking and to provide compelling reasons why "the best sustainable designs are not just environmentally responsible. They also produce buildings where employees can thrive and productivity can soar."

The Bottom Line

One primary reason that those in the green building industry advocate building green is the financial benefit in terms of both capital costs and operating costs. According to a study released in fall 2003 of green buildings in California,[5] the benefits of building green included cost savings from reduced energy, water, and waste; lower operations and maintenance (O&M) costs; and enhanced occupant productivity and health. As shown in the figure above, net total financial benefits of green buildings were about $50 per square foot ($540 per square meter) for Certified and Silver buildings and about $65 per square foot ($700 per square meter) for Gold buildings—more than ten times the average initial investment required to design and construct a green building. Energy savings

alone exceeded the average increased cost associated with building green (see Chapter 2 for further definition of the business case for green building and its financial benefits).

Making People More Productive

One more answer to the question "why build green?" is the increased productivity of workers. In 1994, RMI's study, *Greening the Building and the Bottom Line: Increasing Productivity through Energy Efficient Design*, in large part brought to light the relationship between green building and workers' productivity. The study showed that by improving lighting, heating, and cooling, workers can be made more comfortable and

Numerous studies have documented the beneficial effects of natural sunlight, indoor air quality, and personal control over heating and cooling on employees' productivity. At PNC Firstside in Pittsburgh, tall windows, skylights, the elimination of walled offices, and low workstations help to bring light into the center of the building—even with its large floor plates. Astorino & Ed Massery

Practical and environmentally preferable materials and furnishings contribute to a healthy and attractive interior at the National Wildlife Federation headquarters in Reston, Virginia. Shimer © Hedrich Blessing and/or improved the quality of the work performed. These cases show that productivity gains from energy-efficient design can be as high as 16 percent, providing savings far in excess of the energy savings.

Several other groups and individuals have conducted more rigorous studies on this subject over the last decade. Carnegie Mellon's Advanced Building Research, led by Vivian Loftness, provides an online database on productivity gains and economic benefits. Recently, the U.S. General Services Administration launched WorkPlace 20•20 to analyze 22 pilot projects on productivity. GSA is focusing on high-quality workplaces that can help attract top employees in the "war for talent."[6] Dr. Judith Heerwagen, an environmental psychologist studying workplace ecology at the University of Washington and a former senior scientist at the Pacific Northwest National Laboratory, is examining why natural features seem to improve workers' health and productivity. A growing body of scientific research illustrates that the human brain and behavior are intricately linked to the natural world.

The Heschong Mahone Group's work[7] describes and quantifies productivity gains in schools and stores. In one study, the firm evaluated the effect of daylighting on human performance, specifically focusing on skylighting to isolate daylight as the source of illumination. The evaluation established a statistically compelling connection between skylighting and retail sales. Of the 108 stores analyzed, Heschong Mahone found that retail sales were 40 percent higher in daylit stores. Large chains such as Wal-Mart continue to experiment with daylighting and have realized increased sales (as well as employee satisfaction) in the daylit parts of stores. In another study, Heschong Mahone looked at the academic performance of more than 8,000 students in high-performance schools. In those schools, students' test scores were 7 to 18 percent higher than their contemporaries' scores in conventional schools. If green schools were implemented across the country, some $6 billion could be saved annually.[8]

Green benefits such as energy efficiency and indoor air quality are selling points for the Solaire in New York City. Cesar Pelli and Associates

productive. An increase of 1 percent in productivity can generate savings for a company exceeding the entire energy bill. Efficient design practices are cost-effective just from their energy savings, but the resulting gains in productivity make them indispensable. The study documented eight cases in which efficient lighting, heating, and cooling systems have increased workers' productivity, decreased absenteeism,

Heschong Mahone was also a primary researcher in the groundbreaking Integrated Energy Systems: Productivity and Building Science Program, released in October 2003 as part of the Public Interest Energy Research program funded by the California Energy Commission and managed by the New Buildings Institute. The Sacramento Municipal Utility District (SMUD) was the subject of two studies conducted for this research. The first study tracked 100 workers at the SMUD incoming call center, continuously tracking their performance by a computer system and measuring it in terms of time to handle each call. The second study assessed 200 office workers on a series of short cognitive assessment tests. The results indicate a biophilic response. At the call center, calls were processed 6 to 12 percent faster when people had the best possible view, compared with those who had no view. The office workers performed an impressive 10 to 25 percent better on tests of mental function and memory recall when they had the best possible view, compared with those who had no view.[9]

Publicity and Marketing Benefits

The publicity about green buildings with its contribution to marketing is one of the most underestimated benefits of green building. Green building has numerous real benefits that can offer increased value to tenants and buyers. According to John Gattuso, senior vice president for Liberty Property Trust, "Real estate continues to be regarded as a commodity. LPT is making the commitment to sustainable development now. Rather than a marketing ploy, we see it as an integrated component of quality management for our developments."

Albanese Organization, the Durst Organization, and the Tower Companies specifically draft their marketing materials and advertisements to highlight the high performance of their office and residential properties. Albanese and Northwestern Mutual created a publication called "Live Healthy—Live Green" for the Solaire, a residential tower in New York City. The colorful booklet describes the many amenities offered by green buildings: clean air, more light, a rooftop garden, natural materials, and clean water. Developers realize that enlightened clientele want these kinds of things in their living spaces. Efforts have paid off: the Solaire was occupied quickly (in a reluctant market after September 11, 2001) and appears to have captured a 5 percent rent premium. The project also cuts peak energy use by 67 percent.

The Language of Sustainable Design

Considerable attention is paid to design details and performance of green offices. For that reason, it is important to understand the building features and equipment commonly associated with green offices. The language of green building is not complicated, but it helps to be aware of some commonly used terms.

A collaborative approach among members of the design and engineering teams of a green project is encouraged through intensive charrettes.
Jenifer Seal

Detention ponds can help control stormwater runoff as well as provide outdoor amenities.
JohnsonDiversey

The design, construction, and postconstruction phases in the development of a green building emphasize a coordinated approach. Design charrettes, also known as ecocharrettes, are intensive, multidisciplinary integrated design sessions in which all members of the design and engineering teams meet. Many successful developers point to these sessions as instrumental in creating a truly high-performance design. After a building is completed, a commissioning process tests the operating systems before it is occupied to ensure that a building operates at its best.[10]

During site planning, a variety of techniques can help meet the goal of sustainability. Detention basins help avoid flooding by holding back stormwater until peak flows pass and then releasing the water back into the system. Bioswales act as minidetention basins to hold and filter water through the use of plants and gravel beds.

Xeriscaping involves the use of low-maintenance, drought-tolerant plants for landscaping to help conserve water.

Both passive and active energy conservation techniques are used in green buildings. Passive systems include proper building orientation, the size and placement of windows, the use of landscaping, and other techniques that are integrated into the overall building design. Active systems generally rely on specialized equipment such as photovoltaics or energy-efficient air conditioning and lighting systems.

Photovoltaic (PV) cells work as semiconductors to convert solar energy to electricity. They may be integrated in the building envelope through the roofing system or windows, or they can be added as panels or modules. The single-crystal cell is the most common type of PV cell in use today.

Heating, ventilation, and air-conditioning systems often account for the majority of the energy used in commercial buildings, so these systems receive particular attention in green buildings. When designed and specified correctly,

HVAC systems can provide healthy, comfortable indoor environments at reduced energy costs. The American Society of Heating, Refrigerating and Air-Conditioning Engineers (ASHRAE) publishes standards and guidelines for the industry. For example, ASHRAE 62 sets minimum ventilation air supply rates for commercial and institutional buildings. ASHRAE Standard 90.1–2004 provides minimum requirements for energy-efficient HVAC in large buildings. California's Title 24 sets strict energy efficiency standards for residential and nonresidential buildings.

Materials such as insulation used to prevent heat loss or gain in a building are rated by their resistance to heat flow, called R-value. The higher the R-value, the greater the thermal resistance.

High-performance materials such as low-emissivity ("low-e") window glazing have thin coatings to help control heat loss or gain.

Raised floor systems for air distribution are often used in green buildings. They can be more efficient than top-down forced-air systems, because they require less velocity and can deliver air at hotter and colder temperatures.

Green roofs are specially designed roofs covered with soil, drainage systems, and landscaping. They can help decrease the amount of water runoff on a site and help reduce the "heat island" impact caused by dark roof surfaces that absorb and radiate heat.

A combination of natural lighting and individual task lighting is generally used in green building interiors. T-8 lamps are energy-efficient fluorescent lights that have been shown to provide significant energy savings. (The "T" designation for fluorescent lamps indicates the tubular shape of the lamp, and the number indicates the diameter in eighths of an inch.)

Many traditional construction materials such as paints and adhesives contain volatile organic compounds (VOCs) that produce noxious fumes. The use of low- or no-VOC materials can significantly improve indoor air quality. Another factor to be considered in the choice of materials is the amount of embodied energy necessary to extract, manufacture, and transport the materials or products to the site.

Fly ash, a waste product of coal-burning power plants, is sometimes used to replace a portion of the cement used in a project. The manufacture of cement releases large amounts of carbon dioxide into the atmosphere; thus, replacing a portion of the cement used with fly ash is preferable.

A life-cycle assessment or analysis evaluates the environmental merits or performance of a process or product over its life cycle. This analysis measures the energy, water, and materials flowing into and out of the process or product over its lifetime. It also measures the impact of a product or process on environmental indicators.

Review of Chapters

Chapter 2, "Cost-Effectiveness of Green Buildings," discusses what green buildings cost and the costs and benefits of green buildings. As background to dispelling the myth that green buildings cost more than standard offices, the chapter provides cost data on 40 U.S. buildings. It addresses the benefits of green buildings, including reduced energy requirements and emissions, savings in operations and maintenance and insurance costs, and increased well-being for employees.

Chapter 3, "Sustainable Land Planning," emphasizes that green office development starts with land planning. It describes the practical steps to be followed in site selection, site analysis, and site planning. Landscape architecture considerations such as open space, vegetation, water conservation, climate mitigation, and wind control are described.

Chapter 4, "Green Office Design," addresses the building systems and exterior design features that must be considered in a sustainable project. It discusses elements of interior design, including space planning and materials, and provides background on identifying and selecting green products.

Your Real Estate Company *Can* Go Green

Dan Heinfeld

Green development is not the wave of the future—the future is already here. Many local, state, and federal agencies currently support and even mandate sustainable development through green building incentives and by setting basic standards of sustainability that real estate developers, architects, and other consultants must meet to have their projects approved.

Most developers, however, are not prepared to catch—and profit from—the green wave because they know relatively little about sustainable development. Some developers can in fact talk the green talk, but rarely can they plan and build environmentally friendly office buildings or complexes, particularly when they must work within a real-world moderate budget.

A company's size is not a barrier. Almost any real estate company can go green, although the smallest firms with ten or fewer employees might not be able to support several in-house green experts. Nor is the company's clientele a barrier. Sustainable development works on any building type. The USGBC's comprehensive LEED program has certified, among many other buildings, corporate headquarters, business campuses, federal buildings, schools, and industrial, technology, and research and development facilities.

What must you do to turn your real estate company green?

A Green Culture

First, you must create a companywide green culture, which means institutionalizing sustainable planning, design, and construction practices. How? Educating your in-house staff is of paramount importance.

Invest in your staff with career-long green education such as green conferences and the USGBC's LEED workshops. Many utility companies have educational programs on sustainable practices. ULI provides education about sustainable development through publications, conferences and meetings, its Real Estate School, and its smart growth program. CoreNet Global provides green education through its publications and summits and its executive development program. AIA's Committee on the Environment publishes educational materials and sponsors an annual award program for green design. The U.S. Department of Energy and most state energy and environmental agencies can help developers just embarking on the green path with advice, research, and educational materials. (See the Resource Guide for a list of relevant organizations.)

But education should go even farther. With LEED becoming the unofficial benchmark in the United States for many municipal, state, and federal sustainable development programs, you should educate and train planners and designers to become your in-house LEED certification experts.

Other strategies can help turn your company green. Build on your sustainable development education by incorporating green discussions in your staff meetings. Bring in experts for in-house seminars. Build and continuously update a green library. Become a member of USGBC and other organizations oriented toward sustainability. Create an in-house incentive or reward program for new green strategies. And be sure to practice what you preach. Internalize the green message and act accordingly by, for example, instituting companywide green housekeeping and recycling programs.

A green culture for a real estate company requires moving beyond the four walls of your office. Educate your contractors, engineers, and other consultants about green planning, design, and construction criteria and strategies. You have to both educate and inspire them to look beyond development as usual to green development that serves many stakeholders, including the planet we live on.

Green Planning and Design

A green office requires planning and design. Green is not a gimmick that is overlaid on a project at the end of planning and design. It must be integrated into each project at the very start of work to make it a part of a building's DNA.

Chapter 5, "Sustainable Construction," details the services that an owner or developer should procure from a contractor during the development of a green office project. It also provides background on methods of contracting and the contractor selection process and discusses the role of a contractor for a project where LEED certification is sought.

Chapter 6, "Managing Green," provides easy-to-understand green management techniques to improve the environmental performance of a green office building that can

Designing and constructing a green building require a new way of thinking and a new development process that looks at the entire project—site, exterior, interior—and budget as a whole before planning or designing a single element. You must move beyond the real estate industry's current devotion to specialization to a holistic view of a project that sees how the different parts are connected and how the many elements can work together to create the best sustainable development within the project's budget.

At the very start, the project team must buy into two goals: communication and collaboration. With this approach, the team can also alter planning and design elements and shift budget allocations from one building component to another to meet the larger project objectives of a green building. This process gives the site and building interiors as much or more importance than the facade. You could, for example, decide to spend more on site work and less on the cost of the building skin. Or you could choose to forgo a costly and environmentally insignificant feature such as a showy lobby to set aside more of the budget for extensive site landscaping that will shade the building from the hot summer sun, reduce heat islands in parking lots and on walkways, and increase the overall beauty of the project.

Another key component of building green is knowing where to spend the money. Where do you get the most bang for your (green) buck? Building orientation is a basic and inexpensive sustainable strategy that brings a wealth of benefits such as lower heat absorption and greater natural ventilation, reducing the cost of HVAC. Landscape architecture is relatively inexpensive but pays off in big ways by controlling erosion, reducing or eliminating heat islands, cooling buildings in the summer, creating market appeal, and encouraging people to get out of their cars and walk to another building on the campus.

Trying to squeeze a little more efficiency out of an already efficient mechanical system, however, is an expensive endeavor that brings relatively few benefits. Taking that money and using it instead to increase relatively inexpensive landscaping on the site and shade the building's south facade reduces the entire project's heat islands and has a far greater payoff.

Green Partners

In addition to your company's going green, you must transform your clients into green partners, which, in turn, creates a very different developer/client relationship. As green partners, the real estate company and the client can go far beyond the usual concerns of building appearance and floor plate to analyze and collaborate on what is best for the building, the client, and the environment. This collaboration will ensure the client's quicker buy-in on the final project.

When you first broach the opportunity to construct a green office building or campus, many clients automatically assume that they will face spiraling development costs. They will ask how much more a green design element or building component—recycled rather than nonrecycled carpet, for example—costs than that for a standard building. But that is the wrong question. The cost of building green is not an issue, because green planning and design are simply program elements, like a conference room or a lobby.

This collaborative process continuously generates the value decisions that will determine the extent of the green features ultimately incorporated into the project and still meet the client's budget constraints. Thus, clients' opposition to a green building usually diminishes or disappears because they are partners in the process and because they can see firsthand that building green is not substantially more expensive than conventional construction. This partnership also generates greater satisfaction with the final green product among clients, because they know exactly what to expect and because they end with a cost-saving, efficient, and attractive facility that meets many needs.

Green Tools and Resources

Real estate companies can draw on a wealth of existing green tools and resources to build

result in cost savings from energy conservation, lower life-cycle costs, and improved employee productivity.

Chapter 7, "Financing, Leasing, and Investment," provides guidance on how to evaluate green projects for loan and equity financing, how to structure leases to promote the development of green projects, and how to persuade conventional investors that green buildings can create long-term value. The chapter considers green real estate against the backdrop of conventional real estate risk-modeling techniques. This approach is significant for two reasons:

and support their new green culture and planning and design for it. USGBC's Web site, for example, has abundant information, including a resource list of green building materials, systems, and technology suppliers. USGBC's LEED rating system provides step-by-step guidelines for green planning and development, covering everything from site selection to development density, stormwater management, indoor air quality, and construction processes. The Internet has literally tens of thousands of Web sites devoted to sustainable development, from basic and cutting-edge information to companies specializing in one or more particular aspects of sustainable development (see the Resource Guide). Other resources include value engineering software that can compare short- and long-term costs and the efficiency of green alternatives with standard systems and building materials.

Green Construction

The construction process is a critical part of green development. And a key part of green office development is guaranteeing that the project's contractors consistently use these and other green construction practices. In addition to educating your contractors about sustainable development and the green construction process, your real estate company should have specific green construction criteria in your contracts, a standard green construction management plan that can be adapted to each project, and green construction oversight processes.

Green Marketing

To gain more clients, attract and retain skilled staff, and enhance your company's reputation among local and state agencies (which, it is hoped, will help speed the entitlement process), market your green building track record on the company Web site, at conferences and conventions, and through magazine and newspaper articles.

Consider undertaking a green outreach program that sends your firm's experts to area elementary and high schools and colleges to begin educating younger generations about sustainable development, which will garner interest from parents (potential clients) and the media.

The real estate companies that have already transformed themselves and are actively marketing their green orientation are now profiting handsomely from it. Even clients who could not care less about the environment understand the many ways a green office building can benefit them—from recruiting and retaining employees to fostering goodwill in the community.

■ Green buildings compete for financing against conventional projects, and lenders and investors understandably seek those projects that provide the highest likelihood of repayment or return.

■ Consideration of the elements of risk or return included in the conventional ten-year valuation model can help developers of green projects to communicate more effectively with potential lenders and investors and more readily obtain financing for their projects under more favorable terms.

Chapter 8, "U.S. Federal Government Green Policies and Programs," describes programs related to sustainable construction of the General Services Administration (GSA), EPA, Department of Energy (DOE), and Department of Defense (DoD). The U.S. federal government has a 30-year history of environmentally friendly building construction, and the private sector can learn much from federal agencies. Many published and online resources are available from these agencies, including best practices, product information, and case studies.

The case studies in Chapter 9 illustrate the wide variety of green offices found around the world, ranging from a renovated low-scale historic structure in Portland, Oregon, to high-rise offices in Chicago and New York City, to a mixed-use development in Germany, to a building in Zimbabwe that features a distinctive ventilation system. Photographs, site plans, and detailed project data provide a practical reference.

Chapter 10, "Outlook and Trends," summarizes the key issues and trends that will affect green office buildings in the future.

Notes

1. From a 1966 speech by James Rouse.

2. James Wines, *Green Architecture: The Art of Architecture in the Age of Ecology* (Cologne, Germany: Taschen, 2000).

3. See American Farmland Trust, www.farmland.org, and Colorado Cattlemen's Agricultural Land Trust, www.yampa.com/Routt/CSU/CCALT.html. Some progress has been made toward land conservation. In the 2002 election, 75 percent of state and local conservation-related ballot measures were passed, generating $10 billion.

4. Alex Wilson, Jenifer L. Seal, Lisa McManigal, L. Hunter Lovins, Maureen Cureton, and William D. Browning, *Green Development: Integrating Ecology and Real Estate* (New York: Wiley, 1998).

5. Greg Kats, with Leon Alevantis, Adam Berman, Evan Mills, and Jeff Perlman, "The Costs and Financial Benefits of Green Buildings: A Report to California's Sustainable Building Task Force," October 2003. Available at www.cap-e.com.

6. See www.gsa.gov/sustainabledesign.

7. Heschong Mahone Group, *An Investigation into the Relationship between Daylighting and Human Performance,* August 1999. Available at www.h-m-g.com.

8. Heschong Mahone Group, *Daylighting in Schools,* 1999. Available at www.h-m-g.com.

9. Heschong Mahone Group, *Windows and Offices: A Study of Office Worker Performance and the Indoor Environment* (Sacramento: California Energy Commission, October 2003). Available at www.h-m-g.com.

10. See Department of Energy, "Building Commissioning: The Key to Quality Assurance," *U.S. DOE Rebuild America Guide Series,* p. 9. Available at http://www.rebuild.org/attachments/guidebooks/commissioningguide.pdf.

Interior vegetation will "scrub" the air as it rises inside the Jie Fang Daily News & Media Group corporate headquarters in Shanghai. KMD

Costs
Benefits

The Costs and Benefits of Green Buildings

Gregory H. Kats

It is widely believed that green design is significantly more costly than conventional design. But with more hard information available on the costs and benefits of green buildings, it is likely that more private companies and public agencies will commit to green construction as a design principal. For example, a major study conducted for more than 40 California state agencies in 2003 convinced several agencies to commit to building green and also helped persuade the University of California Board of Regents to adopt a university-wide policy for the design of green buildings.[1]

As background to analysis of the costs and benefits of green buildings, this chapter provides cost data from 40 U.S. buildings for which information is available, comparing costs if they were built as green buildings and as conventional buildings. In addition, this chapter describes several financial benefits

The Ford Motor Company Premier Automotive Group at the Irvine Spectrum Center in southern California illustrates that it is possible to construct a large-scale green building within the strict design guidelines of an existing office park on a mainstream budget.
LPA, Inc./Adrian Velicescu, Standard

of green buildings. Half of them—including reduced energy requirements and emissions and savings in operations and maintenance (O&M)—include calculations for financial benefits. The estimates are typically conservative and represent the low end of a range of reasonable estimates. In the past, inability to quantify the exact value of the benefits has encouraged many to assume a zero value, but that tactic is clearly wrong. Other benefits described with no calculations include insurance, the impact on employment, and spiritual and moral benefits.

A number of other studies document measurable benefits derived from enhanced daylighting, natural ventilation, and improved indoor air quality (IAQ) in buildings. For example, a Lawrence Berkeley National Laboratory study found that U.S. businesses could save as much as $58 billion in lost sick time and an additional $200 billion in workers' performance if IAQ were improved.[2]

Chapter Approach and Assumptions

Life-cycle costing is used in this analysis to evaluate and integrate the benefits and costs associated with sustainable buildings.[3] Many substantial information gaps prevent a full life-cycle cost assessment of green buildings. For example:

■ Analysis and data on the full cost of water use are incomplete.

Green Buildings Used as Background for Cost Analysis

Project	Location	Type	Date Completed	Green Cost Premium	Green Standard
Energy Resource Center[1]	Downey, CA	Office	1995	0.00%	Level 1-Certified
KSBA Architects[1]	Pittsburgh, PA	Office	1998	0.00%	Level 1-Certified
Brengel Tech Center[1]	Milwaukee, WI	Office	2000	0.00%	Level 1-Certified
Stewart's Building[2]	Baltimore, MD	Office	2003	0.50%	Level 1-Certified
Pier One[3]	San Francisco, CA	Office	2001	0.70%	Level 1-Certified
PA EPA South Central Regional[1]	Harrisburg, PA	Office	1998	1.00%	Level 1-Certified
Continental Towers[11]	Chicago, IL	Office	1998	1.50%	Level 1-Certified
CA EPA Headquarters[3]	Sacramento, CA	Office	2000	1.60%	Level 1-Certified
EPA Regional[4]	Kansas City, KS	Office	1999	0.00%	Level 2-Silver
Ash Creek Intermediate School[10]	Independence, OR	School	2002	0.00%	Level 2-Silver
PNC Firstside Center[1]	Pittsburgh, PA	Office	2000	0.25%	Level 2-Silver
Clackamas High School[10]	Clackamas, OR	School	2002	0.30%	Level 2-Silver
Southern Alleghenies Museum[2]	Loretto, PA	Office	2003	0.50%	Level 2-Silver
DPR-ABD Office Building[14]	Sacramento, CA	Office	2003	0.85%	Level 2-Silver
Luhrs University Elementary[2]	Shippensburg, PA	School	2000	1.20%	Level 2-Silver
Clearview Elementary[2]	Hanover, PA	School	2002	1.30%	Level 2-Silver
DPR/ABD Office building[14]	Sacramento, CA	Office	2003	1.37%	Level 2-Silver
West Whiteland Township[2]	Exton, PA	Office	2004	1.50%	Level 2-Silver
Management Building, Technology Square[16]	Atlanta, GA	Office	2003	1.50%	Level 2-Silver
Twin Valley Elementary[2]	Elverson, PA	School	2004	1.50%	Level 2-Silver
Licking County Vocational[2]	Newark, OH	School	2003	1.80%	Level 2-Silver
Seattle Justice Center[13]	Seattle, WA	Office	2002	1.90%	Level 2-Silver
Public Building[1]*	Portland, OR	Office	1998*	2.20%	Level 2-Silver
Public Building[1]*	Portland, OR	Office	1998*	2.20%	Level 2-Silver
Public Building[1]*	Portland, OR	Office	1998*	2.20%	Level 2-Silver
Nidus Center of Science[1]	Creve Coeur, MO	Office	1999	3.50%	Level 2-Silver
Municipal Courts[1]	Seattle, WA	Office	2002	4.00%	Level 2-Silver
4 Times Square[6]	New York City	Office	1999	5.00%	Level 2-Silver
St. Stephens Cathedral[12]	Harrisburg, PA	School	2003	7.10%	Level 2-Silver
PA DEP Southeast[2]	Norristown, PA	Office	2003	0.10%	Level 3-Gold
The Dalles Middle School[10]	The Dalles, OR	School	2002	0.50%	Level 3-Gold

■ Available data on emissions from energy use should (but generally do not) reflect life-cycle emissions from energy extraction, transportation, use, and disposal as well as the generation of energy.

■ In the last decade, no publicly available, comprehensive studies have been published that calculate the full benefits (such as avoided transmission and distribution costs) of reduced energy demand, such as from on-site generation and energy efficiency.

Despite the gaps, a large and compelling body of evidence is available to draw from. The objective of this analysis is to provide a brief review of the available data to provide a reasonable net present value (NPV) estimate of the costs and financial benefits of green buildings.

Project	Location	Type	Date Completed	Green Cost Premium	Green Standard
McCaw Hall[13]	Seattle, WA	Office	2003	0.70%	Level 3-Gold
Development Resource Center[8]	Chattanooga, TN	Office	2001	1.00%	Level 3-Gold
PA DEP Cambria[2]	Ebensburg, PA	Office	2000	1.20%	Level 3-Gold
PA DEP California[2]	California, PA	Office	2003	1.70%	Level 3-Gold
Toyota South Campus Headquarters[15]	Torrance, CA	Office	2003	4.00%	Level 3-Gold
TomoTherapy Headquarters[17]	Madison, WI	Office	2002	4.50%	Level 3-Gold
East End Complex[7]	Sacramento, CA	Office	2003	6.41%	Level 3-Gold
Botanical Garden Administration[9]	Queens, NY	Office	2003	6.50%	Level 4-Platinum
UCSF Osher Center for Integrative Medicine[3,18]	San Francisco, CA	Office	2004	7.10%	Level 4-Platinum

Notes

1. Cost data from "Resource Guide for Sustainable Development in an Urban Environment: A Case Study in South Lake Union, Seattle, WA," prepared by UEI, Oct 22, 2002, p. 42. http://www.usgbc.org/Resources/research.asp. Note that many of these 33 data points came from more than one source and/or were checked with more than one source.

2. Cost data from presentation and discussions with John Boecker, vice president, L. Robert Kimball & Associates, November 20 and December 20, 2002, and May 2003.

3. Cost data from Anthony Bernheim, "Saving Resources," *Urban Land,* June 2001; Anthony Bernheim and Scott Lewis, "Measure and Cost of Green Building," presented at the AIA National Convention, May 2000; and conversations with Anthony Bernheim.

4. C. C. Sullivan, "Off-the-Shelf Ecology," *Building Design & Construction,* May 2001, pp. 57–60.

5. Communication with David Gottfried, WorldBuild, December 27, 2002. Forwarded information from Craig Greenough, DPR Inc.

6. Communication with Bob Fox, Cook + Fox, principal architect for the project, February 2004.

7. Jim Ogden, 3D/I, "Summary of Green Building Costs—Block 225," 2003.

8. Communication with Randy Croxton, Croxton Collaborative, November 20, 2002.

9. David Kozlowski, "Urban Green," Building Operating Management, December 2001. Indicated cost increase is 5 to 8 percent.

10. Communication with Heinz Rudolf, principal, BOORA Architects, November 2002 and June 2003; and with Bill Harper, associate principal, BOORA Architects, May, 2003. For more information, see http://www.energy.state.or.us/school/highperform.htm.

11. Communication with Kevork Derderian, Continental Offices Ltd., November 21, 2002.

12. Communication with Vern McKissick, architect, McKissick Associates. Building may become gold at some future date.

13. SBW Consulting, Inc., "Achieving Silver LEED: Preliminary Benefit-Cost Analysis for Two City of Seattle Facilities," Seattle Office of Sustainability and Environment, April 2003. Additional resources for McCaw: http://seattletimes.nwsource.com/news/entertainment/mccaw/story_overview22.html; and for the justice center: http://www.cityofseattle.net/courts/sjc/justicecenter.htm.

14. "DPR/ABD Office Building," www.dprinc.com.

15. Steven Kendrick, LPA, December 2004. Note that a 1 to 2 percent late charge cost was factored out, with Kendrick's agreement.

16. http://gtalumni.org/buzzwords/pastissues/oct03/articles.html.

17. Ken Pientka, chief operating officer, planning, Design Build, Inc., "Sustainable Design: What's the Bottom Line?"

18. Scheduled completion for the Osher Center has been delayed to 2007.

* Without more information than that the buildings were completed between 1994 and 2001, the completion was designated as 1998 in this analysis.

Green buildings may cost more to build than conventional buildings, especially when incorporating more advanced technologies and attempting to achieve higher levels of LEED or other types of certification. But they may also offer significant cost savings over time. This chapter describes the current value of green buildings and components on a present value or NPV basis. (Present value is the present value of a future stream of financial benefits. Net present value reflects a stream of current and future bene-fits and costs, and results in a value in today's dollars that represents the present value of an investment's future financial benefits minus any costs.)

This analysis assumes an inflation rate of 2 percent per year, in line with most conventional inflation projections,[4] and assumes that costs (including energy and labor) and benefits rise at the rate of inflation. This statement is reasonable though a simplification: for example, energy costs

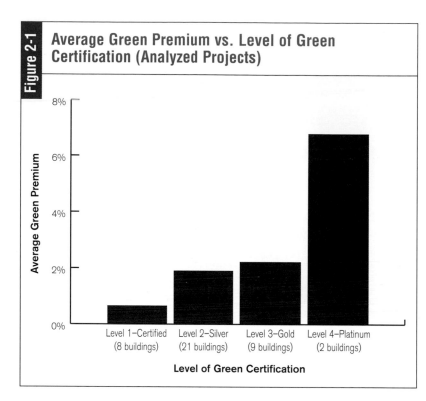

Figure 2-1

Average Green Premium vs. Level of Green Certification (Analyzed Projects)

Average Green Premium

8%

6%

4%

2%

0%

| Level 1–Certified (8 buildings) | Level 2–Silver (21 buildings) | Level 3–Gold (9 buildings) | Level 4–Platinum (2 buildings) |

Level of Green Certification

are relatively volatile, although electricity prices are less volatile than primary fuels, especially gas.

To arrive at present value and NPV estimates, projected future costs and benefits must be discounted to give a fair value in today's dollars. The discount rate used in this analysis is 5 percent real (i.e., 5 percent plus inflation), which is higher than the rate at which states and the federal government borrow money[5] and is about the rate at which many corporations borrow.

In buildings, different energy systems and technologies last for different lengths of time: some energy equipment is upgraded every eight to 15 years, while some building energy systems may last the life of a building. This analysis conservatively assumes that the benefits of more efficient sustainable energy, water, and waste components in green buildings will last 20 years, or somewhat less than the average between

envelope and expected equipment life. This approach is conservative: many buildings last 50 years or longer.

The Cost of Building Green

The perception is widespread in the real estate industry that green buildings cost more than those constructed by traditional methods. Evidence is growing that this perception is not necessarily true, but comprehensive data are still unavailable. Many developers keep cost information proprietary. In addition, even if developers are willing to share their cost data, determining a precise "green premium" for a given project is often difficult for several reasons:

■ Developers typically issue only specifications and costs for the designed building, not for other design options.

■ Some green buildings being built today are showcase projects that may include additional and sometimes costly finish upgrades that are unrelated to greenness but nonetheless are counted toward the increased green building cost.

■ Design and construction of the first high-performance building for a client or design/architectural firm are often characterized by significant learning curve costs and schedule problems such as late and costly change orders.

For this analysis, cost data were gathered on 40 individual LEED-registered projects (32 office buildings and eight school buildings) whose actual or projected dates of completion were between 1995 and 2004 (an expansion of the 33 buildings in the 2003 Kats/California study described in Footnote 1). These 40 projects were chosen because relatively solid cost data for both actual green design and conventional design were available for each building.

A table containing each project name, location, building type, date of completion, green premium, and certification level or equivalent can be found at the end of this chapter. Many of these buildings were not yet USGBC certified at the time of this research. In these cases, the LEED level indicated is an assessment by the architect and/or client team of its potential level of certification reflecting very detailed analysis and modeling, which is viewed as a relatively accurate prediction of final LEED certification.

The eight certified buildings averaged a cost premium of 0.7 percent. Twenty-one Silver-level buildings averaged a cost premium of 1.9 percent. The nine Gold buildings averaged a premium of 2.2 percent, and the two Platinum buildings averaged 6.8 percent. The average reported cost premium for all 40 buildings was almost 2 percent (see Figure 2-1).

The trend of declining costs associated with increased experience in green building construction has been experienced in Pennsylvania[6] and in Portland and Seattle on the West Coast. Portland's three reported completed LEED Silver buildings were finished in 1995, 1997, and 2000; they incurred cost premiums of 2 percent, 1 percent, and 0 percent, respectively.[7] Seattle has seen the cost premium for LEED Silver buildings drop from 3 to 4 percent several years ago to 1 to 2 percent today.[8]

This information implies that the cost of green buildings generally rises as the level of greenness increases, while the premium to build green is coming down over time. Development of multiple green buildings by a particular corporation or public entity can be expected to result in declining costs per building to that organization. Assuming conservative, relatively high commercial construction costs of $150 to $250 per square foot ($1,600 to $2,700 per square meter),[9] a 2 percent premium for a green building is equivalent to $3 to $5 per square foot ($32 to $54 per square meter). Using lower construction costs in these calculations tends to increase the reported cost-effectiveness of green construction.

Quantifiable Financial Benefits

A range of financial benefits typically are associated with green buildings. This chapter deals with some of them, including lower energy bills, reduced waste and water costs, more efficient O&M, and financial benefits associated with improved health and productivity.

Energy Use

Energy is a substantial and widely recognized cost of building operations that can be reduced through energy efficiency and related measures that are part of green building design. The average annual cost of energy in California state buildings is approximately $1.47 per square foot ($15.80 per square meter), while the national average in office buildings is $1.55 per square foot ($16.70 per square meter).[10]

The first commercial office building to receive LEED certification in New York City, 7 World Trade Center uses ultraclear glass technology, steam-to-electricity turbine generators, and variable-speed fans to conserve energy. Silverstein Properties/SOM/dbox

Figure 2-2

Reduced Energy Use in Green Buildings Compared with Conventional Buildings

	Certified	Silver	Gold	Average
Energy Efficiency (above standard code)	18%	30%	37%	28%
On-Site Renewable Energy	0%	0%	4%	2%
Green Power	10%	0%	7%	6%
Total	28%	30%	48%	36%

Source: USGBC, Capital E analysis.

A detailed review of 60 LEED-rated buildings demonstrates that green buildings, when compared with conventional buildings, are:

■ On average, 25 to 30 percent more energy efficient (compared with ASHRAE 90.1-1999 and, for California buildings, Title 24 baselines);[11]

■ Characterized by even lower electricity peak consumption;

■ More likely to generate renewable energy on site; and

■ More likely to purchase grid power generated from renewable energy sources (green power and/or tradable renewable certificates (see Figure 2-2).

Green buildings use an average of 30 percent less purchased energy than conventional buildings. In addition, green buildings are more likely to purchase "green power" or green certificates for electricity generated from renewable energy sources.

The environmental and health costs associated with air pollution caused by electric power generation and on-site fossil fuel use are generally not considered when making investment decisions.[12] This analysis seeks to quantify some of the costs and benefits, including the value of peak power reduction (in this section) and the value of emissions reductions associated with the energy strategies integrated into green building design.

Reduced Peak Power Demands

Because the design and construction process of green buildings is relatively integrated and holistic, interactions between competing building systems (lighting versus cooling, fresh air versus humidity control, for example) can be analyzed simultaneously, allowing the building designers to reduce peak power demand by downsizing building systems, particularly air-conditioning and lighting loads, while providing a comfortable indoor environment. For most of the United States (especially in the South and Midwest), air conditioning is the dominant energy user during peak loads. By encouraging integrated design and awarding credit for optimization of building energy systems, LEED provides strong incentives to cut both of these peak demand uses.

LEED encourages:

■ Integrated design: Project teams consider building systems in total to optimize competing demands.

■ High-performance lighting: Incorporating more efficient lights, task lighting, using sensors to cut unnecessary lighting, and using daylight harvesting and other advanced lighting techniques and technologies can significantly reduce power demand and heating loads in a building, which in turn reduces required air conditioning.

■ More effective ventilation: Helps cut air-conditioning load during peak demand.

■ Heat island reduction: By increasing the reflectivity of roofs and other typically dark surfaces, it is possible to lower building and urban temperatures, in turn reducing air-conditioning loads and peak demand.

■ On-site generation: Two of the eight LEED Gold buildings reviewed use photovoltaics to generate 20 percent of their power on site. The use of PV is coincident with peak power use and thus helps to reduce peak demand.

Data are insufficient to precisely determine peak demand reduction in green buildings. Uncertainties result from a limited data set, inconsistencies in documentation, incomplete documentation, technical issues such as fuel switching, and the large variability between building designs. Nonetheless, the available green building data are significant and collectively indicate that high-performance buildings on average reduce peak demand generally more than average.

Evaluation of LEED certification documentation for more than a dozen buildings[13] indicates an approximate average reduction in energy use of 30 percent but an average peak reduction of up to 40 percent.[14] The data set is limited, and this is a rough estimate.

Benefits of Reduced Peak Consumption

Utility transmission and distribution (T&D) systems generally run at less than 50 percent capacity.[15] During periods of peak electricity use, however, the generation and T&D systems may be close to overloaded. The benefits of reduced consumption are largest during periods of peak power consumption: avoided congestion costs, no reduction in power quality and reliability, reduced pollution, and additional capital investment to expand generation and T&D infrastructure.

The cost of additional transmission and generating capacity has been rising steeply as a result of increased population, pressure to bury lines underground, and local opposition. San Diego Gas & Electric has been planning to build a 31-mile (50-kilometer), 500,000-volt transmission line in south Riverside County at an expected cost of $300 million, or nearly $10 million per mile ($6.2 million per kilometer)—higher than historical costs for large transmis-

During the first nine months of operation, the Plaza at PPL Center used only 70 percent of the energy predicted, roughly equivalent to exceeding ASHRAE requirements by 50 percent. Peter Aaron-Esto/Liberty Property Trust

sion line extensions. A public utilities commission administrative law judge ruled, however, that the cost of the line would not be justified over the next five years based on projected electricity demand growth.[16] The explicit recognition of the link between projected electricity demand growth and approval of costly new power lines highlights the potential value of green buildings in reducing or even eliminating the large capital costs of line expansion.

Conclusion

As discussed earlier, green buildings provide an average 30 percent reduction in energy use, compared with minimum energy code requirements. For energy costs of $1.47 per square foot ($15.80 per square meter) per year for California public buildings, the savings is about $0.44 per square foot ($4.75 per square meter) per year,[17] with a 20-year present value of $5.48 per square foot ($59 per square meter). This result indicates an average of $1.55 per square foot ($16.70 per square meter) for commercial buildings, or a present value of $5.78 per square foot ($62.20 per square meter). Energy savings alone exceed the average additional cost of green over conventional construction.

In addition, green buildings help to reduce peak demand. Based on limited data from the California Task Force's report, the annual peak demand reduction savings attributed to green buildings is an estimated $0.31 per square foot ($3.35 per square meter), or $0.025 per square foot ($0.27 per square meter) per year at a 5 percent discount rate over 20 years.

Thus, the total 20-year present value of financial energy benefits from a typical green California public building is $5.79 per square foot ($62.30 per square meter). For U.S. commercial buildings, the present value of energy savings is $6.09 per square foot ($65.50 per square meter). On the basis of energy savings alone, investing in green buildings appears to be cost-effective.

Energy Emissions

Value of Pollution Associated with Energy

Air pollution from burning fossil fuels to generate electricity imposes very large health, environmental, and property damage costs. Demonstrated health costs include tens of thousands of additional deaths per year and tens of millions of respiratory incidents and ailments.[18] The health, environmental, and property damage costs associated with pollution from burning fossil fuels—commonly referred to as externalities—are only partially reflected in the price of energy.[19]

The Madrid headquarters of Endesa, one of the world's largest private electrical companies, uses photovoltaic cells to supplement its energy needs. H.G. Esch

Reducing electricity and gas use in buildings means lower emissions of pollutants (because of the avoided burning of fossil fuels to generate electricity) that are damaging to human health, to the environment, and to property.[20]

Air pollutants that result from the burning of fossil fuels include:

■ Oxides of nitrogen, a principal cause of smog;

■ Particulates, a principal cause of respiratory illness (with associated health costs) and an important contributor to smog;

■ Sulfur dioxide, a principal cause of acid rain; and

■ Carbon dioxide, the principal greenhouse gas and the principal product of combustion.

Additional fossil fuel–related pollutants include reactive organic compounds and carbon monoxide. (VOCs may have significant value but are not calculated in this report.) A more comprehensive analysis should evaluate the costs of a fuller set of these additional pollutants, including mercury.

Estimated Costs Associated with Pollution from Power Generation

California values for traded emissions are used in this analysis as a relatively simple and imperfect approach to estimate emissions values. These prices reflect the actual marginal cost of emission reductions in relatively liquid and well-established trading markets covering the majority of California's population. For some pollutants, including oxides of nitrogen and sulfur dioxide, a well-established, liquid market exists in California; these market prices serve as a measure of the marginal cost of emission reductions and, to a greater extent than in the rest of the country, the value society places on them (see Figure 2-3).

The market values of California emissions are generally higher than other prices nationally—where markets exist. It is important to note that because the current market for emissions is driven by caps set by regulations and not the actual costs (for example, the morbidity effects of emissions), it does not directly reflect the externalities of health impacts and the value of reductions is therefore generally understated. In addition, important pollutants such as mercury and smaller particulates have large adverse health effects that are not addressed in this report. Even California emission prices, which are far higher than average prices nationally (where markets exist), generally underestimate the full costs of emissions.

The Cost of Carbon: Putting a Price on Carbon Dioxide Emissions

The vast majority of the world's scientists who study climate change have concluded that anthropogenic emissions—principally from burning fossil fuels—are the root cause of global warming.[21] The United States is responsible for almost one-quarter of global greenhouse gas emissions. According to a recent study, U.S. buildings alone are responsible for more carbon dioxide emissions than those of any other country in the world, except China.[22]

Figure 2-3

20-Year Present Value of a 36 Percent Reduction in Pollution for California Buildings (per Square Foot)

Pollutants	Price of Carbon Dioxide	
	$5/ton	$10/ton
Nitrogen Oxides	$0.54	$0.54
Particulates	$0.41	$0.41
Sulfur Oxides	$0.16	$0.16
Carbon Dioxide	$0.07	$0.14
Total	$1.18	$1.25

A recent United Nations study found that in 2000, some of the adverse effects of global warming caused an estimated 150,000 deaths globally.[23] A report published in July 2002 warns that the "increasing frequency of severe climatic events, coupled with social trends, has the potential to stress insurers, reinsurers, and banks to the point of impaired viability or even insolvency."[24] John Fitzpatrick of Swiss Re (see Chapter 9), maintains that "climate change and substantial emissions reductions—like any other strategic global business challenge—ultimately become a financial issue."[25] The U.N. estimates the potential cost of global warming at more than $300 billion per year, and insurance firms are becoming concerned about the possibility of lawsuits as a result of damage from human-induced global warming.[26]

The potential cost of climate change is extremely large but uncertain and extending for generations, making it very difficult to attribute a current cost to climate change. Recognizing the cost of global warming by assigning a dollar value of some amount is preferable to the current practice of assigning no value—effectively zero dollars—to reductions in carbon dioxide. It is also economically efficient for states and public bodies to explicitly recognize a value for carbon dioxide to ensure a more cost-effective decision-making process about building design.

Green buildings typically use half as much water as conventional buildings. An attractive water feature at the Kelsey-Seybold Clinic Medical Center campus in Houston, Texas, also serves as a stormwater detention basin. Tom Fox, SWA Group

Assigning a Cost to Carbon

Determining a value for reductions in carbon dioxide is a difficult proposition (see Figure 2-3). For example, a recent report cites a range of values between $5 and $125 per ton ($4.50 and $113 per metric ton) of carbon dioxide.[27] Carbon dioxide trading programs are emerging in the United States,[28] with the value of trades typically ranging from under $1 to $16 per ton ($0.90 to $14.50 per metric ton), with most trades at under $5 per ton ($4.55 per metric ton). The general trend is rising prices.

Despite the uncertainties and large credible range of possible prices, some value per ton should be assigned to carbon dioxide for the purposes of calculating the benefits of green buildings, and estimated future prices of $5 and $10 per ton ($4.55 and $9.10 per metric ton) are used in this analysis.

Conclusion

Detailed calculations indicate a present value of a reduction in emissions of the four pollutants discussed above of about $1 per square foot ($10.75 per square meter). This estimate is almost certainly very low.

Water Conservation

Green buildings typically use half as much water as conventional buildings and can therefore play a substantial role in cutting the costs of water supply and the costs of wastewater treatment.

Strategies to conserve water in green buildings generally fall into several categories:

■ More efficient use of potable water through better design and technology;

■ Capture of graywater—nonfecal wastewater from bathroom sinks, bathtubs, showers, washing machines, and so forth—to use for irrigation;

■ On-site capture of stormwater to use in place of potable water or to recharge groundwater; and

■ Use of recycled or reclaimed water.

Taken together, these strategies can reduce water use below building code standards and common practice by more than 30 percent indoors and more than 50 percent for landscaping.[29] Of 21 reviewed green buildings submitted to the USGBC for LEED certification (including six in California), all but one used water efficiently for landscaping, cutting outdoor water use by at least 50 percent. Seventeen buildings, or 81 percent, used no potable water for landscaping. Over half cut water use inside buildings by at least 30 percent.[30] Typical green buildings cut water use by about half.

The actual value of water conservation is not simply the avoided cost of retail water rates. Rather, it is the added cost of obtaining new marginal water supplies and the cost of wastewater treatment facilities for that water. A 1999 empirical study in Canada estimated that the price charged for fresh water was only one-third to one-half the long-run marginal supply cost and that prices charged for sewage were approximately one-fifth the long-run cost of sewage treatment.[31] A 2002 study released by the EPA suggests that future costs will likely rise much more rapidly than in the past.[32] The city of Portland, Oregon, expects wastewater rates to rise by about 7 percent annually over the next decade, significantly higher than the 2 to 3 percent annual increase experienced over the past several years.[33]

The 20-year present value for water savings from green buildings in California is an estimated $0.51 per square foot ($5.50 per square meter). These costs are very likely conservative and can safely be used as a proxy for national approximation for the value of water savings in green buildings. A more comprehensive analysis can be expected to result in significantly higher estimated savings.

Waste Reduction

Waste reduction strategies such as reuse and recycling, as promoted in green buildings, help to divert waste from landfills and result in savings associated with avoided disposal costs as well as in reduced societal costs of creating and maintaining landfills.

Of 21 green buildings submitted to USGBC for certification, 17, or 81 percent, reduced construction waste by at least 50 percent, while 38 percent reduced construction waste by 75 percent or more.[34] Renovated projects can often use 75 to 100 percent of a building envelope and shell (excluding windows) and up to 50 percent of nonshell elements such as floor systems by retaining and reusing these features.

Green buildings recycle and divert substantially higher levels of waste and incorporate greater amounts of recycled or reused materials than conventional buildings. Estimating the relative increases in waste recycling, diversion, and use of green buildings compared with conventional buildings, however, is difficult and tenuous.

The value of diverting materials from landfills includes direct economic benefits as well as avoided environmental costs. The most comprehensive study quantifying the environmental benefits of recycling was conducted in Massachusetts in 2000. The study found the average total net environmental benefit of recycling at $63 per ton ($57 per metric ton). According to the study, diversion has two primary benefits, compared with disposal:[36]

1. Fewer hazardous substances and greenhouse emissions when products are manufactured with recycled materials instead of virgin wood, metal, and petroleum resources;[37]

2. Fewer hazardous substances and other pollutants released when materials are collected for recycling instead of disposal in a landfill or incineration.

The commissioning process undertaken at the LEED Silver-certified North Clackamas High School in Oregon identified a variety of issues related to the building's operating systems. Resolving these issues lowered the building's annual energy costs and made the interior environment more comfortable for students and teachers. Michael Mathers

As discussed earlier, estimating financial benefits of waste reduction, diversion, and recycling from green buildings relative to existing buildings is difficult. State, city, and other requirements and the degree to which these mandates actually occur vary enormously across the country. Some states—California, for example—have relatively rigorous recycling and waste diversion requirements. For example, waste diversion rose from 17 percent in 1990 to 48 percent in 2002.[38]

In the absence of good data on present rates of waste diversion in green and conventional buildings during both their construction and operation, it is impossible to quantify the full value of green building resulting from lower waste generation. The one-year value of reduced construction waste from green buildings in California is estimated at $0.03 per square foot ($0.32 per square meter), which is the (very low) waste benefit number used here. It appears

probable that the green building waste reduction advantage in California may not exceed about $0.50 per square foot ($5.40 per square meter) because of California's already aggressive waste reduction targets. Nationally, waste diversion and recycling levels are on average significantly lower than in California and the benefits of reduced waste associated with green construction higher, perhaps on the order of several dollars per square foot. This issue warrants further analysis.

Operations and Maintenance

O&M costs represent a large portion of ongoing building costs. Green building design features design elements and practices, including commissioning and measurement and verification, that have a substantial effect on O&M performance and costs.

LEED requires fundamental building systems commissioning, which currently entails hiring a commissioning expert, developing a commissioning plan, and completing a commissioning report. LEED provides credits for additional commissioning. Commissioning:

- Helps eliminate costly change orders;
- Reduces requests for cost information;
- Helps ensure proper system and component selection; and
- Improves performance of building systems.[39]

LEED provides a credit for building performance measurement and verification. The international performance measurement and verification protocol referenced in LEED[40] is also used internationally as a way to demonstrate benefits of carbon dioxide reductions, providing a potentially helpful way to secure financial value through sale of emissions reductions associated with green buildings.[41] Detailed analysis of several hundred million dollars of energy building upgrades demonstrates that rigorous measurement and verification of energy and water efficiency and system retrofits tend to:

- Increase initial savings level;

- Increase persistence of savings; and
- Reduce variability in energy and water savings.[42]

Commissioning and metering allow building mangers to better manage upgrades and maintenance, helping to anticipate and avoid equipment failure, leaks, and other costly O&M problems.

Thus, commissioning and metering contribute to lower O&M costs such as extended equipment life, though how much lower is not known. O&M costs in California state buildings—$3,039 per person per year[43] or $12.25 per square foot ($132 per square meter) per year—are nearly an order of magnitude larger than energy costs. Therefore, any reduction in O&M costs significantly affects financial benefits. For example, a reduction in O&M costs of 10 percent is equal to a savings of $304 per person, or $1.35 per square foot ($14.50 per square meter) per year. Data are insufficient to estimate with any precision the reduction in O&M costs that would occur in green buildings. Clearly, the reduction is larger than zero but probably less than 25 percent. To be conservative, this report assumes that O&M costs for green buildings decline 5 percent per year—a savings of $0.68 per square foot ($7.30 per square meter) per year, or a 20-year present value savings of $8.47 per square foot ($91.15 per square meter).

Productivity and Health

Recognition is growing of the large health and productivity costs imposed by poor indoor environmental quality (IEQ) in commercial buildings. This finding is not surprising, given that people typically spend 90 percent of their time indoors and that the concentration of pollutants indoors is typically higher than outdoors, sometimes by as much as 10 or even 100 times.[44] Measuring the exact financial impact of healthier, more comfortable, and greener buildings is difficult. The costs of poor IEQ and IAQ—including higher absenteeism and increased respiratory ailments, allergies, and asthma—are hard to measure and have generally been "hidden" in sick days, lower productiv-

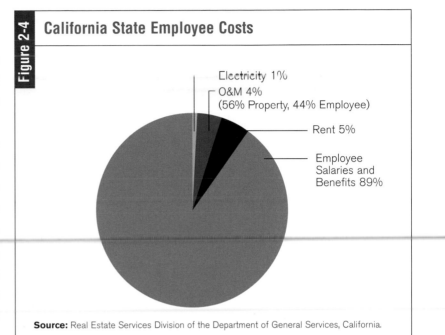

California State Employee Costs

Figure 2-4

Electricity 1%
O&M 4%
(56% Property, 44% Employee)
Rent 5%
Employee Salaries and Benefits 89%

Source: Real Estate Services Division of the Department of General Services, California.

ity, unemployment insurance costs, and medical costs. Health and productivity issues, often addressed separately, are combined here because both relate directly to workers' well-being and comfort, and both can be measured by their impacts on productivity.

Potential Savings

The cost to the state of California for state employees is ten times larger than the cost of property. Figure 2-4 represents state costs for 27,428 state employees in 38 state-owned buildings.[45] Average annual employee costs ($66,478, comprising $65,141 in salary and benefits plus $1,337 in allocated O&M costs) are ten times larger than the cost of space per employee ($6,477).[46] Thus, measures that increase employee costs by 1 percent are equivalent, from a perspective of state costs, to an increase in property-related costs of about 10 percent. In other words, if green design measures can increase productivity by 1 percent, over time it would have a fiscal impact roughly equal to reducing property costs by 10 percent.

The discussion of IEQ and productivity issues in industry publications expanded rapidly in the last decade and has spilled over into the popular media. The cover of *Business Week* for June 5, 2000, for example, features a large, menacing office building accompanying the feature story, "Is Your Office Killing You? The Dangers of Sick Buildings."[47] The article cites potential benefits of up to $250 billion per year from improved indoor air quality in U.S. office buildings.

Gary Jay Saulson, senior vice president and director of corporate real estate for PNC Realty Services (see Chapter 9), describes the benefits of the LEED Silver PNC Firstside Center building in Pittsburgh as follows: "People want to work here, even to the point of seeking employment just to work in our building. Absenteeism has decreased, productivity has increased, recruitment is better, and turnover [is] less." Two business units experienced 83 percent and 57 percent reductions in voluntary terminations after moving into the new Firstside facility.[48]

What Do Tenants Want?

Given the large impact that poor IEQ has on the health and comfort of office workers, it is not surprising that surveys of workers suggest that IEQ is one of the most important components of job satisfaction. Conducted by the Building Owners and Managers Association (BOMA) and the Urban Land Institute, the study, *What Office Tenants Want,* is based on questionnaires from 1,800 surveys of office tenants in 126 metropolitan areas.49 Survey respondents attributed the highest importance to tenant comfort features, including comfortable air temperature (95 percent) and indoor air quality (94 percent). Office temperature and the ability to control temperature are the only features that were both "most important" and also on the list of things with which tenants are least satisfied. The BOMA/ULI study found that the number-one reason that tenants move out is because of problems with HVAC.

Studies indicate that increased daylighting and high-quality supplemental lighting can have a positive effect on the productivity of building occupants. For buildings located in hot, sunny climates like Edificio Malecon in Buenos Aires, Argentina, careful planning is necessary to maximize sunlight and views while protecting against excessive heat gain and glare in the interior. Daniela Mac Adden

Some relevant attributes common in green buildings promote healthier work environments:

■ Much lower source emissions from measures such as better siting (for example, avoiding locating air intakes next to outlets such as parking garages) and better control over building materials. Certified- and Silver-level green buildings achieved 55 percent and Gold-level LEED buildings achieved 88 percent of possible LEED credits for use of less toxic materials, low-e adhesives and sealants, low-e paints, low-e carpets, low-e composite wood, and control over use of indoor chemicals and pollutants.[50]

■ Significantly better lighting quality, including more daylighting (half of 21 LEED green buildings reviewed provide daylighting to at least 75 percent of building space),[51] better daylight harvesting and use of shading, occupants' greater control over light levels, and less glare.

■ Generally improved thermal comfort and better ventilation.

■ Commissioning, use of measurement and verification, and carbon dioxide monitoring to ensure better performance of HVAC systems.

A large body of technically sound studies and documentation links health and productivity with specific building design operation attributes—for example, indoor air quality and tenants' control over their work environment, including lighting levels, air flow, humidity, and temperature. A National Science and Technology Council project entitled Indoor Health and Productivity provides a valuable database of 900 papers on the subject.[52] Seattle City Light has compiled information about more than 30 projects that document productivity, increased retail sales, and increased student learning resulting from incorporation of green design elements.[53]

Two studies of more than 11,000 workers in 107 European buildings analyzed the health effect of worker-controlled temperature and ventilation. They found significantly reduced illness symptoms, decreased absenteeism, and increased perceived productivity over workers in a group that lacked these features.[54]

Productivity Benefits for Specific Worker Control and Comfort Upgrades

One of the leading national centers of expertise on the benefits of high-performance buildings is the Center for Building Performance and Diagnostics at Carnegie Mellon

University. The center's building investment decision support (BIDS) program has reviewed more than 1,000 studies that relate technical characteristics of buildings such as lighting and ventilation to tenant responses such as productivity.[55]

Collectively, these studies demonstrate that better building design and performance in areas such as lighting, ventilation, and thermal control correlate to increases in tenants' and workers' well-being and productivity. The BIDS data set includes a number of controlled laboratory studies where speed and accuracy at specific tasks were measured in low- and high-performance ventilation, thermal control, and lighting control. The studies used a range of speed and accuracy performance measures, including typing, addition, proofreading, paragraph completion, reading comprehension, and creative thinking.[56]

Increases in tenants' control over ventilation, temperature, and lighting each provide measured benefits from 0.5 percent up to 34 percent, with average measured workforce productivity gains of 7.1 percent with lighting control (see Figure 2-5) 1.8 percent with ventilation control, and 1.2

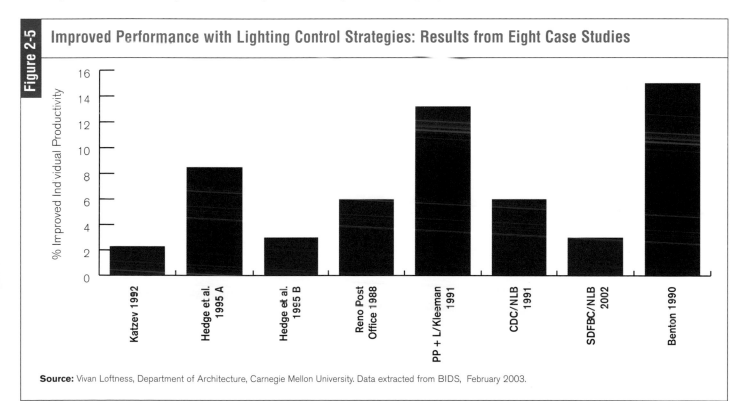

Figure 2-5

Improved Performance with Lighting Control Strategies: Results from Eight Case Studies

% Improved Individual Productivity

Source: Vivan Loftness, Department of Architecture, Carnegie Mellon University. Data extracted from BIDS, February 2003.

percent with thermal control. In addition, measured improvements have been found with increased daylighting, as discussed in the following section.

Increased Daylighting

A study conducted by the Heschong Mahone Group evaluated test scores of more than 21,000 students in three school districts in California, Colorado, and Washington. It found that in classrooms with the most daylighting, students' learning progressed 20 percent faster in mathematics and 26 percent faster in reading than similar students in classrooms with the least daylighting. The overall findings show that increasing daylighting and generally improving the quality of lighting significantly improve students' performance on tests.[57] A follow-up study, employing an independent technical advisory group to reanalyze the data, confirmed the initial study's findings with a 99.9 percent confidence level.[58]

The kind of work done by "knowledge workers" is very similar to the work students do: understanding what they read, synthesizing information, writing, calculating, and communicating. Large-scale studies correlating daylighting with students' performance on standard tests therefore provide relevant insights about the impact of increased daylighting on employees.

This study is important for its size, rigor, and large measured impact of lighting quality on standardized test performance. Note that the study compares performance between students with the greatest amount of daylighting and those with the least—two extremes. The productivity benefits that could conservatively be expected are much less than 26 percent (which reflects extremes in daylighting), perhaps on the order of 2 to 6 percent.

Conclusion

No standard exists for estimating the exact impact on productivity of a green building. Each green building has a different set of technologies and design attributes, and each building population has different health attributes and comfort needs.

At least four of the attributes associated with green building design, however—increased ventilation control, increased temperature control, increased lighting control, and increased daylighting—have been positively and significantly correlated with increased productivity. Quantifiable gains for green buildings have also been shown in attracting and retaining a committed workforce, an aspect beyond the scope of this report.

LEED is designed specifically to address the materials, designs, and operations affecting the productivity and health issues discussed above. Fifteen credits directly relating to productivity are included in the IEQ section, with two prerequisites (about 22 percent of total credits). A preliminary review of green buildings submitted for USGBC certification confirms that these buildings consistently include a range of materials, designs, and operations that directly improve human health and productivity. Gold- and Platinum-level LEED buildings are more comprehensive in applying IEQ-related measures and therefore should be viewed as providing larger productivity and health benefits than certified- or Silver-level green buildings.

Given the studies and data reviewed above, this chapter attributes a 1 percent gain in productivity and health to certified- and Silver-level buildings and a 1.5 percent gain to Gold- and Platinum-level buildings. These percentages are at the low end of the range of productivity gains for the individual specific building measures—ventilation, thermal control, light control, and daylighting—analyzed above. They are consistent with or well below the range of additional studies cited above.

Green buildings such as 7 World Trade Center in New York City are ideal candidates for demand response energy programs, because they typically include advanced utility metering and management systems that help reduce energy demand during peak loads.

Silverstein Properties/SOM/dbox

For example, for state of California employees, a 1 percent increase in productivity (equal to about five minutes per working day) is equal to $665 per employee per year, or $2.96 per square foot ($32 per square meter) per year.[59] A 1.5 percent increase in productivity (or slightly more than seven minutes each working day) is equal to $998 per year, or $4.44 per square foot ($47.75 per square meter) per year. The pres-

ent value of the productivity benefits is about $35.00 per square foot ($377 per square meter) for certified- and Silver-level buildings and $55 per square foot ($592 per square meter) for Gold- and Platinum-level buildings. Assuming a longer building operational life, say, 30 or even 50 years, would result in substantially greater benefits.

Additional Financial Benefits Not Calculated

Green buildings provide or may provide a range of significant additional benefits that are addressed in this chapter for which data are limited. Evaluating the financial benefits of these aspects of green buildings is beyond the scope of this report.

Insurance

Green building design has multiple, potentially significant impacts on insured and uninsured costs, and these costs—and the potential benefits of green buildings—are rising.[60] For example, according to the chief economist at the Insurance Information Institute, most insurers reported a tripling of mold-related claims in 2003. More than 9,000 claims related to mold are pending in the nation's courts, though most involve family homes.[61] Improved ventilation and greater commissioning in green buildings are likely to combat mold.

The Lawrence Berkeley National Laboratory has mapped approximately 80 energy-efficient and renewable energy measures onto specific "lines" of insurance benefited by their use.[62] Of the 64 LEED points possible in design areas one through five (excluding "Innovation and Design Process," which is nonspecific), 49 (77 percent) are associated with measures that could potentially reduce the cost of risk management and insurance. These benefits, though potentially large, are not calculated in this report. Doing so would increase the recognized financial benefits of green design.

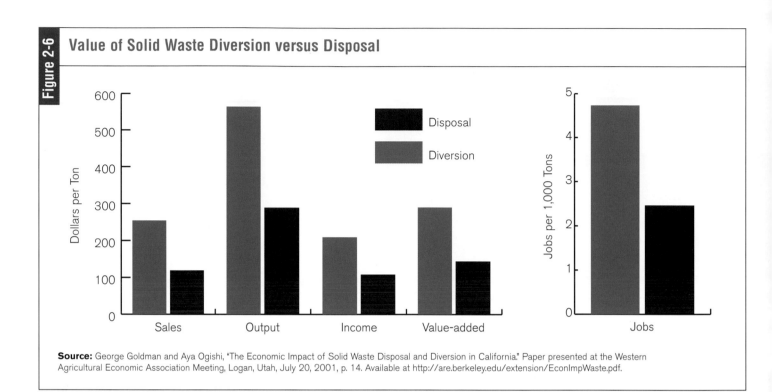

Figure 2-6

Value of Solid Waste Diversion versus Disposal

Source: George Goldman and Aya Ogishi, "The Economic Impact of Solid Waste Disposal and Diversion in California." Paper presented at the Western Agricultural Economic Association Meeting, Logan, Utah, July 20, 2001, p. 14. Available at http://are.berkeley.edu/extension/EconImpWaste.pdf.

Reduced Heat Island Effects

Extensive studies conducted by the Lawrence Berkeley National Laboratory, the California Energy Commission, and others have documented large energy and health benefits derived from lighter color roofs, lighter color paving, and trees. Darker surfaces absorb more sunlight, increasing temperatures inside buildings and creating "heat islands" and an associated need for increased air conditioning. More air conditioning requires more energy, which in turn leads to the release of more pollutants. In addition to increasing their own temperatures, dark roofs and surfaces raise the temperatures of surrounding areas, further increasing their needs for air conditioning. Since 1950, increased absorption of sunlight by dark buildings and roads and the loss of tree coverage have played a large role in increasing the average temperature of Los Angeles by about 34 degrees Fahrenheit (about 1 degree Celsius) every 15 years.[63]

The medical cost of poor air quality in Los Angeles is about $10 billion per year, of which 70 percent is from particulates and 30 percent from ozone.[64] High temperatures are a primary condition for the creation of smog (ozone). When ambient urban temperatures are decreased, the reduced heat island effect directly contributes to reduced ozone creation, in turn lowering the large human health costs associated with smog.[65]

Impact on Morbidity and Hypertension

A recent national study calculates the relationship between denser community design promoted by green design and important human health factors.[66] The study evaluated health attributes of 380,000 survey respondents living in 530 counties or metropolitan areas. It draws on a national health survey maintained by the Centers for Disease Control and Prevention. The authors note that "excess weight and physical inactivity are reported to account for over 300,000 premature deaths a year, second only to tobacco-related deaths among preventable causes of death."[67] The study found that

Toyota Motor Sales's new South Campus office development at its U.S. headquarters in Torrance, California, cost no more than speculative low-rise office development in the area. The 624,000-square-foot (58,000-square-meter) building has been certified by the U.S. Green Building Council as a LEED Gold building.

LPA, Inc./Adrian Velicescu, Standard

obesity and hypertension are substantially higher in areas characterized by sprawl.

Common current community design inhibits walking or cycling and often provides little or no alternative to driving. Green structures tend to encourage building and community design associated with significant improvements in health, including reusing buildings, increasing density and proximity to walkable destinations, building at a higher density and closer to public transport, and providing bicycling racks and showers for pedestrians or cyclists.

Green building clearly helps address costly national health challenges of obesity and hypertension. The impact is probably significant, given the size and cost of the problem. Although it is beyond the scope of this report to quantify these benefits, excluding them underestimates the value of green buildings.

Impact on Employment

A shift to more renewable energy would significantly increase employment nationally. Compared with a business-as-usual fossil fuel–dominated energy growth mix through 2020, expanding renewable energy use up to 20 percent nationally by 2020 would create roughly 100,000 net new jobs.[68] The majority of jobs would be in manufacturing and construction and would be relatively well distributed (all states would show positive employment growth, particularly in sectors currently suffering from relatively high unemployment.

A recent University of California–Berkeley study found that total economic impacts from diversion are nearly twice as large as those from disposal (see Figure 2-6). One ton (0.9 metric ton) of waste diverted as recyclables generates about twice the impact of a ton of waste disposed in a land-fill. Only 2.5 jobs are created for every 1,000 tons (905 metric tons) of waste disposed, while 4.7 jobs are created for waste diverted as recyclables.[69] Placing a financial value on these benefits is beyond the scope of this report, but excluding these benefits underestimates the financial benefits of green buildings.

Even more ambitious clean investment scenarios developed by a coalition of labor movements, public entities, nongovernmental organizations, and businesses called Apollo envisions a larger national program. The Apollo jobs study models a $300 billion investment over a decade in high-performance green buildings, rebuilding public infrastructure, increasing energy diversity, and investing in industries of the future such as clean technologies that would directly create 460,000 jobs.[70]

Spiritual and Moral Benefits

Major religious faiths all emphasize the moral importance of environmental stewardship of the earth. For example, a pastoral statement from the U.S. Catholic Conference states that "Catholics look to nature, in natural theology, for indications of God's existence and purpose. . . . Nature is not, in Catholic teaching, merely a field to exploit at will or a museum piece to be preserved at all costs. We are not gods, but stewards of the earth."[71]

The National Council of Churches, in a full-page letter to the president in the *New York Times* on April 28, 2004, wrote, "In a spirit of shared faith and respect, we feel called to express grave moral concern about your 'Clear Skies' initiative—which we believe is the Administration's continuous effort to weaken critical environmental standards that protect God's creation. . . . We have a solemn duty to the future well-being of Earth and all life within it, . . . yet we believe that the Administration's energy, clean air, and climate change programs prolong our dependence on fossil fuels, deplete Earth's resources, poison its climate, punish the poor, constrict sustainable economic growth, and jeopardize global security and peace."

Federal efforts in green design could help address many of these concerns by cutting bills for the poor, decreasing pollution, and increasing employment. Not surprisingly, many religious groups advocate broader adoption of green design as a way to address these types of spiritual values and concerns. For many, the large reduction in resource consumption and waste and the reduced health damages associated with green design have real moral and spiritual value that, though difficult to quantify, is of central and even compelling value for many Americans.

Demand Response Benefits

Several dozen utilities across the country provide financial incentives to customers to decrease power consumption as a way to cut costs, increase system efficiency, and create a more intelligent and efficiently used electricity grid.[72] These utility programs typically help businesses install metering and control systems to cut power use through such measures as load shifting, moving air conditioning to other than peak periods, and lowering lighting levels. The Electric Power Research Institute estimates that these types of programs can potentially reduce national peak power requirements by 45,000 megawatts, or about 6.4 percent.[73] Green buildings are ideal candidates for demand-responsive load management because they already typically include relatively advanced metering and energy management systems. If, as seems likely, green buildings and demand response programs continue to grow rapidly, green buildings should account for a significant part of the utility strategy to address rising peak power, and transmission and distribution demand at very low societal cost.

Conclusions

Most benefits described in this report, including lower energy and water costs, lower O&M costs, some waste reduction benefits, and most health and productivity benefits, accrue to the first tenants of a building. As the brand value of LEED buildings increases, builders may be more likely to expect their green building investment to translate into higher occupancies, higher lease rates, lower O&M costs, and/or higher asset values.

Although a government entity should care about the environmental or power grid benefits its building may have for society, a private commercial entity may not. Private building owners, for example, may be less likely to care about health and environmental impacts and hence might perceive lower financial benefits of building green. In addition, because of higher capital costs and hurdle rates, private entities generally discount future financial benefits more heavily than public ones, potentially further reducing the perceived value of future green building financial benefits for the private sector. These differences help explain the significant disparity between the public sector's and the private sector's adoption of green building design.

This analysis began with an aggregation of data on actual or modeled costs for 40 green buildings. Largely derived from several dozen conversations with architects, developers, and others, the data indicate that the average construction cost premium for green buildings is about 2 percent, or about $4 per square foot ($43 per square meter), substantially less than is generally perceived.

The body of this report focused on determining the financial benefits of a range of green building attributes (see Figure 2-7). As summarized above, net financial benefits of green design are estimated to be about $50 per square foot ($540 per square meter) for Certified- and Silver-level green buildings and about $65 per square foot ($700 per

Figure 2-7

Summary of Saving (per Square Foot) Financial Benefits of Green Buildings

Category	20-year NPV
Energy Value	$5.79
Emissions Value	$1.18
Water Value	$0.51
Waste Value (construction only)—1 year	$0.03
Commissioning O&M Value	$8.47
Productivity and Health Value (Certified and Silver)	$36.89
Productivity and Health Value (Gold and Platinum)	$55.33
Less Green Cost Premium	($4.00)
Total 20-year NPV (Certified and Silver buildings)	**$50.00**
Total 20-year NPV (Gold and Platinum buildings)	**$65.00**

Source: Capital E analysis.

square meter) for Gold- and Platinum-level buildings. These amounts are more than ten times larger than the average 2 percent cost premium—about $3 to $5 per square foot ($32.30 to $53.80 per square meter) for the 40 green buildings analyzed.

The relatively large impact of productivity and health gains reflects that the direct and indirect costs of employees are far larger than the costs of buildings and energy, so even small increases in employee productivity translate into large benefits. Payback from most green buildings is on average one to several years.

City, state, and local entities can potentially gain a great deal from increasing the portion of new construction and retrofit of existing buildings to meet high performance standards. These benefits may include:

■ Lower peak demand and reduced pressure on T&D systems, including lower line losses and avoided or delayed construction;

■ Improved power quality and reliability;

■ Reduced emissions (including oxides of nitrogen and particulates) from lower energy use, lower peak use, and consequently lower use of dirty backup diesel;

■ Lower water use and water treatment and avoided or delayed required investment in water treatment and supply costs;

■ Improved health and productivity for occupants; and

■ Greater gridwide and system reliability and security.

Tools that public entities can use include accelerated permitting, increasing floor/area ratios (FARs), and permitting denser construction around public transport stations and corridors.

These broader benefits, many of which may be substantial, are not quantified in this chapter. But quantification and inclusion of these additional benefits would generally increase the recognized benefits of green design and reinforce what is already a persuasive case for the cost-effectiveness of green design.

Notes

1. The author of this chapter served as principal author of that study; this chapter draws largely on that report, which was the first to attempt to develop a rigorous analysis of the costs and benefits of green buildings. See Greg Kats, with Leon Alevantis, Adam Berman, Evan Mills, and Jeff Perlman, "The Costs and Financial Benefits of Green Buildings: A Report to California's Sustainable Building Task Force," October 2003. Available at www.cap-e.com. The report was developed for the Sustainable Building Task Force, a group of more than 40 California state government agencies. Funding for this study was provided by the Air Resources Board; the California Integrated Waste Management Board; the California Departments of Finance, General Services, Transportation, and Water Resources; and the Division of the State Architect. This collaborative effort was made possible through the contributions of Capital E, Future Resources Associates, task force members, and the U.S. Green Building Council.

2. William Fisk, "Health and Productivity Gains from Better Indoor Environments," Lawrence Berkeley National Laboratory. Figures inflation-adjusted for 2002 dollars and rounded.

3. For an extensive international listing of green building evaluation and life-cycle related tools and programs with related URLs, go to http://buildlca.rmit.edu.au/links.html.

4. See, for example, http://oregonstate.edu/Dept/pol_sci/fac/sahr/cf166503.pdf and http://www.jsc.nasa.gov/bu2/inflateGDP.html.

5. The *Wall Street Journal* lists discount rates daily, depending on credit rating. See "Market Data and Resources," at http://online.wsj.com/public/site_map?page=Site+Map. See also http://oregonstate.edu/Dept/pol_sci/fac/sahr/cf166503.pdf and http://www.jsc.nasa.gov/bu2/inflateGDP.html.

6. Data provided by John Boecker, L. Robert Kimball and Associates. See http://www.lrkimball.com/Architecture%20and%20Engineering/ae_experience_green.htm.

7. Data provided by Heinz Rudolf, BOORA Architects. See "Portfolio/Schools" at http://www.boora.com/.

8. Lucia Athens, Seattle Green Building Program, November 2002. See http://www.cityofseattle.net/light/conserve/sustainability/. Seattle is reviewing more than a dozen green Seattle buildings and specific costs premiums for those buildings.

9. This is a reasonable, somewhat high (that is, conservative) estimate as confirmed by Oppenheim Lewis Inc. and Anthony Bernheim, principal, SMWM. It includes hard and soft costs (including design fees) associated with construction, but not land acquisition.

10. U.S. Department of Energy, Office of Energy Efficiency and Renewable Energy, "2003 Building Energy Databook," August 2003. Figures in 2001 dollars.

11. Based on analysis of Energy and Atmosphere Credit 1—Energy Optimization points awarded to all LEED-NC v2 Certified projects.

12. See Amory Lovins et al., "Small is Profitable," RMI, 2002. Available at http://www.rmi.org.

13. Data provided by USGBC, analysis by Capital E with USGBC. November and December 2002.

14. Because USGBC does not require peak-load reduction data to be submitted, the quality of data is mixed and includes some buildings that specify peak-load demand reduction and some building data that indicate it indirectly (for example, through large reductions in air-conditioning load). Additional building information reviewed provided no useful data on peak demand reductions.

15. Electricity generation and distribution assets are less than half used most of the time. See Amory Lovins et al., "Small is Profitable," RMI, 2002, at http://www.smallisprofitable.org/.

16. "SDG&E's Plan for Power Line Dealt Blow," Energy Info Source, California Energy Report, October 21–November 3, 2002. Available at http://www.energyinfosource.com/.

17. Thirty percent of $1.47 per square foot ($15.80 per square meter) per year total energy costs at 5 percent discount rate over 20-year term.

18. See, for example, "The Benefits and Costs of Clean Air Act, 1990 to 2010," 1991. Available at http://www.epa.gov/air/sect812/1990-2010/fullrept.pdf; and Jonathan Samet et al., *The National Morbidity, Mortality, and Air Pollution Study.* Part II: Morbidity and Mortality from Air Pollution in the United States, Health Effects Institute, 2000. Available at http://www.healtheffects.org/Pubs/Samet2.pdf.

19. For a valuable introduction and overview of past studies on externality costs and costs of emission reductions, see Jonathan Koomey and Florentin Krause, "Introduction to Externality Costs," LBNL, 1997. Available at http://enduse.lbl.gov/Info/Externalities.pdf.

20. Other forms of power, such as nuclear and hydro, also have environmental costs, though it is not within the scope of this report to evaluate these issues. Note that emissions intensity can vary by time of day and season and other factors such as peak versus baseload power (an issue that is addressed elsewhere in this report).

21. Intergovernmental Panel on Climate Change, World Meteorological Association and United Nations Environmental Program, "IPCC Third Assessment Report: Climate Change 2001." Available at http://www.ipcc.ch/. A valuable publicly available overview of the status of climate change, developed by Harvard professor John Holdren, is available at http://www.incr.com/InvestorSummit_JPH_N03a.pdf.

22. Kinzey, et al., "The Federal Buildings Research and Development Program: A Sharp Tool for Climate Policy," 2002 ACEEE Proceedings, Section 9.21.

23. World Health Organization, World Meteorological Organization, "Climate Change and Human Health: Risks and Responses," 2003.

24. Innovest, for the United Nations Environmental Program, Finance Initiatives Climate Change Working Group, "Climate Change and the Financial Services Industry," 2002. Available at http://www.unepfi.net/.

25. "Climate Change–Related Perils Could Bankrupt Insurers," Environmental News Service, October 7, 2002. Available at http://www.campaignexxonmobil.org/news/News.OneWorld100802.html.

26. Katharine Q. Seeley, "Global Warming May Bring New Variety of Class Action," New York Times, September 6, 2001. Available at http://www.commondreams.org/headlines01/0906-03.htm.

27. IPCC Working Group III, "Summary for Policymakers: The Economic and Social Dimensions of Climate Change," 2001. Available at http://www.ipcc.ch/pub/sarsum3.htm.

28. Carbon Trade Watch, Briefing No. 1. "The Sky Is Not the Limit: The Emerging Market in Greenhouse Gases," January 2003. Available at http://www.tni.org/reports/ctw/sky.pdf. For a list of existing registry and emission reduction programs, see also http://www.nescaum.org/Greenhouse/Registry/state_matrix.html.

29. U.S. Green Building Council, LEED Reference Package Version 2.0, June 2001, p. 65, and analysis of green buildings submitted to USGBC. Available for purchase at http://www.usgbc.org/LEED/publications.asp.

30. Data provided by USGBC.

31. Steven Renzetti, "Municipal Water Supply and Sewage Treatment: Costs, Prices, and Distortions," Canadian Journal of Economics, May 1999, p. 688.

32. The EPA reports that the expected gap between future revenues (based on historical price increase) and infrastructure needs will be approximately $148 billion over the next 20 years. See U.S. Environmental Protection Agency, "The Clean Water and Drinking Water Infrastructure Gap Analysis," August 2002. Available at http://www.epa.gov/owm/gapfact.pdf.

33. Data provided by the Portland Environmental Services Department, October 2002.

34. Data provided by USGBC.

35. LEED Reference Package, Version 2.0, June 2001, pp. 170–180.

36. Lisa Skumatz and Jeffrey Morris, "Massachusetts Recycle 2000: Baseline Report," prepared for the Commonwealth of Massachusetts Executive Office of Environmental Affairs Recycle 2000 Task Force, December 1998.

37. Estimates of net benefits of greenhouse gas reductions are based on U.S. EPA, "Greenhouse Gas Emissions from Management of Selected Materials in Municipal Solid Waste. Final Report," September 1998, Exhibit ES-4. Available at http://yosemite.epa.gov/oar/globalwarming.nsf/UniqueKeyLookup/SHSU5BVP7P/$File/r99fina.pdf.

38. California Integrated Waste Management Board, "Solid Waste Generation and Diversion, 1989–2002." Available at http://www.ciwmb.ca.gov/lgcentral/Rates/Diversion/RateTable.htm.

39. Chad Dorgan, Robert Cox, and Charles Dorgan, "The Value of the Commissioning Process: Costs and Benefits," Farnsworth Group, paper presented at the 2002 USGBC Conference, Austin, Texas. Available at http://www.usgbc.org/expo2002/schedule/documents/DS506_Dorgan_P152.pdf.

40. See www.ipmvp.org. The principal author of this report (Greg Kats) cofounded IPMVP and served as its chair until 2001.

41. Edward Vine, Gregory Kats, Jayant Sathaye, and Hemant Joshi, "International Greenhouse Gas Trading Programs: A Discussion of Measurement and Accounting Issues," Energy Policy, January 2003. Available at http://www.ipmvp.org.

42. Greg Kats, Art Rosenfeld, and Scott McGaraghan, "Energy Efficiency as a Commodity: The Emergence of a Secondary Market for Efficiency Savings in Commercial Buildings," 1997 ECEEE Conference Proceedings. Available at http://www.ipmvp.org/info/ece397.pdf.

43. Data provided by the California Department of General Services, Real Estate Services Division, December 2002.

44. U.S. EPA, "Indoor Air Quality," January 6, 2003. Available at http://www.epa.gov/iaq/.

45. O&M costs ($3,039) are allocated 44 percent for labor and 56 percent for property-related expenses. Data provided by the California Department of General Services, Real Estate Services Division, December 2002.

46. Ibid.

47. Michelle Conlin, "Is Your Office Killing You?" Business Week, June 5, 2000. Available at http://www.businessweek.com/2000/00_23/b3684001.htm

48. Compared with a control group that experiences an 11 percent reduction. "Shades of Green: 2002 Report of the Pittsburgh Green Building Alliance." Available at http://www.gbapgh.org. This report provides a clear overview of green building benefits and valuable references and quotes on productivity and related green building benefits. See also William Browning, "Successful Strategies for Planning a Green Building," Planning for Higher Education, Society of College and University Planners, March–May 2003, pp. 78–86.

49. "What Office Tenants Want: 1999 BOMA/ULI Office Tenant Survey Report." To order, call 1-800-426-6292, or order online at www.boma.org, item #159-TENANT-029.

50. Capital E analysis of USGBC data (based on analysis of points actually achieved in building performance data submitted to USGBC), November and December 2002. For more details on achievable reductions from some of these indoor emissions sources see A.T. Hodgson, "Common Indoor Sources of Volatile Organic Compound Emissions Rates and Techniques for Reducing Consumer Exposures," University of California, Lawrence Berkeley National Laboratory, 1999. Available at http://www.arb.ca.gov/research/apr/past/indoor.htm#Toxic%20Air%20Contaminants.

51. Capital E analysis of USGBC data, November and December 2002.

52. An online bibliography as well as more information about this project can be found at http://www.dc.lbl.gov/IHP/. The Web site includes five useful brief reviews of key findings in the areas of health, productivity, and school test scores that were published in ASHRAE Journal, May 2002.

53. See "High-Performance Building Delivers Results," The Sustainable Demand Project: A Project of the Urban Consortium Energy Task Force of Public Technology, City of Seattle, Seattle City Light, December 2000. Available at http://www.cityofseattle.net/light/conserve/sustainability/SDPFRa.pdf.

54. Judith Heerwagen, "Sustainable Design Can Be an Asset to the Bottom Line," expanded Internet edition," Environmental Design & Construction, posted July 15, 2002. Available at http://www.edcmag.com/CDA/ArticleInformation/features/BNP__Features__Item/0,4120,80724,00.html.

55. Vivian Loftness et al., "Building Investment Decision Support (BIDS)," ABSIC Research 2001–2002 Year End Report. See http://nodem.pc.cc.cmu.edu/bids. Carnegie Mellon's BIDS™ is a case-based decision-making tool that calculates the economic value added of investing in high-performance building systems, based on the findings of building owners and researchers around the world.

56. Communication with Vivian Loftness, Carnegie Mellon University, February 2003.

57. Heschong Mahone Group, "Daylighting in Schools: An Investigation into the Relationship between Daylight and Human Performance," 1999. Available at http://www.h-m-g.com.

58. Heschong Mahone Group, "Daylighting in Schools Re-Analysis," 2002. Available at http://www.newbuildings.org/pier/index.html.

59. Average California employee compensation in 2002 was $66,469, and average space per employee was 225 square feet (2,420 square meters).

60. Evan Mills, "Green Buildings as a Risk-Management Strategy," Energy Associates, December 2002, which draws on a report written by Evan Mills, senior scientist at the Lawrence Berkeley National Laboratory.

61. Ray Smith, "Mold Problems Grow in Shops, Hotels, Offices," Wall Street Journal, December 4, 2002. Available at http://www.iuoe.org/cm/iaq_bpconc.asp?Item=356.

62. Edward Vine, LBNL Report No. 41432, 1998. Available at http://eetd.lbl.gov/insurance/LBNL-41432.html.

63. A.H. Rosenfeld, et al., "Cool Communities: Strategies for Heat Island Mitigation and Smog Reduction," Energy and Buildings, 28, 1998.

64. J.V. Hall, "Valuing the Health Benefits of Clean Air," Science, 255, 1992.

65. In addition, cool roofs also experience less expansion and contraction than dark roofs, extending the life of the roof.

66. Reid Ewing, et al., "Relationship between Urban Sprawl and Physical Activity, Obesity, and Morbidity," American Journal of Health Promotion, September/October 2003, and Wall Street Journal, "Study Links Urban Sprawl to Obesity," October 15, 2003. See also "Measuring the Health Effects of Sprawl," Special Report, Smart Growth America. Available at http://www.smartgrowthamerica.com/healthreportes.html.

67. Ibid.

68. Kammen et al. See http://socrates.berkeley.edu/%7Erael/papers.html#econdev

69. George Goldman and Aya Ogishi, "The Economic Impact of Solid Waste Disposal and Diversion in California." Paper presented at the Western Agricultural Economic Association Meeting, Logan, Utah, July 20, 2001, p. 14. Available at http://are.berkeley.edu/extension/EconImpWaste.pdf.

70. The Apollo Jobs Report, "For Good Jobs and Energy Independence: New Energy for America. See http://www.apolloalliance.org/docUploads/ApolloReport.pdf.

71. From "Renewing the Earth: An Invitation to Reflection and Action on Environment in Light of Catholic Social Teaching," pastoral statement of the U.S. Conference of Catholic Bishops, November 14, 1991. See http://www.usccb.org/sdwp/ejp/bishopsstatement.htm; and http://www.nrpe.org/.

72. See Arthur Rosenfeld, Michael Jaske, and Severin Borenstein, "Dynamic Pricing, Advanced Metering, and Demand Response in Electricity Markets," Hewlett Foundation Energy Series, October 2002. Available at http://ef.org/energyseries_dynamic.cfm.

73. "The Western States' Power Crisis: Imperatives and Opportunities," EPRI White Paper, June 2001.

chapter 3

Sustainable
Land Planning

Sustainable Land Planning

Kalvin Platt and Patrick Curran

To get it right, it is essential to start green office development with sustainable land planning for the site. Doing so can produce positive benefits for all aspects of project development—energy use, water conservation, the indoor environment, open space, and alternative choices of transportation. Planning a site with sustainability in mind can also help ensure easier approval and entitlement in environmentally minded jurisdictions with green requirements, and it can reduce costs over the life of a project.

To take full advantage of these benefits, green planning and design require the professional expertise of landscape architects and planners plus a multidisciplinary analysis of the full spectrum of site issues, large (global, regional, and community) to small (property specific), followed by a collaborative process in which the developer, architect, planner, landscape architect, engineer, and other consultants are partners in environmentally responsible planning and design decisions.

The site of the San Rafael Corporate Center required environmental remediation, but it offered easy access to regional transportation and downtown San Rafael's shops and restaurants. Tom Fox, SWA Group

Site Selection

Ideally, the first step in green site planning is to select a site appropriate for sustainable office development. In many cases, the site may have already been purchased or selected, but in those cases where a property has not yet been acquired, site selection is one of the most powerful tools for a truly sustainable development.

In selecting a green site, the developer should examine regional and community issues that could affect development, including the location of the site in relation to man-made community facilities and transportation and natural systems such as open-space networks. Preferably, office sites should be near existing residential areas or within a compact development to lessen employees' commutes and to lower the resulting energy use and air pollution. The community's utility capacity should be examined to ensure that capacity is sufficient to support office development on the site. Utility capacity that must be enhanced with on-site or off-site measures directly affects the green land plan and potentially lessens the project's sustainability.

Realistic Brownfield Development Opportunities

Stuart Miner

Brownfield sites are often found in prime real estate markets where well-located property is scarce or unrealistically expensive. Many of them—ripe for development—would make attractive locations for infill projects. Some older brownfield properties such as those that formerly housed heavy industrial operations and old gas or power operating plants are in locations that historically were most suitable for industrial development—in the core of larger cities, along waterfronts, and near major transportation routes. A later generation of brownfield properties is found in inner-ring suburbs. These properties tend to house newer, lighter industries or original 1950s- and 1960s-era retail centers that have become lightly contaminated from spills and leaks as a result of their use for gasoline sales, tire and auto repair centers, or dry cleaning facilities.

Real estate developers have warmed up slowly to the opportunities presented by brownfield development—with a number of good reasons for this reluctance. First, the strict joint and several liability standards established by the 1980 Superfund Law and similar state statutes make any owner liable for cleanup, regardless of how the problems originated. No traditional developer would assume this responsibility knowingly unless the cost of remediation could be built into the economics of the deal. The history of environmental cleanup has shown that it is

very difficult to forecast accurately the cost of a cleanup. Time, which is money to developers, is an issue. In many cases, a property must be cleaned up before development can begin, and experience has demonstrated that most cleanups take longer and cost more than originally estimated.

Liability is also a factor. Individuals or companies can suffer damages as a result of a contaminated brownfield property that was purchased by a developer otherwise innocent of any responsibility for the problem.

Yet another challenge is the need to coordinate the remediation of the property with its development. A common disconnect occurs when a purchaser assumes that modest soil contamination can be capped with a parking lot without a realistic site development plan that actually places the parking lot where the soil contamination on the property is found.

Despite these challenges, developers appear to be embracing the concept of land recycling, and it is a major factor in site location for green buildings. Led by firms specializing in the acquisition and development of brownfield properties, the evidence suggests a growing willingness to take on the challenges of these sites.

Although location and pricing may be sufficient motivation to prompt the development of some brownfield properties, in many cases additional supports and incentives are needed before brownfield development

The PNC Firstside Center was built on the site of an abandoned rail yard along the riverfront in downtown Pittsburgh, Pennsylvania. PNC Financial Services Group chose the Baltimore & Ohio railway terminal site because the site would not contribute to urban sprawl or waste green space, it provided the ability to create a new light-rail station for its employees to commute to work, and PNC was able to use existing roads, sewers, and bus stops. Astorino & Ed Massery

becomes commonplace. Other motivating factors play a role, one of the most important of which is the evolution of state and local programs to manage and mitigate environmental liability. More than 35 states have established some form of voluntary cleanup programs that make it easier for owners of contaminated property to develop, receive approval, and implement remedial action. Many states have specific brownfield programs aimed at spurring the development of formerly contaminated property. These programs contain a range of provisions, but typically they include some form of public subsidy such as grants or loans to help defray the costs of site analysis and cleanup as well as various forms of tax incentives to offset the cost of dealing with pollution on brownfield properties. A key component of a number of brownfield programs is the provision of some form of liability relief for "innocent" purchasers.

Although a number of brownfield developments have included the developer's assumption of responsibility to complete cleanup and retain liability for pollution, concern about environmental liability still deters most developers from pursuing brownfield projects. Although government programs are available that provide protection from liability claims from third parties alleging damages resulting from pollution on a brownfield property, they are not common or widespread—critical for many purchasers of brownfield properties.

One of the most important factors supporting the development of brownfield properties is the evolution of sophisticated environmental insurance programs to help manage the major financial uncertainties and residual liabilities that may remain, even after

cleanup and development are completed. During the 1990s, risk-retention agencies and smaller insurers began developing specialized forms of insurance targeting environmental risks. Unlike traditional commercial general liability policies, these new forms of environmental insurance were priced to provide coverage against a range of environmental risks. These policies have evolved and grown in number since their inception, and different forms of environmental insurance coverage are available today from a number of major U.S. insurers.

Regardless of how each insurer structures the coverage, these policies typically address two basic types of risks. The first is the risk of increase in the cost to clean the property. Insurance for this risk is typically referred to as cost cap or remediation stop loss. Remediation stop loss insurance provides coverage against increases in the remediation cost above a defined amount typically termed the attachment point. The second principal type of environmental insurance provides coverage for liability claims. The standard term for this type of coverage is real estate environmental liability insurance.

These policies mainly provide protection against monetary claims from third parties for property damage or bodily injury resulting from pollution present at the insured location. Coverage under these policies usually is triggered after the lead environmental regulatory agency has issued some type of "no

further action" determination documenting that the cleanup has been completed to the satisfaction of the agency. Some insurers, however, provide coverage before this determination is issued for unknown conditions or for a specific schedule of known conditions.

Most major insurance markets also provide coverage under the liability policy for additional cleanup costs (for known or unknown conditions) that can arise after the remediation is completed. Such a problem can arise if, for example, cleanup requirements change or additional contamination is discovered during development.

Development of brownfield properties is moving slowly into the mainstream of the development business. The growing acceptance of it is a result of the range of new tools that provide financial incentives and liability protection for those companies willing to take on this challenge and of the demonstrated success of a handful of developers and specialized brownfield companies that first rose to the challenge. New technical, legal, and financial tools will continue to be developed, and, it is hoped, environmental regulations and guidance will evolve in a direction that supports this effort. It is good not only for the environment but also for communities—and it is good business.

Stuart Miner is a partner with Brownfield Partners LLC in Denver, Colorado.

Recognizing the city's interest in reducing vehicular traffic, Veritas Software's corporate campus was oriented toward the southeast corner of the property, directly across from the light-rail station. In addition, pedestrian pathways provide direct circulation to destinations within the campus, to the transit station, and to adjacent businesses so Veritas employees and nearby workers can walk to work, lunch, and meetings. Tom Fox, SWA Group

Choosing to build within an existing community or on previously developed land helps to avoid sprawl and to maintain existing open-space patterns, both key environmental considerations. Many infill sites and brownfields, for example, have excellent access to both public transportation and utilities, and they may be large enough to also provide good solar access. The site analysis addresses whether environmental remediation is needed, what action should be taken to protect adjacent properties from contamination, and what buildings and infrastructure can be recycled or used.

The 15-acre (six-hectare) site selected for the 450,000-square-foot (41,800-square-meter) San Rafael Corporate Center in Marin County, California, for example, was adjacent to a regional transportation center and within walking distance of downtown shops and restaurants. The property, however, had previously been used by an electric substation, leaving behind many different toxins in the soil that had to be remediated. In addition to environmental remediation, the green land plan also included restoration of the adjacent Mahon Creek habitat, which provides new recreational opportunities, primarily trails, along the creek.

Any green office development should be planned to enhance the surrounding neighborhood. To that end, site selection should examine issues such as the impact of the development on surrounding areas and on local streets.

Veritas Software, the single largest vendor of storage management software, built its corporate campus in Mountain View, California, south of San Francisco, on a 20-acre (eight-hectare) site adjacent to a new light-rail station. As the property was surrounded by offices but no shops or restaurants, the land plan provided commercial services (a café, a health club, and convenience retailers) in an on-campus public zone adjacent to the station. Pedestrian pathways throughout the campus now enable Veritas and nearby workers to walk to lunch rather than drive.

Site Analysis

Whether a property has been acquired specifically for the development of a sustainable office project or the land was already part of a developer's or corporation's portfolio and is now slated for development, green land planning and development begin with a comprehensive site analysis before a single plan is drawn.

An environmental sensitivity analysis begins with a site survey that looks at the property's geology, climate, topography, soils, hydrology, and biology. An effective tool for the site survey is Geographic Information Systems (GIS), which identifies regional and site issues that should be addressed in the sustainable land plan. One product of the analysis is a development suitability map of the site, of paramount importance for a green land plan. The map guides decisions about where development should be located on the site.

Careful study of the property's natural systems helps to determine the carrying capacity of the land and the site's sensitivity to development. Some portions of the property, for example, will likely be more suitable for buildings and parking than others. Determining the most appropriate land for development also usually ensures an easier permitting process and helps to begin defining the property's open space.

The site analysis should also include a sensitive lands assessment to identify plant and wildlife habitats and set aside (or create) habitat conservation areas, safeguard indigenous plants and trees, and specify areas for office development on noncritical habitat lands. The law requires developers to protect endangered species, but green land planning should go far beyond the law to protect site-specific species.

A site survey identifies potential hazards—earthquake faults, slide areas, underground caverns, rock outcrops—as well as the location of the water table and groundwater and aquifer recharge areas. It also helps to locate and record topographical features, including subsurface rock formations (which are expensive to build on), elevations, utilities that serve or cross the property, trees, rights-of-way, property lines, and other issues that directly affect green land planning. The site survey should include a slope analysis that details how the site's topography connects to larger landforms as well as the property's sun and view orientation. Thus, the green planning team can use the land's features to establish the site's development patterns and help save dominant ridges, prominent high points, and the overall integrity of the land and its environment.

Soil borings provide data on the condition and weight-bearing capacity of the land, which affect building foundation and roadway design, and identify the presence of haz-

ardous materials, salinity, fertility, compaction, and ease of grading. Healthy soils that are full of life and appropriate for development can support strong vegetation, easier on-site drainage systems, and more reasonable development costs.

The regional hydrology systems—from the watershed to underground aquifers, streams, lakes, and floodplains—affect a site in many ways, from supplying water that can be pumped by wells, to creating wetlands that cannot be developed but can provide an important amenity, to periodic flooding. Land development can also affect the

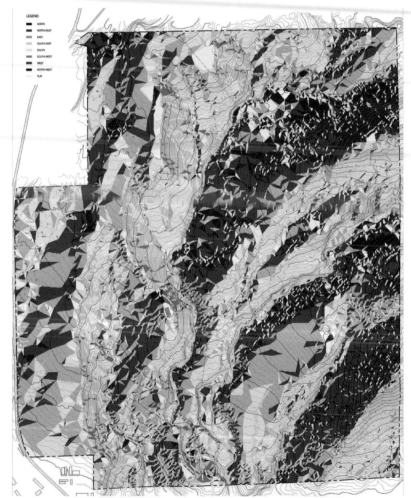

An aspect map, such as the one shown here for Stone Ridge Ranch in Chico, California, provides an analysis of solar conditions at various points throughout a site to guide the design process. SWA Group

The Impact of Regulatory Issues on Site Selection

Kalvin Platt and Patrick Curran

In the United States, federal, state, regional, and local regulations substantially affect site selection for a green office. They usually take the form of constraints on development, but green land planning can turn these regulations into opportunities. Developers of a site adjacent to wetlands or a creek, for example, can mitigate those constraints by creating on-site open space or green corridors that protect the environment and enhance the project's value. Looking beyond regulations helps to find a site's hidden opportunities.

The main impact of land development on land, water, air, plants, animals, and insects is usually destruction. Over the last 300 years, human beings have decimated 97 percent of the ancient forests in North America. Today, however, government agencies like the U.S. EPA and state fish and wildlife departments often enforce promotion of biodiversity and maintenance of the integrity of the environment, which can affect the pattern of development on a property.

Wetlands and Water Quality

The U.S. Army Corps of Engineers and the U.S. EPA comanage the Clean Water Act, which regulates wetlands, streams, and other natural hydrological features. These agencies must review any proposed modification or potential impact on the areas, and, when

required, the modification or impact must undergo the permitting process. Floodplains are documented by federal mapping and may have special requirements for ground and building elevations.

Endangered Species

The Endangered Species Act requires review of any habitat that potentially could serve listed species of plants and animals. Some regions, like San Diego County in California, have prepared Multiple Species Conservation Programs that meet the requirements of the Endangered Species Act by identifying habitat areas and those locations free from endangered species. Some other regions have adopted Habitat Conservation Plans for selected species. Developers can use both tools to identify areas that can be developed intensely without triggering habitat and endangered species issues.

Habitat Conservation

Habitat conservation regulatory issues affect site selection in many ways. Office facilities can be successful neighbors to identified habitat areas. The professionally managed and controlled environment of green office developments has a low risk of intruding on habitat, and, in turn, the visual open spaces of habitat areas are amenities for tenants and visitors.

Clean Air

The Federal Clean Air Act has mandated traffic control measures to reduce the discharge of pollutants from automobiles. Clean air regulations can significantly affect site selection. The proposed development, for example, can add to already peak traffic flows, which would exacerbate air pollution in some areas. Such a site would therefore not meet green land planning and development criteria unless multiple trip reduction technologies and strategies were implemented.

Energy

Some states offer incentives for the construction of renewable energy systems such as wind turbines or solar panels on site. The California Public Utilities Commission, for example, offers rebates of up to 50 percent on project costs for solar systems. When studying sites, therefore, the developer or corporation should look for land that would support renewable energy systems.

Infill and Brownfields

Many local jurisdictions now enact policies that favor infill and brownfield development. Often, they offer incentives, such as easier permit processing. As green land planning addresses some of the most pressing problems of infill and brownfield development, lessening an office facility's impact on existing infrastructure, these sites can increase the supply of land in metropolitan areas suffering from a scarcity of available and buildable sites. They greatly expand opportunities for green site selection.

The federal government's Small Business Liability Relief and Brownfields Revitalization Act has expanded infill housing and economic development opportunities by protecting purchasers of contaminated sites from future federal action if they meet specific criteria for buying, maintaining, cleaning up, and preventing future threats of contamination on the land.

Local Regulatory Issues

Local regulations identify sites that are suitable for office development as well as the density, floor/area ratio (FAR), height limit, setbacks, parking, service areas, open space, and character of permitted facilities. Sustainable planning and design have to work within those constraints. Most local communities require an environmental impact statement (EIS) or environmental impact report (EIR) that sets out all the adverse and beneficial impacts of the proposed project.

Zoning

Zoning is a critical component of green planning. Mixed-use zoning that allows some multifamily housing on an office or business park site can greatly support sustainable development by putting homes close to jobs, thereby reducing vehicular trips. Hacienda Business Park, a large business park in Pleasanton, California, for example, has successfully integrated housing on the business campus.

Some large cities give zoning bonuses to transit-oriented developments by expanding allowable uses or increasing the FAR when a project is built near transit facilities or increases access to transit. Some cities also offer transfers of development rights, which preserve historic structures by selling the office density to other certified sites.

Water and Sewer

Some local communities require documentation that adequate water and sewer capacity exists for the site, while others require special allocations for water and sewer where capacity is in short supply. In still other areas, recharging the aquifer may be an important community issue with its own regulations. The emphasis of sustainable planning and development on hydrological uses may lead a municipality to approve a green project for a sensitive site where a traditional development would be vetoed.

Stormwater Management

Many communities require zero runoff or no net increase in runoff to downstream neighbors from a two-year storm. They also generally require that runoff from buildings and paved areas, and nonpoint source pollution such as nutrients, sediments, and petroleum compounds be treated and detained on site.

Transportation

Easy access to transit is a key criterion in green land planning. Office identity is enhanced by a location along a main street or in the community's preferred office district. Such locations are usually the most affected by peak traffic flow, an important consideration in green development. Some communities require substantial monetary or in-kind contributions to local road networks for development on these locations. By investing in measures to reduce the number of trips, costly off-site road contributions could be reduced.

Balance between Jobs and Housing

Many local jurisdictions mandate constructing mixed uses—housing and workplaces, for example—on the same property or assess fees that are used to construct affordable housing or require large developments to be sequenced to balance jobs and housing Local government was very receptive to Apple Computer's choosing to build a major R&D manufacturing facility on a site near Sacramento, California, adjacent to a supply of affordable housing.

Exxon Mobil preserved existing woodlands and wetlands, added new water features, and reforested greenways at the company's headquarters campus in Irving, **Texas.** Tom Fox, SWA Group

regional hydrology system in many, usually negative, ways by, for example, draining an aquifer, paving over a floodplain (which increases flooding), and redirecting water flow outside the natural system.

Conducting a watershed analysis helps to identify the prevailing hydrologic patterns of the region and how they affect a particular site. The EPA now has a Web site (www.epa.gov/surf) that locates any property's watershed. Essential data include the quantity of water entering and leaving the site and identification of any natural waterways, streams, or drainageways on or adjacent to the property, as well as flood zones and FEMA (Federal Emergency Management Agency) mapping or other sources that provide insight into periodic upstream events. By understanding these patterns, the planning and design team can quickly and easily determine what hydrology strategies are

necessary and what development is and is not appropriate for the land to minimize or avoid any negative impact to the regional watershed.

Green land planning also includes preserving the water regime or, if it has been altered or damaged, restoring the natural system. This requirement could involve renovating drainageways, revitalizing stream corridors, and reintroducing appropriate vegetation to filter and retain any additional runoff created by planned buildings and parking. A site survey helps to determine if such work is necessary.

Rainfall patterns affect green land planning. A property in an area that has a heavy annual rainfall, for example, needs engineering water systems like detention basins and bioswales to retain and clean the water and help avoid flooding. In drier climates, engineering water systems are needed to capture rainfall and recycle water for irrigation. As the green land plan must ensure a zero net increase in stormwater runoff, a rain analysis is of great importance and can be extensively used in planning the site's hydrology and stormwater management systems.

Green land planning includes the promotion, maintenance, and perhaps the restoration or reestablishment of native vegetation on the site. Thus, the environmental sensitivity analysis should include a study of the historic patterns of native vegetation and critical habitat on the site and a survey of existing native plants and invasive vegetation that may harm the quality of the habitat. This analysis guides land planning and design so that they provide high-quality habitat for terrestrial species, aquatic species, and underground species in the form of corridors and patches (stopping places for hunting and migratory species).

A site's animal species require a certain character of ecosystem in which to live or move through. A regional study identifies endangered species and their habitats, and local environmental agencies determine what habitat planning and design should be done. Nonendangered species also require a specific ecosystem. A study of those species on site will form the basis for the planning and designing of suitable habitat.

Sustainable Site Planning

Once a site suitable for sustainable development is acquired and the various site analyses have been studied, the planning team can begin creating a site plan for the project using information provided by those analyses in conjunction with market research, a tenant needs assessment, and an understanding of broader regional issues.

The USGBC's LEED program can help guide the project. LEED evaluates and certifies a facility's sustainability and environmental performance over a building's life cycle based on five broad categories: site, water, energy, materials, and indoor air quality (see Chapter 1). To earn LEED certification, new office facilities must address six different categories—sustainable sites, water efficiency, energy and

atmosphere, materials and resources, indoor environmental quality, and innovation and design process—potentially earning a total of 69 points. "Sustainable Site" makes up 14 of those points.

LEED criteria address major site planning issues—erosion and sedimentation control, alternative transportation and public transportation access, brownfield redevelopment, the reduction of light pollution—and they provide guidance on how to earn the necessary points for certification. LEED, for example, requires that the office site be located within one-half mile (0.8 kilometer) of a commuter rail, light-rail, or subway station or within one-quarter mile (0.4 kilometer) of two or more public or campus bus lines.

To meet the goal of reduced site disturbance, LEED requires limiting greenfield site earthwork and the clearing of vegetation to 40 feet (12 meters) beyond the building perimeter, five feet (1.5 meters) beyond the primary roadway curbs, walks, and main utility branch trenches, and 25 feet (7.6 meters) beyond constructed areas with permeable surfaces. To reduce light pollution, LEED requires that the project meet or provide lower light levels and uniformity ratios than those recommended by the Illuminating Engineering Society of North America by using full cutoff luminaries, low-reflectance surfaces, low-angle spotlights, and appropriate building orientation, interior design, and landscaping.

Additional LEED products are now under development, including one that will address neighborhood development, Smart Growth criteria, and site criteria for streets, infrastructure, and historic and ecological restoration.

Building Location and Orientation

Sustainable site planning balances the environmental sensitivity and amenities of the site with building configuration, parking needs, access, views, and regulatory requirements (maximum density, height, and setback) to create a green land plan that is functional and also responsive to users' needs. The developer, architect, engineer, and other project consultants must collaborate on siting the buildings and their overall form and orientation. A critical goal in this exercise is to allow for flexibility in the site and building program for future uses in anticipation of shifting priorities and changing market dynamics.

By following the footprint of the industrial building previously on the site, site grading was minimized in the construction of Kunming Communities in Kunming, Yunnan Province, China. Tom Fox, SWA Group

Buildings and other major structures should be located only on those portions of the site found suitable in the site analysis for intensive development. If the overall site is adjacent to transit or compatible mixed uses, buildings should be located to reinforce those positive relationships and forge connections to adjoining developments.

When land planning green on a previously developed site, look for opportunities to locate facilities on already disturbed lands to conserve existing open space. Disturbed lands can range from building foundations to parking lots or exotic landscape. In Kunming, China, for example, the land plan for a 20,000-square-foot (1,860-square-meter) multiple-use building on the site of a former brick-making

factory follows the same footprint as the factory, which saves existing ravines and open meadows on the site from grading and potential degradation.

Solar intensity, exposure, and orientation on the land partially determine where buildings and other facilities are sited on the property. In cooler climates, buildings and main outdoor spaces should be given a southern orientation to reap the sunlight's warmth. In hot climates, buildings and main outdoor spaces should be given a northern or east-west orientation (with the use of sunshades on facades with the most solar exposure) to avoid the greatest impact from the sun.

Depending on regional wind patterns, the green land plan should orient internal streets, pedestrian paths, and other facilities to take advantage of the wind or to protect those facilities from the wind. Generally, tenants and visitors need to be protected from northerly and other prevailing winter winds and cooled by summer breezes. If the site has hillsides, for example, or is adjacent to hillsides, buildings can be sited so that the hills provide protection from the wind.

Views and opportunities for access to open space, whether a hill, meadow, river corridor, or woods, are important amenities for building occupants. A viewshed analysis helps determine building location and orientation to reap the best views from locally or regionally significant land forms. The Gap building in San Bruno, California, for example, was oriented to give tenants views of the nearby golden hills.

When green land planning a major office project, remember that how much you build is just as important as what you build. Sustainable planning should minimize the amount of on-site infrastructure, from roads to utilities, limit large areas of impermeable paving to reduce peak stormwater runoff flows and promote groundwater recharge, reduce the development footprint, and focus on compact building development. LEED criteria for urban redevelopment (building, roads, parking) encourage a minimum density of 60,000 square feet per acre (13,775 square meters per hectare) or a floor/area ratio of 1.38, which in most cases would require structured parking.

Density in a green land plan is about creating a smaller development footprint and increasing the opportunities for high-quality, connected open space. Building up rather than sprawling out is typically the best choice for a sustainable site plan, because it helps mitigate potential environmental, regional, and neighborhood issues.

Topography and Grading

The property's topography—including slopes, dominant land forms, and soil composition—has a dramatic impact on green office development. The green land plan should create an office development that seems to have grown out of the land, which is achieved primarily through landscaping and grading that respects and mimics the surrounding landscape. A slope analysis and elevation study provides a critical guide for how the site should be used and where

development should occur to minimize any negative impact from development.

More and more often, office construction takes place on previously developed land or on land previously used for agriculture. Thus, the green land plan should include (in some jurisdictions it is mandated) reconstruction of the site's natural topography and replanting of the native vegetation. This reconstruction also affects where development occurs on the property and how it is built so that the property once again becomes part of the functioning regional open space and habitat system.

The former Orlando Naval Training Center in Florida is being redeveloped into a 1,100-acre (445-hectare) mixed-use community that includes business parks. A key component of the master plan is the restoration and expansion of wetlands and lakes on the former base and the extension of that system to a larger regional lake and park system, creating important wildlife habitats, open-space corridors, and community amenities.

At the Horizon Paris mixed-use development outside Paris, buildings are placed along the natural contours of the sloping site to minimize grading. Tom Fox, SWA Group

Sustainable land planning sets a building into the site in a manner that causes the least possible disturbance to the land. The less grading required by building construction, the less money is required to import dirt and restore the natural conditions of the site. LEED criteria limit site disturbance to less than 50 percent of the property.

Grading can be minimized with strategies like locating buildings on less steep land and using contour grading; that is, roadways and building sites follow the topographical contours of the land, reducing the amount of grading, maintaining a sense of the natural land forms, avoiding large retaining walls, and supporting revegetation and thereby reduce erosion, protect the natural environment, and maintain natural hydrology processes, open-space patterns, and wildlife habitat.

Grading can also be used to strengthen a green land plan by creating drainage swales to handle stormwater runoff or building berms that can act as noise and/or wind barriers. The grading strategy for the 68-acre (27.5-hectare) McCarthy Ranch business campus in Cupertino, California, met the city's mandate for no net increase in stormwater runoff through a series of gently graded surfaces that meet at drainage swales, where water is polished and allowed to settle before groundwater is recharged. This grading strategy worked with the landscape plan to create a pattern of terrain—a series of fingers at the lowest elevation—in a landscape plan that gives the parking areas a softer aesthetic. It also saved construction costs on infrastructure components such as pipes.

In most metropolitan areas, much of the prime flat land has already been developed, so design teams often must create a green land plan for a hillside parcel. In this case, the land plan and architectural design must work together. A thorough slope map should help clarify what portions of the property have the capacity to support development.

Strategies to minimize the negative impact of development on a hillside include pier-on-grade foundations (in which the uphill side of a building is on grade and the downhill side is supported by piers), retaining walls, and split-level architecture.

The Horizon Paris is a mixed-use development under construction on a 53-acre (21.5-hectare) infill parcel at the eastern end of Marne-la-Vallée near Mont d'Est outside Paris, France. The site has slopes of up to 10 percent, quite steep for the high-density development planned for the property, and clay soils that exacerbate stormwater runoff from the site, causing flooding into the nearby Marne River. The land plan, however, has successfully surmounted these challenges. First, to mitigate the steep slope without leveling it, the planners specified the development of traditional European-style office buildings, which are usually just 50 to 60 feet (15 to 18 meters) wide. The architects then elongated and curved the buildings and located them along the natural contours of the slope, minimizing both the grading and excavation that had to be done.

Second, to better manage stormwater, the planners again turned to French tradition. The drainage system is a series of flat surface canals that move back and forth across the site along the natural contours of the hill. Cascades (stairs or steps) also carry water down the slope. Holding or detention basins further slow the flow of water through Horizon Paris. A walkway system ties the canals and cascades together, helping to both unify the site and provide an important pedestrian amenity. This combination of old and new stormwater management systems not only helps prevent flooding but also creates a distinct identity for the mixed-use development.

Erosion Control

Erosion can be controlled during and after construction with green strategies like silt fencing (a textile fence attached to wooden stakes) and straw bails to reduce sediment runoff

A manmade system of lakes, wetlands, and a central greenway serves as both an amenity and a stormwater management system at the Meridian Business Campus in Aurora, Illinois.

Tom Fox, SWA Group

during construction. In addition, rapidly growing but temporary plants help hold the slopes. Over the long term, it is helpful to implement erosion control strategies that provide dual benefits. Landscaping with deep-rooted plants, for example, helps hold the slopes and beautifies the property.

Bioengineering—the use of groundcovers, shrubs, and trees—can help control erosion on sloped areas. Live-staking uses bundles of natural materials held in place, or staked, by deep rooted plants to help hold the slope in place. Willow waddles, for example, combine willow cuttings with quick-growing willow plantings.

Erosion control devices such as open-core concrete blocks or textile fences can hold the slopes while plants are developing root systems. Geosynthetic materials like Enkamat are an alternative to the use of rigid concrete or rip rap to stabilize the slope and control erosion. These products support the growth of strong vegetation for permanent erosion protection of slopes, rivers, banks, ditches, channels, spillways, landfills, shorelines, and other vulnerable or erosion-prone areas.

Bioswales, water detention devices, gravel filters, and other stormwater management strategies can reduce the velocity of water flowing over the site, minimizing erosion and supporting absorption.

Stormwater Management

The overall goal of a green land plan's stormwater management system is no net increase in the rate and quantity of stormwater runoff from the site. The basic strategy is to reduce the amount of stormwater peak flow, runoff volume, sediments, and pollutants generated on site.

Several planning strategies discussed earlier can support this strategy; for example, a reduced development footprint, which allows the natural processes of evaporation and infiltration to continue on site, or the reduction of impervious surfaces. Other solutions include the construction of water detention and retention systems on site.

Flood risk can be minimized by setting aside areas on large campus-style office developments for detention basins, which hold back stormwater until the peak flow passes and then release the water slowly back into streams, rivers, and bayous, avoiding flooding and protecting habitat. Some of the water held in a detention basin can be retained on site for irrigation, water features, and other reclaimed or non-potable water uses.

Detention basins take two forms. Off-line basins are separate from a stream channel and remain empty until the stream reaches a certain level and the water is diverted into the basin. In-line, or in-stream, basins widen the flood bench of a stream channel to expand its capacity to manage stormwater and to help slow the flow of that water.

Detention basins can also be designed to serve as park areas and real estate magnets. Houston's Willow Water Hole, for example, is actually a series of detention basins in the form of lakes and streams surrounded by open space, creating wonderful recreational opportunities. The master plan for the Kelsey-Seybold Clinic Medical Center Campus, also in Houston, created a two-acre (0.8-hectare) park with a water feature that accommodates more than 50 percent of the site's stormwater detention requirements and provides a view, recreational amenities, and a beautiful place for both campus users and the surrounding community to cool off in Houston's hot and humid climate.

Instead of curb and gutter systems and storm sewers, a sustainable land plan can use bioswales to help slow stormwater, acting essentially as minidetention basins that can hold and store water from smaller storms.

The property's open space can be dedicated to mitigating peak flows and the associated flooding, improve water quality, and promote infiltration while providing a community open-space amenity. The green land plan for an office park or corporate campus can also use that regional watershed for open space, a natural wastewater treatment system, a power resource, and a view.

The Meridian Business Campus, for example, turned the requirement for a stormwater management system into the organizing land planning element for the entire campus. Water-holding requirements were transferred from the more than 80 individual parcels into the site's open-space common areas to form a wetland, five manmade lakes, and a central greenway. Consolidating the open space gave Meridian a focus and a sense of place, creating a cohesive whole rather than a patchwork quilt of individual parcels. This consolidation also created open space for the tenants and the surrounding community, generated a high-quality image for the entire campus, and added value to the individual parcels.

On small and large sites, bioswales lined with grass and plants that filter stormwater can be used to clean stormwater runoff from paved parking areas. Vehicular areas should be graded toward the parking stall separators—the bioswales—which should be cross-sloped with gravel beds and lined with plants. This approach slows stormwater and allows sediment loads to drop out and be broken down by the microbial species and used in the plants' biological processes before the water enters the site's larger hydrology system.

On larger office sites where the water table is sufficiently deep, infrastructure costs can be reduced and the property's open-space system enhanced by treating stormwater on site. Such treatment would involve a local system incorporating biological functions such as renovated natural channels or constructed bioswales, gravel or sand deposits, and natural or manmade wetlands that reduce or remove pollutants and filter and treat the water before releasing it into the site's natural systems (ravines, a creek, wetlands, or open water). These natural water filtration systems can also be used for wildlife habitat, recreational areas, trails, and views.

The developer of Playa Vista—a new 1,087-acre (440-hectare), environmentally sensitive mixed-use community, including a 114-acre (46-hectare) business campus, under construction in greater Los Angeles—is creating a new 26-acre (10.5-hectare) freshwater marsh that, in addition to vitally needed wildlife habitat, will also provide flood control and the first natural stormwater management system in Los Angeles County. The marsh will act as Nature's sponge, absorbing large quantities of water (including stormwater and urban runoff), cleaning it, and slowly releasing it into Santa Monica Bay.

Manmade products can also improve water quality. Storm chambers, for example, are part of an underground system in which micro-organisms form on the soil and stone underlying the chambers and then metabolize pollutants and convert them and nutrients to noncontaminating byproducts. The filtered runoff can then reenter the larger hydrology system.

The water generated from these and other stormwater management strategies can be recycled and reused for nonpotable applications such as landscape irrigation, fountains and other landscape water features, toilets, commercial laundry facilities, and car washes, reducing the use of potable water on site and helping to maintain groundwater levels.

The Santa Monica Water Garden, a 1.6 million-square-foot (149,000-square-meter) business campus in Santa Monica, California, has an on-site wastewater treatment plant and a graywater recycling system that supported the creation of a 1.4 acre (0.6 hectare) lake with fountains and cascading waterfalls in the midst of a dry landscape, creating a distinctive image for the Los Angeles–area business park. The system collects all the site's stormwater and graywater and reuses it for landscape irrigation, the campus's lake and fountains, and the water gardens.

Wastewater Treatment and Management

When it comes to wastewater treatment and management, the goal of the green land plan is to reduce the office facility's burden on the municipal infrastructure and to reuse cleaned wastewater rather than potable water on site.

An important and increasingly popular strategy is to include biotreatment of localized wastewater, if the office property is large enough, and recycled wastewater facilities to reduce the use of potable water. Constructed wetlands, for example, treat wastewater before returning it to the ground and can be used with septic tanks or biological treatment units.

One biotreatment strategy, typically referred to as Living Machine, moves wastewater from a facility into an anaerobic reactor, which is much like a septic tank. The reactor uses biological processes to treat waste. The Living Machine system at the Ethel M. Chocolates facility in Henderson, Nevada, provides advanced treatment of confectionary process wastewater. The treated wastewater is then reused for on-site landscape irrigation. The sludge is also treated on site by a composting reed bed, making this a zero discharge facility.

Keeping and treating wastes on site requires that waste management is local and closer to the source—a goal of paramount importance in sustainable development. It also avoids adding larger and larger pipes to the regional network and further burdening the regional wastewater treatment system. Moreover, it provides more water for on-site reuse, such as landscape irrigation.

Energy Reduction

A green land plan can help reduce energy use. Siting an office on the north-south axis, for example, floods the interior with northern light without heat gain. With careful siting of a building, natural light can be the single interior light source during the day, which significantly reduces energy use and costs. Similarly, solar orientation can also lower HVAC use and energy costs.

The Capitol Area East End Complex in Sacramento, California, is expected to exceed the 1998 energy efficiency standards mandated in California's Title 24. It does so through a combination of photovoltaic panels on the parking structure roof that shade the parked cars and the roof and provide electricity for the garage, high ceilings and an interior floor plan to generate the greatest use of natural daylighting, automated lighting controls, high-efficiency mechanical systems, two-story arcades that shade the lower building levels, and high-efficiency window glazing that reduces cooling requirements. This complex is forecast to generate $400,000 annually in energy savings alone (see Chapter 9).

The Arvida Park of Commerce in Boca Raton, Florida, includes an 18-hole public golf course that provides a major amenity for the community and business park tenants while also serving as an on-site stormwater retention system and supporting aquifer recharge. SWA Group

Innovative technologies such as photovoltaic panels on buildings, accessory structures, and parking areas provide power for site lighting and landscape irrigation systems and help reduce a project's mechanical heating and cooling loads and overall energy consumption. The new 624,000-square-foot (58,000-square-meter) South Campus Office Development expansion of the 135-acre (55-hectare) Toyota Motor Sales North American Headquarters in Torrance, California, for example, has the single largest commercial installation of photovoltaic panels in California, which provide 20 percent of the buildings' energy requirements. With this and other strategies, energy performance of the south campus exceeds both the California Title 24 energy code and the minimum LEED requirements by more than 42 percent (see Chapter 9).

Advances in fuel cell technology, gas turbine engines, microturbine generators, and energy management systems all support a sustainable land plan and energy conservation. Wind generation to provide electricity may be practical where windmills on towers can be safely installed on landscape ridges or coastal areas.

Heat Island Reduction

A green land plan should avoid creating heat islands generated by the use of asphalt and other dark nonreflective surfaces on roofs, walkways, patios, roads, and parking lots that absorb sunlight and heat during the day and then slowly release the heat at night, which increases surrounding temperatures by as much as 10 degrees. Heat islands make the climate less comfortable for humans, and they increase HVAC loads for buildings and water needed for exterior landscaping. Heat islands also negatively affect nearby wildlife habitats, making them unlivable for some plants and animals that require cooler conditions.

Strategies to minimize or avoid heat islands include a compact development footprint and alternatives to impermeable paving, such as an open-grid roadway system with gravel, not asphalt paving, which also reduces stormwater runoff. At the Philip Merrill Environmental Center, headquarters of the Chesapeake Bay Foundation, the roof is made of a recycled light-colored material to reflect the sunlight and its associated heat. Approximately 25 percent of the parking spaces are underground, and the at-grade parking lots are paved with gravel. The emergency vehicle access roads are covered in grass pavers rather than asphalt. Paved pedestrian areas are made of light-colored concrete that minimizes solar reflection (see Chapter 9).

The choice of roofing material can also reduce heat islands. Roofing materials should be highly reflective (reflecting solar light and heat back into the atmosphere rather than absorbing it) and highly emissive (shedding infrared radiation and any absorbed heat). Two of several choices are membrane roofing—a modular roof with a single layer of fabric material that has a high reflection ratio—and metal roofing of steel or aluminum, which also has a high reflection ratio as well as low emissions. A light-colored reflective ENERGY STAR roof on an office building reduces the heat island effects and heat absorption of a darker standard roof surface, in turn lowering air-conditioning needs and costs (see also "Landscaped Roofs" below and "Sustainable Roofs" in Chapter 4).

Open-Space Planning

Open-space planning can add significant value to an office property through its aesthetic appeal, habitat conservation, and recreational amenities. Native vegetation, for example, can be turned into buffers, screens, shade canopies, usable open space, and water management systems. Enhanced wildlife habitats and natural resources on the site provide a setting and sense of place that can make a project specific to the surrounding community. LEED recommends exceeding local code open-space requirements by more than 25 percent.

The green land plan should focus on conserving existing natural areas and restoring damaged areas to enhance local habitat and open-space patterns when possible. The mowed lawn on the AT&T Network Systems Campus in Lisle, Illinois, was restored to native prairie, which created and restored wildlife habitat, connected that habitat to the larger regional systems, and reduced AT&T's maintenance costs through the elimination of irrigation and lawn mowing.

Urban wildlife is very adaptable to different habitats and often can acclimate to a variety of native or naturalized restoration projects. Thus, created or restored habitat patches and corridors function at a high level—particularly if they connect to larger open-space systems—while adding value and providing important amenities to the office property.

Open space can be expensive. The combination of high land costs, building costs, and open-space management might make sustainable land planning's emphasis on preserving abundant open space seem wholly unrealistic. But green land planning also emphasizes getting multiple uses from almost every master plan component, including open space, which significantly affects a project's cost/benefit analysis.

Stormwater management systems like bioswales, detention basins, and wastewater wetlands, for example, can support aquatic species, provide stopover habitat for migrating birds, serve as environmental educational facilities for the community, and even provide some recreational amenities such as jogging paths. Existing creeks, streams, and rivers can also be used to clean and manage stormwater flows. Large swaths of forest can be planted as visual buffers or wind screens for the office campus, and they also provide wildlife patches or corridors.

The green land plan must ensure that office development will not negatively affect environmentally significant adjacent or nearby open spaces, bodies of water, wildlife habitat, or views to and from the property. The open space, landscape, and hydrology plan, for example, can help control pollution and protect habitat on site. At the same time, adjacent natural resources like a lake, marsh, meadow, or forest can add significant value to the project if the land plan protects, maintains, and celebrates that resource.

Planning for Parking

As parking can consume vast amounts of space—more than 400 square feet (37 square meters) per vehicle is allocated in some cases and ratios of three and one-half to four spaces per 1,000 square feet (93 square meters) of rentable space are typical—parking reduction is a key component of green land planning.

Parking requirements can be reduced with a shared parking program and an increase in opportunities for alternative transportation such as preferred parking areas for vanpools and alternative fuel vehicles, and shuttle, bicycle, and pedestrian links to nearby transit lines, residential neighborhoods, and commercial areas. LEED credits are earned by, among other strategies, limiting parking to the minimum required by local codes, providing designated carpool parking for 5 percent of a building's occupants, and providing showers and bicycle racks for more than 5 percent of a building's occupants.

Surface parking lots are certainly cheaper to build, but they are massive heat islands, they create a huge development footprint, leaving less room for open space and other amenities, they are aesthetically displeasing, and they can create problems with stormwater runoff. Structured parking is more expensive and has environmental issues as well, but it significantly reduces the development footprint and number of heat islands.

Partially or fully underground parking conserves the development footprint, but it is the most expensive type of structured parking to construct, it blocks natural light and ventilation, and it consumes the most energy per space. Parking constructed under buildings helps minimize the development footprint, but the necessary building foundation and columns make it less efficient than a freestanding or attached garage, and it also lacks natural light and ventilation.

Native landscaping covers almost half of the Veritas campus in Mountain View, California, including parking areas. Tom Fox, SWA Group

Several strategies and products can mitigate many of the challenges parking brings to sustainable land planning. Pervious paving materials like porous pavement, gravel, and patented block surfaces such as grasspave in at-grade parking lots reduce stormwater runoff and encourage water absorption. Gravel beds in parking areas can filter stormwater runoff into recharge systems.

In addition to shading techniques such as street trees, a newly emerging strategy is to shade parking lots with freestanding photovoltaic panels that also collect the sun's energy and reuse it on site, reducing the facility's energy costs.

Circulation and Transportation

The circulation network is the framework on which the entire built environment is laid out: that framework must do much more than simply move people from one location to another. Green land planning integrates many modes of transportation on a site to serve a variety of needs, avoid conflicts, and reduce vehicle trips and impermeable surfaces on site. Ideally, roads should be located only on those portions of the site that are suitable for intensive development. In a business park or corporate campus, it is desirable to create an east-west axis for the streets so that buildings have southern and northern solar exposures, allowing them to use more photovoltaic panels for heating and electricity.

Streets should be friendly to pedestrians and bicyclists, not just cars. Overly wide streets should be avoided. Narrow streets slow traffic, and they leave space for pedestrian sidewalks to encourage walking rather than automobile use. Street trees planted near the curb and in the median can help to shade the pavement, reduce the heat island effect, and provide a beautifully landscaped environment for pedestrians that visually and physically separates them from traffic, creating in effect a safe zone.

The circulation of vehicles, bicycles, and pedestrians should be planned to avoid conflicts between these different modes of access. The primary road system for automobiles should remain distinct from parking lot access drives. Truck routes should not go through employee or visitor parking areas.

Pedestrian and bicycle systems should have preference, be clearly marked, and connect surrounding areas and parking to building entrances in the most direct manner with clearly marked crosswalks. Buses, shuttles, and vanpools should have direct access to building entrances and pull-off areas for loading and preferred parking.

Silicon Graphics's 26.6-acre (10.8-hectare) R&D campus in Mountain View, California, includes a five-acre (two-hectare) public park and provides public access through the campus to a nearby regional park and a planned trail along the Permanente Creek corridor. Tom Fox, SWA Group

City Center Oakland, at the edge of downtown Oakland, California, provides pleasant pedestrian routes to nearby transit facilities. Dixi Carrillo, SWA Group

The fire lanes or extra paving necessary for large trucks and emergency vehicles and their turning radii can be made of permeable materials such as paving blocks, grasscrete, grasspave, and sod reinforced with appropriate subbases to reduce the heat island effect and the site's paving footprint and associated costs, and to support stormwater management and groundwater recharge. Loading docks or zones should be out of view from the project's entry and surrounding properties and screened from the office building by landscape, walls, or fences.

One key component of the green land plan is the connection between the property and the existing regional transportation infrastructure. Within a major office park, for example, internal streets can be extended to the existing street grid to create pedestrian and vehicular paths that connect directly to regional transit (bus stops, train stations, freeways), services, and/or open space and trails.

A green office land plan should include strategies to reduce the number of vehicle trips such as maximizing the ease of site access for those tenants and employees who do not drive to work, designating priority parking for carpool users, and locating buildings near services (that is, within a five- to ten-minute walk).

On larger properties such as a corporate campus or office park, higher-density development should be focused on areas accessible to transportation nodes such as bus stops or a commuter train station to encourage the use of alternative means of transportation and to make the development less dependent on automobiles. Large developments may wish to provide shuttles to and from local transit stops.

The 3 million-square-foot (278,800-square-meter) City Center Oakland, completed in downtown Oakland, California, in 2002, is an urban complex of four mixed-use buildings ranging from 11 to 24 stories. The center was constructed directly above the 12th Street rapid-transit station. A 1.5-acre (0.6-hectare) plaza provides attractive pedestrian connections to several different bus lines.

The green land plan should include alternative transportation and pedestrian routes that connect to adjacent transit and land uses. City Center Oakland, for example, extends the existing Clay Street pedestrian corridor with street-level storefronts given a similar height and scale as existing retail along the corridor. The Veritas Software headquarters in Mountain View, California, received a density bonus for setting aside 45 percent of the site as open space and for providing easement and pedestrian connections between the adjacent Netscape Campus and the local mass transit station.

Bicycles are a popular form of alternative transportation that support sustainable development. On an office campus, bicycle circulation paths should be provided that connect to the neighborhood's existing street (and, it is hoped, bicycle) system. Generous bicycle parking and employee showers promote the use of bicycles. LEED certification requires that a "security apparatus and changing/shower facility must be accommodated for more than 5 percent of the building occupants."

Landscape Architecture

Landscaping is a critical green planning tool that influences almost every major green consideration—climate mitigation, erosion control, power, water, environmental protection, enhanced wildlife habitat, encouraging pedestrian rather than vehicular activity. Effective landscape architecture can also help to improve employees' morale, create an attractive image, help win public support for the project, and establish a sense of community. Properly planned and designed, green assets can appreciate over time as they mature and integrate with larger natural systems.

Open Space and Vegetation

Open spaces designed and landscaped to provide wind protection and shade or sun as the season requires can serve as outdoor rooms for a range of activities from meetings to eating lunch and relaxing. To make the project more green, the landscape plan should incorporate native plants to reduce long-term landscape maintenance costs and water use and to lure wildlife attracted to indigenous landscape.

On-site trails wind through conserved ranchland, connecting the corporate facilities at Fidelity Investments' campus in Westlake, **Texas.** Tom Fox, SWA Group

Native grasses and other vegetation, such as those used at the Exxon Mobil Headquarters campus in Irving, Texas, require less water than nonnative landscape materials. Tom Fox, SWA Group

The land plan for the 650,000-square-foot (60,400-square-meter) Westlake Corporate Campus of Fidelity Investments in Westlake, Texas, preserved the terrain, existing forested areas, and on-site wetlands; planted wildflowers to create meadows; and added 1,000 trees to create a natural retreat of outdoor rooms and recreation areas. In another example, the green land plan for the ground-hugging, prairie-style 200-acre (81-hectare) Exxon Mobil Headquarters in Irving, Texas, placed the building in an area that minimized its impact on both the land and natural habitats of the site's rolling mesquite woodland. The plan incorporated the extensive use of native grasses and plants like sumac and red yucca, and a Texan evergreen, suitable for the property's specific soil, shade, and water conditions. The plan also preserved the existing woodland and wetland areas, greatly reforested the property, and added two new ponds.

The use of native plants creates a distinctive and attractive identity for an office facility and provides an important amenity for workers. The site plan for the 172,000-square-foot (16,000-square-meter) Nature Conservancy Headquarters in Arlington, Virginia, includes a half-acre (0.2-hectare) native plant garden that serves as a gathering space for employees and a forum for company events. The garden was designed to show how vegetation patterns in the Arlington region evolved through many stages and many different plant species before culminating in the area's

dominant ecosystem—the Oak Woodland. This design provides both education and interest for workers and a landscape that requires minimal maintenance.

Landscape architecture in the form of berms, groves of trees, shrubs, and green walls (trellises planted with vines, ivy, flowers, and other plants) can be used to screen noise from and views to adjacent or nearby uses (traffic, trains, buildings) and on-site service areas and loading docks. It can also be used to screen buildings, pedestrian pathways, roadways, and parking lots to reduce heat islands and beautify the office development.

A primary strategy to mitigate the emissions from mechanical systems and automobiles and improve on-site air quality is the use of tree canopy cover throughout the development. Urban trees absorb carbon dioxide and pollutants from the air and reuse them in the trees' biological processes. According to Washington, D.C.–based American Forests, a 40 percent canopy cover in an office or other development substantially reduces air pollution. A tree canopy cover is an important planning tool to improve on-site air quality and help prevent heat islands while also beautifying the property.

Water Conservation

As water becomes more and more a precious resource, water conservation strategies become a key component of green office planning. Many communities, in fact, now mandate water conservation in new developments. To earn LEED certification, new developments must reduce standard water use by 20 to 30 percent. New strategies, tools, and technologies have been created to meet this growing need, from the increasingly widespread use of waterless urinals and low-flow fixtures in restrooms to the now-standard use of drip irrigation in the office landscape.

Both stormwater and wastewater can be recycled for office use, conserving potable water for the community as a whole. LEED certification requires the reduction of the use of municipally provided potable water for building sewage conveyance by a minimum of 50 percent or the treatment of 100 percent of wastewater on site to tertiary standards.

The office facility can use a system, for example, that catches stormwater runoff in cisterns above and below grade for reuse in the irrigation and fire suppression systems. An on-site local treatment system can incorporate biological functions—including the use of plants, gravel, or sand deposits—to clean the water before releasing it, generally into a natural or manmade wetland. Recycled water can also be used for on-site nonpotable applications such as water features like fountains and landscape irrigation.

Landscape design using indigenous plants requires an understanding of the historic plant species found on the specific site and of the site's microclimate. Accustomed to the various precipitation patterns of the site's environment, these plants tolerate and flourish in both dry and wet times and often need irrigation only during the period when they are becoming established on the site.

Xeriscaping—landscaping with slowly growing drought-tolerant plants—has become an effective and popular water conservation strategy in dry climates like California and Arizona. Xeriscaping (from the Greek *xeros,* which means dry, and landscaping) eschews grass lawns, which practically inhale water, fruit trees, and other water-hungry plants and uses instead indigenous drought-tolerant plants like sage, cactus, sumac, red yucca, and buffalo grass.

A xeriscaped property does not mean a landscape devoid of color. Many drought-tolerant ground covers and flowering plants and trees can be used—for example, lead-plant (which has purple flowers in the summer) and crocus, New Mexican locust, and Japanese pagoda trees—in addition to hardy oaks, evergreens, and juniper.

In some cases, the choice of plants must be tailored to the final quality of water from the property's recycled water systems, but the opportunities to reduce potable water use greatly outweigh the need to exclude certain plants from the landscape design.

Climate Mitigation and Wind Control

In a region with a hot, humid climate, the landscape architecture should provide shade and encourage breeze to make the property more comfortable and to reduce requirements for air conditioning and energy use. In a hot, dry climate, however, the landscape architecture should encourage shade

Native landscaping directs winds to cool waterfront office buildings at the Shenzhen Central Business Park. SWA Group

but not necessarily breeze, as the winds are hot and dry out people, animals, and plants, which then require an infusion of humidity, mainly through the greater use of a precious resource—water.

Strategies to address different climates can be quite simple. Planting deciduous trees in a more temperate climate, for example, lets sunlight and warmth into office buildings and onto parking lots and outdoor amenities during winter, while in summer they create the canopy that shields

Native grasses and wildflowers on the rooftop reestablished a coastal savannah ecosystem at Gap Inc.'s corporate campus in San Bruno, California. Tom Fox, SWA Group

people and buildings from the sunlight, glare, and heat but allows breezes to come through. In contrast, evergreens like junipers create shade and block breezes year-round.

Overall, the green land plan should work with the site's climate to reduce a building's requirements for HVAC. The landscape can be designed to support climate control and energy conservation. Using green screens and other land-scaping on and near building facades, for example, reduces heat islands and lowers the amount of air conditioning needed. Creating a 30 percent canopy cover at 75 percent full tree growth on all paved surfaces also greatly reduces heat islands and reflection from paved surfaces. It is estimated that a single mature tree can provide the same cooling effect as ten room-size air conditioners that run 24 hours a day.

Landscape architecture can be used to mitigate the impact of wind on a site. Evergreens, for example, can be used as a windscreen for northern or other undesirable wind exposures. Multiple layers of deciduous trees can also be used as windscreens. The 660-acre (267-hectare) Meridian Business Campus outside Chicago, for example, uses "wind rows" (swaths of trees) running across the property as both an organizing and an aesthetic element to help keep major wind impact away from buildings and tenants.

Although landscaping can help ameliorate the impact of heavy winds, wind can be used to ameliorate humidity. The Shenzhen Central Business Park for a new mixed-use city block covering 49 acres (20 hectares) in downtown Shenzen, China, for example, uses rows of trees to capture and focus the prevailing winds to cool the central area of the development.

Landscaped Roofs

Landscaped or green roofs offer many benefits, starting with superior building insulation. The thicker and cooler roof membrane required for a green roof reduces the amount of heat that penetrates the interior of the building, which lowers requirements for air conditioning and therefore lessens energy loads and saves money. It also decreases the amount of heat loss in the winter, saving heating requirements and reducing energy loads.

Landscaped roofs also eliminate the heat island effect of most roofs, absorbing solar heat in the same healthy manner of a meadow. This kind of green roof also reduces the total area of impervious dark paved surfaces in the sustainable land plan, a significant environmental benefit.

Brightfields: Clean Energy from Dirty Land

Mark Burger

Brightfield™ is a concept for effective use of a brownfield that can improve the community and bring economic value and a revenue stream to the property. The concept, coined by the U.S. Department of Energy, is an economic development strategy in which nonpolluting energy such as solar electricity is generated on the brownfield.

Beyond the conversion of a community eyesore into a productive, safe asset, brightfields serve another valuable purpose. Electricity from solar photovoltaic installations on the site can alleviate peak power requirements during the daytime and summertime. Brightfields can also generate other forms of renewable energy such as wind power or solar heat.

Potential brightfield sites are often located near major electrical infrastructure that can transmit power; otherwise, the power can be generated locally as part of community revitalization.

A range of financing entities is available for brightfields. Besides generic brownfield programs, funding can come from federal, state, local environmental, renewable energy, or utility sources, or municipal bonds or tax increment financing. Revenue can come by selling the electricity as well as its nonpolluting value, which has been captured by the market-based tradable credits called "green tags" or "renewable energy certificates." Selling the energy and green tags in a long-term power purchase agreement package has the best potential for making brightfields an economically feasible solution.

One of the first brightfields in the world is the Chicago Center for Green Technology, located on the city's west side. By the 1990s, the 17-acre (seven-hectare) site with a 34,000-square-foot (3,160-square-meter) building was abandoned and contaminated, primarily with construction waste. Under Chicago Mayor Richard Daley's leadership, the city instituted a two-year cleanup and rehabilitated the building into a state-of-the-art example of environmental design, construction, and operation. The building is highlighted by arrays of solar photovoltaic panels totaling 115 peak kilowatts. The largest concentration of solar energy technology in the Midwest at this time, the panels supply a large portion of the building's energy needs.

Other U.S. brightfield projects include a large-scale photovoltaic installation at a 27-acre (11-hectare) site in Brockton, Massachusetts, the first phase of which consists of 500 peak kilowatts (eventually to reach one peak megawatt) and, under consideration, the Miramar Landfill in San Diego.

The city of Chicago and the U.S. Department of Energy identified an underused and polluted site, cleaned it up, created new jobs, and integrated solar energy technologies into its development plans, turning a Chicago brownfield into the nation's first brightfield. Mark Farina

For more information about brightfields, see http://www.eere.energy.gov/brightfields/about.htm.

Mark Burger works for Spire Solar Chicago and is president of the Illinois Solar Energy Association.

Source: Article reprinted with permission from *The Brownfield News* (www.brownfieldnews.com).

Such roofs are even a front line in reducing stormwater runoff quantity and improving the quality of stormwater runoff. The roof's plants absorb and store stormwater, reducing the amount of runoff. They also filter the runoff before it enters the site's larger hydrology system. Green roofs improve air quality by producing oxygen and catching airborne particulate matter.

Landscaped roofs can provide wildlife habitat for several species, particularly birds that can use the roof as a rest stop on their wildlife corridor or migratory path, or as an island habitat in an urban environment. And a green roof provides a view amenity for tenants on the upper floors of other buildings. The Gap building in San Bruno, California, for example, has a vegetated roof planted to mimic the surrounding rolling hills.

Green roofs can be designed in many ways. They can use only a few inches of soil and drainage; be planted with tough cover plants; be intensively landscaped with ornamental trees, shrubs, and flowers; or incorporate hardscape and softscape areas to support passive rooftop recreation.

The majority of the product development wing's roof at the Ford Motor Company Premier Automotive Group headquarters in Irvine, California, has been landscaped with more than 30 different native plant species. The landscaping uses rainwater for drip irrigation, requires 67 percent less water than standard campus landscaping, helps insulate the upper floors of the wing, saves on future roofing costs, and provides increased energy efficiency. The rooftop landscaping also serves as a bird sanctuary (see Chapter 9).

Recycled Materials

The use of recycled materials can support landscape architecture for a green land plan. On-site boulders, for example, can be reused for new retaining and seat walls. Existing plants can be stored in a temporary on-site nursery for reuse in the new landscape architecture plan. The plan must specify that landscape materials such as paving, pipe, edging fabrics, and outdoor furniture contain recycled content. Renewable resources such as plantation-grown woods and biological rather than chemical fertilizers should be used.

Opportunities exist for recycling materials from previous development on the site into the new landscape, reducing waste and saving energy and money. Balancing cut-and-fill on site, for example, lessens the need to import or export soil. On-site plant materials can be reused as mulch or compost. Even concrete, glass, wood, and other existing and on-site construction materials can be recycled into landscape areas as paving aggregate, gravel, or mulch. Crushed aggregate from previously constructed roads that have been removed and crushed glass from demolished buildings can be used as road base for the site's new circulation system.

Monitoring and Follow-Up

Management of the office building or complex once it is completed should, in addition to normal financial and property management, include the monitoring of critical environmental functions and systems. Building and landscape maintenance should consider a life-cycle approach for material and energy use and pollution control.

The project's master plan should include a sustainable landscape maintenance plan to be implemented when construction is completed. Organic or biological fertilizers and weed and pest control products without potentially toxic contaminants should be used. Graywater should be tested periodically to ascertain whether salts or other mineral concentrations have accumulated in the soils. Energy budgets should be prepared for pumps and maintenance machinery. Air and water quality, energy and water use, and water recycling systems should be monitored continuously and periodically reviewed, and management procedures adjusted accordingly.

chapter 4

Green Office Design

Green Office Building Design

Ron Nyren

Sustainable design involves more than simply installing photovoltaic panels on the roof, laying down carpeting made of recycled material, or specifying energy-efficient lighting. Sustainable design is a holistic way of looking at the opportunities for minimizing a particular structure's impact on the environment and its future occupants. Green design is also sensitive to its context and climate; a green building in Houston requires very different solutions from a green building in London or Hong Kong. The developer's values, the program for the building, and the local office market are also significant factors.

The Benefits of Collaboration Early in the Design Process

Successfully addressing environmental issues requires a more collaborative, integrated design approach than designing a conventional building. A project team in which all members are committed to sustainability will produce a much more successful result than one that features only a few green design champions. Team members whose input is valuable early in the design process include

Designing the under-floor air displacement system for Endesa's new headquarters in Madrid, Spain, was a bilingual, collaborative effort among Battle McCarthy consulting engineers, local engineering consultants Rafael Urculo, and Endesa. H.G. Esch

architects; landscape designers; civil, mechanical, electrical, plumbing, and structural engineers; contractors; facility management, human resources, and marketing staff; and (depending on the project's specific goals and the team's depth of knowledge) outside specialists such as sustainability consultants, energy consultants, indoor air quality (IAQ) consultants, and native landscaping and forestry consultants. If the project involves building commissioning, a building commissioning agent should be selected and involved early as well (see Chapter 5 for more information on commissioning).

Many green design strategies rely on the developer's and the design and construction team's early brainstorming and goal setting. Otherwise, opportunities may be lost. For instance, if an architectural team designs a building with solar shading and other methods of mitigating heat in a hot climate, the possibilities for maximal energy savings will be undercut if the mechanical engineers have already designed a standard-size HVAC system typical for a conventional

The innovative and adaptable design of 40 Grosvenor Place, located in the shadow of Buckingham Palace, is a direct result of HOK's research-led facility consultants, architects, technicians, and interior designers' working as an integrated team. Peter Cook

building in the area. Coordination between the two teams could have resulted in smaller fans, filters, and ducts, which could have been just as effective and yet lowered initial costs, future utility bills, and maintenance. Collaboration among design participants can also result in potential synergies for daylighting, which can be significantly enhanced if the interior designers specify light-colored finishes and furniture rather than dark colors that absorb light. If lighting designers work with interior designers, the project can realize additional energy savings. Contractors are also valuable participants early in the process. They can contribute to sustainability, which is important because they assess the cost and build the structure. If they are not part of the decision-making process, they may not understand or follow the choices made, for example, substituting conventional materials when recycled ones were specified, simply because the recy-

cled ones are less familiar to them or require more work to obtain. Early coordination reduces errors, saves time, and allows for more innovative solutions.

Early involvement of the whole team also helps cost estimators create a more realistic budget. The budget for a green building often looks different from that for a standard building; even if the overall cost is not higher, individual amounts for aspects such as the exterior wall structure, structural system, HVAC system, and finishes may vary from the standard budget amounts for those categories. For complicated or ambitious projects, the developer should allocate more time during the conceptual and schematic design phases for the design team to undertake research, perform energy modeling or daylight simulations, and choose the most cost-effective strategies. Energy analyses are not generally part of the traditional scope of services designers provide to their clients, but for a relatively small upfront cost, they can save a great deal of money in utility bills over the years.

Some architects integrate green approaches into the standard design process. Sandra Mendler, sustainable design principal at HOK (Hellmuth, Obata + Kassabaum), says, "Ideally, the design team sees the project as a whole; it's about weaving green design into the overall process. How does the building relate to the context? What is the long-term use? How can we create a healthy workplace? These are fundamental to the criteria for making design decisions." Others recommend that the entire team participate in sustainability workshops or charrettes to generate ideas and develop sustainability goals first. Charrettes, a series of collaborative meetings usually spread over several days, offer a chance for members of different disciplines to exchange ideas and give each other feedback. This method is particularly useful if team members have varying degrees of experience with sustainable design, allowing those who are more knowledgeable to make presentations on relevant topics or previous building projects that met sustainable goals. During these sessions, the team should prioritize environmental goals (which may differ depending on the region—water conservation, for instance, may be more important in Phoenix than in Connecticut), what the challenges and opportunities of the specific site are, and which sustainable measures will be most costly. Some may not add to the building's cost at all. The team may also choose to follow a particular third-party standard or pursue third-party certification of the project's level of sustainability (see Chapter 1).

Anthony Bernheim, principal of SMWM, recommends a series of at least three workshops involving the whole team—developers, engineers, landscape architects, contractors, marketing staff, and other specialists as appropriate. "At the first workshop, we discuss what sustainability is and what the goals are—globally, locally, and specific to the project," Bernheim says. "These discussions provide the basis for decision making for the rest of the project. In the second workshop, we brainstorm how to achieve those goals. The third workshop focuses on what we can realistically accomplish, given the budget and schedule."

Early in the design phase, it is important to establish the reasons for seeking sustainable solutions and the goals for the project. Energy conservation and efficiency strategies are popular, because they result in quantifiable savings on utility bills. Factors such as sustainable site planning, water efficiency, conservation of materials and resources, and indoor environmental quality (IEQ) can be even more significant, depending on the particular project. Lee Polisano, president of Kohn Pedersen Fox Associates, notes that the largest expense for office tenants is staff, so improved IEQ may be the greatest economic benefit a sustainable building design can offer. "Energy is less expensive in the United States than in Europe, so the cost benefits of energy-saving measures are not as great in the United States," Polisano says. "The real reason to apply sustainable design is to increase occupants' comfort and productivity. Do employees have choices about their environment? Do they have fresh air, daylight, control of the temperature around them, the ability to open windows?"

Studies have demonstrated that IEQ, which includes the quality of air, lighting, temperature, humidity, and acoustics, has a significant impact on occupants' health; improving IAQ, for example, results in fewer sick days and greater productivity.[1] Other studies have confirmed that daylighting also increases productivity, and workers with views of nature experience less stress.[2]

Sustainable measures may also help to gain approvals for a project. In areas with limited water supplies, a building that features low-flow water fixtures or water reclamation will likely have an edge over a similar project that does not. In cities where parking and traffic are issues, office projects that encourage the use of public transit or carpooling have an advantage.

Once goals are established, the next step is to prioritize them and perform cost-benefit analyses to determine which approaches are most advantageous and realistic given the schedule and budget, and which offer the most advantages. When all parties reach consensus about the most appropriate solutions for a project, they have a foundation for making decisions later in the process, when the unexpected occurs. For instance, for the Capitol Area East End Complex in Sacramento, the state of California expressed a desire for indoor materials that offered high recycled content and zero or low volatile organic compound (VOC) and formaldehyde emissions. A specification section, Special Environmental Requirements, was used as a way to screen building products before selection, procurement, manufacture, and installation. The requirements include guidelines for energy, materials, and water efficiency, IAQ, nontoxic performance standards for cleaning and maintenance products, and sustainable site planning and landscaping considerations, among other measures. At the time, however, it was not possible to obtain carpet with low formaldehyde as well as high recycled content. Because the team members had already established

Building Green on a Budget

Dan Heinfeld

Contrary to popular opinion, green development does not have to cost more than standard development—and sometimes it can cost less. A wide variety of tools and strategies has successfully turned office projects green on a budget and ensured long-term savings through reduced power and HVAC costs, water conservation, and greater satisfaction and productivity for workers.

Green tools and strategies encompass every aspect of office development, from site selection and planning to building design and construction management. Adopting these tools and strategies ensures that an office project stays on budget and fulfills the developer's or client's green objectives.

Site Selection

Site selection can have a major impact on a project's short- and long-term costs at little or no cost. The optimal site for a green building is in an urban or suburban area with existing infrastructure and a minimum development density of 60,000 square feet per acre (13,800 square meters per hectare). The site should be within a half-mile (0.8 kilometer) of a commuter rail, light-rail, or subway station or one-quarter mile (0.4 kilometer) from two or more public bus lines.

A suburban or urban infill site has much of the existing infrastructure an office building or campus needs, from power to sewers and adjacent public transportation systems, requiring less infrastructure work and therefore a smaller portion of the project budget.

Infill sites typically offer major green pluses and financial advantages, because they are near (or are already served by) costly infrastructure like power and sewer lines and roads. These locations are also often near the housing and services that attract workers to an employer.

Similarly, a brownfield site already has infrastructure and commuter access, and funds may be available for environmental remediation. Selection and rehabilitation of a brownfield site is also an important way to meet broader environmental objectives such as reducing development pressure on greenfields.

Site Planning

Site planning is one of the most cost-effective ways to turn an office project green. Buildings can be oriented, for example, to lessen the creation of heat islands, which lowers HVAC costs. Building orientation can also maximize solar exposure to support the use of photovoltaic panels to generate electricity.

The site plan should focus, in particular, on minimizing the office development footprint. The less land used by buildings, roads, and parking, the less stormwater management system required and the more land available for open space. More open space enhances property value while supporting wildlife habitat and natural (less costly) stormwater management.

To minimize the development footprint, the project should be built up and down, not out. Plan shared facilities, like conference centers and food services, to reduce space requirements and development costs. Meet parking needs with underground garages, shared parking facilities, and preferred parking for carpools or vanpools that serve at least 5 percent of the building's occupants.

The site plan should limit earthwork to 40 feet (12 meters) beyond the facility's perimeter. Minimize earthwork by building into the landscape rather than leveling it. On sites that were previously developed, construct the new office facility on the existing development footprint to limit the project's impact on the rest of the site.

The new Long Beach Maintenance Facility in southern California was constructed on the same site used by the facility for more than 50 years. The new 150,000-square-foot (14,000-square-meter) complex of four separate buildings—including parking for more than 1,000 impounded vehicles, parking for the city's refuse vehicles, and a full truck wash facility—stretches almost four blocks. Approximately 30,000 square feet (2,800 square meters) of new office space was planned on the site's north-south axis to give the interiors northern light without heat gain. Sun screens and translucent panels on the building's south facade protect the interiors from glare and heat gain and disperse the sunlight. This orientation made it possible to use natural light as the single interior light source during daytime hours in many areas, generating significant cost and energy savings.

An office site plan should conserve natural features like streams and vegetation, particularly trees. These features not only add property value but also can be incorporated into the landscape architecture plan to significantly increase the project's sustainability and to lower costs.

Landscape Architecture and Open Space

Trees, flowers, shrubs, hedges, and grass are some of the most important and cost-effective tools for creating a green office building or campus. Landscape architecture can significantly reduce heat islands, which in turn lowers HVAC requirements and costs. A green screen along a building's western facade, for example, can limit heat absorption, which reduces air-conditioning needs. A landscaped

The National Wildlife Federation headquarters in Reston, Virginia, capitalizes on solar energy sources to reduce energy expenditures and uses native plantings to support local wildlife while reducing the need for irrigation and frequent mowing. © Alan Karchmer

roof provides both insulation and beauty and reduces heat absorption. Placing trees along the south facade of a building provides shade and heat reduction in the summer.

Planting deciduous trees that drop their leaves every fall means that the facility will be able to enjoy warmth and sunlight during cold winter months, in turn reducing energy use and lowering heating bills. Trees planted around and throughout a parking lot minimize or prevent heat islands and turn parking lots into attractive and welcoming tree-shaded courts. Trees, which absorb air pollution, can also be used to significantly improve air

quality, an important LEED requirement. In regions where water is a precious commodity, drought-tolerant and native plants can conserve water, reduce maintenance costs, and beautify the property.

On an office campus site, the property's open space can be used to cost-effectively meet stormwater management requirements. A 60-acre (24-hectare) site within the larger 400-acre (162-hectare) McCarthy Ranch master-planned community being developed by the Irvine Company in Milpitas, California, uses a water-purifying and -retention system of bioswales (open channels with a dense cover of grasses and leafy plants) along the perimeter of the entire property. The first of its kind in Silicon Valley, this system naturally slows, cleanses, and reduces the amount of stormwater runoff from the site.

Building Design: Interior Planning

Interior planning—floor layout and use—is also a cost-effective means of turning a building green. The use of long, narrow floor plates wherever possible maximizes the use of natural daylighting and lessens the need for artificial illumination, reduces energy consumption, minimizes heat gain from artificial lighting, and lowers the need for air conditioning. Fixed elements like stairs, mechanical systems, kitchens, and bathrooms should

be placed in the middle of a floor plate, with the perimeter left open, so everyone on that floor can receive natural daylighting.

Green Building Technology, Products, and Materials

Selecting green building technologies, products, and materials can help to keep an office project on budget.

Green building systems, fixtures, and furniture have become far cheaper and more widely available in the last few years. As recently as the mid-1990s, a bare 10 percent of building products were made from recycled materials. Now, that figure has risen to 50 percent, and it should grow to 100 percent within five years.

High-performance glass has become much more cost-effective. A low-e coated glass with dual glazing, for example, allows light into the interior of the building while keeping infrared rays (heat) out, lowering lighting and HVAC requirements and costs.

A raised-floor air distribution system, which delivers air to the space at a lower level and allows natural stratification to occur, was twice as expensive at the turn of the century as it is today. This system, which supports under-floor electric and cable conduits, uses significantly less energy than the traditional system of forcing air down from the ceiling plenum.

Similarly, indirect lighting—which illuminates the ceiling and bounces off the walls, provides a higher light level with less energy and less heat, reduces air-conditioning costs, and makes it easier to read—was priced at a premium at the turn of the century and was offered by only a few manufacturers. Today, its cost is comparable to standard parabolic lighting on a two-by-four grid, and products are available from a wide variety of manufacturers. Of equal importance, improvements in technology mean that indirect lighting no longer requires a more expensive ten- to 11-foot (three- to 3.4-meter) ceiling. It can now work with a 9.5- or ten-foot (2.9- or three-meter) ceiling without compromising lighting efficiency.

Green building systems—those that use less energy to provide better performance and generate less pollution—require particular attention. A greater variety of demand-based energy controls for lighting and HVAC systems is now available. These controls, which lower mechanical and HVAC requirements and costs, have become much less expensive and more efficient in the last few years.

Water conservation is a critical component of any green facility. Newer technologies that help minimize water consumption at a moderate cost include reclaimed water systems that recycle all irrigation and/or plumbing wastewater for reuse on a campus or in a building and systems that capture and use rainwater to support drip irrigation.

The advances, variety, and number of green interior products—from furniture to flooring and paint—are literally changing daily.

City, State, and Federal Incentive Programs

While green planning, design, and construction tools and strategies can go a long way toward keeping an office project at or under budget, government incentive programs from tax credits for LEED-certified buildings to rebates for energy-efficient equipment can be used to push a building or campus well into the black.

Incentives are everywhere. Maryland offers a green building tax credit for non-residential projects. The New York State Green Building Tax Credit Program gives tax incentives to commercial developments that incorporate specified green strategies. Oregon's 35 percent Business Energy Tax Credit, also for commercial development, is tied to LEED certification and ranges from $105,000 to $142,500. Idaho provides loans up to $100,000 at 4 percent interest for commercial or industrial installation of energy-efficient systems. Massachusetts lowers permitting fees by 15 percent (up to $10,000) for LEED-certified buildings. Seattle, Washington, provides reimbursement for energy-efficient windows, insulation, refrigeration, pumps, and energy controls in commercial buildings. The Green Incentive Program in Gresham, Oregon, provides tax credits to qualified stormwater design projects. Santa Barbara, California, expedites plan review for projects that exceed California Title 24 energy requirements. Arlington County, Virginia, awards developers added density or height bonuses if they meet the LEED Silver rating.

Many utility companies also provide local incentives, which can help pay for green components. California's Pacific Gas & Electric, Southern California Edison, and San Diego Gas & Electric have formed a consortium that pays 50 percent of the installation costs for an on-site power system. Progress Energy, the utility company for North Carolina, South Carolina, and Florida, provides free energy consultation and advice on new business construction and a cash-back incentive programs for the installation of high-efficiency HVAC equipment.

Short- and Long-Term Savings

Developers and clients can reap immediate budget and cost benefits from a program to recycle construction waste. Developers and property owners can enjoy long-term payback by incorporating features like photovoltaic panels into an office building or campus or by arranging building orientation to minimize direct west and south sun.

For years, many developers—and even some green-friendly architects—have claimed that going green would never work. Only a handful of environmentally sensitive buildings could be constructed, they maintained, and only with much higher than average constructions budgets. Going green was the right thing to do, but it was out of the question.

Although that myth still persists in some circles, it has been proved wrong by recent buildings that meet rigorous LEED certification standards but cost no more than standard structures. The 624,000-square-foot (58,000-square-meter) expansion of Toyota Motor Sales North American Headquarters in Torrance, California, not only earned LEED Gold certification upon completion in 2003 but also was constructed for no more than standard low-rise office buildings in that region (see the case study in Chapter 9).

In coming years, more and more developers and corporations will study successful projects like the Toyota Motor Sales expansion and will realize that new ways of designing and constructing buildings, when combined with sophisticated yet everyday technologies and fixtures, mean that their buildings can go green at everyday budgets. That day is not too far in the future.

Dan Heinfeld is president of LPA, Inc., an architectural firm in southern California with offices in Irvine and Roseville, and an early member of USGBC.

that indoor air quality was the top priority, the decision did not become a stumbling block; the designers chose a product with low formaldehyde emissions, even though it did not have as much recycled content as other options.

A number of software tools are available to aid in green design. Although they cannot substitute for practical experience in developing sustainable solutions, they can support it. BuildingGreen, publisher of *Environmental Building News*, and Design Harmony have created a software program called "Green Building Advisor" that offers sustainable design strategies, prioritized according to information that users enter about their project (www.greenbuildingadvisor.com). EnergyPlus, a building energy simulation program developed by the U.S. Department of Energy, models the overall consumption of energy in buildings, including heating, cooling, lighting, ventilation, and other components (www.eere.energy.gov/buildings/energyplus). Information about a building's energy flow helps the designer prioritize energy-saving strategies. (Software for assistance in choosing green building products is discussed below in "Sustainable Building Systems.") Computational fluid dynamics programs can model the flow of air within a building. This software can help determine the size, number, and best location of operable windows required for naturally ventilating a building comfortably. For buildings relying on HVAC systems, the software can also model the most efficient HVAC system for a given building, taking into account specific weather patterns and site microclimates.

Sustainable Building Systems
Energy Conservation

Power plants rely largely on burning nonrenewable fossil fuels. Extracting these fuels requires disrupting the environment, and burning them for fuel produces air pollution. A building's demand on the conventional electric grid can be reduced by active or passive design. Active design techniques rely on manufactured systems to reduce energy use: photovoltaics, energy-efficient HVAC and lighting

systems, heat recovery systems, cogeneration facilities that recycle heat from the generation of electricity for use in heating, groundwater coupling or cooling, chilled ceilings or beams, and a combination of natural and mechanical ventilation. Passive design techniques take advantage of the

Light shelves lining the exterior of Shaklee's headquarters direct light into the building while also reflecting excess rays. Gensler

local climate and the environment around the structure to reduce the need for conventional energy resources. For example, strategically sized and placed windows and skylights reduce the need for electric lights. Proper orientation of the building shields the interior from the sun during the hottest part of the day. Reflective roof coverings and high insulation lessen the demand for conventional heating. Double-skin facades use two layers of glass to provide acoustic and thermal insulation, protect the building from the sun using shading systems between the layers, and allow operable windows to be used even in areas of high wind, such as the top floors of high-rise buildings.

Lighting is a significant factor, accounting for one-third of the energy use in office buildings. Electric lighting should be considered holistically, integrating energy-efficient lighting, daylighting, and interior design strategies.

Occupancy sensors and light-level sensors use electric lights intelligently. Occupancy sensors use infrared or ultrasonic detectors (or both) to turn off lights after occupants have left an area. They make the most sense in areas that are not heavily used: lavatories, hallways, storage areas. Light-level sensors detect the amount of light in a room. They can be set to adjust artificial lighting levels depending on the amount of daylight in a room. As a result, energy is not wasted during the brighter portions of the day. A building automation system can be programmed to turn lights off and on at set hours, saving energy when the building is unoccupied overnight. A less expensive solution is to place switches for controlling different zones in easily accessible areas, so building occupants can turn lights off when not needed.

Natural Daylight

Using natural daylight is a passive design technique that can translate into significant energy savings—the more daylight entering a space, the less electric lighting required. Moreover, several studies suggest that exposure to daylight-

On sunny days, the stairwells at the Toyota Motor Sales' new South Campus office development in Torrance, California, can be lit solely by sunlight.
LPA, Inc./Adrian Velicescu, Standard

ing increases productivity. Making the best use of natural light can be far more complicated than simply increasing the size and number of windows, however. Daylighting requires carefully thought-out solutions that take into account the region's climate, as increasing the amount of sunlight entering a building affects heating and cooling requirements. It is essential to involve daylighting consultants, interior designers, and mechanical engineers early in the design process. Daylighting studies and scale models or computer models play a vital role in ensuring that the building's orientation, thermal mass, and windows work in harmony with each other and with the climate. Glass on the east and west facades is the most difficult to shade properly, whereas glass facing north allows diffuse daylight to enter the building. Such studies and models also help determine the placement and design of electric lights.

Along with heat gain, glare has to be taken into account. One solution is to place light shelves (horizontal overhangs) on the exterior of the building, usually above windows at about eye level. A highly reflective upper surface reflects light through a transom window above the shelf. In combination with a highly reflective ceiling, light shelves can significantly extend daylight's reach while reducing glare and shading occupants near windows. Direct sunlight can be mitigated in other ways: flanking windows with vertical fins to block low-angle sunlight, setting windows back from the building's skin, adding sunscreen structures to the exterior or combining them with the structure, and installing interior blinds or louvers. However, blinds and louvers require more maintenance, add to the cost of hardware, and must be adjusted depending on the time of day. Strategically placed trees, vine-covered trellises, and bushes can also shield a building.

Skylights seem like an obvious choice for increasing daylight, but they must be used carefully, especially in regions where high temperatures are likely. They provide the most light in the middle of the day, coinciding with the hottest part of the day, which can result in higher cooling costs. One alternative is to use light monitors, sections of flat roof raised above the surrounding roof and connected by vertical glazing around the perimeter. Clerestory windows are another possibility: these vertical panes, placed high on interior walls, are easier to shade than light monitors, either with an exterior overhang or interior shading devices.

Atriums are often used to bring light into a building. The Genzyme Building in Cambridge, Massachusetts, enhances daylighting with an atrium whose skylight is topped with mirrors that automatically track the passage of the sun across the sky and reflect sunlight into the atrium. Redirectional louvers increase the amount of natural light in the office spaces. The atrium doubles as a return air duct; fans bring fresh air in at the bottom and exhaust warm air out the top.

Photovoltaic Systems

When photovoltaic systems were initially introduced in the 1970s, they offered the possibility of providing free energy from the sun, but they also earned a reputation of being prohibitively expensive compared with conventional power supplies. Today's technology, however, is

A variety of techniques are used to promote energy efficiency at the Capitol Area East End Complex in Sacramento, California: photovoltaic panels, natural daylighting, automated light controls, window glazing, and shading devices. ©Erhard Pfeiffer 2003

much more cost-effective. Moreover, PV systems have no moving parts and so have a long life span, with minimal maintenance requirements.

PV technology uses either a single-crystal or thin-film system. The former is currently the more commonly used and is more efficient in converting sunlight to energy. New PV systems made with thin-film cells generate less electricity per square foot but offer the potential for lower costs overall, because they use much smaller quantities of semiconductor material than single-crystal cells.

PV systems can also serve double duty, providing shade even as they generate energy. PV systems can shade roofs, extending the roof's life span, reducing heat gain, and lowering the strain on the air-conditioning system. They can be used to shade individual windows in the form of awnings.

The building's orientation and configuration play key roles in the success of a PV system. The building should be placed on the site so that the panels receive unobstructed sunlight between 9 a.m. and 3 p.m. Because the periods of most intense sunlight correspond to the times of peak energy demand, PV systems relieve the strain on the power grid. Photovoltaic systems connected to the power grid can send excess electricity back to the utility, often earning the building owners utility credits. Connecting the system to the grid also eliminates the need for a battery system to store excess electricity.

PV systems can be placed in arrays on flat roofs or incorporated into sloped roofs. Either way, the panels must be tilted correctly to provide the maximal amount of energy. A recent trend is building-integrated photovoltaics (BIPV), in which the PV system is integrated into the building's curtain wall glazing (the skin). This approach reduces building material costs, both for conventional exterior building materials and for the mounting hardware associated with conventional PV systems. The Condé Nast

Building at Four Times Square in New York City supplements the energy it receives from the power grid with BIPV on the top 19 floors of the south and east facades. The BIPV system supplies approximately 1 percent of the building's energy. The building uses another alternative source, two 200-kilowatt hydrogen fuel cells, which generate electricity from a chemical reaction. The fuel cells provide all the building's power during the night, releasing hot water in the process, which helps the building's heating system during cold months (see the case study in Chapter 9).

Determining how much a PV system costs depends on a variety of factors. The region's particular energy costs and the average amount of sunlight each day play a role. In some cases, tax credits and special financing are available. Considering PV systems early in the process can reduce costs greatly, offering more possibilities for incorporating them into the design and integrating them with other energy-saving solutions. Because photovoltaics are one of the most widely known components of sustainable design, the increased potential for marketing to potential tenants should be considered in determining overall costs. Using other energy-saving measures in tandem with photovoltaics also plays a significant role in reducing energy use.

Heating, Ventilation, and Air-Conditioning Systems

Specifying energy-efficient HVAC systems in combination with other sustainable solutions that allow smaller mechanical systems can help reduce a building's energy use. Usually a number of methods are employed in combination to reduce energy use. At 40 Grosvenor Place in London, several strategies combine to reduce energy costs by an estimated 20 percent. All workstations are located within 25 feet (7.6 meters) of natural light, made possible by extensive glazing throughout, a large glazed atrium facing southwest, and two secondary atriums. The building's concrete structure provides thermal mass, which, in combination with translucent glass mullions, light shelves, recessed win-

An atrium rising from the ground-floor level to the rooftop of the Jie Fang Daily News & Media Group's building facilitates a breathing effect by drawing hot air out of the office spaces and venting it out the top. KMD

dows, and exterior fins, reduces solar heat gain. The displacement ventilation system operates without the need for fans, and chilled ceilings provide radiant cooling to further reduce energy use.

Mechanical systems for office buildings are often larger than necessary. As a result, they cost more to install and consume more energy than they need to. Certain measures can permit the use of a smaller HVAC system: the correct building orientation, a building envelope that enhances daylighting while avoiding excessive solar heat gain, insulated walls, thermal glazing, and high-performance lighting. In a cold climate, well-insulated walls and insulated glass can reduce the heat loss around the perimeter of a building, which means that HVAC ducts around the perimeter could potentially be eliminated—saving construction costs and energy. In climates with significant periods of mild temperatures and low humidity, natural ventilation may be an option. Sustainable HVAC solutions not only can work more efficiently and reduce capital and life-cycle costs but also can enhance workers' health and satisfaction by giving occupants more control over their environment, improving IEQ and reducing sick days, increasing productivity, and creating greater job satisfaction.

Before the advent of mechanical HVAC systems, all buildings had to rely on natural ventilation. Natural ventilation relies on a combination of breezes and the stack effect (the movement of air as it warms, rises, and draws cooler air in from lower vents). The placement of the building on the site plays a key role in natural ventilation. The building should be placed so that its longest facades are perpendicular to the direction of prevailing winds in the summer. Trees or other sheltering site elements may be required on the side exposed to cold winds in winter. Narrow building forms, wings, and/or courtyards enhance the flow of air through the building.

The most effectively designed rooms have at least two separate openings, one for air to enter and the other for air to exit (preferably higher than the intake opening). The interior should be designed to avoid obstructions to airflow. Large pieces of furniture should be placed so they do not block windows. Open-plan offices with low privacy screens provide for the freest movement of air. If interior

In the summer, the outer envelope of the World Trade Center in Amsterdam screens the office space from solar gain and acts as a thermal buffer. In the winter, excess heat gain is naturally expelled using the thermal stack effect. Eamonn O'Mahony

walls are required, high louvers, transoms, and doors that stay open most of the time can help airflow.

Buildings can be designed to rely on a combination of natural and mechanical ventilation. In some cases, HVAC systems are installed only for particular areas of the building. In other cases, HVAC systems and natural ventilation operate alternately, depending on the time of day, occupancy levels, and the seasonal climate. The latter approach requires a solution for ensuring that the HVAC system does not oper-

ate while windows are open, which would waste energy. The Chesapeake Bay Foundation's Philip Merrill Environmental Center in Annapolis, Maryland, designed by SmithGroup, relies on a sophisticated energy management system that monitors outdoor temperatures and humidity. When the climate on the outside is comfortable, the system turns off the HVAC system, and a green light signals occupants that windows can be opened. A red light indicates when windows should be closed. The system also automatically opens and shuts windows that are out of human reach.

Another approach is displacement ventilation, a method of air distribution currently more common in Europe than in the United States, with the potential to improve IAQ. Cool air (usually 100 percent outside air) is brought into rooms at low levels. The air may enter through wall ducts below windows or through vents in the floor. The air flows up to ceiling return grilles, carrying pollutants upward and away from occupants. The direction of air currents corresponds with the natural rising action caused by the heat from office equipment and occupants.

Under-floor air distribution systems have existed for decades. Originally designed for areas that generate high heat loads, such as computer rooms, they are particularly widespread in Europe and Japan. Buildings with an under-floor air system have a raised floor. The two distinct systems of under-floor air distribution—ducted and non-ducted (or plenum)—offer advantages in terms of cost and serviceability. For instance, ducted systems typically require a deeper floor void to accommodate the required duct sizes and coordination between the various services in the floor. Nonducted systems suffer from decompression and loss of air delivery every time the void is accessed for work on data, electrical, or communication cabling. With nonducted systems, dust collects in the floor void and is distributed into the atmosphere with the supply air, lowering air quality and staining floor finishes.

Nonducted systems are less expensive, however, and more flexible in terms of space planning than a ducted system. Because they provide space to house all phone, data, and electrical cabling, it is much easier and faster to reconfigure spaces to accommodate changing employees and their changing needs; for example, lifting modular floor panels is easier than retrofitting the wiring in furniture systems and walls. Widely available adjustable outlets allow occupants to adjust their environment individually. In some systems, occupants can take their personally adjusted air vent with them to their new location. Because air enters the room near occupants, the air does not have to be cooled as much as in conventional buildings to provide the same level of comfort. Typically, air delivered through an under-floor air system at about 65 degrees Fahrenheit (18 degrees Celsius) works just as well as air delivered through a conventional system at 55 degrees Fahrenheit (13 degrees Celsius).[3] HVAC fans might be necessary, however, to increase air speeds.

With careful planning and coordination among the design team, under-floor air distribution systems can be implemented with the same floor-to-floor heights as those required with a conventional system. With the elimination of overhead HVAC ducting, floor-to-floor heights can be reduced in some cases.

All HVAC systems need a method of producing cool air: choosing natural gas–fired chillers instead of electric ones can reduce the cost of cooling and result in the emission of fewer greenhouse gases. Gas-fired chillers tend to be more expensive than electric chillers, which can increase capital costs, and they are most effective when the chilled water system is highly efficient overall. Purchasing high-end efficiency lighting, improving insulation, and optimizing the rest of the HVAC system all help reduce cooling loads.

Radiant heating and cooling systems provide a good level of comfort for occupants. They consist of tubes concealed in the ceiling, floor, or walls. Water, heated by a boiler or cooled by a chiller, circulates through the tubing. Like an old-fashioned radiator, these tubes can radiate or absorb heat without air circulation. Radiant systems can be more energy efficient, avoiding the reliance on fans and pumps of conventional air-conditioning systems. In some cases, a separate ventilation system may be necessary, depending on the requirements for providing adequate quantities of outside air in a space.

Pier 1 in San Francisco required an unusually creative approach to heating and cooling. Architect SMWM and preservation architect Page & Turnbull faced the challenge of converting a 1930s warehouse on the bay into a 140,000-square-foot (13,000-square-meter) office building; historic preservation requirements precluded architectural changes to the exterior walls and roof, so passive design techniques such as adding insulation and high-performance glazing were not possible. The solution was to place a heat exchanger in San Francisco Bay; the bay water cools water that flows through a closed loop radiant tube system that provides cooling as the water flows through tubes in the building's concrete floor slabs, carrying away heat generated by the building. The amount of heat is small, not enough to create a problem for the bay's ecology. The system cost less than a standard HVAC system to install, and it performs about 20 to 30 percent better than required by California Title 24.

In climates with a significant difference between day and night temperatures, nighttime ventilation is an excellent way to cool buildings during warmer months. At night, either the natural ventilation system takes advantage of breezes or the HVAC system draws in outside air, cooling the building's mass. During the day, as temperatures rise, the building's windows and vents are closed to allow the building's mass to provide radiant cooling. Concrete frame buildings offer greater thermal mass than steel frame buildings and so are more effective for radiant cooling.

Atriums can play a key role in ventilation. The atrium of the Endesa headquarters building in Madrid, Spain, links the building's two office blocks. To develop the best solution, engineers undertook dynamic thermal analysis and computational fluid dynamics studies to simulate temperature and air flow during different times of the year. The atrium serves as a transition zone between the controlled air of the office spaces and the outside. Two underground ducts bring in fresh air. Aided by evaporative spray cooling and heat exchangers, these "earth tubes" take advantage of the earth's thermal mass to cool the air in warm months and heat it in the winter. Solar chimneys exhaust air from the atrium at different airflow rates, depending on seasonal temperatures.

When designing HVAC systems for energy efficiency, it is important to avoid taking measures that reduce indoor air quality. The U.S. EPA studied the relationship between energy-efficient HVAC measures and indoor air quality and found that relying solely on energy-saving measures that did not affect indoor environmental quality resulted in a 42 to 43 percent savings in energy costs for its model office building.[4] Methods such as reducing the flow of outdoor air, reducing the hours the HVAC system operates, and permitting temperature or humidity levels to exceed common comfort levels resulted in negligible additional energy savings while compromising the office building's indoor environmental quality.

Once the building is occupied, ongoing maintenance is essential to ensure continued good air quality. For this reason, it is a good idea to ensure that HVAC systems are easy to clean and maintain.

Plumbing

Conserving water is becoming increasingly important as new and existing sources of fresh water become scarcer and water rates rise. Water conservation measures lower water and sewage bills, save resources, and reduce energy use related to water heating. In areas with scarce water supplies or an overtaxed municipal wastewater treatment infrastructure, implementing water-saving methods can also help a project gain approvals.

Flushing toilets and urinals consumes the most water in office buildings. Since 1997, U.S. federal law has required that toilets installed in commercial buildings use no more than 1.6 gallons (six liters) per flush (one gallon [3.8 liters] per flush for commercial urinals). Ultra-low-flush toilets and urinals are available. Pressure-assisted toilets can use as little as 0.5 gallon (1.9 liters) per flush. Waterless urinals, as the name implies, use no water at all. Low-flow faucets and faucet sensors are also options. Sensors turn water on only when they detect hands underneath the faucet, eliminating wasted running water while users lather or dry their hands.

Adding a graywater system to a building saves resources by recycling water from the building's sinks, drinking fountains, and other sources. Water is collected and treated on site for nonpotable uses, such as flushing toilets. The cost varies, depending on how much the system reduces the need for fresh water and how the graywater is used. In addition, some wastewater treatment plants allow access to treated water for nonpotable uses. A separate set of pipes is required to carry the water to the building.

Solar hot water systems can reduce pollution and the use of fossil fuels by providing as much as 75 to 80 percent of the building's hot water requirements. A wide variety of solar water heating systems is available. They can provide as little or as much of a building's hot water needs as desired, depending on the size of the system. Generally, solar hot water systems feature a roof-top collector that absorbs solar rays and a well-insulated storage tank. Active, indirect systems are the most commonly used. Active systems rely on electricity to operate the pumps, valves, and controls. Passive systems do not require pumps or electricity, relying instead on the natural circulation of water as it heats. In direct systems, the collector directly heats the potable water. In indirect systems, the collector heats a freeze-resistant fluid, which then transfers heat to the potable water, usually by passing through tubing in the storage tank.

It is always a good idea to have a conventional water heating system as a backup to provide supplemental heat during extended cloudy periods, at night, or while the solar water heater is being serviced.

The 19-story Jie Fang Daily News & Media Group corporate headquarters in Shanghai, China, is shaped with a concave arc on its main facade to reduce wind load on the building and to channel wind away from pedestrians below. KMD

Basic Building Configuration

Reinforced concrete and steel are the most common structural materials for office buildings, and they each have their advantages and disadvantages. Concrete structures offer the advantages of greater thermal mass. Buildings with greater thermal mass change temperature more slowly than conventional buildings, which can reduce energy costs required to heat or cool the interior: the building's mass absorbs the rays of the sun, keeping the inside cool even on very hot days, and releases heat slowly during the night. Usually, thermal mass is enhanced with additional insulation for greater effectiveness. Trombe walls are one option; they consist of several layers—a thick masonry wall (lined with a dark material that absorbs heat), an air space, and an exterior layer of glass. Concrete frame buildings, particularly with thick flat slabs or coffered slab/beam construction, offer significant advantages, especially when no suspended ceilings are used. Thermal mass can also be provided by natural or artificial heat sinks such as a swimming pool, rammed earth wall structures, or deep basements with concrete foundations.

Concrete production does have a negative impact on the environment, mostly because the Portland cement used to bind concrete requires the burning of large amounts of fossil fuels, which produces greenhouse gas. The amount of Portland cement can be reduced, however. Fly ash, a byproduct of coal-burning power plants, is plentifully available in landfills and can be substituted for a portion of the Portland cement. Autoclaved aerated concrete is another option. Aluminum powder is added during the formation of the concrete, causing it to expand dramatically. A unit of aerated concrete requires one-fifth the amount of concrete as a similarly sized unit made the conventional way.

If a project involves demolishing an existing concrete building, the concrete can be crushed and recycled as fill material. Edificio Malecon in Buenos Aires, Argentina, designed by HOK, reuses the 3.2-foot-thick (one-meter-thick) foundation walls of the warehouse that previously occupied the site as foundation bearings for the building's podium and underground parking and service space for the mechanical and electrical systems. In addition, the concrete frame consists of locally mined and manufactured materials, mixed either on site or close by, lowering the environmental impact of transporting materials to the site.

Steel also requires considerable energy to manufacture, but unlike concrete, structural steel is available with close to 100 percent of recycled content. Recycling rather than using new steel reduces waste and pollution. Two kinds of steel with recycled content are available—postindustrial and postconsumer. The former is recovered during the manufacturing process; the latter is recycled after it has served its intended use. Recycled postconsumer waste is the more sustainable of the two because it keeps material out of landfills. Steel mills provide information on the percentage of recycled steel from each category. Buildings with steel structures can also be adapted cost-effectively for new uses, because steel can be easily modified and reinforced. Specifying steel from local manufacturers requires less transportation, thereby saving fossil fuels.

Climate also plays a role. Hot, dry climates with significantly cooler nights benefit from exterior walls with high thermal mass, which mitigate the effect of strong temperature swings. In hot, humid climates, however, lower thermal mass is preferable. Light-colored, highly reflective wall materials help lower cooling costs. Cold climates in particular call for high-quality insulation.

Exterior Design
Building Form

Building orientation and building form in relation to the site's characteristics are the two most significant factors in sustainable design. They can make far greater contributions to energy efficiency and occupants' comfort than any other active or passive system. Tall, narrow buildings occupy smaller footprints than low-rise buildings of the same volume. By occupying less space, they displace less stormwater, help reduce disturbance of the site, and leave more room for landscaping and public plazas. Building shape also affects how much natural light is introduced into a building's interior, letting daylight penetrate into as much of the office space as possible. Edificio Malecon in Buenos Aires has wide convex facades on the north and south and very narrow facades on the east and west; the curvature and orientation maximize exposure to daylight through the full-height glazing. Sunshades are designed to block direct sun during the hottest months. During the cooler months, however, the sun is low enough in the sky to shine directly into the building, providing heat. The building's shallow depth also allows prevailing breezes to naturally ventilate the space, providing a nonmechanical means of cooling.

Clad in glass and metal curtain walls, the towers of the Poly Guangzhou Complex face north, allowing natural light and views to reach through the full depth of the 49-foot-wide (15-meter-wide) floor plate without the problems of excessive solar heat gain an equivalent south-facing facade would incur. SOM

Building form can be used innovatively to enhance the context and to allow more efficient structural systems. For example, the 40-story Swiss Re Headquarters in London has a highly unusual shape that is more than just aesthetically striking (see Chapter 9). The circular form widens slightly above the base and then tapers to a rounded point at the top, a shape that reduces wind loads on the building. As a result, the building structure is more efficient. The design team's wind tunnel research indicated that the aerodynamic form will lessen wind conditions for pedestrians in the area. The shape also encourages the flow of fresh air for natural ventilation.

Poly Guangzhou Complex, a speculative office complex in Guangzhou, China, designed by Skidmore, Owings & Merrill (SOM), features an open-air terrace as a refuge floor in the middle of each 33-story tower. The terrace not only provides a shaded outdoor area for gatherings and meetings but also relieves wind pressure on the facade. Oriented to

face north, the two buildings have narrow floor plates, 50 feet (15 meters) wide, which, combined with glass and metal curtain walls, allow natural light to penetrate fully into the floors. The building relies on two layers of X-bracing that doubles as part of the structural system and as a sun shade on the south side, reducing heat gain.

Glazing

The choice of glazing influences heat gain as well. Useful in hot climates, spectrally selective glazing lets most of the visible portion of the light spectrum through, while blocking most of the infrared radiation that raises temperatures. Spectrally selective glazing allows wider expanses of glass while still keeping cooling requirements low. For cooler climates, however, it may be more important to keep heat in or even to encourage solar heat gain. In these instances, several layers of glazing with low-e coatings to reduce heat loss are more appropriate. Inert low-conductivity gas between layers increases the insulating properties even more.

Sustainable Roofs

A vegetated or "green" roof is a roof assembly that includes soil above the roofing membrane and is planted with live plants, often drought-tolerant varieties. These roof systems—popular in Europe, notably Germany—have withstood the test of time. Green roofs offer a number of advantages for the environment compared with their black tar counterparts. Traditional roofs shed rain completely, which, during long periods of inclement weather, can lead to overflowing city sewers and drainage systems. Green roofs generally absorb most stormwater. Black tar roofs absorb heat from the sun and radiate it for hours afterward, raising temperatures in urban areas and significantly contributing to increased pollution and destructive weather patterns. The plants on green roofs make use of the sun's energy, keeping upper floors cooler and reducing outdoor temperatures. The process of photosynthesis removes carbon dioxide from the air, also reducing pollution. The layer of plants protects the underlying membrane from harmful ultraviolet rays and intense heat, which cause standard roofs to degrade. As a result, green roofs often last two to three times longer than conventional roofs.

The initial cost of green roofs in the United States is currently significantly higher than conventional roofs because of the extra materials involved and because support industries for green roofs are not yet as fully established as they are abroad. Lower HVAC costs, greater longevity, and reduced costs for extensive storm drain systems counterbalance some of the initial costs. In addition, maintenance is minimal, confined to occasional weeding, fertilization, and, depending on the climate, some irrigation. The green roof of Gap, Inc.'s office headquarters in San Bruno, California, designed by William McDonough + Partners, includes wildflowers as well as native grasses. The roof has an undulating form that helps the building fit into the surrounding context of rolling hills. With six inches (15 centimeters) of soil, the living roof not only provides significant thermal insulation but also serves as an acoustic barrier, muffling the noise of air traffic from the nearby San Francisco International Airport.

Other sustainable roof options include metal roofs, cool roofs, and solar shingles. Copper, steel, and aluminum roofs can be made of recycled material and recycled at the end of their life. They also last much longer than asphalt. Cool roofs are made of white reflective materials that block ultraviolet rays and reduce heat gain, lowering cooling costs and slowing roof degradation. Solar shingles are made of

Green roofs, such as this one at the Bank One Corporate Center in Chicago, absorb stormwater and use the sun's energy to reduce outdoor and upper-floor temperatures. Kildow Photography

PV cells and turn solar radiation into electricity. High-quality insulation is key for all kinds of roofs, saving energy costs for heating and cooling.

Interior Design
Space Planning

Daylighting design should be coordinated with interior design. If windows are arranged to let light penetrate deep into the building but then high partitions are erected or private offices are arrayed along the perimeter, the value is lost. In addition, dark interior finishes can absorb light instead of reflecting it, requiring higher-wattage bulbs. Open workstations along the windows allow for the most light to penetrate. Private offices should be grouped farther from windows; glazing, where possible, allows even these areas to receive the benefit of some natural light. Tasks that require the most light should be grouped near windows, oriented to avoid glare. Flexible floor plans maximize the use of space and eliminate the cost of retrofitting (and the accompanying disposal of waste) when space needs change. Office plans that encourage the use of shared space are more efficient, requiring less overall square footage, which can reduce the building's overall footprint. Creating dedicated areas for employees to recycle paper and other office supplies supports recycling programs.

Daylighting and ceiling lights provide general lighting, but task lighting is also essential for offices. Lighting designers can analyze lighting requirements and develop the best solutions for integrating task lighting into the overall lighting design, reducing the need for ambient electric lighting and thereby saving energy.

A wide variety of energy-efficient lighting fixtures is available. Maintenance and operating costs over the product's life cycle should be taken into account when choosing among them. Long-lasting fixtures need fewer replacements, saving resources and money over the long term.

Reducing the amount of materials used in the design also lessens the impact on the environment. "Try not to build anything if you don't have to," advises Nellie Reid, LEED coordinator at Gensler. "Avoid having offices surround the perimeter, cutting off natural light. By avoiding perimeter offices and nonstandard-sized rooms as much as possible, you can make room for more flexible spaces that don't have to be

Natural daylighting can be complemented by energy-efficient artificial lighting. Toyota Motor Sales North American Headquarters uses both task lighting and overhead indirect lighting, as seen in the dining area at left. LPA, Inc./Adrian Velicescu, Standard

The reception area of Shaklee's corporate headquarters in Pleasanton, California, displays the company's commitment to sustainability. Designers chose certified sources for all wood surfaces, recycled carpet yarns, workstation fabrics, and floor and ceiling materials. Gensler

torn down as needs change." Melissa Mizell, a LEED-accredited workplace designer at Gensler, adds, "Avoid finishes where you don't need them. Try to expose ceilings; use the structure as the finish. Ask yourself why you're covering it up. If it's for acoustic reasons, is there another way to achieve the same result? Downsize materials: place carpet only beneath workstations; keep acoustic tiles over workstations." Mizell notes that exposed ceilings, walls, and floors are common ways to avoid unnecessary finishes. Acoustic materials can be applied strategically only where needed—below and above workstations, for example.

Emissions from materials and finishes can increase the concentration of chemical compounds in indoor air and contribute to an unhealthy environment, resulting in lower productivity and more sick days. Volatile organic compounds vaporize over time at room temperature from building materials such as solvents, paints, adhesives, sealants, composite wood boards, wall and floor coverings, and ceiling materials. They can cause short-term health

problems known as sick building syndrome; symptoms include respiratory irritation, nasal congestion, dizziness, and headaches. Long-term health effects, known as building-related illnesses, include Legionnaires' disease and cancer. Manufacturers are increasingly responding to the call for low-VOC- or non-VOC-emitting products. (See "Selecting Green Products" at the end of this chapter for information about the wide variety of product claims and solutions.)

Floors and Carpets

Floors and carpets can be sustainable in a number of ways. Those made of recycled materials save resources that might otherwise end up in landfills; those made of sustainably harvested woods or plants, or rapidly renewable materials such as bamboo or wool, avoid depleting resources. Floors and carpets made of low-emitting VOCs contribute to improved indoor air quality. Architect William McDonough has designed a line of recyclable carpet tiles in collaboration with Shaw Industries: all chemical components of the carpet's materials and manufacturing processes have been analyzed for their effect on human and ecological health and optimized for maximal safety.

Bamboo grows much more rapidly than wood, making sustainable harvesting easy. It is also harder than oak and highly durable. Cork floors are sustainable because cork derives from the bark of cork trees, which naturally peels off and continues to grow. Most cork is used for stoppers; cork that would otherwise be waste material from the production of stoppers can be turned into flooring. Also highly durable, cork has the added benefit of strong thermal and noise insulating abilities. Linoleum is made of solidified linseed oil mixed with other natural materials and does not require much energy for extraction. Floors made from recycled rubber are another option but should be used only after verifying that the VOC emissions will not contribute to increased indoor air concentrations.

Endesa's glass ceiling allows daylight to enter the atrium, while shading devices on the roof protect the ceiling from direct solar gain. H.G. Esch

In the United States, more than 2.5 million tons (2.3 million metric tons) of carpet ends up in landfills each year.[5] Governments and manufacturers have combined to create the Carpet America Recovery Effort (CARE), a third-party organization that establishes ways to collect carpet at the end of its life and serves as a resource for information about carpet recycling. Manufacturers have devel-oped a number of ways to recycle carpeting at the end of its life cycle into other products, such as carpeting, carpet backing, plastic building materials, and floor tiles. Some manufacturers are also using recycled materials such as plastic bottles or nylon in the production of carpeting. Natural wool carpets last a long time, they insulate well, and they are easy to clean.

Some conventional carpet backing contains polyvinyl chloride (PVC), which is toxic to produce and does not biodegrade easily in landfills. Some scientific studies suggest that the plasticizers used in PVC may emit phthalates that in turn may increase the incidence of asthma and allergies in children.[6] Carpet backing made without PVCs or from up to 100 percent recycled content is now available. The adhesives and padding used in carpet can also emit VOCs that increase concentrations of indoor air chemical compounds and may also harbor mold and mildew. Manufacturers are now beginning to make low-VOC adhesives that also have antimicrobial properties, but a debate persists about their benefits. Another alternative is carpets that rely on a high-friction coating rather than adhesives to stay in place. This approach is particularly advantageous in buildings with under-floor plenums for air distribution, data, and electric cables, because without adhesives, it is easier to lift the carpet to access the plenum when changing workstation configurations.

Because carpet can absorb VOCs from paint, adhesives, and other building materials and subsequently release these chemical compounds back into the air at a slower rate than the original materials did, carpet should be installed late in the construction process—after VOC-emitting work is completed and when emissions have slowed to a very low rate.

Ceilings

Leaving ceilings exposed is the option that saves the most resources. Sometimes, however, ceiling tiles are necessary for acoustic, health, or aesthetic reasons. Conventional ceiling tiles may emit formaldehyde or other VOCs, which are released into the air, particularly when the product is new (during installation and shortly thereafter). Ceiling products should be tested for emissions and selected based on low VOC emissions.

Ceiling tiles containing recycled content are readily available as well. Acoustic ceiling tiles may contain recycled newsprint, slag wool from steel manufacturing plants, and/or recycled fiberglass; some tiles consist of more than 80 percent recycled material. Because acoustic ceiling tiles are usually porous, they can absorb VOCs from other building materials or paints during construction and release them later, so it is a good idea to arrange to have them installed late in the construction process. Aluminum ceiling tiles made of recycled metal are another option, as they do not absorb VOCs at all. Several manufacturers are now recycling old ceiling tiles at the end of their life span, which not only helps the environment but also may be less expensive than relying on landfills for disposal.

The potential of ceilings to enhance both daylighting and electric lighting is strong. Specifying highly reflective ceiling tiles significantly extends the reach of daylight and allows fewer lighting fixtures to achieve the same level of brightness; fewer lighting fixtures translates to reduced initial costs, lower energy use, and less maintenance. In addition, they boost indirect lighting, softening sharp shadows and reducing glare on computer screens.

Furniture

Several elements should be considered in the choice of furniture for an office. Many products with recycled metal, wood, and fabric are available. Manufacturers incorporate recycled tire rubber, plastic, waste paper, and nylon. But it is also important to factor in the energy required to produce or transport the materials. An office system containing 30 percent recycled steel that has to be trucked from across the country may not

Various furnishings, furniture systems, fabrics, and carpeting throughout the Ford Premier Auto Group's office building are made of recycled materials. LPA, Inc./Adrian Velicescu, Standard

The Gradual Progression toward Green Furniture

Scott Lesnet

Contemporary office furniture is designed using a relatively small number of materials. Steel, aluminum, and composite wood account for most structural components, while laminates, polyester fabrics, and plastic trim provide aesthetics. The recycled content ranges from 30 percent for steel to 100 percent for cast aluminum and some polyester fabrics. Nearly 100 percent of the composite wood products used by the industry are manufactured from sawdust generated during the milling of dimensional lumber and/or plantation trees grown for pulp.

Over the past 20 years, furniture manufacturers have worked to eliminate occupational hazards and provide clean, safe workplaces for their employees. At the same time, the cost of environmental compliance has encouraged the development of people-friendly, environmentally friendly materials such as solvent-free powder paint and hot-melt adhesives. The effect of these combined efforts is a workplace essentially free of chemical exposure for employees and office workers.

In early 2000, designers began to understand that incorporating environmental considerations in planning workplaces could improve workers' productivity, thus improving business profitability. Amenities such as daylight views, elimination of glare, and temperature control became requirements for effective workplaces.

In response to the need for factual information, various certifications and certifying organizations have evolved to validate claims of environmental performance. Current certifications tend to be narrowly focused on individual areas such as energy efficiency or recycled material content; obtaining third-party certification is time-consuming and often expensive. For example, a single test of indoor air emissions of a standard workstation runs $15,000 to $20,000 and may not satisfy the needs of every end user, making it difficult to make quick choices among green offerings.

Some excellent examples of unified specifications are available, however, such as the State of California Green Specification for Open Office Furniture Systems, which sets minimum criteria for bidding on state contracts. In addition, industry groups and standards organizations such as the American Society for Testing and Materials (ASTM) and International Organization for Standardization (ISO) are working to establish uniform definitions of terms and to harmonize the efforts of the various certification programs. When combined with the LEED rating system, these emerging standards provide facilities managers with the necessary resources for making logical, cost-effective decisions that lower the environmental impact of the building and workplace, improve productivity, and enhance the bottom line for a business.

So what do we do now? If you are asking this question, then you have started the process of recognizing and reducing the environmental impact of your current and future workspace projects. It is important to select vendors early in the process who take the time to understand your goals and provide clear answers to your questions. Qualified manufacturers will provide factual

Herman Miller, Inc., an industry leader in environmentally responsible product design and manufacturing, uses its own sustainable furniture at its LEED-certified MarketPlace in Zeeland, Michigan. Christopher Barrett© Hedrich Blessing

and informative information on their products: indoor air quality evaluations, environmental data sheets summarizing recycled content, and of useful life management, descriptions of the manufacturer's environmental commitment. Your choice of provider, whether for flooring, lighting, or furniture, helps determine how quickly we green America's workplace.

Reprinted with permission from **Buildings, *December 2003*.**

Sustainable Renovation: Turning Existing Office Buildings Green

Dan Heinfeld

"Green" need not be restricted to new construction. Existing buildings can be renovated into green facilities. In fact, the USGBC has released LEED standards for existing buildings that address indoor air quality, energy efficiency, water efficiency, and cleaning and maintenance, among other operational issues. Green renovation is critical in today's commercial market, because tenants are looking for healthy, attractive workplaces with lower energy costs—something commercial buildings often cannot provide.

Green renovation is also a cost-effective strategy. The new southern California headquarters of LPA, for example, involved green renovation of 28,000 square feet (2,600 square meters) in an existing two-story building at University Research Park in Irvine, California, based on a standard tenant improvement allowance for Class A office buildings in Orange County of $30 per square foot ($323 per square meter). The sustainable design reduces water use by 21 percent compared with similar buildings at the research park, exceeds California's Title 24 energy standards by 22 percent, and used building materials, flooring, and furnishings with a high content of recycled materials.

Turning existing buildings green requires action in five broad categories: site, water, energy, materials, and indoor air quality.

Working from the outside in, restore open space on the site and use landscape architecture to control erosion, minimize heat islands, and screen the building(s) to prevent heat absorption. Use drought-tolerant plants to beautify the property and to reduce water use. Turn open space into a natural stormwater management system that both slows and cleanses stormwater runoff.

Create a water recycling system that directs nonpotable water to on-site water features like fountains and waterfalls. Create a weather satellite–connected drip irrigation system—which is now the norm—for the landscape that uses the recycled nonpotable water and rainwater. Simply switching to waterless urinals and low-flow fixtures in the restrooms reduced water use in the headquarters building by 21 percent compared with other buildings in the research park.

Provide an on-site landscaped bicycle and pedestrian circulation system, one that connects to local transit and the community's street grid, to support alternative transportation choices. Add electric vehicle recharging stations to the property. Encourage a reduction in vehicle trips with those choices and a reconfiguration of the on-site parking system to favor shuttles and carpooling.

Green renovations to a building facade begin by understanding what the existing facility has to offer and then building on that. A wall with many windows and a southern exposure, for example, can be given sunshades designed to support the overall architectural treatment while also reducing interior glare and heat absorption. On the other hand, adding sunshades to an exposure without the right solar orientation will not be as effective as installing high-performance glass in the windows. The roof may support the installation of photovoltaic panels, skylights, or daylight monitors—or even landscaping to provide insulation and minimize heat absorption.

Renovation can adopt one of several green roofs to lower heat absorption and reduce HVAC loads. An Energy Star roof, for example, reduces the heat exchange,

lowers the HVAC requirements, and decreases the amount of insulation needed.

A green interior renovation should focus first on increasing the amount of natural daylighting, generally with an open-space plan that creates the greatest level of flexibility. This approach will support future changes in function and use while also bringing more daylight to the interior of the floor, lowering requirements for and use of artificial lighting, and reducing energy costs. Renovation of the existing office building that would house LPA's new headquarters involved eliminating private offices and moving all fixed walls to the interior of the space. As a result, all the firm's employees receive natural daylighting.

A key part of any green renovation is the installation of energy-efficient products and equipment and energy-generating equipment. Green lighting systems such as indirect light fixtures coupled with daylighting controls not only improve lighting and vision in the workplace but also improve energy performance, often significantly. This lighting strategy also reduces HVAC requirements, because the fixtures generate less heat, lowering the cooling load.

HVAC systems are changing. The main conference room of LPA's new headquarters, for example, uses a thermal displacement ventilation system—a highly sustainable air distribution system and one of the first of its kind in California—that delivers conditioned air at a lower velocity just above floor level. The conditioned air rises naturally and disperses throughout the space. This delivery system uses lower fan pressure and speeds, and therefore less energy, than comparable HVAC systems.

Installing photovoltaic panels generates sufficient energy to further lower utility costs. The use of other energy-generating systems

The World Resources Institute's green office in Washington, D.C., was built within a conventional leased office space and within a standard budget. ©Alan Karchmer

is growing. LPA, for example, plans to add three 60-kilowatt micro turbine generators to the headquarters building that will provide 80 percent of the firm's energy requirements.

Green renovation does not limit color or material selection. Building and finish materials meeting a variety of green requirements, from wood to paint and linoleum, are now widely available at or near the cost of standard materials. Wood-based materials certified in accordance with guidelines of the Forest Stewardship Council can be used for structural framing, flooring, bracing, and even pedestrian construction barriers. Linoleum is now made from a wide variety of natural materials, including linseed oil and wood flour with a jute backing.

More than 50 percent of building products and furnishings—from carpets to desks—now have recycled content. LPA used recycled materials throughout its new headquarters building. Carpet in the main conference room, for example, is made from 100 percent recycled materials. Signage throughout the head-

quarters is made from 100 percent recycled plastic, and all the accent woods in the main entry doors, reception desk, and built-in furniture are made from medium-density fiberboard, a 100 percent recycled material. Desk and work surfaces at workstations are made from 100 percent recycled wood, and filing cabinets are made with 40 percent recycled steel.

Ensuring high-quality indoor air is critical in green renovation, and that quality can now be achieved easily and cost-effectively. Many manufacturers of paints, adhesives, sealants, coatings, composite wood products, and carpets now meet or exceed the requirements for VOC off-gassing set by the South Coast Air Quality Management District, the Bay Area Air Quality Management District, Green Seal, and/or the Carpet and Rug Institute's Green Label Indoor Air Quality Test Program.

Newer HVAC equipment and systems can significantly improve indoor air quality at a lower energy cost and at a much shorter buyback period. Heating, fire suppression, ventilation, air conditioning, and refrigeration

equipment that does not use ozone-depleting hydrochlorofluorocarbon-, Halon-, or chlorofluorocarbon-based refrigerants is now widely available. Copy rooms, which do not require natural light, can be relocated to the building core and ventilated separately to further improve indoor air quality.

The renovation construction process itself is an opportunity to go green. Existing materials from concrete to furnishings can be reused or recycled on site, significantly reducing construction waste and trips to the local landfill. A waste management provider can recycle waste. More than half the construction waste from LPA's headquarters project was recycled.

A number of strategies and tools are already available for protecting indoor air quality during construction—flushing and sealing HVAC equipment, for example. For its new headquarters, LPA created and followed an indoor air quality construction plan that included such strategies as coordinating the construction sequencing of wet and dry activities to avoid contaminating dry materials that would absorb moisture and become a breeding ground for mold or bacteria.

As both the public and businesses recognize the important savings and environmental and energy benefits of green buildings, recycling existing facilities into sustainable buildings will become a win-win situation for owners and tenants and a vital market strategy that will change the real estate industry and help address the pressing environmental issues we face.

Dan Heinfeld is president of LPA, Inc., an architectural firm in southern California with offices in Irvine and Roseville, and an early member of USGBC.

be as sustainable as one with less recycled content that is made locally.

A project's life cycle should also be taken into account. The more durable a project, the less frequently it needs to be replaced. Some furniture is more easily designed to be disassembled, which aids recycling at the end of its life. Furniture that can be easily repaired or has readily available parts for replacement will also consume fewer resources. Furniture is one of the biggest contributors to poor IAQ, as its VOC emissions contribute significantly to the indoor chemical compound concentrations in a completed building. All furniture should be tested for emissions and selected based on low-VOC emissions. A two-week building flush-out with 100 percent tempered outside air should be considered to dissipate emissions from the furniture.

To reflect its mission, the Gordon and Betty Moore Foundation relocated its headquarters to a historic building in the Presidio area, a former military base in San Francisco, California. Gensler/Chris Barrett/Hedrich Blessing

Office Equipment

Copying and printing areas can be harmful to occupants, as standard photocopiers and laser printers emit VOCs and ozone, which can irritate eyes and mucous membranes and cause respiratory problems. Low-emission copiers and printers are available; others have ozone filters. Offices requiring clusters of such equipment should have them in a separate area, away from other work areas, and should provide a direct exhaust system to the outside.

Building Renovation

Renovating existing buildings is a sustainable solution in itself, as it reuses materials that would otherwise be discarded. Many of the same principles for designing new buildings apply, including energy-efficient lighting systems and controls, high-performance HVAC systems, increased natural light, selection of recycled and low- or no-VOC materials, and introduction of water-efficient plumbing fixtures. Early involvement of contractors ensures a plan for recycling construction debris and identification of building materials that can be salvaged. The design team should look for as many opportunities as possible to reuse features of the existing building to conserve resources. Tanner, Leddy, Maytum, Stacy Architects, designers of the 75,000-square-foot (7,000-square-meter) Thoreau Center in San Francisco's Presidio, adapted historic hospital wards for reuse as office space for nonprofit organizations working on environmental and justice issues. The narrow floor plates had originally been designed with daylighting and natural ventilation in mind, and the mild northern California climate permitted the renovation to avoid adding a mechanical HVAC system. Other measures that minimized site disruption and saved resources included rehabilitating historic plants and even excavating historic drainage systems to catch stormwater runoff.

A building's orientation and form are generally set by the existing structure, but courtyards can be transformed into atriums, and light shelves, clerestory windows, and skylights can be added. On the interior, restructuring the floor plan to place open offices around the perimeter enhances the penetration of natural light. Removing false ceilings and leaving ceilings exposed instead of replacing ceiling tiles saves resources.

Parking Structures and Transportation

Automobile traffic and parking have a tremendous impact on the environment, not only because of air pollution and the reliance on fossil fuels but also because of their negative impact on the quality of life. As freeways become more congested, city streets become less hospitable for pedestrians and more open space is paved over with streets. Office buildings can incorporate sustainable transportation measures in a number of ways, starting with the choice of site. A site that is close to public transit makes it easier for employees to leave their cars at home, especially if the design provides easy access to transit systems. Limiting the number of parking spaces also encourages carpooling or public transit. Some office buildings offer preferred parking for carpools as well. Telecommuting is another way to reduce the use of automobiles; office buildings that provide video-conferencing facilities can make traveling unnecessary for some meetings.

Conventional parking lots are problematic because large areas of asphalt surface parking radiate heat absorbed from the sun, raising temperatures significantly enough to contribute to harmful climate change. Nonporous parking surfaces increase stormwater runoff, which can overwhelm urban sewer systems and pollute local waterways. Strategies to minimize the environmental impacts of surface parking include light-colored paving, porous paving, landscaping islands, and curbless parking lots that allow runoff to drain into vegetated swales that treat stormwater.

Parking structures use space much more efficiently, as they reduce the footprint devoted to parked cars. Equipping

The World Trade Center in Amsterdam has a new underground storage facility for up to 2,500 bicycles. H.G. Esch

these structures with green roofs is one way to alleviate the radiated heat and stormwater runoff problems.

Parking garages can incorporate living vegetation in other ways as well. AC Martin Partners has designed a new parking structure for California State University at Fullerton that features vines growing on three of the exterior walls, helping to absorb carbon dioxide produced by automobiles. A stormwater management system diverts rainwater to help irrigate the plants.

Parking garages can also work in tandem with alternative transportation options to reduce the environmental impact of automobiles. They can house bicycle lockers, encouraging workers to bicycle to work, especially if shower facilities and changing areas are also provided. Separate garages devoted entirely to bicycles are common in Europe and Asia. Partnering with a car-sharing program may be a possibility in dense urban areas; employees can drive these cars to work and park them in the garage, while other members of the car-sharing program can use them during the day. The parking garage for the Genzyme Center in Cambridge, Massachusetts, offers recharging stations for electric cars and preferred parking spaces for carpoolers.

Photovoltaic cells on the roof of the garage can generate electricity and save energy resources. Inside the garage, energy-efficient lighting and motion detectors further lower energy bills.

Selecting Green Products

Selecting green building materials involves a number of strategic issues; each project's overall sustainable goals provide the criteria to guide selection through the maze of possibilities. Some materials are sustainable because they come from renewable sources, others because they offer zero- or low-VOC emissions. In addition, the amount of embodied energy—the energy required for extracting, manufacturing, and transporting the material to the site—is a factor to consider, although it is still small compared with the energy consumed in a building's operation. Choosing products that come from sources that do not exploit any social or racial group is another possibility.

Determining the truth of product claims can be time-consuming, costly, or both. Comparing different products by different manufacturers can also be confusing. A number of groups provide certification of the sustainability of products and materials. Some are trade associations that rely on collectively developed standards. More reliable sources are third-party certifiers, which have created their own standards. Scientific Certification Systems, for example, is a third-party certifier that has been in existence for more than 20 years, testing and certifying not only product manufacturers' environmental claims about industry products but also forest management and marine habitat management

practices. Certifications include biodegradability, formaldehyde, ozone-depleting chemicals, indoor air quality performance, recycled content, and salvaged wood, among other categories. A number of organizations certify wood that derives from sustainable forests. The Forest Stewardship Council, an international nonprofit organization, offers one of the most respected programs, inspecting and certifying forest products that meet its standards. The GREENGUARD Environmental Institute, an independent nonprofit organization that tests products for their effect on air quality, offers a certification program for those that meet their standards.

The California Department of Health Services now provides "Special Environmental Requirements, Section 01350," as a guide for architects to include in their project specifications. It requires material manufacturers to test their products for emissions and to provide data on their products' impact on the indoor chemical concentration. The purpose of the Section 01350 specifications is to reduce and limit emissions of airborne VOCs documented to have long-term health effects for occupants of new public buildings. It relies on current peer-reviewed health risk assessments conducted by the California Environmental Protection Agency's Office of Environmental Health Hazard Assessment to establish guidelines for long-term exposures of the general population.

Green Seal, another independent nonprofit organization, conducts a life-cycle evaluation examining major environmental impacts from resource extraction to recyclability. Green Seal certifies products and services that produce less pollution and waste than comparable standard products, conserve resources and habitats, and minimize global warming.

A number of software products and online and print directories provide assistance. BuildingGreen, publisher of *Environmental Building News,* offers *GreenSpec,* an online and print directory of more than 1,750 green building products, with environmental data, information about manufacturers, and links to additional resources (www.building green.com/menus). The California Integrated Waste

Management Board offers its "Recycled-Content Product Directory" online at http://www.ciwmb.ca.gov/RCP, naming thousands of recycled products along with information about the companies responsible for them (see also "Environmentally Preferable Purchasing Policies" in Chapter 6 for more information about product certification).

Life-cycle assessment evaluates environmental performance over the whole life cycle of a product, building, or process, taking into account the extraction of raw materials, manufacturing, construction, building occupancy, demolition, and eventual recycling or disposal. Life-cycle assessment tools are in their infancy, because the information they rely on is still limited: information on many products has not been obtained, and different manufacturers or researchers use different methods to develop data, making comparisons across products or manufacturers difficult. Nevertheless, these tools can still provide useful guidance. BEES (Building

40 Grosvenor Place in London, contains only sustainable veneers, magnetic carpet tiles to eliminate toxic adhesives, and work surfaces made of recycled yogurt containers. "Write-on" walls eliminate the need for whiteboards. Peter Cook

for Environmental and Economic Sustainability) software provides assistance with choosing cost-effective building products that have less negative impact on the environment than their standard counterparts. Developed by the National Institute of Standards and Technology Building and Fire Research Laboratory with support from the U.S. EPA, BEES lists environmental performance data for nearly 200 building products. The ATHENA software program allows designers to compare the environmental trade-offs of different design alternatives, based on a life-cycle analysis of building products. Developed by the Athena

Wooden benches in the atriums of the Gap, Inc., office in San Bruno, California, were constructed entirely of eucalyptus from the site; carefully designed daylighting allows plants to grow inside. Mark Luthringer Photography

Sustainable Materials Institute, a not-for-profit organization, it assesses environmental impacts in all stages of a product's life cycle, analyzing energy use, solid waste emissions, air pollution, water pollution, global warming potential, and use of resources.

For assistance in identifying energy-saving office machinery, the U.S. EPA's ENERGY STAR program provides the ENERGY STAR label for products that meet its stringent energy efficiency guidelines.

Because selecting green products and materials can be more involved and time-consuming than choosing standard products, it is essential to begin selecting them early in the design process. Some products have longer lead times because they are not yet produced in the same large volumes as standard products.

Sustainable design is still an evolving discipline, and even though it has become much better known in the United States in recent years, the relatively limited availability of materials, performance data, and technologies (limited at least in comparison with their conventional counterparts) can pose real challenges. At the same time, green design is not entirely new and untested; for most of history, human ingenuity was required to design comfortable structures for living and working despite the lack of electricity, mechanical ventilation, and modern plumbing. By encouraging the use of local materials and climate-specific strategies, green design results in buildings that respond more specifically to their site and region, often taking more distinctive forms than many of the standard office boxes of the late 20th century. The new emphasis on sustainability inspires a more creative approach that pays off in increased comfort and productivity—for the planet as well as for the occupants of any individual building.

Notes

1. W.J. Fisk, "Health and Productivity Gains from Better Indoor Environments and Their Relationship with Building Efficiency," *Annual Review of Energy and the Environment,* 2000, Volume 25, No. 1, pp. 537–566.

2. Joseph J. Romm and William D. Browning, *Greening the Building and the Bottom Line: Increasing Productivity through Energy-Efficient Design* (Snowmass, Colorado: Rocky Mountain Institute, December 1994).

3. Monta Monaco Hernon, "Churn Down the Heat: Underfloor HVAC Systems Allow Easy Space Reconfiguration and Improve Comfort," *Journal of Property Management,* March/April 2004, pp. 40–44.

4. U.S. Environmental Protection Agency, *Energy Cost and IAQ Performance of Ventilation Systems and Controls: Executive Summary,* Indoor Environments Division, Office of Air and Radiation (Washington, D.C.: U.S. Government Printing Office, January 2000), p. 16.

5. Christine L. Grahl, "Beyond Recycled Content," *Environmental Design & Construction,* March 2002, pp. 20–24.

6. J.J. Jaakkola, P.K. Verkasalo, and N. Jaakkola, "Plastic Wall Materials in the Home and Respiratory Health in Young Children," *American Journal of Public Health,* May 2000, pp. 797–799.

chapter 5

Sustainable
Office Construction

Sustainable Office Construction

Rod Wille

In the United States, general contractors historically have competed for building construction projects by submitting lump-sum bids based on completed drawings and specifications. More recently, construction management became a popular delivery methodology involving a qualifications-based selection process that brought the contractor onto the project team early in the design phase to provide preconstruction services to the owner in reaction to the design that was being created. The services generally include cost estimating, value engineering, and scheduling as the design evolved. At or near the completion of contract documents, the contractor would consolidate all estimated construction costs into a final estimate and proceed on a "cost-plus" basis or provide a fixed guaranteed maximum price (GMP) and proceed into construction on an "at-risk" basis. Both the lump-sum and construction management approaches are sequential processes in which the construction professional provides services that parallel the designer's and owner's activities.

Sites in dense urban locations such as Thames Court in London, England, require careful planning to ensure they meet sustainability goals during construction. H.G. Esch

Likewise, the design team and the owner's team all fed information into the program and design "on queue," and, when the first shovel of dirt was overturned, they hoped for a coordinated, buildable design that met the owner's needs and was within his budget. This "budget" was nearly always an internal appropriation of dollars based on a cash flow extending through final payment to the contractor at the completion of his construction.

In today's world of sustainable development, with green design and environmentally sensitive construction practices, it is no longer acceptable to allow all these talented players to spend months proceeding on parallel paths. And one must remember that this process does not end until the building functions in total accordance with the owner's program and the designer's intent. If an owner has done his due diligence and determined that he will develop a sustainable project, he must consider bringing together professionals for an integrated team whose mission is to create a project that meets the needs of the present without compromising the ability of future generations to meet their own needs.

If the traditional sequence of plan-design-bid-build-occupy-operate-maintain is considered, the contractor historically has been involved with the bid-build, possibly design-bid-build, segment and with construction management. Now, if sustainable development is the goal, then the contractor needs to be a member of an integrated project team from concept through functional operation and maintenance.

The same process necessarily applies to all other project team members: they should be retained early, and those relationships should be maintained until the building is functioning in accordance with the owner's sustainable program. From a contractual standpoint, all services must be procured on the basis that they will support and complement the services being provided by other team members.

Key Services Provided by the Contractor

Assuming that an owner retains a general contractor from early project concept through the commissioning of a functional building, many key services must be procured for a green project. During the design phase, these services might include comprehensive cost estimating, system value analysis, green product and regional material identification, master scheduling, constructability reviews, and an overall market analysis of the project's green capabilities. Moving into construction, the contractor must have a proactive green procurement plan, site logistics studies, manpower analyses, lead-time verification, detailed scheduling, and a green quality assurance/quality control program and administrative procedures in place for documentation. A general contractor with previous green experience should have the in-house capability to provide these services, or, at worst, the contractor may need to retain a subconsultant to provide any services he himself is not capable of providing.

Several photovoltaic installation options were discussed before construction began on the Endesa corporate headquarters building in Madrid. Although the building does not include photovoltaic panels at present, its design will allow Endesa to choose from a number of options in the future. H.G. Esch

Preconstruction

The first activity in which a contractor should actively participate is the design charrette. If the owner has decided to develop a green project but is unsure just how green to make it, a charrette allows all stakeholders in the project to brainstorm ideas for sustainability. Typically, charrettes are set up by a third party who becomes the facilitator of this one- or two-day activity. If the project team includes a green consultant, that person should be able to organize and facilitate the charrette. Invitees might include representatives from the owner's facility, financial, maintenance, and user groups, all architectural and engineering consultants, and the contractor. In addition, city officials, lenders, neighboring property owners, and other interested parties might be invited for all or portions of the event.

The ultimate goal of the charrette is to establish the criteria for sustainability for the project that the team has evaluated. Issues discussed include environmental impact, energy consumption, health and productivity of occupants, available technology, and cost (both initial cost and life-cycle costs). Perhaps a mission statement for the project is created that will serve as the litmus test for green features being considered. Assignments are delegated at the charrette and follow-up meetings held to fine-tune the information that eventually becomes the basis for green design and construction. Meeting minutes are kept of all discussions, and follow-up responsibility and time frames are set forth as a road map for the design process.

At a recent charrette for a major big-box retail project, Turner Construction Company, in the role of designer/builder, served as the catalyst to brainstorm a shopping list of more than 150 sustainable ideas in a two-day session.

The contractor played a key role in estimating the cost and evaluating the feasibility of a rooftop heliostat system for the Genzyme Corporation headquarters in Cambridge, Massachusetts. Turner Construction Company

With the entire team contributing design, cost, and feasibility information over the next six months, the final list was fine-tuned to 45 items. Accepted items had to be justified as conforming to the owner's mission statement and were supported with life-cycle analyses or their positive impacts on store operations and customers.

The contractor is a key participant in the charrette, not only as a contributor of ideas for sustainability but also as the resource for developing cost data, availability of materials, local market analysis, lead times for delivery, evaluation of trade-offs (value engineering), analysis of constructability, and overall scheduling for the project. The contractor's contribution to these issues, in fact, becomes the major focus of his continued contributions to preconstruction.

Although excellent cost estimating is a prerequisite for any good contractor who provides preconstruction services, it is even more critical for the evaluation of green buildings. First, the owner wants to know upfront what the new building will cost to construct, including the value of its green components. The contractor estimates this "first cost" for construction using historical data (particularly in the concept stage of design) as well as local unit pricing that considers labor productivity, material prices and availability, and other market conditions. Green products, materials, equipment, and systems must be carefully evaluated and priced using these same factors: Is the material locally available? Is local labor familiar with installing this green material? Is it a proprietary product with no competition? For example, substituting recycled fly ash for cement in ready-mix concrete should result in no cost premium, if fly ash is readily available from local fossil fuel power plants and if local labor knows how to work with a fly ash mix.

As green design and construction continue to join the mainstream, the availability of accurate first cost and life-cycle cost data increases. Moreover, increased competition among suppliers and qualified subcontractors as a result of more green projects reduces any green cost impact. Nevertheless, ongoing research by the contractor is required to identify separate costs for manufactured goods as well as their installation cost. Many subcontractors are willing to invest effort into gaining a better understanding of green technology and to educate their workers. A good general contractor minimizes the impact of any resulting learning curve by clearly delineating and explaining the green requirements in supplementary specifications.

The life-cycle cost analysis for a product or system involves the first cost as well as cost factors for energy savings, maintenance, replacement, and operating efficiency. The life-cycle analysis is based on assumptions for interest rates, energy costs, and operations and management costs for a fixed term; for example, a 50-kilowatt wind turbine was recently proved to have a 12-year payback at the cost of $0.08 per kilowatt-hour for electricity, with no incentives or rebates. In California, with its higher electricity rates and significant incentives for renewable energy, this technology would be even more cost-effective. Owners must be willing to evaluate the long-term return on investment, however, because based strictly on first costs, this technology is quite expensive. When life-cycle costs are considered in the evaluation of building design, the benefits of green features become abundantly clear, and the owner can make conscious decisions on how green the facility should be. The contractor must be capable of providing high-quality cost data and work with the team (usually the engineering consultant) to prepare these analyses.

Another specific area where green cost estimating is important is in the analysis of trade-offs. Trade-offs come into play in two ways; first, they could simply involve the substitution of one product or material for another. An example might be the substitution of a rapidly renewable bamboo floor in lieu of a cherry wood floor. In this case, the first cost of each material is an issue, but certain environmental issues related to the foresting of these woods are more subjective and difficult to quantify.

Perhaps more important in the green building arena is the analysis of building systems—in fact, the analysis of the integrated building as a whole—as they relate to trading off the additional cost of one material for another (for example, insulation with higher "R" value versus the savings generated by a reduction in chiller capacity). If this simplistic example is extrapolated to an evaluation of every building component affected by a potential revision to one material or piece of equipment, the complexity and importance of the comprehensive analyses of trade-offs become obvious. If the architects and engineers are creating an integrated design for the project, then the contractor needs to work in parallel with them, providing accurate cost estimates that become the basis for the owner's essential decisions. Only by following this integrated process can an owner be assured that the project envisioned is high performance, energy efficient, and environmentally friendly.

For the headquarters of Genzyme Corporation in Cambridge, Massachusetts, Turner Construction Company offered comprehensive input on costs, constructability, product availability, and scheduling for a complex system of rooftop heliostats that track the sun's path across the sky, reflect the sunlight through stationary mirrors, and redirect it into the building's atrium, where the light is deflected horizontally by a prismatic chandelier into adjacent offices. A truly integrated design using European technology required Turner to carefully manage the process to bring it all together in the field.

Because of the relative newness of the green movement, the identification of green products and materials can become a significant task for the team. For traditional projects, the architect has intimate knowledge of these items and

The Santa Monica Water Garden in California has an on-site wastewater treatment plant and a graywater recycling system that supports a lake and other water features. Tom Lamb, SWA Group

writes specifications to incorporate them into the design. For green projects, the architect retains overall design responsibility, but it is incumbent on the contractor to assist with this task. Trade journals are filled with advertisements by new manufacturers of green products and materials claiming excellent performance. But these upstart companies are also responsible for a significant number of business failures. Team members need to collaborate on the identification of reputable and financially capable suppliers of green products before they specify products. Factors such as regional availability, local subcontractors' familiarity with installation, lead times for manufacturing and delivery, the supplier's track record, and agency test requirements must all be considered—and the contractor must play a key role in this analysis.

The project team must also decide during preconstruction whether the design will feature "leading" or "bleeding" edge technology. The contractor's review of systems will help educate the team on any risk factors that must be considered. Risk may be associated with a product or system that is not suitable for the application being considered. Or, it may be associated with the ultimate goal (for example, energy savings), which is not achievable. Because many green products, equipment, or materials are so new, the track record associated with traditional buildings may not yet be established.

Scheduling for a green building takes on added significance early in the design phase. The argument for additional design and construction management costs to coordinate a green design can essentially be eliminated if the schedule keeps the project team on its integrated design path. The road map from the initial charrette to ground breaking must be drawn in detail to avoid costly redesign, unnecessary studies, budget overruns, and a lack of timely decision making. If these delays can be eliminated because the team buys in to a comprehensive preconstruction schedule, then fees and reimbursable costs can be reduced and the projected occupancy date maintained.

The contractor should be charged with creating the master development schedule and monitoring and updating it at every team meeting. As concepts envisioned during the charrette start to take form, all project team members will have scheduled activities that must be completed on time to bring the concept to reality. An example might be an underfloor air distribution system that has many sustainable advantages. Activities involving aesthetics, energy modeling, life-cycle cost analysis, equipment trade-offs, noise, air quality and health/productivity factors, controls, and even the effect of the building's height for planning and zoning approvals must be coordinated and accomplished on schedule to enable a fully integrated (and cost-effective) design.

Further, the master development schedule must take into consideration the construction phase. Issues such as lead times for manufacturing, shop drawings, and delivery must be carefully researched for specialty green products or equipment. Also to be considered is whether items such as building-integrated photovoltaic modules require certification by Underwriters Laboratories or whether the local building department requires extra time to approve the use of a fuel cell on the project. Besides the traditional bricks and mortar, an experienced contractor has to anticipate the special scheduling requirements of a green building and its special features.

Turning Waste into Profit

Rod Wille

It is a fact that construction projects contribute more than 136 million tons (123.4 million metric tons) of demolition and construction waste each year to landfills that are quickly becoming overburdened. Many of these waste materials can be recycled or reused, which ultimately would require less new raw material to be extracted from the earth. Recycling waste can save costs on many projects. Taken together, these facts strongly point to the need for a well-designed construction waste recycling program on every project, green or not.

Even before construction begins, the contractor should develop a waste avoidance program. Many materials—metal studs, gypsum wallboard, and dimensional lumber, for example—can be ordered precut to save on cutting and waste in the field. Packaging for all materials arriving on the jobsite should be minimized and returned to the supplier for reuse or recycling. Subcontractors should be encouraged to specify exact sizes and precise quantities of materials to minimize excess and waste.

An owner should look to his contractor to investigate the local and regional markets to determine the cost of hauling unsorted debris to a local landfill compared with identifying sources (and cost factors) for various construction waste materials that might be recyclable. Materials might include metal, wood, concrete, masonry, drywall, glass, cardboard, plastic, and more. Typically, when the cost of dumping debris at a landfill exceeds $50 per ton ($45 per metric ton), a recycling program makes good economic sense.

If local haulers already have experience in recycling, then the program is easy to create. In certain locations, however, the contractor must make the market for recycled

Construction waste can be sorted on site as shown or at an off-site collection facility. With disposal fees steadily rising across the country, waste management can provide both short-term and long-term payoffs.
Turner Construction Company

materials by searching out users for the materials. The debris can be sorted on site by using separate Dumpsters, or off site, where haulers sort it.

The steps to creating and implementing a recycling program might include:
- Preparing a cost/benefit analysis;
- Creating specifications;
- Soliciting bids from haulers who recycle (or making the market);
- Educating subcontractors at the site;
- Setting up separate Dumpsters and monitoring sorting;
- Documenting debris leaving the site; and
- Tabulating results.

At the Toyota Motor Sales North American Headquarters in Torrance, California, Turner Construction Company developed a waste-recycling program that diverted 96 percent of all construction waste from landfills (1,130 tons [1,025 metric tons]) and saved more than $35,000 when compared with traditional hauling and tipping fees.

If demolition of existing structures is a component of a project, then the recycling program takes on an added dimension. First, the existing structure should be analyzed to determine whether all or part of it can be reused or disassembled and recycled. Certain materials such as ceiling tile and

carpet often can be recycled directly with manufacturers, and materials such as brick and stone have a direct market for reuse. Concrete and asphalt can be processed for use as a high-quality subbase or as aggregate in new building materials. The contractor needs to explore all avenues to ensure an efficient and cost-effective program.

The design of new buildings should be considered as to their ultimate evolution. Are high-tech products more durable, and do they offer long-term benefits through avoided maintenance and replacement? Are new building components manufactured from recycled materials, and can they, in turn, be recycled and reused? Is modular design implemented to maintain flexible space and to save on remodeling waste (and cost)? Can the building itself be designed to ultimately be disassembled or renovated for other uses? The contractor can be a major contributor to the ultimate life of many natural resources.

Recycling construction and demolition waste is the one green activity that is totally under the contractor's control, and it should be implemented on all projects. As an added incentive, the USGBC, under its LEED rating system, awards one or two credit points for recycling 50 percent or 75 percent, respectively, of construction waste.

Construction

Two important green activities occur during the transition from the preconstruction to the construction phase. The first entails the preparation and implementation of an environmentally friendly site logistics plan. A site in an urban environment has its own idiosyncrasies and constraints that somewhat limit the environmental aspects of planning. A downtown site surrounded by other buildings and city streets can host successful construction operations if they are contained within the property lines.

Keeping ducts clean during construction and flushing out HVAC systems at the completion of construction can help ensure high air quality standards in a newly completed building. LPA, Inc./Adrian Velicescu, Standard

By the same token, if a contractor can build a 50-story building on a tight urban site, he does not need to spread out and disrupt the ecology of a suburban or rural site for a simple three-story building. Access roads, laydown areas (minimized by just-in-time delivery), trailer complexes, and trade parking should be carefully planned to minimize disruption to the existing natural environment. A prudent owner looks to preserve existing low- or no-maintenance vegetation and animal habitats by requiring a site logistics plan for construction operations that is considerate of existing conditions. And, in so doing, he also saves construction dollars (see Chapter 3).

A second aspect of a good site logistics plan is the control of stormwater runoff and erosion during construction. Although the civil engineer is charged with the design of an erosion control plan during construction, it is the contractor who must maintain it, properly sequence sitework to prevent runoff from leaving the site, wash down vehicle wheels, use temporary seeding, maintain dust control, and generally use good common sense to avoid mishaps that will pollute waterways, affect the environment, and be offensive to the neighborhood. The green contractor must have in place a plan to recycle construction (and demolition) waste to keep these materials from further overburdening landfills (see the accompanying feature box).

Procuring trade subcontracts is another of the contractor's very important activities that in essence kicks off the construction phase of the project. This activity effectively leads to the implementation and documentation of green activities on the site.

As shop drawings and material samples are submitted for approval, the contractor must ensure that the standards for all specified green products, materials, equipment, and systems are maintained. Frequently, subcontractors and vendors offer substitutions that do not meet the rigid guidelines

Commissioning

Rod Wille

Perhaps one of the most worthwhile investments that any building owner can make is to have his project properly commissioned. Commissioning a building should be an organized process ensuring that the building performs in accordance with the design intent and the contract documents. If commissioning is undertaken during the design phase (as it should be), it will also ensure that the design itself is commensurate with the owner's operational needs. With the sophistication of modern building designs and the technology incorporated into a building's systems and equipment, it is more important than ever for commissioning to take place. If not, the owner runs the risk of having his high-tech building underperform—resulting in unnecessary costs for more energy, high maintenance, and potential early replacement of expensive equipment.

Commissioning has historically involved a simple process of starting up the mechanical and electrical systems, balancing air and water flow, undertaking minor testing and adjusting, completing the punch list, and passing the baton to the owner's facility staff to operate the building. As systems became more complex, it was common for the owner's staff to "disconnect" the sophisticated controls and operate the building manually because they were unfamiliar with the technology required.

Today's buildings, green or not, are being designed to conserve energy by integrating all aspects of the building and sizing the systems accordingly. The controls need to be designed to optimize this efficiency. Equipment is no longer oversized and therefore must be run as intended to maintain a comfortable indoor environment. And commissioning needs to extend to the building envelope that is integrated into the mechanical design to truly ensure performance.

Building commissioning needs to examine all equipment to ensure that it was installed correctly and is working in accordance with the specifications by measuring temperatures, flow rates, power consumption, and calibration. The sequence of operations for the controls must be verified to create the proper interaction between systems and equipment. The process requires documentation of results, a training program for ongoing performance, and perhaps a longer-term (one year or more) validation of continuous efficient performance.

Typically, the owner retains a third-party agent to commission the building. Having a third party tends to ensure an unbiased evaluation of the design and installation. The cost to commission the entire building (mechanical and electrical equipment, controls, and envelope) tends to run between 0.5 percent and 1.5 percent of the construction cost, but the paybacks on this investment can be almost immediate—energy and water savings, operational and maintenance efficiency.

The typical steps involved in basic commissioning include:

■ Retaining a commissioning agent early in the design phase;

■ Evaluating the owner's operational needs to create an intent for the design;
■ Ensuring that an integrated design conforms to the design intent;
■ Including a commissioning plan and its requirements in the contract documents;
■ Monitoring installation of systems;
■ Verifying and documenting startup, functional testing, samplings of performance data, and calibration of components;
■ Verifying (or conducting) training of the owner's personnel;
■ Reviewing operation and maintenance manuals;
■ Preparing and submitting a commissioning report; and
■ Verifying continued performance after 11 months or longer (optional).

The contractor, at a minimum, is a key participant in the commissioning process. He also could serve as the commissioning entity if commissioning is performed by experienced staff who are independent from the project staff. The contractor should view commissioning as a service that will assist him in delivering a project that conforms to the contract documents and will save callbacks after construction. The contractor must engage his key subcontractors and suppliers in the commissioning process so that all technical expertise is available to the commissioning agent. Commissioning is not a substitute for a good quality control program, so completing punch lists and normal testing and balancing must occur before verification. Commissioning is a team activity that is necessary to ensure a high-performance building.

for energy efficiency, recycled content, low-VOC emissions, and other criteria. The contractor must monitor the source of locally manufactured materials to ensure that standards for embodied energy are maintained. And the on-site installation process requires careful field inspection to ensure provision of an energy-efficient and environmentally friendly building. These activities require that a contractor have staff assigned to the project who are knowledgeable and familiar with the intent and implementation of a sustainable design so that costly rework or delays are avoided.

Depending on the owner's intentions for verification of all green features on a project (either LEED certification or an informal self-certification), the level of documentation varies. The LEED rating system has a very well-defined process for documentation to which all team members contribute. This documentation begins early in design, extends through construction, and continues through turnover and building operation. The contractor relies on his subcontractors and vendors for much of the information, which ideally should be collected during construction so that at completion, a well-maintained binder of information is available for review and analysis. A less formal program (other than LEED) should be established during the design phase so that a clear definition of documentation requirements is established before procurement of trade subcontracts. Although the development of a sustainable project may make the project team feel good, it is much more rewarding to be able to share design intentions, quantified results, and lessons learned with the public and to educate others about the project's specific green attributes.

Another area under a contractor's control during construction is "general conditions." A contractor entertains many items while planning how to manage the project. A clean building during construction optimizes indoor air quality after occupancy. Temporary protection of the work and stored materials minimizes damage from moisture, which also affects air quality. Flushing out the completed building, including replacing all air-handling unit filters and wrapping the ends of all ductwork before use, also affects air quality. A well-thought-out program of temporary lighting (including trailers) saves energy and money. Two other general conditions for the contractor to address are recycling waste paper and using vehicles for the project that use alternative fuels or are hybrid designs.

Postconstruction

Certainly one of the most important activities in the overall development of a green building is commissioning. Commissioning, put in simple terms, is a process that ensures the owner that the completed building and its systems function in accordance with the intent of the design. The contractor is a key player in commissioning from design through occupancy. He must ensure that systems are buildable and cost-effective, procure technical assistance from subcontractors and vendors, carefully monitor submittals to ensure they strictly meet the specifications, and inspect the installation for quality control. As the project nears completion, the contractor assists the commissioning agent and designers with starting, calibrating, and testing systems, and training the owner's operations staff. Once all systems are performing as designed, a performance manual is prepared, comparing as-built results with the original intent (for example, whether the chiller is producing the desired flow of water at the design temperature while consuming a predetermined amount of energy). Warranties and as-built drawings are included.

One last activity to consider is a walk-through 11 months after completion—just before the one-year warranty period expires. The walk-through identifies items that may need to be repaired or replaced and allows analysis of how the building's systems have been performing over the course of four climatic seasons.

The San Mateo County Forensics Laboratory in California was constructed under the design-build method. The project's success encouraged the county to require LEED certification for all new facilities. HOK

Selecting a Green Contractor

Perhaps the first factor to consider when selecting a contractor to construct a green building is the timing. The list of services suggested during preconstruction indicates the need to bring a contractor on board very early in the process—no later than the schematic design phase—to provide input that will allow the project team to make informed decisions. Although many preconstruction services could be provided by third parties (quantity surveyors or scheduling consultants, for example), an integrated approach to sustainable development is best achieved by a project team that is seamless from concept through occupancy.

One of the most cost-ineffective situations is for an owner to decide late in the design phase (or, worse, during construction) that he wants to develop a green building. Such timing would involve a costly redesign with associated delays or a "glue-on green" approach that attempts to incorporate green features without total design integration. If an owner is truly committed to sustainable development, he should assemble the project team early so that an organized and integrated design is possible with intelligent input from all team members.

With a program and possibly design concept in hand, the owner must decide how to contract for the construction of the project. Several contracting methodologies might be considered: a lump-sum bid, construction management (at risk or not at risk), and design-build.

A lump-sum bid process does not lend itself to green building construction for three reasons. First, by its nature, a lump-sum bid does not include preconstruction services, as the contractor submits a fixed-price bid based on completed design documents. Second, it does not allow for the important continuity from design to construction, thus losing the concept of an integrated approach. Third, a lump-sum bid does not promote an atmosphere of teamwork, so essential in a successful green project.

Construction management offers the owner comprehensive preconstruction services at a reasonable cost. It allows the owner to control the design and receive meaningful input from the eventual builder so he can make informed decisions. Contractors typically provide preconstruction services "at cost," looking to earn their profit from a fee for the actual construction.

Upon completion of design, the owner may elect to have the contractor provide a fixed price for the construction ("construction management at risk") or proceed to construction based on a firm cost estimate on a "cost-plus" basis. Most owners need a firm price before beginning construction and therefore prefer construction management at risk, usually with a guaranteed maximum price (GMP).

The benefits of construction management at risk include a GMP comprising competitively bid trade subcontracts using a list of prequalified bidders. This process ensures the owner that a team of financially stable subcontractors with experience in building green projects is available. Quality control and adherence to the strict intent of sustainable design are issues that many subcontractors are not familiar with. A successful green building requires experience and commitment from every subcontractor and worker on site.

Other benefits of a GMP contract include an "open book" approach to costs (that is, there are no hidden secrets about the cost of any item), a return of any savings to the owner, and a complete price that fills any gaps in the documents required to meet the intent of a sustainable design. This methodology should be considered the most compatible with achieving a successful green project.

Another option to be considered is design-build. In this case, the owner needs a program, a conceptual design, and preferably an idea of the level of greenness that he hopes to achieve (for example, LEED Silver certification). The designer-builder then develops the design within a predetermined budget and delivers the project under a sole source

of responsibility. Another option with design-build is to base the selection of a design-builder on a preliminary design and price proposal that also commits to achieve a certain LEED rating. In this way (with all other factors being equal), the owner could choose a team that could produce a LEED Gold rating versus one, say, that targets only LEED Silver.

The benefits of design-build include full design and preconstruction services, a fixed price before construction begins, and a single point of overall accountability. A disadvantage might be the owner's perceived loss of control over design.

If lump-sum bidding is excluded as an option, the selection process for a green contractor usually follows the following path: prequalification of firms; request for proposals; presentation of staff, services, and experience; evaluation based on selection criteria; and award.

A consensus is growing that the first costs of building green tend to decrease in proportion to the experience of the project team members, including the contractor and designer, with this building type. Therefore, from the perspective of the bottom line, an owner should select a contractor based more on his experience with green building rather than a low fee. This factor also applies to LEED documentation required from the contractor, which is not a big deal if he has been through the process a few times.

Another selection criterion to consider is the contractor's procurement process. The key issue is having a centralized purchasing group that is familiar with the green marketplace—that is, vendors of products and subcontractors familiar with green construction and with the lead times and availability of these specialty materials. It is a very dynamic market, and the person responsible for procurement needs to understand the pulse of the market.

Concrete Performance

Kevin Flynn

Concrete has been used for more than 2,000 years—since the Romans discovered that mixing pozzolana cement, lime, gravel, and sand yielded a durable, high-strength material that could be produced inexpensively and locally. They used concrete to build much of their empire, and it was so durable that many of the structures still stand today.

Not only durable, concrete also can offer significant thermal mass. It is wind and fire resistant, a sound performer in seismic events, dimensionally stable, readily recyclable and able to contain recycled products in its manufacture, and capable of being produced locally. A versatile material that can be colored, molded, and shaped, concrete can be formed in the field or purchased in a variety of shapes and sizes for panelized construction. The basic components of concrete have changed very little since the Romans first used it, but it has been improved over time.

A highly regarded environmental material, concrete has a durability that makes it an obvious choice from the perspective of embodied energy alone. But Portland cement, a material used when concrete is manufactured, contributes close to 7 percent of the world's carbon dioxide greenhouse gas emissions during its production. Concrete reabsorbs some of this carbon dioxide as it cures but generally not more than 10 percent. To address this issue, the Farmington Hills, Michigan–based American Concrete Institute formed a committee in 2000 to find ways to produce more environmentally sustainable concrete.

One way to achieve this goal is by using less Portland cement in the manufacture of concrete and by substituting other aggregates and cementitious materials in its place:

■ *Coal fly ash.* A byproduct of burning coal, fly ash is created from impurities found in coal that evaporate and then condense into very tiny glass spheres. This waste product can be used to replace up to 55 percent of the Portland cement found in concrete. The use of fly ash aggregate makes concrete lighter and less expensive while reducing the amount of fly ash headed to landfills and the amount of greenhouse gas emissions.

■ *Blast furnace slag.* Consisting of limestone and other impurities that float to the surface as byproducts of melting iron ore, slag becomes granulated when cooled quickly with water. The slag granules are then ground into a powder that acts much like cement. Because it is a waste material from other processes, it requires less energy to manufacture than Portland cement, and, like coal fly ash, it helps reduce greenhouse gas emissions and waste product sent to landfills. The use of blast furnace slag, already widespread in Europe, is growing in popularity in the United States.

■ *Rice hull ash.* Burning rice hulls, which contain significant amounts of silica, yields an ash that can be ground into a powder and used as an additive to concrete to reduce its permeability while increasing its strength. Because of the relatively small amounts produced, rice hull ash is more expensive than traditional cement. A mixture of rice hull ash and coal fly ash, however, is affordable and can produce a high-performance concrete for the same cost as standard concrete.

■ *Glass.* Mixed, colored, and broken glass can be used in concrete as a coarse or fine aggregate that can lead to lower permeability and prevent leaching of metals or other compounds to and from concrete. When used as a replacement for sand, glass should be used with fly ash when concrete is being used for structural purposes.

In many instances, however, concrete is used for finish work or decoration, and its structural load-bearing performance is less important. The use of concrete for pavers, table- or countertops, and flooring can all benefit from glass, which provides an interesting visual and decorative element within the concrete itself. Similar effects can be achieved with a wide range of other materials such as old tires, plastics, stone chips, bricks, tiles, marbles, metals, wood, and nearly anything else that is inorganic and can be broken, ground, or polished.

Concrete can absorb the atmospheric pollutant nitrogen oxide and convert it to harmless ions that can be washed away by rain when an ultrafine powder with photocatalytic properties is added to the cement mixture. Studies are being conducted in Japan and Norway in which normal concrete forms such as sidewalks, retaining walls, sound barriers, and even roadways act as giant air cleaners and pollution control devices when this special concrete mix is used. It is all part of a process to make higher-performance and less-expensive concrete that actually makes a positive contribution to the environment by reducing waste and improving the health of the planet.

Kevin Flynn is a senior designer and director of sustainable design at HGA, Inc., a national firm in Minneapolis, Minnesota, that uses a multidisciplinary approach encompassing architectural, engineering, and planning solutions.

Reprinted with permission from **Urban Land,** *June 2004.*

The contractor's staff—both his on-site staff and the depth of green expertise available in house—is a major factor. On-site supervision by those with green building experience is important for many reasons: scheduling (what is the lead time to fabricate a fuel cell?), constructability (why does a bamboo floor need room for movement?), trade jurisdiction (who installs building-integrated photovoltaic modules?), and quality control (does the label on the paint can really state "no VOCs"?).

A final factor to consider is whether the contractor has truly embraced a green culture. Is there a companywide commitment to sustainability demonstrated by internal training, participation in organizations like USGBC, dedicated green resources, and other telltale signs that the commitment goes beyond a few staffers who may have a personal interest in sustainability? This factor is important, because too often, a contractor's traditional approach to construction might tend to treat green buildings as second-class citizens. An owner deserves a commitment that all the contractor's resources will be pointed in the same direction to create a cost-effective, energy-efficient, and environmentally friendly project.

The key issues to consider when selecting a green contractor include retaining him or her early in the design phase to take advantage of his or her preconstruction expertise and to allow for continuity to construction. Green qualifications and experience under a construction management form of contract are criteria that will result in a cost-effective project and a top-to-bottom commitment to sustainability.

Green Procurement Plans

In any type of construction, a contractor's performance is directly proportional to the performance of subcontractors and material vendors. Therefore, it is critical that the contractor have in place a procurement plan or process that identifies and awards work to firms that are the most qualified and financially stable and have experience with previous green buildings. The list of experienced firms, however,

is rather limited (although rapidly growing), and no owner or contractor wants to risk failure by retaining someone who is not committed to or familiar with the design intent of sustainability.

Like the selection process for the contractor, the first issue to consider with subcontractors and vendors is timing. On many green projects, the subcontractors or vendors for high-technology or integrated systems need to be on board during design to lend their expertise to the design team. Examples might include providers of geothermal systems, photovoltaic modules, or green roofs. A contractor could retain these providers on a design-build or design-assist basis: the difference is that with design-build, the provider becomes the "designer of record," and with design assist, the provider collaborates with the architect and engineer of record and offers technical advice so that the documents are ultimately complete and functional for their systems.

The trick is obtaining competitive bids when the design is based on one specific provider's system or technology. The contractor must solicit proposals early in the design process, based on schematic layouts and a performance specification. The prequalified subcontractors or vendors then submit their not-to-exceed proposals either to design or assist with the design of the system, obtain any necessary governmental or agency approvals, and then when the design is complete, convert their not-to-exceed price into a lump sum (at or below their original proposal). This process allows the contractor to creatively maintain competition early in the design phase and yet be protected by a lump-sum price before entering into a formal subcontract agreement or purchase order at the time construction begins. A similar process can be followed for proprietary items of work, even if design assistance is not required. Competition must be maintained in some form for the contractor to obtain the best pricing on behalf of the owner.

Timing of trade buyouts is also related to the lead times required for bid, award, shop drawings, fabrication, and delivery. With green construction, the contractor needs a special understanding of these time frames as they relate to specialty products or equipment. How long will it take to obtain finished wood paneling from a sustainable forest and document its travels from forest to building site? In many cases, green products are manufactured in small facilities, and their availability is a function of backlogged orders. So the contractor must have the resources to investigate such issues so that procurement is accurately scheduled to allow for delivery to the site when required.

On traditional projects, a contractor can usually rely on the designer's specifications to ensure that he is buying materials that conform to the intent of the design. On green projects, however, the contractor must reinforce the scope of work being procured, because even minor deviations (or substitutions) can cause a well-designed integrated system to miss the mark. Subcontractors are very adept at using the "or equal" provision in the general requirements of most specifications to their advantage. The contractor, to prevent any misunderstandings, must therefore develop project-specific special conditions and individual trade requisitions that clearly spell out the scope of work. In fact, it is sometimes necessary to have the subcontractor list the manufacturers and products on which he is basing his bid so their acceptability can be evaluated. More than one green project has been seriously delayed when a product shows up on site ready for installation and then it is discovered that it does not conform to specifications. Sometimes getting the correct product delivered at this point is a major issue.

Many designers have third-party testing agencies verify in the field that the contents of products (recycled content or chemical composition, for example) are in fact the same as the contents the manufacturer claims. It is surprising the amount of misleading information (intentional and unintentional) that causes products to fall short of expectations. Several trade associations claim to monitor the quality and greenness of their members' products, but investigative

research by the designers and contractor is the only way to ensure that standards are being maintained. The lack of universal green standards is an area that continues to create confusion and must be addressed in the near future.

Performance is clearly the bottom line of green products and systems. The contractor must be aligned with the owner and designers to demand that subcontractors and vendors stand behind their products. The responsibility for design normally rests with the architect and engineer, but they must be able to rely on the integrity of suppliers and the contractor must support this reliance. If products fail to perform as the manufacturer claims, then there must be recourse for them to be replaced or repaired. Warranties must be carefully written to ensure longer-term performance. Performance bonds are a wise investment: they can help alleviate the financial pain when a subcontractor or vendor becomes insolvent, an all-too-frequent occurrence with many upstart green firms.

The procurement process takes on a special meaning for green buildings. Time and money can be wasted or saved as a direct result of the contractor's ability to create a common-sense plan early in the design phase. Owners should be satisfied that their green contractor has met this obligation.

Integrating Certification in the Construction Process

The contractor plays a significant role in the process of certifying a building's greenness, and a building owner should be aware of this role when selecting a contractor for a project that is seeking to be certified.

A variety of certification programs are used around the world, and the process of integrating them into the construction process is similar. In the United States, the LEED rating system for green buildings as developed by the U.S. Green Building Council is the predominant evaluation tool used to verify how green a project is.

The first consideration should be the experience the contractor has with LEED or the relevant certification

At the McCarthy Ranch in Cupertino, California, sensitive grading, drainage swales, and land-scaping help reduce stormwater runoff.

Tom Fox, SWA Group

process. It is widely acknowledged that the cost and time required to design and build a LEED-certified project can be significantly reduced when the contractor and other team members have prior experience with LEED. It is an even greater issue for projects seeking a higher level (Gold or Platinum) of certification. A learning curve clearly is associated with conforming to the LEED requirements and the follow-up documentation, which can be eliminated with prior experience.

To achieve LEED certification, the owner should consider retaining a facilitator or consultant who will lead the project team through the process. An experienced contractor could serve in this role if a staff person has the required experience and leadership skills. The USGBC has developed a program to train and certify an individual with an understanding of the principles of sustainable design and construction. The result of this program is becoming a LEED

Accredited Professional. Large contractors have such individuals available for LEED-certified projects; they also maintain national resources that support the process.

It is important to retain the contractor early in the design phase to arrange about LEED credits. A LEED credit matrix should be created at the charrette and monitored by the contractor through design and construction. Input to this matrix includes first cost and life-cycle cost data that allow the project team to evaluate which LEED credits are worth pursuing and whether trade-offs should be considered to gain the highest possible LEED rating. As the design evolves, the targeted credits may change as they are continuously evaluated in comparison with the whole building design in terms of cost, schedule, availability, and constructability. As the design is finalized, the contractor

The Greening of Fort Bragg: Creative Use of a New Construction Site

Lynda S. Pfau

Construction at Fort Bragg, North Carolina, is moving in a new direction. Rethink, reduce, reuse, and recycle are keywords in the new environmental culture evolving there. By operating in a manner today that will enhance our ability to operate in the future, Fort Bragg continues to set the standard in environmental sustainability.

At the new design-build Combat Aviation Barracks Complex completed in late 2004, Caddell Construction Company of Montgomery, Alabama, took additional steps to help Fort Bragg meet one of ten strategic environmental goals: reducing landfill waste toward zero by 2025.

By converting unmarketable natural resources to usable materials such as mulch, landfill waste and energy consumption are reduced. "If we have the ability to use land-clearing debris," says Timothy Jackson, project manager for Caddell, "then why not use it? We try to use common sense on what's being developed from the jobsite."

Common sense has been used from the very beginning on the 70-acre (28-hectare) site. The U.S. Army Corps of Engineers took extra care to mark and remove only the trees necessary for construction rather than clear-cutting the site. Even then, the trees that had to be removed were not just hauled away to a landfill. The Corps took greening one step further and called in Harvesting and Reforestation Company of Castle Hayne, North Carolina.

Bobby Smith, manager for Harvesting and Reforestation, brought in a tub grinder capable of handling trees up to 14 feet (4.3 meters) wide and 12 feet (3.7 meters) long. The 1,000-horsepower engine turns approximately 28 diamond-tipped teeth at 20,000 revolutions per minute to produce 120 to 160 tons (109 to 145 metric tons) of mulch per hour.

Smith says the huge investment in the tub grinder was an investment in the environment as well as a necessity. Raleigh, Durham, and New Hanover are no-burn counties, according to Smith, and many counties are going in that direction. To keep it out of the landfills, they had to go to grinding. "We make it usable for somebody," says John Melton, an employee with Harvesting and Reforestation. "It's all about recycling. The tub grinder is another recycling tool." Mulch from the downed trees has been stockpiled at the site for use in the future as ground cover. It is free of charge to installation organizations and agencies as well as soldiers and their families.

William Squire, solid waste manager at Fort Bragg's Public Works Business Center, estimates Harvesting and Reforestation has diverted more than 240 tons (218 metric tons) of land-clearing debris from the Fort Bragg landfill with this initiative. But reducing the amount of waste going to the landfill is important beyond reaching the strategic goal. Over the last seven months, more than 50 percent of total solid waste disposed of on Fort Bragg was land-clearing debris.

According to Robert Ford, project engineer for the Army Corps of Engineers at Fort Bragg, additional mulch generated from one area of the construction site will be mixed with soil and turned on a regular basis so that in three years the stockpile becomes fertile topsoil to be incorporated in the final phases of the project.

tabulates the total LEED credits available that, if validated by the USGBC, will result in a LEED rating at completion. It is a good idea to create a cushion when tabulating these credits in the event that certain criteria are not met in the final submittal.

Documentation of criteria needed for LEED certification is another important activity undertaken by the contractor. It is preferable to have an early understanding of the documentation required, because it is very difficult to retrieve this type of information after the project is completed. Even though the designer may spell out the documentation requirements in the specifications, it is also necessary for the contractor to reinforce them in the solicitation of bids from subcontractors and vendors. Many LEED requirements stipulate that technical data and certifications on products and materials be incorporated with shop drawings. As these materials arrive on the jobsite, the contractor must verify that they are the same as those previously approved. At the project's closeout, the party responsible for gathering and submitting project documentation to the USGBC for LEED certification will expect the contractor to have an orderly and complete package of information.

After removing the trees, Caddell took further steps to reduce and reuse debris. Topsoil stripped from the site for grading and excavation was also stockpiled for reuse at the site, cutting down on hauling requirements and unnecessary depletion of soil from Fort Bragg's borrow pit or purchasing new topsoil.

Jackson says undertaking construction in an environmentally sound manner is a win-win situation. "This type of practice helps Caddell, helps with the storage situation, and helps keep usable material out of the landfill. It also helps the Corps of Engineers and the government."

Protected wetlands, covered by state and federal regulations, surround the construction site. Proper erosion control measures have been taken to protect the wetland areas by use of silt fencing, sediment ponds, and diversion ditches.

Jackson says more rethink, reduce, reuse, and recycle practices may develop on the construction site in the future. "As a design-build project, more environmental practices may evolve as construction progresses," says Jackson.

Fort Bragg's Environmental Compliance Branch is aggressively working with the Construction Management Division and the Corps of Engineers to identify other design and construction initiatives that will not only preserve resources but also make good business sense. Many of these ideas will be incorporated in the *Installation Design Guide,* which provides requirements and standards for all construction on Fort Bragg and is currently being revised.

Christine G. Hull, sustainability planner at Fort Bragg, believes procedures employed for the Combat Aviation Barracks Complex are just the beginning in the journey toward environmental sustainability. "Environmentally sound procedures such as those used at the new complex ideally will be built into future contracts," she says. "Everyone from designers to backhoe operators to carpenters will become an essential tool, even a stakeholder,

Fort Bragg's construction team recycles timber debris and stockpiles the mulch just outside the construction area to be used later. Lynda S. Pfau

in this program. Recycling and reuse will be the norm, expected. The implementation of sound environmental practices and sustainable design concepts, paired with the size of the installation's construction program and the significant number of upcoming projects, present a golden opportunity for Fort Bragg to effect change at a much more rapid pace."

Lynda S. Pfau is environmental resource coordinator at Fort Bragg.

The contractor can directly influence several LEED credits associated with the construction process that are different from design credits. They include minimizing the impact on natural areas adjacent to the actual building, maintaining a proactive erosion and stormwater control plan during construction, recycling construction (and demolition, if any) waste, building commissioning, and monitoring indoor environmental quality as a result of construction activities. Although LEED prescribes strict criteria to be achieved in these areas, they really all entail good common sense and should be a part of every experienced contractor's tool kit. But documentation is again required to meet the LEED credit criteria. And like most other construction activities, these credits need to be identified and planned for early in the design phase.

The contractor is a key player in the development of any green building. By engaging the contractor early in project development, a truly integrated approach to design and construction can be achieved, leading to a cost-effective project that reflects development to meet the needs of the present without compromising the ability of future generations to meet their own needs.

Sustainable Management

Managing Green: Sustainable Facilities Management

Ann Moline

According to the International Facility Management Association (IFMA), facilities management (FM) is a profession encompassing multiple disciplines to ensure functionality of the built environment by integrating people, place, process, and technology. The Building Owners and Managers Institute (BOMI) says further that facilities management is a profession incorporating long-range facility planning, annual facility planning, tactical planning, facility financial forecasting, real estate acquisition and/or disposal, interior space planning, work specifications, installation and space management, architectural and engineering planning and design, and new construction and renovation. All these tasks—as well as operations and maintenance (O&M) of the physical plant, telecommunications integration, security, and general administrative services such as food services, reprographics, and transportation—fall under the umbrella of facilities management.

The offices of the Gordon and Betty Moore Foundation in San Francisco are "paperless," so spaces that would normally be occupied by storage files are available as staff meeting areas. Gensler/Chris Barrett/Hedrich Blessing

Sometimes, facilities management is outsourced to an outside contractor; other commercial real estate firms employ in-house teams. In either case, the role of the facilities manager from the very beginning of a green building project cannot be understated. The facilities manager takes the longer view of the costs associated with constructing a new building. It is not just about least cost upfront and how to negotiate the lowest bids on all components of a building project. Rather, the issue for the facilities manager is how to design and outfit a building so that it functions in the most efficient, economical way over its life cycle. And because green buildings can lower utility costs, reduce waste disposal, improve productivity, and enhance the work environ-

ment, the facilities manager can provide valuable input early in the process so that such goals are achieved.

Sheila M. Sheridan, former chair of the IFMA board of directors, points out that sustainability is becoming more and more important to facilities managers. "A recent survey of IFMA members found that an overwhelming 95 percent agree that sustainability will become a significant issue for facilities management and almost 90 percent already are recycling solid waste," says Sheridan. "In addition, nearly half are contributing to environmental responsibility by reusing materials, and half already have an employee education program in place."[1]

Elements of an Effective O&M Program

■ Ensure that up-to-date operational procedures and manuals are available.
■ Obtain up-to-date documentation on all building systems, including system drawings.
■ Implement preventive maintenance programs, complete with maintenance schedules and records of all maintenance performed for all building equipment and systems.
■ Create a well-trained maintenance staff and offer professional development and training for each staff member.
■ Implement a monitoring program that tracks and documents the performance of building systems to identify and diagnose potential problems and track the effectiveness of the O&M program. Include cost and performance tracking in this analysis.
■ Conduct O&M on HVAC systems and equipment, cleaning equipment and products, water fixtures and systems, waste systems, and landscape maintenance

Source: Alex Wilson, ed. *Greening Federal Facilities*, second edition, May 2001, http://www.eere.energy.gov/femp/pdfs/29267-9.1.pdf, p.188.

Sheridan also notes that awareness is the key. Even doing a little can make a great deal of difference. Facility managers are responding to environmental challenges with plans of action. Moreover, they are doing so for the right reasons: cost savings, corporate mandates to be environmentally friendly, governmental mandates, public opinion, and the need to provide a healthy and productive work environment for their employees and the customers they serve.

The bottom line is that the facilities manager cares about what happens to the building after the construction crews disappear and people begin to use it daily. What goes on before the first person reports for work on the first day of operation has a critical impact on the ability to maximize efficiencies and meet the goals of sustainability.

Planning Ahead for Sustainable Facilities Management

It is best if the facilities manager is part of the project development team, involved in management issues before the building is even built. He or she can add a practical perspective to the process. For example, the FM can help ensure that mechanical specifications are written so as to favor vendors that offer energy-efficient, space-saving, and bacteria-fighting models. The FM can work closely with the architect, adding a dose of reality to a design concept that might look spectacular but might not suit the functions that will be needed daily from the facility over the long haul.

But it is not only the facilities manager who should champion the green cause. During planning and design, the team should establish green policies and standards together, with leadership from the top. Buy-in from all participants in the planning and design phase is critical to ensuring maximal benefit of the greening effort.

The FM should help address several issues:
■ The project budget and schedule;
■ Incentive programs for reducing energy demand and using resources efficiently;
■ Architectural design from the standpoint of efficient cleaning and maintenance;
■ Sustainable construction practices such as making sure ducts are vacuumed;
■ The design of utilities and HVAC systems;
■ Materials and products that are preferable from an environmental standpoint;
■ Landscape design and materials; and
■ Monitoring systems.

The LEED guide to new building construction can also help during planning and design. The facilities manager who is part of the team might also want to check out the USGBC's rating system, specifically designed as a guide for facilities managers. Although the guide, called "LEED-EB" (LEED for existing buildings) does not focus on new buildings, it does offer suggested technologies and strategies that will improve a building's performance over its life cycle.[2] And tools such as ENERGY STAR's financial value calculator can help determine potential savings from a project.[3] Such tools will help make the business case that upfront investments can be recouped by savings down the road. In

To ease the strain on local landfills, the Gordon and Betty Moore Foundation has created a closed-loop system that handles all waste on site, including large-scale composting of all landscape materials, salvage and reuse operations for trees and woody materials, and an intensive recycling program. Gensler/Chris Barrett/Hedrich Blessing

tion. FMs must juggle many balls at the same time to keep a building running smoothly. In fact, it can be hard to know where to start, particularly because so much information is available that sifting through the material can be a full-time job in itself. To start, FMs might consider breaking down the integration of sustainability to more manageable tasks (some of which will affect multifunctional areas):

- waste management;
- efficient use of water;
- energy efficiency;
- indoor air quality;
- groundskeeping;
- purchasing policies;
- green policies and training; and
- monitoring performance.

As the action plan for a sustainable building moves forward, a strong operations and maintenance program plays a critical role in all the activities listed above. O&M is the first line of attack after tenants move in, as the FM takes steps to make the building even more efficient, reduce energy consumption, enhance the building's performance, and increase employees' comfort and productivity.

addition, grant moneys, rate reductions, or tax incentives might be available, depending on the nature of the project.

Forming a cross-functional team—pulling from all levels of the company's organization chart during all stages of a green project—helps ensure that the work will continue to go forward and that changes initiated during construction, such as recycling construction waste, will become a routine part of the job for all employees.

The FM should be involved from planning and design through the submission of bids and award of contracts through construction through closeout to building opera-

Waste Management

Reducing waste is probably one of the simplest steps a facilities manager can take and among the easiest activities workers can embrace, especially if incentives are offered. Recycling and waste-reduction programs and their supporting hardware need frequent attention and maintenance to function at peak performance. (And workers need frequent reminders about their importance.) Auditing the waste stream will help determine what the facility and its occupants are using. The information from this audit can serve as a benchmark to measure the effectiveness of waste reduction and recycling efforts.

At PNC Firstside Center in Pittsburgh, water-conserving plumbing features are used throughout the building; even the decorative water features use recirculated water. Astorino & Ed Massery

The following actions will help manage waste:

■ Purchase recyclable products and office supplies, particularly those with a high content of recycled products.

■ Set aside easily accessible areas to collect and store recyclables.

■ Set aside a bin near copiers and printers for scrap paper that can be reused.

■ Recycle glass, plastic, office paper, newspaper, cardboard, metals, batteries, and fluorescent lamps; divert them from disposal in landfills by finding local handlers to dispose of or reuse them.

■ Install cardboard balers, aluminum can crushers, and recycling chutes to encourage maximum recycling.

■ Recycle debris from construction and renovation projects.

Efficient Use of Water

One of the simplest ways to improve a building's water efficiency is to make sure pipes do not leak. Some estimates suggest that a building loses close to 50 percent of its water through old or corroded pipes and up to 10 percent through faulty toilet tank valves and tap washers. One leaking toilet can cost a company more than 50 gallons (189 liters) of water per day.[4] As with the building's HVAC system, a good O&M budget and schedule contribute to peak performance and less water loss throughout the facility.

Flushing toilets uses the most water in residential and commercial buildings. Installation of low-flow systems can save from 60 to 90 percent of water used in a traditional toilet, because older toilets use four to eight gallons (15 to 30 liters) of water per flush, while all new toilets must use no more than 1.6 gallons (six liters) per flush.[5] Low-flow systems include low-flow toilets and sinks, waterless urinals, dual-flush and composting toilets, and sensor-operated sinks and toilets. Low-flow fixtures, automatic controls, and dry fixtures such as composting toilets and waterless urinals can be used to reduce sewage volume.[6]

Reusing roof runoff and so-called "graywater"—nonchemically tainted industrial wastewater or wastewater from bathroom sinks and flush toilets—for flushing or landscape irrigation can also improve the building's water efficiency. Another method is to collect rainfall in on-site cisterns for reuse.

Although such efforts might seem costly, one company, Gangi Brothers Packing Company in Santa Clara, California, estimates a net savings of $40,000 per year after implementing water conservation measures that saved approximately 91 billion gallons [344 billion liters] of water.[7] In general, Greenerbuildings.com estimates, "In a typical 100,000-square-foot [9,300-square-meter] office building, low-flow fixtures coupled with sensors and automatic controls can save a minimum of 1 million gallons [3.8 million liters] of water per year, based on 650 building occupants each using an average of 20 gallons [75 liters] per day."

In addition, the local water company might offer incentive programs for implementing water conservation. Such programs can reduce water costs even more. For example, the Contra Costa (California) Water District offers a 100 percent material rebate when commercial customers replace older toilets with new ultra-low-flow toilets (ULFTs).

The following eight ways can be used to conserve water in a facility:

1. Use less water.

2. Inventory water use for all water-consuming fixtures, equipment, and seasonal conditions to identify significant potable water demands and determine methods to minimize or eliminate those demands.

3. Use water-conserving plumbing fixtures that exceed the fixture requirements stated in the Energy Policy Act of 1992. Consider ultra-high-efficiency fixture and control technologies for toilets, faucets, showers, dishwashers, and cooling towers. A variety of low-flow plumbing fixtures and appliances are currently available and can be installed in the same manner as conventional fixtures.

4. Develop a wastewater inventory and determine areas where graywater can be used for functions that are conventionally served by potable water: sinks, showers, toilets, landscape irrigation, industrial applications, and custodial applications, for example. Estimate demand for these applications and the availability of graywater generated on the site. Check with the health department for guidelines regarding reuse of graywater. Determine the amount of wastewater that will require treatment and select the most suitable treatment strategy.

5. Consider an on-site wastewater treatment system such as constructed wetlands, a mechanical recirculating sand filter, or an aerobic biological treatment reactor. On-site wastewater treatment systems transform perceived "wastes" into resources that can be used on the building site. Reducing the treatment required at the local wastewater treatment plant minimizes the use of public infrastructure, energy, and chemicals.

6. Install a roof-water or groundwater collection system. Use metal, clay, or concrete-based roofing materials and take advantage of gravity flows whenever possible. But be aware that roofs made of asphalt or lead-containing materials can contaminate collected rainwater and render it undesirable for reuse. Check with your local health department for guidelines on the collection of rainwater.

7. Rethink your landscaping plans by monitoring how much water you use. Can plants be replaced with ones that require less water? Could the lawn be watered once a week—or not at all—instead of every day?

8. Stay current on new technologies. Investigate products or systems that can help lower or eliminate water consumption. Research the availability of waterless urinals, dual-flush toilets, composting toilets, manual or electronic sensors to activate sinks, and low-flow showerheads.[8]

Energy Efficiency

Reaching maximal resource efficiency involves an initial assessment to determine where other similar buildings are located and where changes could benefit energy conservation. The U.S. Department of Energy and some local power companies will conduct energy audits to determine where improvements can be made. In addition, the DOE offers downloadable tools to conduct in-house energy audits. It is also possible to simulate the impact of a variety of energy-saving measures on your building by using software, downloadable for free from the Internet. For example, eQUEST, a site sponsored by the California Public Utilities Commission and developed by Energy Design Resources, is an easy-to-use tool for analyzing a building's energy use.[9]

Mechanical Systems

Critical to both efficient energy use and substantial cost reduction is a good budget and regular schedule for O&M on HVAC systems. Heating and cooling issues most likely form the basis for the majority of workers' complaints as well. In fact, from a purely financial—and daily hassle—standpoint and separate from the green aspects, regular maintenance and upgrading of equipment contribute to reduced operational costs and increased satisfaction for workers. According to Houston-based maintenance consultant David Tod Geaslin, "The penalty for deferring maintenance is not more, not twice as much, not four times as much. The real penalty for deferring maintenance that becomes a breakdown event is 15:1 minimum and often exceeds 40:1!"[10]

HVAC equipment must be well maintained for the complex array of chillers, boilers, air handlers, controls, and other hardware to function at peak performance. Easy access to HVAC systems for ongoing maintenance and repair is critical (it must be considered during design). A well-thought-out, well-executed O&M program can provide huge savings in equipment and energy costs.[11] Installing computerized controls can maintain temperatures at desirable levels during peak and nonpeak hours, reducing energy costs a great deal.

"On our HVAC systems, we have installed energy-efficient chillers, air-handler units, and cooling towers with variable frequency drives," says Blake Real Estate's Joan Berman. "We have sophisticated energy management systems in our buildings, and we exercise strict maintenance

The Howard Hughes Tower in Los Angeles relies on efficient lighting, HVAC, and building automation systems to run at peak efficiency. Arden Realty

A Green Roof in Washington, D.C.

Ann Moline

A 13-story building in the heart of the Washington, D.C., business district recently unveiled a new addition—not another lobbying firm or multiname law practice, but a 3,500-square-foot (325-square-meter) rooftop garden featuring three inches (eight centimeters) of soil, 9,730 plants, a weather station, and a monitoring center with an unplanted area to compare temperature and water runoff.

According to Joan Berman of property owner and manager Blake Real Estate, the green roof will alleviate the problem of massive water runoff and sewer backups that occur during big storms. In addition, the moderating effect of the garden on the building's temperature is expected to reduce the building's energy needs and thus operating costs.

Berman says one of its tenants, an environmental organization, approached the company about the project. Initially skeptical, she and her management team raised questions about the safety of the project and whether the roof would leak. "We were really concerned for our building and for our tenants—particularly the ones on the top floor," she says. But worries about damage from plant root systems were mitigated because the plantings are succulent sedums with shallow root systems. In addition, technicians wired an electronic field around the roof's perimeter that can detect any leaks and pinpoint their exact location. Thus far, the roof has not leaked at all, according to Berman.

But the process was not cheap. Berman estimates that, not counting the extensive contribution of company time and discounts from contractors and vendors, the green roof cost approximately $12.50 per square foot ($135 per square meter). The firm received a $60,000 grant from an environmental organization—a tenant in the building—for the project. "If we had not received the grant, I'm not sure we would have done it, because the roof on the building was relatively new," says Berman. Actual installation was a compli-

A green roof at 1425 K Street, N.W., in downtown Washington, D.C., will alleviate water runoff and help moderate the building's internal temperature. Casey Trees

cated process, involving removing the existing ballast and hoisting dirt up many stories to reach the roof. She has some words of advice for property managers considering such a project. "Due diligence is critical, especially when retrofitting," she says. "Talk to the experts and keep in mind that this is a fairly new technology in the United States. Everything must come together—structural approval, the choice of root barrier, the type of plant material, and design installation and maintenance."

programs on all our mechanical, electrical, and plumbing equipment to ensure maximum efficiency."

Commercial equipment manufacturers have recognized the importance of this connection. Some, like Carrier, have extended their offerings beyond air-conditioning units. The company has teamed with other service providers to retrofit lighting fixtures, install super windows, and otherwise upgrade customers' buildings so they will ultimately need less air conditioning and thereby use less energy while providing more comfort for occupants.[12]

Other ways to conserve energy include:

■ Turn off equipment when not in use. According to research conducted by the Xerox Corporation, up to 90 percent of the energy consumed by office equipment can be saved by turning it off when it is not needed.

■ Install energy-efficient light fixtures such as compact fluorescent lights, T-8 lamps, and lights that incorporate electronic ballasts. Using fixtures with the ENERGY STAR label helps ensure that efficiencies are being achieved.

■ Use renewable energy: techniques such as daylighting and solar heating can improve efficiencies and enhance productivity. The U.S. DOE's extensive Web site on renewable energy and technologies offers a compendium of resources as well as links to procuring items such as solar heating panels. Much of the information on solar heating involves photovoltaics—electricity produced from the sun—or solar thermal systems that produce heat for climate control or water heating. The DOE's Office of Energy Efficiency and Renewable Energy (EERE) has developed a solar technologies program that offers a wide range of resources for commercial building managers who want to make use of solar technologies.[13] Energy also can be generated on a building site by using technologies that convert energy from the wind and biomass into usable energy.[14]

■ Install automatic lighting controls: controls such as occupancy sensors, photosensors, and timers can save energy by turning lights off when they are not needed. This approach is particularly effective for security lighting and lighting in infrequently used rooms. Dimmers also save energy by allowing building occupants to adjust the light output to suit their needs.[15]

■ Add task lighting: office lighting is one of office workers' biggest complaints. Offices generally are overlit, leading to headaches, irritability, and high energy and cooling costs. Hallways, computer environments, paperwork areas, and meeting areas all need different levels of light. Installing indirect, ambient lighting and user-controlled task lighting with compact fluorescent lamps helps reduce costs, employees' error rates, and sick days.[16]

■ Replace computer screens, exit signs, and the like with LED (light-emitting diode) panels that use less energy than conventional screens.

■ Install white or reflective roofing materials—or those with the ENERGY STAR label—to mitigate the urban heat island effect.

■ Retrofit windows. Solar control window film can reduce a building's heating and cooling costs while preventing ultraviolet rays and glare; low-e glass can improve energy efficiency.

■ Turn down thermostats.

■ Insulate and block unused windows.

■ Seal cracks and holes in the building.

■ Use solar water heaters.

■ Seal heating and cooling ductwork.

■ Reduce hot water temperature to a maximum of 106 degrees Fahrenheit (41 degrees Celsius).

■ Wrap hot water heaters in insulation.

■ Replace air filters regularly.

■ Remove lighting and lamps that are not needed.

Using Renewable Energy Sources

Some companies have harnessed renewable energy resources to reduce heating and cooling costs for their facilities. For example, Honda's Northwest Regional Facility in Gresham, Oregon, uses the strong Columbia Gorge winds from the east. The 212,888-square-foot (19,800-square-meter) mixed-use building uses external vents and a raised access floor in the office to draw air in from outside, filter it, and adjust it for temperature. The air is then distributed via 22 personal controls throughout the office area, allowing for maximal flexibility in temperature control. The interior air is drawn up and out through large gravity ventilators on the roof. The facility's reliance on natural light and careful monitoring of electricity for lights and heating have reduced energy consumption by 51 percent.[17] The facility uses 120 translucent Kalwall skylights, making artificial lighting unnecessary on sunny days.[18] Annual energy savings from the combined efficiencies are estimated at

Fifteen Mechanical Improvements to Save Energy

Rick Fedrizzi

1. Central plant energy efficiency opportunities include installing higher-efficiency chillers (or other air-conditioning systems). New chillers are 25 to 50 percent more efficient than chillers that are ten or more years old. Because many facilities with central chillers must replace them to comply with the phaseout of chlorofluorocarbons, it pays to invest in a new, high-efficiency unit. The new chillers also have vastly improved controls that make it easier to optimize chillers' efficiency.

2. Consider installing a larger cooling tower to improve efficiency and reduce the tower return temperature. Cooling towers are rarely sized to handle "worst case" conditions. As a result, the entire cooling system is very efficient on the warmest days. An oversized cooling tower results in lower return water temperatures and higher chiller efficiency.

3. Install variable-speed drives on cooling tower fans. A variable-speed fan allows the cooling tower to operate efficiently, using less fan energy and reducing fan maintenance by eliminating on-off fan cycling.

4. Install high-efficiency condensing boilers for heating hot water. All gas- and propane-fired boilers should be modulating condensing boilers with efficiencies higher than 90 percent—about 30 percent more efficient than most older boilers. Moreover, condensing boilers operate very efficiently at low loads. Most new installations use two or more smaller, modular boilers rather than a large boiler.

5. Install a high-efficiency hot water heater. New high-efficiency hot water heaters use much less energy to heat water.

6. In warm months, reduce outside air intake, especially when enthalpy is high. Many facilities bring in too much outside air during warm and humid periods.

7. Repair (and upgrade where necessary) insulation on steam, hot water, and chilled water piping. Consider "wicking" insulation on chilled water piping (to help move water away from the pipe so it can evaporate). Much of the installation on existing steam, hot water, and chilled water piping was installed when energy was cheaper. Additional insulation will further reduce losses.

8. Install variable-speed drives on the hot water pumping systems. All continuously operating hot water pumps should have variable-speed drives that reduce pumping energy during periods of low hot water use.

9. Obtain "free" hot water from the chiller(s) or other air-conditioning units. Consider adding a new "heat recovery" chiller to produce hot water. Facilities that require cooling most of the year can obtain "free" hot water from their refrigeration equipment by using double-bundled heat exchangers in the chillers or a plate heat exchanger in the condenser-cooling loop going to the cooling tower.

10. Install variable-speed drives on all constant-speed fans that are throttled back in response to variable loads. Fans controlled by dampers should be retrofitted with variable-speed drives. A speed reduction of only 20 percent will reduce fan energy by nearly 50 percent.

11. Install premium efficiency motors on pumps and fans with long run hours. Oversized motors should be replaced with smaller motors that operate more efficiently than the oversized motor they replace.

12. Consider geothermal heating and cooling. Using the ground (or a nearby body of water) for a heat source or heat sink can result in high heating and cooling efficiency, especially during peak conditions.

13. Install an ozone water treatment system for the water tower. It will keep chiller heat exchanger surfaces clean and efficient while reducing cooling system chemicals.

14. Install upgraded HVAC controls to include intelligent new technologies. The latest generation of energy management systems is much easier to use while delivering more consistent savings than earlier energy management control systems. They can deliver a substantial savings while also improving comfort.

15. Consider installing a desiccant HVAC system. Desiccant technology (which dehumidifies air) has become a valuable tool in space-conditioning options. In certain cooling applications, desiccant cooling units provide advantages over the more common vapor-compression and -absorption units. For example, desiccant units do not require ozone-depleting refrigerants, and they can use natural gas, solar thermal energy, or waste heat, thus lowering peak electric demand. They are particularly effective in treating the large humidity loads resulting from ventilation air in much of the country.

Rick Fedrizzi is president of Green-Think, Inc.; president and CEO of the U.S. Green Building Council, of which he is also founding chairman; and president of the World Green Building Council.

Source: www.buildings.com.

Energy savings can be achieved by lighting interior spaces with a combination of natural sunlight, efficient user-controlled task lighting, and automatic lighting controls such as occupancy sensors. Peter Aaron-Esto/Liberty Property Trust

Indoor Air Quality

U.S. companies could save as much as $58 billion annually by preventing sick building illnesses plus $200 billion in improved performance from workers by creating offices with better indoor air, according to researchers at Lawrence Berkeley National Laboratory. The financial benefits of improving office climates can be eight to 17 times larger than the costs of making those improvements.[21]

Among the chief culprits contributing to poor indoor air quality are volatile organic compounds, found in many common building materials such as adhesives, and sealants, paints, coatings, carpeting, cleaning materials, and composite wood. Another leading cause of poor indoor air quality is dampness in a building, which can cause mold.

Sometimes, efforts to improve a building's energy efficiency by adding insulation or stepping up the repair of cracks or energy leaks can inadvertently have an adverse effect on indoor air quality. Although tighter buildings minimize heat loss and save energy, they can also trap indoor air pollutants. Odors and gases can build up. Microscopic contaminants continue to circulate through heating and cooling ducts.[22]

In recent years, well-publicized legal actions have drawn more attention to problems related to sick building syndrome caused by poor indoor air quality. Even if greening the building were not a priority, some experts suggest that facilities managers should focus on IAQ—because of liability. Attorney James Witkin, author of *Environmental Aspects of Real Estate Transactions*, suggests that building managers must pay increased attention to water leaks, drainage, and similar issues. "A problem that would have been treated as a simple plumbing leak ten years ago can result in a lawsuit in today's mold-conscious environment."[23]

The good news is that many companies have produced a variety of environmentally friendly products for use inside offices. Office furniture manufacturer Steelcase,

more than $36,000, with $34,000 in electricity savings and the remainder in natural gas.[19]

In some cases, incorporating renewable energy technologies in commercial buildings could make the facility eligible for a variety of tax incentives. Federal incentives include the solar and geothermal business energy tax credit, the renewable electricity production credit (also known as the wind energy production tax credit), and the solar wind and geothermal modified accelerated cost recovery system.[20]

based in Grand Rapids, Michigan, produces chairs and other furniture crafted with low-VOC-emitting materials. Several of the company's furniture lines have received GREENGUARD Institute certification, and it is moving more of the lines in this direction. Paint manufacturer Sherwin-Williams recently introduced the "Harmony" paint line that contains no VOCs and is odorless. As a result, according to the company's marketing materials, the paint can go on in areas where people are working without having to vacate the space. And HVAC supplier Carrier Corporation offers antimicrobial coatings and germicidal lamps on its air handlers to prevent the buildup of mold. The company has also developed a new air handler for commercial applications that helps eliminate water buildup that can breed mold and bacteria. Its heat-recovery ventilator can exchange stale indoor air for fresh outdoor air up to eight times a day. New electronic air cleaners remove most airborne dust, dirt, and pollen, as well as significant amounts of bacteria, mold, and other contaminants.[24]

Industry groups, too, have gotten involved. The Carpet and Rug Institute—an association of carpet and rug manufacturers—launched "Green Label Plus" to help builders and facilities managers identify carpets that are tested by an independent, certified laboratory and meet stringent criteria for low chemical emissions.[25]

Improvements to indoor air quality might include:

■ Frequently checking air ventilation and distribution systems and regularly inspecting them for biological and chemical contaminants;

■ Coordinating air-distribution systems and furniture layouts to make sure furniture does not block vents;

■ Switching to biodegradable and least-toxic cleaning products and equipment (and writing the requirements into maintenance contracts);

■ Isolating copying/print/fax rooms and ensuring appropriate ventilation in those areas;

■ Increasing the circulation of outdoor air; and

■ Installing high-efficiency filters rated at MERV 13 or higher for outside air intakes and for recirculating inside air.

Groundskeeping

Minimizing the water requirements of plants around a building reduces water costs. Depending on a building's height, strategically planted trees can serve as a windbreak during strong storms and keep the building shaded—and cooler—during the summer. Other suggestions:

■ Use drought-resistant native plants because they need less water and pest control to keep them healthy (xeriscaping).

■ Collect rainwater (perhaps in a rooftop cistern) and use it for irrigation, watering plants, and flushing toilets.

Using native prairie landscaping rather than Kentucky bluegrass saves money by eliminating the need for mowing, irrigating, and applying fertilizers, herbicides, and insecticides. JohnsonDiversey

There's a Fungus among Us!

Stachybotrys, Aspergillus, Penicillium, Hyphae . . . no, we aren't talking about the latest types of pasta. Each of these is a type of mold that can permeate your facility and cause building damage ranging from minimal inconveniences to structurally unsafe conditions. As well, mold can create hazardous IAQ conditions that can affect the physical well-being of your tenants.

You may think that, because your facility is in a low-humidity area or a region that is fairly arid, your risk of mold and mold-related problems may not be as great as a facility in a more humid region. But mold growth does not require the presence of high humidity or standing water. Growth can occur when the relative humidity or the hygroscopic properties (the tendency to absorb and retain moisture) of building surfaces allow enough moisture to accumulate. In addition, the age of your building can affect your susceptibility to mold.

No matter what part of the country you may work in, potential mold growth is a pervasive problem that every facility manager must address.

Put quite simply, the key to controlling mold is controlling moisture.

Determining Whether You Are at Risk for or Currently Have Mold in Your Building

Your first step in keeping mold out of your facility is to determine your risk level. No one can completely eliminate the possibility of mold growth; mold spores are almost always present in both outdoor and indoor air, and almost all commonly used construction materials and furnishings can provide nutrients to support mold growth—but you can take steps to reduce growth opportunities. If you are concerned that mold growth might be present in your building(s), perform a walk-through to look for some of the common indicators listed below. If you wish to incorporate preventive measures as part of your overall facilities management plan, adding these indicators to your routine maintenance inspection checklist should be sufficient.

Everyday factors to look for that can indicate whether mold is present in your building include:

- black growth on or under restroom tiles, in maintenance rooms or basements, or around windows and doors;
- blocked gutters;
- complaints of increased allergy or respiratory symptoms among building occupants;
- condensation and cracking, peeling paint;
- flooding (either past or present);
- high humidity;
- leaky roof;
- loosening of drywall tape;
- mildew or musty odors;
- poor ventilation;
- presence of wet materials;
- rusting;
- visible spores and growth;
- warped wood;
- water leaks/pipe leaks;
- water stains on walls.

If your property has recently sustained water damage or flooding, you are clearly at a much greater risk for mold growth. In addition to the myriad other tasks involved with cleaning up water damage, you must keep a sharp eye for mold growth. Mold growth can begin in as little as 24 hours. The type of water damage is another factor in growth potential as well. Damage from clean water may be less and easier to clean than that from water possibly contaminated by sewage, chemical, or biological pollutants.

Not all mold growth is visible, however. The back sides of drywall, wallpaper, and paneling; the top of ceiling tiles; the underside of carpets and pads; utility tunnels and air-handling units may all have hidden mold. If a visual inspection yields no signs of mold but you still suspect mold growth, it is advisable to call in a professional to conduct a more thorough inspection.

Steps You Can Take to Reduce Moisture and Mold-Friendly Conditions

Reducing moisture and inhibiting mold-friendly conditions can and should be part of your current facilities management plan.

- Assess current drainage and slope direc-

- Consider reducing the amount of lawn area—which requires more water and more upkeep—and replacing it with plants that need little water to survive.
- Maintain lawn and garden; cut grass to a minimum of two to three inches (5 to 7.5 centimeters).

- Use integrated pest management that relies on non-chemical techniques to decrease the need for hazardous chemicals and pesticides and reduce overall O&M costs.[26]
- Water gardens and lawns only when needed.

tions. As much as possible, drainage and slope should head away from the foundation of your building. If your building is located at the bottom of a hill, make sure internal and external drainage systems are adequate, clean, and functioning properly.

■ Perform HVAC system inspections and routine maintenance. Properly inspected and maintained HVAC systems affect your building operations on many levels, including positive IAQ—a key factor in moisture control. Humidification and dehumidification systems must be kept clean to prevent the growth of dangerous bacteria and fungi. Poor or no water treatment in cooling towers can result in the growth of hazardous organisms that will then filter into the HVAC supply ducts. An accumulation of water anywhere in the system can result in harmful biological growth that can be rapidly distributed throughout the entire building. Drip pans for equipment must always be clean and unobstructed to ensure proper water flow.

■ Perform unscheduled maintenance. If you have recently experienced flooding, water leakage, or heavy rains, don't wait for your scheduled inspections to look for mold growth. Remember, mold can begin to grow in as little as 24 hours, so don't delay. The extra effort you put forth immediately can save you from major building damage, significant money output to clean up mold, and the headaches and stress involved in a full-blown mold remediation process.

■ Ensure proper housekeeping. Dirt on surfaces supplies mold with the nutrients it needs to grow. Cleaning and disinfecting with non-polluting cleaners and antimicrobial agents can provide protection against mold growth.

■ Respond quickly. Fix leaky plumbing and building envelope leaks as soon as possible. If wet or damp spots appear, clean and dry them within 48 hours. Depending on the size of the damp areas, you may need to rent professional drying and ventilation equipment. Make sure you have a list of resources available in your overall facilities management guidelines.

■ Ensure proper IAQ and humidity levels. The ideal range for indoor relative humidity is 30 to 50 percent. To increase or decrease moisture levels in the air, increase ventilation if outside air is cold and dry, or dehumidify if outdoor air is warm and humid. The air around windows and doors is more difficult to keep balanced; keep a watchful eye on condensation levels around these areas. If condensation lingers, you may need to consider using additional humidity control equipment for these specific areas, or updating or upgrading your door and window units to better modulate condensation.

■ Communicate with and listen to your tenants. Tenant activities can positively or negatively affect your efforts to keep mold in check. Tenants who have a significant number of plants clustered together may not be aware of the increased potential for mold growth in that area. Blocking off air-circulating vents can alter your HVAC system's performance. Tenants who have access to working windows may intentionally or unintentionally leave them open, allowing humidity and airborne dirt to settle in their offices. Some tenants may complain about musty odors or increased allergy symptoms, two key indicators of mold growth.

You Found Mold in Your Building—Now What?

The steps you take to clean existing mold and prevent new growth will vary based on several conditions. Among others, the extent of the damage to the structure as well as the building materials (such as carpet, tiles, or drywall) and contents (like furniture and equipment); the amount of mold; and tenant schedules will all factor into your cleanup planning and activities. The EPA has written several highly informative guidebooks and information packets that can help you determine the extent of the cleanup procedures you will need to perform. This information is available online at http://www.epa.gov/iaq/molds/moldresources.html.

Source: http://www.fmlink.com/ProfResources/HowTo/article.cgi?BOMI%20Institute:howto0104.htm. Used with permission.

Purchasing Policies

Companywide policies that require all purchasing decisions to consider sustainable development can contribute to a substantially greener environment. Several organizations offer seals of approval to indicate good environmental performance and provide information on specific products that meet their environmental specifications.

The U.S. EPA's ENERGY STAR program certifies a broad array of energy-efficient products (see Chapter 8). The EPA has developed its own environmentally preferable

A variety of certification programs can help identify environmentally preferable materials for building construction and ongoing O&M. At the Shaklee headquarters, certified sources were used for all wood sources, ceiling materials, workstation fabrics, and recycled carpet yarns. Gensler

to buy everything from copier toner to food service supplies to refrigerant to cleaning materials.

Other certifying groups include Green Seal, an independent organization that scientifically tests products for environmental friendliness. The group offers certification of items ranging from electric chillers to paints and coatings to plumbing fixtures to windows and doors to toilet paper and coffee filters. Green Seal also recommends products based on scientific study and reports recommendations through its series of "Green Reports," downloadable from the group's Web site at no charge to the public.[27]

The GREENGUARD Environmental Institute is a nonprofit organization that has established environmental industry standards for manufacturers of a wide variety of commonly used products. The group also certifies products, but with a more narrowly defined focus on indoor environmental quality, and provides specifications for low-e products as well as management plans to improve IEQ.

Several general guidelines help in purchasing green:

■ Give preference to products with as high a proportion of recycled content and postconsumer waste as feasible. Share your corporate purchasing policy with suppliers.

■ Choose products that contain few or no toxic substances and minimize pollution in the manufacturing process, such as water-based markers and aqueous cleaners.

■ Precycle by choosing products that are more easily recycled; for example, use white paper instead of colored paper and corrugated board instead of plastic packaging.

■ Buy products designed for reuse such as rechargeable batteries and reusable mugs.

■ Select products that consume fewer resources in their manufacture, use, and packaging such as two-sided copying and printing equipment, more fuel-efficient vehicles, and bulk purchases that require less packaging.[28]

■ Circulate a list of recycled or environmentally friendly products to purchasing staff. Set out clear guidelines to follow.

■ Train purchasing agents to understand the issues.[29]

purchasing program for government users and offers extensive resources to the public on its Web site, with information and training on where to buy, what to buy, and how

Green Policies and Training

Following through on a green construction project includes a focus on all aspects of the building's function. But green facilities management is also about changing behavior. Behavioral change starts with setting standards and establishing policies that employees can understand clearly such as routine participation in the recycling program or switching to environmentally preferable purchasing. Setting these new standards is not a decision that a facilities manager can make unilaterally. It involves the entire team—and significant commitment from senior management.

Another aspect of changing behavior involves proper communication of the changes. This communication might include development of new handbooks for employees and new maintenance manuals for technical staff. Training—for maintenance staff on ways to maintain equipment at peak efficiency and how to spot potential problem areas and for building occupants on how they can do their part to keep the building green—is critical as well. For example, if the janitorial staff does its own purchasing, the staff requires extensive information on buying chemically benign cleaning supplies. If, on the other hand, this function is outsourced, specifying in the contract that the janitorial staff will use environmentally friendly products helps ensure that green housekeeping goals are met.

The maintenance staff also might need additional training related specifically to keeping equipment properly tuned and repaired. All occupants of the buildings should be reminded frequently—through newsletters and posted signs—about policies regarding recycling or energy reduction methods such as turning out the lights and turning off computers.

Monitoring Performance

As part of the planning process, the green team should have set up appropriate mechanisms to monitor performance and to track improvements. In this way, it will be easier to quantify savings and to document efficiencies. Results should be compared with benchmarks established before the project began. Frequent monitoring can help assess what is working and what is not, allowing changes to be made to improve performance. For example, to monitor water and indoor air quality, Blake Real Estate routinely tests systems twice a year.

Regular evaluation allows the FM to make informed decisions about future projects and to reward teams or individuals who have contributed to the cause. To monitor energy improvements, ENERGY STAR's Delta Score estimator can help estimate the amount of energy reduction needed to go from current energy use to a targeted reduction. Such tools should be used at the beginning and

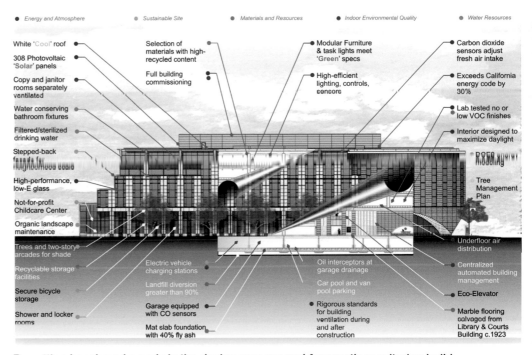

● Energy and Atmosphere ● Sustainable Site ● Materials and Resources ● Indoor Environmental Quality ● Water Resources

White 'Cool' roof
308 Photovoltaic 'Solar' panels
Copy and janitor rooms separately ventilated
Water conserving bathroom fixtures
Filtered/sterilized drinking water
Stepped-back façade/Atrium walls
High-performance, low-E glass
Not-for-profit Childcare Center
Organic landscape maintenance
Trees and two-story arcades for shade
Recyclable storage facilities
Secure bicycle storage
Shower and locker rooms

Selection of materials with high-recycled content
Full building commissioning

Electric vehicle charging stations
Landfill diversion greater than 90%
Garage equipped with CO sensors
Mat slab foundation with 40% fly ash

Modular Furniture & task lights meet 'Green' specs
High-efficient lighting, controls, sensors

Oil interceptors at garage drainage
Car pool and van pool parking
Rigorous standards for building ventilation during and after construction

Carbon dioxide sensors adjust fresh air intake
Exceeds California energy code by 30%
Lab tested no or low VOC finishes
Interior designed to maximize daylight
Green roof
Tree Management Plan
Underfloor air distribution
Centralized automated building management
Eco-Elevator
Marble flooring salvaged from Library & Courts Building c.1923

By setting benchmarks early in the design process and frequently monitoring building systems once construction is completed, it is possible to assess the performance of a green building and make adjustments if necessary. © Erhard Pfeiffer 2003

throughout the life of the project to determine whether desired goals have been reached.

New Facilities Management Technologies

Just as computer-controlled electronic systems have increased efficiency, innovations are happening all the time that will make operating a completely green facility easier and less expensive.

Microsystems, also known as MEMS (microelectromechanical systems), are showing promise in the development of new electronic components, with parts measuring the diameter of a human hair that will take up far less space, be more economical to operate, and emit no VOCs.

MEMS is a set of technologies that make it possible to mass-produce large numbers of integrated sensors, actuators, computers, and communication systems that can be embedded in products or spread throughout the environment.[30] Like many innovations, microsystems technology evolved as a result of military research, and its principle application to date has been related to security and defense systems.

In addition to government, defense, and university lab research, manufacturers themselves are investigating new technologies to streamline products and make them cleaner, more efficient, and less expensive to operate. For example, Twenty-First Century Research is an initiative of the Air Conditioning and Refrigeration Institute (a national trade association for HVAC manufacturers) whose mission, in conjunction with the public sector, is to identify, prioritize, and undertake research that focuses on decreasing energy consumption, increasing indoor environmental quality, and safeguarding the environment. The group's emerging technologies subcommittee investigates promising concepts such as MEMS as well as alternative vapor compression cycles and cooling technologies and other emerging technologies that might be applied for a system, instrumentation, self-diagnostics, and enhanced controls.[31]

Similarly, the American Society of Plumbing Engineers through its research foundation is actively researching ways to improve water efficiencies in buildings, including new approaches to heat recovery in plumbing systems.[32]

Companies themselves constantly search for new, more efficient products. Manchester, New Hampshire–based Kalwall teamed with Cabot Corporation, a specialty chemical company, to develop a new roofing material that allows light to pass through for added daylighting but has superior insulation properties as well. The product, Kalwall+ Nanogel, uses translucent aerogel insulation to create a translucent building panel that features R-10 insulation with 20 percent light transmission. The insulating value, usable daylighting performance, and structural integrity of Kalwall+Nanogel elevate the technology to a new level.[33]

And iCurie Labs, a company founded by a former NASA scientist, is building a factory in England to develop a prototype and manufacture its air-conditioning units that incorporate MEMS technology. The company also patented a new computer cooling system that will drastically reduce the drain on energy that multiple CPUs tend to produce.

Notes

1. Personal correspondence, August 19, 2004.

2. For a look at LEED's green guide for existing buildings, see http://www.usgbc.org/Docs/Existing_Buildings/LEED-EBvPilot.pdf. A guide for tenants can be found here as well. As of publication of this book, these documents were in draft form. The final version may contain some changes.

3. See http://www.energystar.gov/index.cfm?c=assess_value.bus_financial_value_calculator.

4. A. K. Townsend, *The Smart Office: Turning Your Company on Its Head* (Olney, Maryland: Gila Press, 1997), p. 75.

5. See http://www.greenbiz.com/sites/greenerbuildings/backgrounders_detail.cfm?UseKeyword=Facility%20Management.

6. Ibid. See also the U.S. Department of Energy's "Greening Federal Facilities" at http://www.eere.energy.gov/femp/pdfs/29267-6.2.pdf for more information about purchasing low-flow toilets for commercial properties.

7. Ibid.

8. Ibid.

9. http://www.energydesignresources.com/resource/130/.

10. "Do the Math," Greener Facilities newsletter, at http://www.buildings.com/Articles/detail.asp?articleid=1980, July 2004.

11. http://www.eere.energy.gov/buildings/info/operate/operate.html.

12. "Real Property Sustainable Development Guide," General Services Administration, at http://www.gsa.gov/gsa/cm_attachments/GSA_DOCUMENT/sus_dev_guide_R2O1X_0Z5RDZ-i34K-pR.pdf, p. 15. For more information on improving the efficiency of HVAC systems, see http://www.energydesignresources.com/category/heating-vent-ac/.

13. See http://www.eere.energy.gov/solar/.

14. http://www.greenerbuildings.com/tool_detail.cfm?LinkAdvID=52675.

15. http://www.eere.energy.gov/EE/buildings_lighting.html.

16. Mark Harrigan, "Facilities Management Resources Sustainability," FMLink, April 26, 2004, p. 2.

17. http://www.greenerbuildings.com/tool_detail.cfm?LinkAdvID=52675.

18. http://www.kalwall.com/news.htm.

19. http://www.betterbricks.com/default.aspx?pid=casestudy&casestudyid=7&sectionname=financialanalysis.

20. For a comprehensive overview of state, local utility, and federal renewable energy incentives, see www.dsireusa.org, the database for State Incentives for Renewable Energy.

21. Rick Fedrizzi, "IAQ," at http://www.buildings.com/newsletters/greener_facilities/2003/may2003.asp.

22. See the Carrier Corporation's Web site at http://www.global.carrier.com/details/0,1240,CLI1_DIV28_ETI16,00.html.

23. http://www.bizjournals.com/washington/stories/2002/06/17/focus12.html?page=3.

24. http://www.global.carrier.com/details/0,1240,CLI1_DIV28_ETI16,00.html.

25. http://www.carpet-rug.com/pdf_word_docs/0406_GLP-fact-sheet.pdf.

26. http://www.eere.energy.gov/buildings/info/operate/index.html.

27. See www.greenseal.org.

28. "A Business Guide to Waste Management," Xerox Corporation, p. 40. www.bushofficesupply.com/pages/detpages/xeroxnews196.shtml.

29. "Real Property Sustainable Development Guide," General Services Administration, at http://www.gsa.gov/gsa/cm_attachments/GSA_DOCUMENT/sus_dev_guide_R2O1X_0Z5RDZ-i34K-pR.pdf, p. 22.

30. Palo Alto Research Center, at http://www2.parc.com/spl/projects/smart-matter/#approach.

31. http://www.arti-21cr.org/.

32. http://www.aspe.org/ASPE_RF/rf_projects.html.

33. http://www.kalwall.com/news.htm.

Financing, Leasing, Investment

Financing, Leasing, and Investment Considerations

Leanne Tobias

Design professionals, public officials, community organizations, and others interested in green real estate development often express frustration with the quantitative focus of developers, lenders, and investors. The emphasis that development and financing professionals place on the financial viability of a project—on whether the deal "pencils"—is seen as a stumbling block to the construction of green real estate projects. But what is perceived as a stumbling block also represents an opportunity. Developers, lenders, and equity investors have no intrinsic ideological resistance to sustainable real estate projects. If they can be persuaded that a green transaction makes financial sense—or, even better, that the deal represents a better opportunity for returns than a conventional project—chances are that the green project will go forward. Thus, advocates of green real estate development must learn the language of real estate investment so that they can communicate the

Even though many green buildings outperform comparable conventional properties, developers must often overcome perceptions of increased risk on the part of lenders and equity investors. In New York City, 7 World Trade Center will provide a range of green features, including improved IAQ, energy conservation, water conservation, and waste reduction.

advantages of green projects to developers, lenders, and equity investors. Central to this challenge is persuading the capital source that the deal pencils when subjected to conventional underwriting analysis.

How Lenders and Investors Underwrite Risk

Permanent lenders, construction lenders, and equity investors assess real estate projects on the basis of their ability to produce annual returns and, ultimately, sales proceeds, in the face of a diverse set of risks. Projects are typically modeled over a ten-year holding period, using a series of varied analytical assumptions to replicate significant sources of potential financial stress. The modeling process is used to derive an estimated value for the project.

Equity investors use the valuation model to compare project value at the end of the holding period to the initial investment amount; this figure, in turn, is used to determine annual return. Lenders use the valuation model in conjunction with their loan-to-value requirements to determine the loan amount and develop other loan terms. In a second test of project viability, the valuation model is used to compare the project's expected net operating income (NOI) to the lender's debt coverage ratio requirements. In sum, the project's estimated value determines loan terms.

Key Risk Elements

The key risk elements for a commercial real estate project include design risk, construction and site risk, and market conditions.

Green Financing: The Color of Money

Dan Winters

The color of money is the greenest of green regardless of whether you are developing a LEED Platinum project or a minimally code-compliant project. Ultimately, capital-market underwriting criteria, capital availability, the return requirements of equity and debt investors, and the dynamics of market supply and demand will drive many development budget decisions along the way.

Deft market positioning, coupled with negotiating savvy and a deep knowledge of the capital market, are prerequisites for creating a debt and equity financial structure that will allow a green building to be a successful investment. In the area of financing green buildings, the experience of the Washington, D.C., office of L.J. Melody & Company includes the following:

■ The $490 million construction financing and bond offering for the 1.35 million-square-foot (125,400-square-meter) U.S. Department of Transportation headquarters, a building that is projected to be LEED certified at its completion in 2007;

■ 1425 K Street, a 218,000-square-foot (20,200-square-meter) Class A trophy office building that has the distinction of being the first office building with a green roof in the District of Columbia's central business district; and

■ The Tower Building, which was designated by the Apartment and Office Building Association of Washington, D.C., as the 2002 Green Building of the Year.

Of particular note is the financing of the Tower Building, a ten-story, 261,500-square-foot (24,290-square-meter), high-performance, Super Class A office building

located in the Rockville, Maryland, submarket along the I-270 corridor in suburban Washington, D.C. Designed in the late 1990s and completed in 2001, the building offers green amenities that in many instances were ahead of their time. These amenities include the following:

■ High-efficiency, double-glazed windows that allow direct light to permeate deep into the building's core while achieving high energy efficiency and associated cost savings;

■ An energy-efficient HVAC system that prefilters outside air and recycles 100 percent of the indoor air every hour, making it possible to maintain a steady indoor temperature and high-quality indoor air;

■ Acoustic controls that minimize exterior roadway noise and interior noise from mechanical systems and workplace activity; and

■ Interior and exterior construction materials consisting of recycled, recyclable, and low-VOC products, which add to the already high indoor-air quality.

■ ENERGY STAR compliance, which results in a 30 percent energy savings and a direct, bottom-line financial benefit.

At the time the Tower Building was delivered, it was (and it remains) the clear leader in its submarket with respect to design, workplace quality, and tenant amenities.[1] The results—including increased employee satisfaction and associated gains in productivity, stronger tenant retention, and lower operating costs—were expected, through proper market positioning, to bring about higher rental rates over the long term.

As with any pioneering project, the question on the minds of tenants, lenders, and investors alike is whether the rental rates

obtained by the project will be sufficient to finance the cost of the design benefits. To achieve such rates, it is vital to have an experienced financial adviser and a strong project leasing team involved from inception. Ideally, the financial adviser and leasing team will be well versed in the benefits of green projects. If the capital-markets team, the leasing team, and the design team collaborate, members of all three teams will develop a deep understanding of how to position the project and educate their respective audiences.

Key Insights

Among the insights gained by the L.J. Melody team while financing the Tower Building, three elements stand out: the quality of the income stream, the lack of comparables, and the value of a track record.

Quality of the Income Stream

The tenants are the most important determinant of project value. Their value is based on their company credit rating as well as factors associated with the lease, such as lease term and lease structure. Secondary considerations are project location and market dynamics, including overall market vacancy and the project's vacancy at the time of construction takeout financing.

A green project, which is high quality and high performance by its very nature, should attract a well-heeled tenant roster, but there is no guarantee. It is essential for the leasing team to understand the project, to know how to position it, and, ultimately, to sell the health, productivity, and ongoing operational cost benefits. The objective is to obtain market rents in the upper quartile for its Class A

The high-performance features of the Tower Building, completed in 2001, added an estimated $700,000 to the construction budget, but an analysis of the annual savings in energy and maintenance costs indicates that the upfront investment made economic sense. The Tower Companies

peer group, as these lease contracts drive the ultimate capital structure and overall financing economics.

The CB Richard Ellis team took the project from speculative development to 84 percent lease-up with major credit tenants, including Bank of America, the U.S. Department of Health and Human Services, and Booz Allen Hamilton at time of financing. The lease rates achieved were at the very top of the Class A market at the time they were signed. Ultimately, the overall rental rates and the tenants' underlying credit ratings drove the financing economics.

The Lack of Comparables

Sales of similar properties and lease comparables substantiate the market value of the collateral—which, in turn, drives the lending decision. Green buildings—as high-cost, high-value pioneers—run into trouble when it comes to compiling market sales and leasing comparables that support the underlying value.

Constructing a Super Class A property narrows the project's comparable list, necessitating creative capital-market positioning. This may require a search for sales and leasing comparables outside the primary market. The financing team will need to refute the "mark-to-market" push by lenders as they attempt to assign a value to the collateral and to make it fit within their debt-service-coverage and loan-to-value underwriting ratios.

Expanding the pie to include high-end Class A leasing and sales comparables outside the submarket might be a start. Another solution is to compare the property to similarly sized and similarly designed green buildings on a national basis, to capture the leasing and sales premiums achieved by these peers.

The Value of a Track Record

Reduced operating costs are one of the key financial benefits to a green building. Once these savings are quantified, they can be valued very simply by applying a market-driven capitalization rate to the amount of annual savings.

Most projects seeking permanent financing to pay down the construction loan have yet to establish an operating track record for a full year. Capturing this value while underwriting the loan necessitates a leap of faith on part of the permanent lender and the appraiser, who must deviate from typical market operating expenses—which, if applied, would not capture the high-performance design efficiencies and cost savings.

For example, the Tower Building's high-performance components were estimated to add $700,000 (1.2 percent) to the budget and were projected to realize $60,000 in annual savings on energy and maintenance costs. The commissioning process and the results from computer-simulation models of energy use demonstrated these savings. The $60,000 ongoing cost reduction, at an 8 percent capitalization rate, yielded an implied value of $750,000, giving the lender comfort that the upfront investment in high-performance features was financially sound.

The capital markets and leasing team's knowledge of issues that drive costs and benefits is vital to achieving the value proposition derived from building green. Lender underwriting is driven by the quality of the future income stream, which is a direct result of the project's tenants, the aggregate rent due under the lease contracts, and the dynamics of supply and demand in the micromarket.

The amount of financing is directly correlated to the success of the leasing team. Shifting the dialogue away from the costs associated with building green and focusing on the benefits inherent in high-performance features sets the stage for the economic underpinnings that ultimately decide financing decisions. Realizing top-tier rents through a Super Class A, Class AAA, or other market positioning is critical to increasing the revenue line. Focusing on the tenant's productivity benefits, by means of the now-numerous case studies substantiating productivity gains in green buildings, should be the leasing team's number-one objective on the way to achieving this goal.

Emerging Financing Opportunities

A number of opportunities are emerging for new debt and equity financing vehicles that recognize and capture the value inherent in high-performance green buildings. Lenders who seek out LEED- or ENERGY STAR–certified properties for debt placements can aggregate these loans, securitize them through a commercial mortgage-backed security (CMBS), and target institutional investors with a security that may demonstrate better risk/reward dynamics, thanks to superior product, strong tenant rosters, and other areas of systematic risk reduction (lower insurance premiums, lower exposure to energy price hikes, etc.).

Green properties are also likely to attract attention from institutions that maintain an underlying social mandate within their investment portfolios, as well as the socially responsible investor network, a highly receptive investor audience consisting of well over $1.5 trillion in investable assets.[2]

Private equity fund vehicles focused solely on acquiring and holding green properties are also on the horizon, as these investors will be in the position to reap additional portfolio-level financial rewards. Diversification reduces market risk, leaving investors with a collection of the highest-quality assets renting at market-leading rates; at the same time, energy savings allow these properties to enjoy lower operating costs than their peer group. Growing the top line while reducing the expense line is a good formula for superior market returns.

Increased financing sources result in increased lender and investor competition for the deal, which ultimately leads to lower project-specific capital costs. The capital-markets group at L.J. Melody sees the development of these types of financial vehicles as the next step in moving ahead with mass-market acceptance of green building standards.

Dan Winters, a real estate finance specialist, is the founder of Evolution Partners. He was formerly with L.J. Melody, the real estate investment banking subsidiary of CB Richard Ellis.

Notes

1. For additional information on the Tower Building, see www.towerbuilding.com.
2. As reported by the Zicklin Center for Business Ethics Research, Wharton School of Business, University of Pennsylvania.

Design risk. Does the project use space efficiently and meet tenant needs in a functional and aesthetically pleasing manner, in relation to project cost? Is the site used efficiently and in accordance with zoning requirements?

Construction and site risk. Is the project likely to be delivered on time and within budget? For a speculative project, is the budget within market parameters? Does the site pose environmental or construction challenges that may adversely affect cost? Does the project team have a track record for delivering projects on time and within budget? Is the contingency budget sufficient to mitigate construction risk, and is the project schedule attainable? Is the land appropriately zoned? Are subdivision approvals in place? Can utilities be run to the site? Have easements and public improvements been obtained? If not, what are the risks associated with obtaining the necessary approvals?

Market conditions. Economic assumptions at the macro, market, and submarket levels form the crux of every real estate valuation model.

Market and Project Assessment

To evaluate market conditions for a proposed project, lenders and investors undertake an economic analysis of the metropolitan area and region. Data typically examined include population, demographic, and employment trends; rates of household and business formation; trends in family and personal income; and salient changes in household and business settlement patterns.

Lenders and investors also evaluate current and future supply and demand for competitive space. The variables considered in this evaluation include available primary and sublet space; planned construction; and recent, current, and projected absorption. The forecast of supply and demand is used, in turn, to interpret overall market trend data, projected rental rates, and the inducements, or "concessions," that landlords will award to attract tenants. Concessions include free rent, moving allowances, and, in some instances, buyout of a tenant's existing lease. Market conditions also determine the level of tenant improvement allowances (also known as "TIs," "buildout allowances," or "tenant work letters") awarded by landlords to finish a vacant space to a tenant's specifications.

Rental rates, tenant concessions, and tenant improvement allowances are typically modeled on comparable transactions—that is, leases executed in the same submarket under similar market conditions. Comparables for recent leases (or "lease comps") are used to develop rental rate, tenant concession, and tenant improvement estimates for the proposed project, along with market averages and trend data developed by local brokerage houses and appraisal firms.

Project-specific information is also considered in developing a financial model for a proposed real estate project. Preleasing (that is, leases that are already in place before construction is completed), proposals developed for tenants seeking space in the market, and assessments of the creditworthiness of proposed tenants are typically incorporated into the project modeling assumptions.

Tenant creditworthiness is an important criterion for projects expected to be leased to a single tenant or to a small number of tenants. Credit analysis is especially critical for build-to-suit projects to be occupied by a single firm for a lengthy lease term.

In addition, leasing and rental assumptions for the project under consideration are adjusted to reflect how the location, functionality, and design of the proposed project compare to those of similar properties in the market. Finally, the track record of the leasing and development team is assessed as a factor that can influence the leasing success of the proposed project.

While the projected revenue stream is the most critical element in evaluating the feasibility of a proposed real estate development, operating costs represent another important element in project performance. Information on operating costs typically includes tax levels; utility expenses; energy costs; maintenance and repair outlays; leasing, marketing, and property management fees; and annual capital-reserve requirements, spread over the average life of the improvements.

The final element in the assessment of a proposed real estate project is the exit strategy for the equity owners and the lenders. What is the likely holding period for the project, and how attractive is the project likely to be to other investors when it is put up for sale? The holding period is typically determined by the owner's preference: some investors "flip" properties after a short holding period, while others prefer to hold properties for the long term. For financing purposes, however, the usual model assumes a five- to ten-year holding period; ten years is the industry standard.

The estimated sales price at the end of the holding period is typically based on sales data for market transactions completed during the previous 18 months. These data are usually expressed on a price per square foot basis or in relation to the NOI for the property. Transactions used to project sales prices are known as sales comparables, or "sales comps." The future sales price for a property can also be forecast using the NOI projected in the year following the end of the holding period. (This approach will be discussed in greater depth later in the chapter.)

Project Valuation, Stress Testing, and Loan Terms

The elements of risk are typically modeled by the lender or equity investor in an internal valuation model. Frequently, an independent appraisal is required to verify the results of the internal model. Whether it is developed internally or by an independent appraiser, a typical valuation model is based on estimates of revenues, expenses, and sales price over a ten-year holding period. When considering a loan, lenders and investors will subject anticipated cash flows to stress testing, to determine the extent to which the project can withstand adverse changes in market conditions such as rental rates, expenses, the pace of project leasing, the length of vacancies between tenants, and interest rates for debt refinancing.

A ten-year valuation model, and its variants under stress assumptions, will generate valuation outcomes for the project. Each potential lender or investor will typically develop a separate model of estimated project value. These estimates, in turn, will be used to determine the terms of debt or equity financing. Lenders and investors typically develop numerous financial ratios in the course of determining the ultimate structure of a real estate transaction. The two key ratios are the loan-to-value (LTV) ratio and the debt coverage ratio (DCR).

The estimated value of the project is used to determine the loan amount. The ratio of the loan amount to the estimated project value is known as the loan-to-value ratio.

Loan-to-value ratio = Loan amount/Estimated project value
and
Loan amount = Loan-to-value ratio x Estimated project value

The standard LTV ratio for a first mortgage loan on a commercial property is typically between 65 and 85 percent. Variations in the LTV ratio are affected by market conditions, the lender's appetite for risk, the interest rate associated with the loan, whether the lender participates in project cash flows or sales proceeds, the length of the loan, special project features (such as preleasing or an outstanding location), and the track record of the developer and leasing team.

Typically, a lower LTV ratio is associated with more favorable loan terms, such as a lower interest rate or a longer amortization period. An LTV ratio that exceeds market standards may increase the interest rate, require lender participation in cash flow or sales proceeds, or reduce the loan term.

Whatever the final LTV ratio, the borrower is responsible for raising the additional capital for the project, whether through equity investment or subordinate debt. Moreover, the primary lender's evaluation of the project will take into account the extent to which the remaining funds represent unleveraged equity or subordinate debt. Because there is a second lender to be paid, subordinate debt puts additional stress on project cash flows, and therefore adds significant risk. As of 2005, however, low interest rates had substantially increased the use (and enhanced the acceptability) of subordinate financing.

The other key determinant of the loan amount for a new real estate project is the project's estimated annual debt coverage ratio. Understandably, the property's ability to pay debt service—the principal and interest payments due on the loan—is a critical aspect of project feasibility for a lender. It is from debt service that lenders derive their repayment and yield. The viability of a project is therefore measured according to whether the NOI is sufficiently in excess of the financing costs to pay the loan principal and interest due to the lender.

Net operating income = Project revenues – Project expenses

Debt coverage ratio = Annual net operating income/Annual loan payments (principal + interest)

Though the lenders and the borrower may negotiate a debt coverage ratio for a project that is as low as 1.05 percent, lenders typically require a debt coverage ratio of 1.25 percent or more. The final ratio is influenced by market conditions, other loan terms, whether the lender is participating in cash flow or sales proceeds, and the borrower's track record and previous relationship, if any, with the lender. Stress testing is used to determine whether reserves need to be established in order to ensure that the property will be able to pay debt service and expenses over the life of the loan.

Real Estate Underwriting: A Summary

The standard underwriting process for real estate is a widely used method of comparing project risks and returns. Many advocates of green building have expressed frustration with the model because it ignores long-term project benefits that extend beyond the typical holding period of ten years, and because conventional underwriting methods do not capture the societal benefits associated with green projects. These concerns are valid to a degree, especially for projects that incorporate relatively expensive design innovations and that are intended to receive a LEED Gold or Platinum rating from the U.S. Green Building Council.

These criticisms, however, ignore the reality that green real estate projects that are financed through conventional financing sources must pass standard underwriting hurdles and produce returns that are at least equivalent to those achieved by conventional projects. The usual underwriting criteria also ignore the fact that green projects *can* pencil— and, in some cases, may be able to outperform—conventional properties. Many green projects built to the specifications of an EPA ENERGY STAR rating or a basic or LEED Silver

certification can be built for the same cost as conventional real estate. In short, the standard valuation model can, in fact, be used to demonstrate the market value represented by green projects. Moreover, lease-based financing for development of a build-to-suit property for a motivated single user can be used to attract financing for potentially more expensive LEED Gold or Platinum projects.

Risks Associated with Green Projects

Green development projects share many of the same risks as conventional development projects. In the absence of state or local incentives for green construction, the project's locational characteristics and site-specific zoning and permitting concerns will be the same, regardless of whether the project is built to green specifications. Area economic analysis and the supply and demand characteristics of the market and submarket will be identical for green and conventional projects. Similarly, green buildings to be leased on a speculative basis will be subject to the same market parameters as conventional projects—although, as will be discussed later in this chapter, these parameters may be modified during the leasing process to the benefit of green projects.

Perceived Higher Risks

In the eyes of a developer or financing source unfamiliar with green building techniques, green buildings typically appear to be associated with higher risk. Innovative design elements and construction methods are likely to elicit concern, particularly if those elements are perceived as increasing construction costs or the length of the development schedule. Donald Moses, vice president of Capital Source, a national real estate financing company, notes that lenders frequently have per-square foot construction cost standards, and that any costs beyond those standards may be viewed as "noneconomic" outlays, against which a lender cannot extend financing.[1]

State and Local Initiatives Supporting Green Building

Leanne Tobias

State and local programs supporting green construction are diverse in nature, ranging from local zoning initiatives to state and local financial incentives and design and construction requirements.

Access and Zoning Initiatives

Thirty-three states and a number of local jurisdictions have enacted legislation promoting the installation and use of solar and other alternative energy systems, according to information compiled by the Database of State Incentives for Renewable Energy (DSIRE).[1] Such regulations provide the underpinnings for green real estate development and can be proactively applied to encourage the development of green projects.

State and local access and zoning regulations on the alternative-energy front take the following forms:

■ *Enabling legislation to permit voluntary contracts between property owners establishing easements for solar or wind access.* States that have adopted such statutes include Iowa, Kentucky, Massachusetts, Montana, Nebraska, New York, North Dakota, Ohio, Rhode Island, Utah, Virginia, and Washington.

■ *Local or state solar easements.* Georgia permits property owners to apply for solar-easement permits, and such easements can be granted at the state level in Minnesota and Wisconsin. Localities in Iowa, Maine, and Tennessee are empowered to grant solar easements.

■ *Enabling legislation permitting local jurisdictions to adopt zoning or other requirements to encourage the use of alternative energy systems.* States with these statutes in force include Kansas, Maine, New Mexico, New York, Oregon, Tennessee, and Utah.

Rhode Island requires that local entities address solar access requirements in their zoning ordinances and regulations.

■ *State legislation preventing localities or subdivisions from enacting regulations that prohibit or unreasonably restrict the installation or use of solar or other alternative energy systems.* State governments that have adopted this regulatory approach include Colorado, Florida, Hawaii, Indiana, Maryland, and Massachusetts. Hawaii also prohibits sales covenants that forbid or restrict the installation of solar energy devices.

Local governments have adopted a variety of zoning and access measures to encourage the installation and use of energy-saving devices:

■ In California, Los Angeles and San Jose exempt solar energy devices from height restrictions. Palo Alto has established subdivision requirements that encourage the installation and use of passive solar devices and other alternative energy systems. San Diego limits the shade that can be cast by new residential development.

■ In an effort to encourage the use of residential solar devices, Boulder, Colorado, has introduced limits on the shade that can be cast by new residential construction.

■ Ashland, Oregon, has established solar set-back requirements for new residential, commercial, and industrial construction. Eugene, Oregon, has introduced similar subdivision requirements for residential construction.

■ Madison, Wisconsin, requires that new streets be sited to facilitate solar access.

Among the more innovative local zoning regulations are provisions adopted by Gainesville, Florida; Ashland, Oregon; and Arlington, Virginia. Gainesville has amended its zoning code to require that all public facilities be sited to provide for solar access. For properties that meet enhanced efficiency standards for energy use, water use, and indoor-air quality, Ashland provides a density bonus for residential construction of up to 15 percent.

Arlington, Virginia, has amended its zoning ordinance to award density bonuses for green properties. The program applies to commercial office buildings, condominiums, and rental apartment projects certified under the LEED standards of the U.S. Green Building Council. The program gives LEED-certified green projects density bonuses according to the following schedule: 0.15 additional floor/area ratio (FAR) for projects with basic LEED certification; 0.25 for projects with Silver LEED certification; and 0.35 for projects with LEED Gold or Platinum certification.

Financial Incentives

Tax incentives to encourage sustainable construction are widespread in the United States, as are rebate programs financed through local utilities.

Property Tax Incentives

According to DSIRE, 25 states have approved the enactment of property tax incentives to encourage sustainable development. Of these, 20 grant the incentives to commercial properties or permit local governments to do so. Such statutes confer an operating-cost advantage on properties that install and use alternative energy systems.

The following states exclude one or more alternative energy systems from all or part of local property taxes: California, Kansas, Indiana, Massachusetts, Minnesota, Nevada, New York, North Dakota, Ohio, South

Dakota, Tennessee, and West Virginia. Alternative energy systems included in such exemptions include solar, wind, photovoltaic, hydropower, biomass, and geothermal systems. Solar, photovoltaic, and wind exemptions are the most common.

A second approach is to reduce the assessed valuations and property taxes on energy systems to bring them into line with those on conventional construction. States that have adopted this requirement include Illinois, Maryland (with respect to special state assessments), North Carolina, Oregon, and Wisconsin.

Other states permit local governments to reduce property tax levies on alternative energy systems or to exempt these systems from property taxation. States using this approach include Connecticut, Iowa, Maryland, and Virginia.

Corporate Tax Incentives

Ten states provide corporate tax benefits to commercial-property owners who install alternative energy systems or construct green buildings. These incentives help to offset higher development costs associated with sustainable projects. Three state programs—in Maryland, New York, and Oregon—are geared specifically to green projects that meet standards established at the state level.

■ California offers corporate and personal tax credits for taxpayers who install photovoltaic or wind energy systems. The credit is limited to the lesser of the capital cost after rebates or other purchase discounts, or $4.50 per watt.

■ Hawaii provides tax incentives for solar, photovoltaic, and wind energy systems in commercial properties. The credit is limited to 35 percent of the cost of solar energy or

photovoltaic equipment for a commercial property, with a ceiling of $250,000. For wind systems, the credit is limited to the lesser of $250,000 or 20 percent of initial costs.

■ Maryland offers income tax credits for taxpayers who construct green buildings of at least 20,000 square feet (1,860 square meters) on brownfield sites or in other priority areas. Also eligible are rehabilitated green facilities that are located in priority funding areas or that increase square footage by less than 25 percent. Costs eligible for the Maryland credit are capped at $120 per square foot ($1,290 per square meter) for base buildings, and at $60 per square foot ($646 per square meter) for tenant improvements. Credits range from 20 to 30 percent of eligible development costs.

■ Businesses located in Massachusetts may deduct from taxable net income up to 100 percent of the costs incurred through the installation of any solar or wind-powered system for climate control or heating. The installation must be used exclusively in the trade or business of the taxpayer.

Massachusetts also exempts from the corporate excise tax solar and wind energy systems for the length of the system's depreciation period.

■ New York State's Green Building Tax Credit program provides for the issuance of up to $25 million in aggregate credits for properties placed in service from 2001 to 2004. Credits may be used to offset design, construction, or rehabilitation costs. Eligible properties include hotels, offices, and multifamily residential dwellings with at least 20,000 square feet (1,860 square meters) of interior space. Credits are phased in during the first five years after the building is placed in service; the taxpayer can carry

unused tax credits forward indefinitely; and successive owners or tenants are entitled to any remaining credits if the building or tenant space continues to meet applicable environmental standards.

■ North Carolina provides income or franchise tax credits of up to $250,000 for commercial or industrial facilities that install alternative energy systems. Eligible improvements include solar, photovoltaic, wind, hydropower, and biomass systems. Expenses that can be covered by the credit are design, equipment purchase, construction, and installation (less any purchase or installation discounts). The credit is taken over a five-year term, and can be extended over a five-year carryover period.

■ North Dakota offers an income tax credit of 3 percent per year for up to five years against the cost of equipment or installation for geothermal, wind, or solar energy devices.

Ohio exempts from the state franchise tax and sales and use tax equipment that is used to replace fossil-fuel energy with alternative technologies. Solar, thermal, and photovoltaic systems are eligible for the exemption.

■ The Oregon Business Energy Tax Credit for Sustainable Buildings, adopted in 2001, provides a 35 percent tax credit for eligible project costs related to developing or retrofitting a property that meets the LEED Silver, Gold, or Platinum standard. The tax credit can cover all costs directly related to the project, including loan fees; permit costs; equipment costs; engineering and design fees; and the costs of materials, supplies, and installation. The size of the credit is determined by the size of the building and the LEED standard achieved; eligible per-square-foot project costs increase according to the LEED designation (see table on next page).

Eligible Costs, Oregon Business Energy Tax Credit for Sustainable Buildings

Building Area	LEED Rating		
	Silver (per Square Foot/Square Meter)	Gold (per Square Foot/Square Meter)	Platinum (per Square Foot/Square Meter)
First 10,000 square feet (930 square meters)	$5.71/$61.46	$9.29/$99.99	$14.29/$153.81
Next 40,000 square feet (3,720 square meters)	$3.57/$38.42	$4.29/$46.17	$7.86/$84.60
Over 50,000 square feet (4,650 square meters)	$2.00/$21.52	$2.86/$30.78	$5.71/$61.46

Source: Oregon Department of Energy, July 2003.

■ Texas offers taxpayers a choice of incentives for the installation of solar or photovoltaic energy systems. The cost of the system can be excluded from taxable capital, or 10 percent of the system's cost can be excluded from taxable income.

■ Utah's renewable-energy-systems tax credit applies to 10 percent of the cost of system installation, up to a maximum of $50,000. Systems eligible for the credit include active and passive solar devices, biomass, hydropower, and wind.

Rebates

Twenty-two states and a number of local jurisdictions offer rebate programs associated with the purchase of energy-efficient lighting, HVAC systems, building-control systems, and weatherization programs. Rebates are generally provided through local utilities and provide a valuable incentive for property owners to install energy-efficient systems in new construction or to replace or upgrade existing systems. According to DSIRE, the following states have rebate programs: Arizona, California, Connecticut, Delaware, Florida, Hawaii, Illinois, Maine, Massachusetts, Minnesota, Montana, Nevada, New Hampshire, New Jersey, New York, Oregon, Pennsylvania, Rhode Island, Texas, Utah, Washington, and Wisconsin.

Austin, Texas, offers a comprehensive rebate and financing program for local businesses interested in installing energy-efficient systems in commercial properties. Austin Energy provides rebates of 50 percent of project costs (up to a maximum of $100,000) for energy-efficient lighting, water heaters, HVAC systems, building-control systems, solar water-heating, reflective roof coatings, roof and ceiling insulation, and solar screening. The Austin program also offers no-interest financing for lighting upgrades. The program is enhanced by technical analysis and assistance provided to property owners by the city of Austin.

Construction and Design Policies

Fifteen states and a number of local jurisdictions have adopted green or energy-efficient standards for public construction or require such standards for the construction of commercial properties. The following initiatives are examples:

■ Arizona has enacted solar design standards for all state buildings. In Tucson, energy consumption in all new municipal construction must be 50 percent lower than the 1995 standard.

■ California has mandated that all state buildings and parking facilities constructed after December 31, 2002, install solar energy equipment no later than January 1, 2007. The city of San Jose requires all municipal buildings measuring 10,000 square feet (930 square meters) or more to meet a San Jose LEED green building standard.

■ Denver, Colorado, has adopted LEED standards for municipal construction, and the city's new civic center is being constructed to the LEED Silver standard.

■ Florida has mandated that all state buildings use solar technologies for heating and cooling if a life-cycle analysis indicates that cost efficiencies can be gained.

■ Hawaii requires all buildings constructed with state funds or located on state land to assess the costs and benefits of solar energy relative to conventional energy systems and to use solar power if a life-cycle analysis so warrants.

■ In Maryland, the design process for the construction of any state facilities must include an evaluation of the use of solar and wind-powered energy versus conventional systems.

■ Minnesota requires the installation of active and passive solar systems and other alternative energy technologies in newly constructed state facilities and in state facilities undergoing substantial (more than 50 percent) renovation.

■ Nevada has adopted legislation encouraging local school districts to employ daylighting, solar energy, and renewable energy sources in their reconstruction programs. A pilot program is underway in Clark County, with completion scheduled for August 2008.

■ In Chapel Hill, North Carolina, energy use in town-owned buildings must be 30 percent

lower than the levels required in the 1997 local code.

■ Portland, Oregon, requires municipal buildings to attain Basic LEED certification, and encourages the attainment of Silver, Gold, or Platinum LEED certification. Portland properties that have received $200,000 or more in local public financing are also required to attain Basic LEED certification.

■ Pennsylvania has constructed two green office facilities totaling over 100,000 square feet (9,290 square meters), has produced a green facilities-maintenance guide for state buildings, and requires state agencies to take green standards into account in property procurement and leasing.

■ Texas requires that construction and reconstruction programs for state facilities include an evaluation of the cost-effectiveness of alternative energy systems; the use of such systems is required if it produces life-cycle savings.

■ Seattle, Washington, and surrounding King County require that public projects meet sustainable standards. All Seattle facilities of 5,000 square feet (465 square meters) or more must be built to the Silver LEED standard. King County has adopted a local LEED standard for all county construction and renovation programs.

Jurisdictions requiring private commercial construction to meet energy-efficient design or construction standards are less common. Localities that require commercial construction to meet alternative energy

standards include Santa Monica, California, and Aspen, Colorado.

Santa Monica mandates that all hotels, motels, and commercial, institutional, and light-industrial buildings meet an annual energy conservation target that calls for energy use to be 15 percent lower than the minimum compliance levels set in 2001. Multifamily residential and retail buildings must meet a target that is 10 percent lower. The ordinance requires building owners or developers to use the Santa Monica Energy Code Compliance Application, a computer simulation, to demonstrate that nonresidential buildings meet the energy conservation target.

The City of Aspen and Pitkin County Efficient Building Program has adopted an energy conservation checklist that must be completed in connection with remodeling, construction, and demolition projects. To obtain a building permit, a project must demonstrate the use of one or more of the following techniques or the presence of one or more of the following characteristics: the reduction of construction waste; efficient building methods; the use of recycled and renewable resources; energy efficiency; high indoor air quality; the use of renewable energy; and water conservation.

Note

1. See www.dsireusa.org.

Careful planning, and the use of architectural, construction management, and contracting teams that have successfully designed and built green projects on time and within budget, can mitigate concerns related to project costs or construction schedules. Cost savings associated with green building practices, including the recycling of construction-site waste and the use of commissioning, should be clearly articulated and included in the project budget.

As successful green builders often note, the construction manager, general contractor, and key subcontractors must be included in the project design and budgeting process, in order to value-engineer the project and incorporate protocols that will save time and dollars during construction. The project should also include an appropriate contingency budget to cover potential cost overruns, an element that will certainly be scrutinized by lenders and investors confronted by innovative design and construction requirements. Careful value engineering, construction-management protocols, and contingency budgeting will help to allay the cost concerns of developers, lenders, and equity investors, as will the use of design, engineering, construction management, and contracting professionals who are experienced with sustainable projects.

According to Donald Moses, if the project team has been associated with comparable projects that achieved replicable savings, these comps are an important piece of evidence for the lender and can help to allay concerns about cost overruns. Comps documenting that green projects lead to energy savings over the investment period will also be helpful to the lender. If green projects can deliver other economic benefits, such as faster lease-up, higher rents, or improved tenant retention, those factors should also be documented, to enable lenders to take these factors into account when considering project financing.[2]

Most important, advocates of green buildings should practice "the art of the possible." Unless the project is a build-to-suit that will be constructed under a long-term, above-market lease for a creditworthy tenant, a green developer who seeks conventional financing is likely to be forced to design the project so that costs fit within the market envelope. As a practical matter, this means that Gold and Platinum LEED projects are most likely to be built on a build-to-suit basis for motivated single tenants with strong credit profiles, at least at the current stage of building technology. With respect to speculative real estate that must compete on a market basis, the cost constraints imposed by the conventional real estate financing model leave significant opportunities for ENERGY STAR and LEED basic- or Silver-rated properties that can be built within conventional market parameters.

Financial Incentives That Offset Risk

A number of states and localities have enacted incentive programs to encourage green construction. Most such programs offer tax credits for properties that meet certain green standards. Examples include the New York State Green Building Tax Credit, the Oregon Business Energy Tax Credit for Sustainable Buildings, and the Arlington County, Virginia, Green Building Incentive Program. (See the accompanying feature box for more details on these and other programs.)

Under the New York State Green Building Tax Credit program, credits can be earned in six categories for green new construction or rehabilitation, and include base building costs for occupied space (7 percent of costs); base building costs for unoccupied space (5 percent of costs); costs for renovating tenant-occupied spaces (5 percent of costs); fuel-cell credits (30 percent of capitalized costs over five years); photovoltaic-module credits (100 percent of incremental costs over five years); and green refrigerant credits for equipment meeting EPA-approved standards for non-ozone-depleting refrigerants (10 percent of costs over five years). For each year in which the credit is claimed, all projects must obtain eligibility certification from a licensed architect or professional engineer.

The first five projects certified under the New York State program were announced in February 2003. The projects, described in the list that follows, secured tax credits totaling close to $18.9 million.

- 1400 Fifth Avenue, New York City: A 225,000-square-foot (20,900-square-meter) condominium in Harlem that includes 30,000 square feet (2,790 square meters) of retail space; tax credit of $1.77 million.
- 959 Eighth Avenue, New York City: The renovation of the Hearst Communications office building at 57th Street and Eighth Avenue; $5 million tax credit.
- 20 River Terrace, New York City: A green condominium project undertaken by Albanese Development Corporation in Battery Park City; $2.71 million tax credit.
- 888 Main Street, New York City: The rehabilitation of a 500-unit apartment project on Roosevelt Island; $6.6 million tax credit.
- 625 Broadway, Albany, New York: A LEED Silver office building housing the New York State Department of Environmental Conservation. The first building to receive LEED certification in New York State.

Under the Oregon Business Energy Tax Credit for Sustainable Buildings program, eligible properties not only must meet LEED certification criteria, but also must meet energy-efficiency requirements set by the state. The 35 percent tax credit must be taken over five years, with 10 percent of eligible costs deducted in the first and second years and 5 percent each year thereafter. Unused tax credits can be carried forward for up to eight years. Owners or buyers of buildings are eligible for the tax credit. A tax-exempt project owner can also transfer the net present value of the tax credit to a third-party partner under a pass-through option.

By helping to defray the costs of developing a sustainable project, the New York State and Oregon programs improve investment returns over the life of the tax credit, and can thereby help to secure investment financing for sustainable projects. Such tax credits are helpful during the underwriting process because they allay concerns about cost overruns and, during the life of the tax credit, create moderate improvements in "below-the-line" cash flows (that is, after-tax cash flows to investors). The New York and Oregon tax-credit programs also contain two particularly attractive features: First, unused credits can be carried forward, increasing their favorable financial impact. Second, unused tax credits can be transferred to new owners, increasing the sales price and marketability of the property. And under the Oregon program, tax credits can be transferred from a tax-exempt owner to a taxable development partner. This feature is particularly useful when tax-exempt owners (pension funds, not-for-profit organizations, or governmental institutions) develop projects in partnership with for-profit entities.

Although tax-credit programs can help get green projects to pencil, they may not guarantee value in the long run. Most tax-credit programs have a life of ten years or less, and the aggregate value of the tax credit is greatest at the start of the program and diminishes each year thereafter. Thus, the upfront value created by the tax credit diminishes during the project's useful life—during which time the property and its investors are likely to be required to compete with newer projects eligible for a new cycle of tax credits. Thus, while tax credits can be helpful in securing initial financing for a project, they should not be relied upon exclusively to generate ongoing project value.

Another public program, however—the Arlington County, Virginia, Green Building Incentive Program—offers a more powerful set of incentives, in the form of density bonuses, to promote green construction. The program requires all eligible projects to have a LEED-accredited professional on the development team, and for LEED requirements to be built into the site-planning and permit-issuance process.

A 220,000-square-foot (20,440-square-meter) headquarters for the Navy League of the United States was completed under the Arlington County program in 2005.

Designed by PageSoutherlandPage and developed by the Keech Company, LC, the project has been designed to meet the Silver LEED standards. Green design features include a stormwater detention system that will catch and store rainwater for nonpotable uses; a CO_2 monitoring system; and energy-saving lighting, HVAC, and electrical systems. Tenant finishes will include LEED-approved carpeting and paint, as well as green wood (new-growth wood, recycled wood, or wood that is not in short supply).

The Navy League Building earned an additional 12,000 square feet (1,110 square meters) of floor space because of its green features. The additional floor area made the project economically viable by adding sufficient rentable space to offset the extra costs associated with LEED Silver certification. (The project's architect and general contractor both estimate that the green design features will increase total construction costs by 3 percent above conventional construction.)

The project is owned by the Navy League of the United States, an educational association whose mission is to be a source of information, both for the general public and for Congress, about the importance of sea power to the nation's political and economic security. According to Howard Siegel, senior director of finance at the Navy League, "the additional FAR granted by Arlington County, the [anticipated] lower operating costs in the long term, and the 'quality of life' " expected to be delivered to the tenants "all worked into our decision as an owner . . . to make the investment in the building and the community. These factors weighed into our investment and financing decisions. On a final note, we encountered no adverse reaction from mortgage brokers or lenders."[3]

As suggested by the example of the Navy League Building, the Arlington program is significant because it will positively affect revenue and sales price over the life of the project, thus providing a competitive advantage over conventional projects. For lenders and investors, the opportunity to realize density bonuses that increase FAR by up to 0.35 is a clear-cut economic advantage in allocating investment dollars. The incentives enhance revenue and sales price, accompany the project throughout its useful life, and can be transferred from the original owner to subsequent buyers, as well as to successive financing sources. By enhancing the revenue potential of a sustainable property over its life cycle, the Arlington County model creates quantifiable and long-lasting investment value.

As indicated by the preceding discussion, public incentives can help to make green projects pencil, thereby maximizing financing opportunities. Tax-credit programs are most helpful in offsetting development costs associated with designing, developing, and renovating sustainable buildings; their financial impact is typically moderate and diminishes over the life of the credit. Programs such as the density bonuses offered by Arlington County provide a more robust financial inducement to develop green projects, in that they enhance the financial performance of the property over its life cycle and can be enjoyed by successive generations of investors and lenders.

As will be seen in the next section of this chapter, leases associated with a green project can also be a source of ongoing project value, and can help to encourage the use of conventional financing for sustainable projects.

Lease Financing
Build-to-Suit

Build-to-suit financing for a single tenant is an excellent way to finance the development of a green building. Development of a build-to-suit project relies on the rental income from a long-term lease to underwrite the cost of the development, the payment of debt service, and the owner's profit over an appropriate holding period.

To finance a green project through a tenant lease, three elements are required: satisfactory tenant credit, a suitable lease structure, and favorable real estate conditions.

Satisfactory Tenant Credit. A creditworthy tenant is defined as a tenant whose operating history and financial profile substantiate the tenant's ability to sustain payments on a long-term lease. The tenant's credit history will be closely examined, and ratio analysis will be performed to assess the strength of the tenant's balance sheet. The tenant must demonstrate profitable and growing operations over time, including a minimum operating history of five years (preferably longer). The track record of the tenant's principals and the competitive position of its key business lines will be assessed to determine the tenant's long-term viability. The tenant's income statement must demonstrate sufficient strength to make lease and operating-cost payments over time. Frequently, credit enhancements—such as letters of credit, financial guarantees from a parent entity or from principals of the tenant, or significant security deposits—will be required to strengthen the security of the lease.

Suitable Lease Structure. The term of a build-to-suit lease is likely to be at least seven years; a term of ten or more years is preferred. A lease term of seven years or more will be necessary to induce the owner to undertake development risk for the project. The owner and the financing sources are also likely to demand a triple-net lease, under which the tenant is responsible for paying the building operating costs over the lease term. In the case of a newly constructed property, rental payments must (1) cover the costs of the building shell and the interior improvements and (2) create an appropriate return for the lender and owner. To preserve the investors' yield after inflation, the financing team will often prefer a lease that incorporates regular rent increases (also known as "steps" or "bumps") over time. Such increases, however, are negotiable and dependent on market conditions. Potential tenants should be aware that developers and owners are often most interested in undertaking a build-to-suit project during a market slowdown, when development opportunities are scarce.

Favorable Real Estate Conditions. Investors in a build-to-suit project will also be concerned with the project's location, market strength, design, and functionality. These parameters must be assessed to determine whether the project will remain viable after the lease expires for the build-to-suit tenant, or in the event that the build-to-suit tenant vacates the space prematurely. Thus, projects located in a strong and growing market will be favored, as will buildings whose design and improvements are likely to be attractive to successive generations of tenants.

Speculative Projects

Efforts to undertake green speculative buildings are still in their infancy, but evidence is beginning to develop that green features can be a selling point with tenants and can reap economic benefits over time. (See the accompanying feature boxes on the Navy League Building and the Brewery Blocks.)

The Investment Benefits of Green Building

Happily, green design and construction can yield quantifiable benefits in the context of the traditional real estate valuation model. As detailed in this section, these benefits are likely to be derived from a variety of variables. While no one variable is necessarily sufficient to confer a financial benefit on a sustainable project, the combination of several factors associated with green construction are likely to produce a favorable valuation relative to a conventional project.

Operating Costs

The most obvious benefit of green construction is in the realm of operating costs: a green real estate project will reduce utility outlays by as much as one-third when compared with conventional construction. Over a ten-year holding period, this factor modestly improves the perform-

The Headquarters Building of Norm Thompson Outfitters

Leanne Tobias

The headquarters building of Norm Thompson Outfitters, a catalog retailer located in Hillsboro, Oregon, is a successful example of a lease-financed sustainable building. The 54,500-square-foot (5,020-square-meter) facility, financed under a ten-year, triple-net lease, was designed to Norm Thompson's specifications and includes the following sustainable features:

■ A southern orientation, to decrease energy consumption;

■ Daylighting, light shelves, light sensors, and a computer-programmed "light sweep" that shuts off all lighting except emergency lighting when the facility is unoccupied;

■ An energy-efficient HVAC system;

■ Operable windows and doors, to maximize the flow of fresh air;

■ Energy-efficient windows;

■ The use of recycled building materials, sustainable woods, and low-VOC paints throughout the facility;

■ Commissioning to test lighting and HVAC during design, and before and during occupancy, to ensure that energy savings are being realized; and

■ Landscaping that conserves water by incorporating wetlands, native plantings, a bioswale, and drip irrigation.

As of 2003, energy costs for the project were 35 percent below area averages, resulting in annual operating-cost savings of approximately $30,000 per year, or $0.55 per square foot ($5.92 per square meter). Several years earlier, the corresponding figures were $22,000, or approximately $0.40 per square foot ($4.31 per square meter).[1]

The Norm Thompson facility was developed by Trammell Crow Company and financed by the Multi-Employer Property Trust (MEPT), a privately held commercial real estate equity fund owned by pension investors. Under the final development agreement, Trammell Crow built the project for a fee and retained a property management contract with MEPT, the equity owner. MEPT acquired the Thompson headquarters under a presale agreement, buying the project upon completion.

Why did MEPT undertake the presale investment? As the manager of MEPT's investment approval process for the project, I can state with authority that the project's green features were incidental to the decision. The fund managers undertook the investment because the transaction penciled and offered the following benefits:

■ The lease terms produced a long-term

return consistent with other investment opportunities available to MEPT at the time. Not coincidentally, the project was conceived, financed, and developed from 1993 to 1995, a period of economic downturn during which speculative development and investment opportunities were rare. For an equity pension investor operating during a real estate recession, the Norm Thompson project represented a prudent, lower-risk project with a market return.

■ A ten-year lease to a creditworthy tenant presented an opportunity to minimize risk during an uncertain time in the real estate economy.

■ The use of a triple-net lease structure minimized the owner's downside risk, as the tenant would bear all operating expenses.

■ The tenant's operating and credit history were highly favorable: at the time the lease was negotiated, Norm Thompson Outfitters had been in business for over 40 years, offered a healthy financial profile, and had been profitable over time; the new headquarters represented an expansion.

■ The project cost met market parameters, and MEPT had significant and successful experience with Trammell Crow. The shared history of the developer and the investment

ance of a sustainable property relative to a conventional one. While it can certainly be argued that energy efficiency is a significant benefit for green projects, particularly as the cost of fuel rises over time, energy costs are not, compared with other risk and return factors, an especially substantial factor in a real estate valuation model. Thus, although energy cost savings represent a "nice to have" advantage for green projects, they might not, independent of other variables, represent a sufficiently important consideration to bring a real estate transaction to fruition.

Time Needed for Initial Lease-up

Sustainable buildings often appeal to a subset of tenants interested in a cleaner, more innovative, or more worker-friendly

The Norm Thompson Outfitters headquarters in Hillsboro, Oregon, located on a protected wetland, is a good example of a lease-financed green building. It was designed and built to the company's specification by Trammell Crow Company. Norm Thompson Outfitters

The building incorporates recycled materials, maximizes the use of natural light, and features a computerized, energy-efficient system that reduces energy use by 35 percent. Norm Thompson Outfitters

team overcame any concerns about the innovative nature of the project design.

■ The Norm Thompson headquarters could offer attractive and functional space to successive generations of tenants. Although the project represented significant risk if Norm Thompson did not renew at the end of its ten-year lease term, the project team considered the facility potentially attractive to the many software and research and development firms that rent space in the Hillsboro area. In addition, the open-plan design would allow the space to be reconfigured to suit multiple tenants, if needed.

In sum, the minimal leasing risk represented by the facility over its first ten years of operation, in conjunction with its per-ceived appeal to successive generations of tenants, was sufficient to persuade MEPT equity fund the project.

It should be emphasized that MEPT's investment was neither enhanced nor impeded by the green features of the project. Simply put, the project offered the success elements necessary for a single-tenant build-to-suit: a cost structure that conformed to market parameters; design and functionality that would appeal to successive generations of tenants; and a long-term lease to a credit tenant that would produce market returns over time. The same set of factors should be sufficient to generate conventional financing for other sustainable build-to-suits. So even if the green character of a project does not guarantee financing, green build-to-suits should be expected to receive favorable treatment by the real estate financing world if the deal makes sense financially.

If Norm Thompson does not renew its lease at its current headquarters, how will the project fare when it is time to release the space to the next generation of tenants? The MEPT project team took a bet that the project would be appealing to other firms in the Hillsboro submarket. That judgment was based on the demand for office and research and development space in the Hillsboro area, as well as on the functionality and the look and feel of the space, rather than on the building's green features.

Note

1. Derek Smith, sustainability manager, Norm Thompson Outfitters, E-mail to author, February 18, 2004, and "Founders of a New Northwest," available at http://www.sustainablenorthwest.org (accessed February 18, 2004).

environment. In the case of the Navy League Building, for example, certain trade associations felt that a green building was "mission congruent." In the case of Block 2 of the Brewery Blocks, certain tenants found green construction appealing and appear to have considered the project's green design elements as indicative of comfort and quality.

Can such potential tenants be effectively targeted to reduce the time needed to fill the building? The evidence is mixed. The time needed to absorb space in a green office building appears to be overwhelmingly dictated by market conditions. Nevertheless, in a soft market, the desire of certain tenants to rent in a green building appears to have a moderate but positive effect.

The Navy League Building, Arlington, Virginia

Leanne Tobias

The Navy League Building, in Arlington, Virginia, completed in mid-2005, offers 220,000 square feet (20,440 square meters) of Class A retail and office space. The Navy League occupies space on the second floor of the seven-story building, and the remainder of the office space, on floors two through seven, is being leased to Class A office tenants. The ground floor features retail uses. According to David Millard, of Cushman and Wakefield, who served as the initial leasing broker on the property, green features appear to have bolstered the project's appeal to prospective tenants during the early phases of leasing.[1]

The two major occupants, the Navy League and the Associated General Contractors of America, both feel that the building's green features clearly reflect their goals and image. The Navy League was inclined to develop a green headquarters facility because both the Navy and the federal government are committed to green construction. The Associated General Contractors of America leased space in the building in part because the green design reflects the organization's emphasis on quality construction; innovation in construction; and clean air, water, and transportation systems. The building's green design has also attracted the notice of other Washington, D.C., trade associations and private firms that feel that green architecture is congruent with their mission or values.

Millard notes that the green features of the Navy League Building have been greeted positively by other prospective tenants, including law firms, consulting firms, and government agencies. While tenants regard the project's green design as only one component of its market attributes (the other key components are location, functionality, and pricing), the green character of the Navy League building is viewed as a tenant amenity that will contribute to tenant comfort and worker productivity over the term of a lease.

The economic impact of the green design is also a selling point for prospective tenants. Millard estimates that when compared with competing conventional properties, water usage will be as much as 53 percent lower and electricity costs 23 percent lower. Office tenants in the Navy League Building will share in these savings. Under the base-year expense-stop lease structure, the building owner pays the first year of operating expenses; in subsequent years of the lease, tenants pay any excess over the base-year expense-stop. Bill Keech, Sr., of the Keech Company, LC, the developer of the Navy League Building, estimates that first-year operating expenses will be $0.50 to $1 per square foot ($5.38 to $10.76 per square meter) lower than they would be in a conventional building, and that expenses will escalate more slowly because of lower water and electricity use.[2] Millard concurs, noting that the end result will be a win-win deal for tenants and the building owner.

For retail tenants in the Navy League Building, the economic advantages of green design are even more clear-cut. Tenants will rent under triple-net leases, which require the tenant to pay all annual operating expenses, including water, sewer, and electricity charges. Thus, all savings in operating costs associated with the property's retail space will be captured by the tenants.

Another consideration in leasing the Navy League Building and other sustainable properties is the cost of tenant improvements. According to Amy Wynne, of PageSoutherlandPage, the LEED architect for the project, tenants who lease in the Navy League Building will be required to meet certain green standards. Current LEED requirements encourage building owners to develop tenant manuals on green improvements, and PageSoutherlandPage has developed a manual for the Navy League Building to educate tenants about options related to the installation of green improvements.

The cost of green tenant improvements is incorporated into the total hard construction costs for the project, which are estimated to exceed conventional costs by approximately 3 percent. According to Wynne and to Kim Pexton, sustainability director at James G. Davis Construction, the general contractor for the project, green tenant improvements will not add expense for many building tenants, but may affect certain retail tenants. Both Pexton and Wynne note that retail tenants with significant energy needs—restaurants, for example—may require energy-intensive, self-contained mechanical systems that are potentially more expensive to construct than conventional systems. In addition, retail chains with standard improvement specifications may have to redesign the specifications for occupancy in a green project, which may increase improvement costs for these tenants.

According to Pexton and Wynne, improvements for office tenants rarely pose the same challenge because they rely on the mechanical systems of the base building and because sufficient supply networks have been developed to deliver green office improvements at the same cost as those for conventional buildings. For tenants who

The Navy League Building, in Arlington, Virginia, earned an additional 12,000 square foot (1,110 square meters) of floor space by complying with the Arlington County Green Building Incentive Program for LEED-certified green projects. This incentive helped to offset additional construction costs associated with the building's green features. Keech Company

require significant wood finishes, however, the project's green wood requirement will require tenant improvement expenditures that exceed those associated with conventional construction.[3]

Tenant improvement allowances for speculative projects are typically dictated by the marketplace. If the cost of green improvements for certain tenants exceeds the market standard, several responses are possible: the owner can offer an above-standard allowance, perhaps in exchange for a higher rental rate; or the tenant can be encouraged to modify the design, to bring the cost of improvements down to the market standard. In addition, the owner may be

able to reduce improvement costs by encouraging tenants to use certain contractors or suppliers who will undertake the improvements for a favorable price. The strategy used by the owner will depend on market conditions. In leasing conventional buildings, owners frequently trade off above-standard tenant improvement allowances for higher rents over the lease term. Whether this strategy is possible in green buildings—and how the Navy League Building and its leasing agents will manage the economics of tenant improvements—remains to be seen.

How will green features affect rental rates at the Navy League Building? Both Keech and Millard agree that rental rates are

a product of numerous features, including location, design, tenant amenities, and market conditions. It is difficult to isolate the impact of green features on rental rates, but Millard is confident that the property will lease at rents above submarket averages; he notes that the Navy League Building's green features are attractive to tenants and offer savings on operating expenses relative to conventional properties. If management opts to provide an above-standard building improvement allowance to accommodate green design features for certain tenants, that economic concession could potentially be used to negotiate higher rental rates for those leases.

In sum, it appears that the green features of the Navy League Building have heightened tenant interest in the property and have led to somewhat faster preleasing. Rental rates for the property are also expected to be positively influenced by the economic benefits and the perception of quality associated with the project's green design, although it is difficult to isolate the effect of the project's green features from the effect of its location, functionality, architectural appeal, and amenities. It remains to be seen how green improvement requirements will affect project economics and whether green design features will enhance tenant retention over time.

Notes

1. David Millard, interview with author, March 5, 2004.

2. Bill Keech, Sr., the Keech Company, LLC, March 1, 2004.

3. Kim Pexton, telephone interview with author, March 5, 2004; and Amy Wynne, telephone interview with author, March 25, 2004.

The Brewery Blocks, Portland, Oregon

Leanne Tobias

The Brewery Blocks is a five-phase, 1.7 million-square-foot (158,000-square-meter) mixed-use development at the northern edge of Portland's central business district. The project was designed and developed by Gerding/Edlen Development of Portland, Oregon, a leader in the development of green commercial and multifamily real estate. The first three phases of the project—all Class A, mixed-use retail and office facilities—were delivered to the market from March 2002 through May 2003. A 15-story luxury condominium development known as the Henry was completed in June 2004. The Louisa, a 16-story rental-apartment and townhouse project with ground-floor retail space, was completed in spring 2005.

The three office/retail blocks of the five phases of the Brewery Blocks are LEED certified, with certification levels ranging from Basic LEED to Silver or Gold. Green features at the Brewery Blocks include the following:

- High-efficiency HVAC and air-filtration systems;
- A district-chilled water system, for more efficient cooling;
- High-efficiency induction lighting in underground parking areas;
- High-efficiency glazing;
- Daylighting incorporated into the building design;
- High-efficiency lighting systems and controls;
- Operable windows in office towers;

- Interior light shelves;
- Solar power incorporated into the design of several buildings;
- Use of low-toxicity building products and resource-efficient building materials.

Energy use at the Bowery Blocks is 30 percent below Oregon code.

The first three Brewery Blocks phases delivered to the market represent approximately 625,000 square feet (58,060 square meters) of office and retail space. As of early 2004, 82 percent had been leased. Phase I, completed in March 2002, is fully occupied. Vacancies are distributed among the mixed-use office/retail phases completed in November 2002 and May 2003. According to Scott Eaton, director of development at Gerding/Edlen and principal commercial-leasing broker for the Brewery Blocks project, leasing for both phases has proceeded more slowly than had been projected before the general retrenchment in the real estate market that began in 2001, but the pace of leasing and the rental rates have significantly exceeded Portland market averages. Eaton notes that during a two-year period in which the amount of leased space in Portland shrunk by 1 million square feet (92,900 square meters), the Brewery Blocks leased over 500,000 square feet (46,450 square meters).

Rents attained by the office/retail phases of the Brewery Blocks exceed Portland averages by 20 percent.[1] The luxury condominiums at Brewery Blocks, which were

completed in June 2004, had been fully sold by September 2003, nine months before their delivery date and at the highest recorded price per square foot for luxury condominiums in the Portland area.[2]

Office tenants at the Brewery Blocks are diverse, and include Perkins Coie, a top-ranked Portland law firm; Tyco Telecom; several financial services and investment management firms; two energy companies; and an international clothing design and marketing firm. The Brewery Blocks is also home to the Art Institute of Portland, the North Face, West Elm, and the Portland flagship store of Whole Foods Market, a national grocery retailer that specializes in organic and specialty foods. The tenant mix is oriented toward firms whose products and services are congruent with the high-quality, innovative image of the Brewery Blocks—an image that is bolstered by the project's green attributes.

Eaton believes that the green features of the Brewery Blocks have contributed to favorable tenant perceptions of the project, and notes that features such as daylighting, the use of low-emission materials, and enhanced indoor air quality have been popular tenant amenities. In sum, the green design of the Brewery Blocks has been greeted positively by tenants and prospective tenants as an indication of project quality, which tenants consider alongside such critical variables as location (the project site is in a highly desirable location in Portland's Pearl District, at the northern edge of the

Rental Rates

Developers and leasing agents insist that tenants are attracted to the idea of renting green space but aren't willing to pay extra for it. In order to lease, a green building must be competitive with prevailing market rents, which typically fall within a range. All things being equal, are green buildings more likely to be priced toward the top of the market range than competing conventional projects? The answer will vary with the particular case, but a cau-

The Brewery Blocks, in Portland, Oregon, is a five-phase mixed-use green development. The mix of retail and office tenants is oriented toward companies whose products and services are compatible with the environmentally sustainable characteristics of the project. Gerding/Edlen Development Company

central business district), functionality (the project boasts extremely efficient floor plates), and rental rates.

Office tenants at the Brewery Blocks have base-year expense-stop lease structures, allowing them to share energy cost savings with the building owners. Retail tenants are on triple-net leases, so all energy savings are passed through to the tenant. Energy costs at the Brewery Blocks are estimated to be 30 percent lower than Oregon code requirements. At the same time, property taxes have been higher than anticipated—in part because of the project's leasing success—which has partially blunted the project's cost advantages in relation to competing properties.

As for tenant improvement allowances, Gerding/Edlen used market standards without making adjustments for additional costs associated with green improvements. However, Gerding/Edlen encouraged tenants to install green improvements by procuring competitive, bulk pricing from suppliers of green lighting and carpeting, and by offering a separate allowance for energy-efficient VAV (variable–air volume) boxes, the devices that regulate air flow to tenant spaces. Gerding/Edlen also encourages tenants to choose green improvements by providing the services of an environmental consultant during design and buildout, and by providing green product specifications, information on the vendors of green products, and guidelines for long-term green operations. The company's Brewery Blocks Tenant Manual, posted on the Internet, is its guide to green tenant improvements. The approach adopted by Gerding/Edlen offers a model for other speculative projects in which the developers wish to encourage green improvements for tenant spaces.

While tenants are not required to incorporate green features in their improvements, several have (following the example of developer Gerding/Edlen and project architect GBD, both of which rent space in the Brewery Blocks). Tenants appreciate the greater floor-to-ceiling heights (13.5 feet [four meters]), the operable windows, and the improved HVAC efficiency. Several tenants have elected not to install dropped acoustical ceilings, and thus enjoy even greater ceiling heights.

To date, the investors in the Brewery Blocks include the Multi-Employer Property Trust (MEPT), an institutional pension trust, and Portland-area private investors. MEPT invested in the Silver LEED-rated Block 2, a mixed-use office and retail project that was designed and built within market cost parameters. Block 2 tenant improvement allowances also followed a strict market standard. MEPT committed to the Block 2 project because of its high-quality design and favorable location in downtown Portland. The Silver LEED-rated green features were noted in the underwriting and judged nonproblematic because (1) the construction budget and schedule were realistic; (2) the design, development, and contracting team had a strong track record; and (3) the project—including contingency line items—could be produced for a cost equivalent to that for competing Class A conventional buildings.

Notes

1. Scott Eaton, telephone interview with author, March 5, 2004.
2. Residential data from www.thehenry.com (accessed March 5, 2004).

tious yes is in order if tenants perceive green properties as high-value propositions. Components of tenant value include lower pass-through expenses to the occupant (in particular, lower utility bills); the greater comfort and potential productivity gains derived from certain features of green design (operable windows, daylighting, enhanced air quality); and the perception that a property constructed and managed according to sustainable principles offers a level of quality that will, over time, lead to higher tenant

Energy-Savings Trust Certificates: Financing Energy-Efficient Improvements through the Capital Markets

Anita Molino and Leanne Tobias

As of early 2005, the U.S. capital markets had financed over $500 billion of commercial real estate debt by pooling mortgages and selling the cash flows to investors, a process known as "securitization."

Securitization is an important source of funds for the commercial real estate market, and frequently results in less expensive financing options for borrowers. While securitization is most frequently used for mortgage

A solar turbine and cogeneration plant supply 90 percent of the energy needs at the Avenal State Prison, in Avenal, California. next>edge

financing, the technique is also being used to finance the construction of energy-efficient improvements employed by government agencies and private companies. Structured correctly, energy-services contracts can be

securitized and achieve low cost of funds, which is likely to increase the number of such transactions that are undertaken.

Bostonia Partners LLC, a Boston-based investment bank, has pioneered the use of capital-markets financing for energy-efficient building systems. Since 2000, Bostonia has issued an estimated $400 million in energy-savings trust certificates. The program allows energy-services companies that enter into long-term contracts with creditworthy corporations or government agencies to borrow in the capital markets the upfront costs of installing energy-efficient improvements. Bostonia's financings have been put in place for a variety of borrowers, including developers, general contractors, and nonregulated subsidiaries of utilities. Among the improvements that have been financed through Bostonia's trust certificates are cogeneration facilities, chiller plants, energy-efficient HVAC systems, energy controls, and building upgrades, including energy-efficient lighting.

Many of Bostonia's transactions have involved improvements undertaken for federal agencies, including the military. The federal government is the largest single energy consumer in the United States. In an effort to reduce energy consumption at federal facilities, the National

Energy Conservation Policy Act (EPACT) and Executive Orders 12902 and 13123 require federal agencies to install and implement energy conservation measures. Under EPACT and the executive orders, federal agencies must reduce their energy consumption (as compared with 1985 levels, and on a per-square-foot basis) by 30 percent by 2005, and by 35 percent by 2010; they must also install all energy-saving measures that have a payback period of less than ten years. These requirements have led the federal government to enter into long-term contracts with energy-services companies. The trust certificates issued by Bostonia turn the payments due under the federal contract into a stream of future cash flows that can be borrowed against—or securitized—in the capital markets.

A federal contract offers a particularly low-risk source of future cash flows, but the Bostonia technique has also been used to securitize energy-services contracts with creditworthy corporations, including Boeing, General Motors, and IBM. An increasing number of corporations and industrial users are looking to energy-services companies, and in some cases building owners, to provide energy-efficient building components and "inside-the-fence" utility services on a contractual basis rather than on a capital-cost basis.

To securitize energy-savings contracts with both public and private sector organizations, the Bostonia financing is structured so

satisfaction. On the basis of available evidence, a green building is likely to command a moderate rent premium relative to submarket averages but will not exceed the market envelope. The experience of the Brewery Blocks and the Navy League Building, for example, suggests that well-located green buildings are likely to rent in the top quartile of market rents—that is, 10 to 20 percent above average rental rates for the submarket.

that repayment of the trust certificates approximates the value and sequencing of the energy savings achieved under the contract. This arrangement allows the contractor to offer "self-financing" of important upgrades and energy-efficient installations. The debt repayment schedule is based on an upfront energy audit that conservatively documents probable savings over the life of the service agreement. The amount borrowed is calculated in such a way that debt service for the securitization does not exceed the energy savings attained under the contract. The term of a particular security is therefore linked to the payback period for the energy improvements: a securitization for a lighting system would typically have a term of five to seven years, whereas financings for chillers or HVAC systems would have 15- to 20-year terms.

Bostonia structures and issues trust certificates on behalf of the energy-services company holding the contract. The debt service on the trust certificates is derived solely from the revenue stream coming from the payments due under the energy-savings agreement with the user. Hence, in structuring the financing, important elements of risk include the contractor's financial strength and ability to perform, as well as the financial strength of the user of the improvements—typically the federal government or a creditworthy private entity. The interest rate paid on the trust certificates is a function of these risk elements. Bostonia pioneered a structuring technique that efficiently isolates and mitigates these risks, thereby achieving pricing on the trust certificates that reflects the creditworthiness of the user entity, an important element when the user is a U.S. government entity or an investment-grade corporation.

Bostonia assigns the payments due under the energy-services agreement to a bank trustee and then enters into a trust agreement, pursuant to which trust certificates are issued. The debt service on the certificates is secured by all payments, revenues, and other income realized from the underlying contract, including casualty insurance; a security interest in the equipment, machinery, and fixtures installed under the energy-services contract, to the extent assignable; and any payment and performance bonds and sureties securing the obligations of the energy-services contractor to construct and install the specified improvements.

Bostonia's trust certificates are typically issued unrated and privately placed with qualified institutional buyers. Because they are private and unrated, the securities typically trade at interest rates of approximately 75 to 150 basis points above the user's own rated corporate bonds of similar maturities, and 125 to 200 basis points above U.S. Treasury securities of similar maturities for government contracts. The securities are very attractive to institutional investors looking for a safe investment that provides a yield pickup over time.

The transactions completed by Bostonia demonstrate that energy-services contracts between reputable contractors and creditworthy real estate owners can be financed in the capital markets, and that debt service on borrowings backed by these contracts can be linked to achievable energy savings associated with energy-efficient improvements. The Bostonia securitizations offer an innovative financing model by which real estate owners can enter into energy-services contracts to finance new green construction or retrofit existing buildings. The model has wide potential use in the financing of green improvements for properties owned or tenanted by federal, state, and local governments; it is also applicable to well-secured energy-services contracts with real estate investors with strong, long-term financial performance. Properties tenanted by creditworthy tenants under long-term leases may also be appropriate candidates for the Bostonia financing vehicle.

Anita Molino is principal and cofounder of Bostonia Partners LLC, a private investment bank that specializes in developing new credit instruments and creative financial solutions for corporate, real estate, and government clients.

Tenant Retention and Downtime

While longer-term research is needed, it seems probable that green buildings will ultimately result in higher levels of tenant satisfaction—which will lead, in turn, to higher levels of tenant retention, shorter downtime between leases, and lower retenanting expenses for landlords. Although these are subtle benefits of green development, they are likely to become value-added characteristics of sustainable development.

Environmental Risk

The impact of green construction on long-term project risk also is an important, if subtle, benefit. Environmental liability—whether from site conditions or from building toxicity—is a growing concern for real estate owners and lenders. Sick building syndrome—and, more recently, contamination by mold—have come to pose substantial, open-ended liability concerns. As a result, property management protocols are increasingly focused on the prevention and remediation of environmental risk. In addition, the building materials and construction industries have begun to develop products and procedures that will reduce environmental risk in commercial real estate. Green buildings, of course, are designed and constructed to minimize sources of environmental risk. As result, these properties are less likely to be a source of long-term environmental risk than are their conventional counterparts.

An environmentally sound project should be associated with a lower likelihood of risk than a conventional building on the same site. Can this element be incorporated in the traditional real estate valuation model? The answer is yes. The conventional real estate investment model incorporates a risk-measurement mechanism known as the "discount rate." The lower the discount rate, the less risky the project and the higher the project's value over the holding period. Discount rates are measured in percentage points, typically in quarter-percent (25 basis-point) increments. As can be seen in a feature box later in this chapter, "A Ten-Year Discounted Cash Flow Analysis," a reduction of the discount rate by 25 basis points on a hypothetical green property increases its value by approximately $308,000.

Effect on Current Sales Price

One method of calculating the value of a commercial real estate property considers the property's NOI in the context of a required return factor known as a "going-in" capitaliza-

tion rate ("cap rate"). The most common way to derive a cap rate is on the basis of market sales, such that

Net operating income/Sales price = Capitalization rate.

Frequently, investors make purchase offers in which pricing is pegged to a desired cap rate, as follows:

Net operating income/Desired capitalization rate = Sales price.

There is an inverse relationship between the cap rate and the sales price: as the cap rate declines, the property becomes more expensive; and as the cap rate increases, the property becomes cheaper. The reciprocal of the cap rate (for commercial real estate, the equivalent of a price/earnings ratio) acts as a multiplier for each dollar of NOI.

1/cap rate = NOI multiplier.

According to the Real Estate Research Corporation, as of winter 2004, the average U.S. capitalization rate for first-tier properties (new or newer properties with good-quality construction in good to prime locations) in central business districts was 7.9 percent. A 7.9 percent cap rate acts as a multiplier of 12.66 per dollar of NOI. The equivalent national average for suburban office properties is 8.3 percent, which indicates a multiplier of 12.05 per dollar of NOI.

Thus, the $30,000 per year energy savings realized by the Norm Thompson Building, a suburban office property, boosts NOI by $30,000 and the sales price by $361,500 [$30,000 times the 12.05 suburban office multiplier], or $6.63 per square foot [$362,500 divided by 54,000 square feet] ($71.36 per square meter).[4]

How would the sustainable nature of a project affect its cap rate? Concerns about the developer's ability to complete construction on time or within budget might increase the cap rate (make the project less valuable). On the other hand, reduction of environmental risks over time, lower operating costs, and improved leasing and tenant performance would tend to decrease the cap rate (make the project more valuable).

Effect on Future Sales Price

The effect of a sale at the conclusion of the projected holding period is also taken into account in the ten-year valuation model used by most lenders and investors. In the conventional model, the sales price is estimated by calculating NOI for year 11 and capitalizing it by a "terminal," "reversion," or "exit" cap rate—the estimated cap rate in ten years. To account for the aging of the property and for unanticipated risk, the exit cap rate is higher than the going-in cap rate. The difference between the going-in cap rate and the exit cap rate is typically determined by investor surveys assessing market conditions and perceived risk.

Net operating income, year 11/Exit cap rate = Year ten sales price.

According to the winter 2004 estimates published by Real Estate Research Corporation, the average exit cap rate for central business district office properties is 8.4 percent (for a multiplier effect of 11.9), and the average exit cap rate for suburban office properties is 8.9 percent (for a multiplier effect of 11.24). To estimate the impact of the Norm Thompson Building's $30,000 energy savings on a sale ten years hence, we would inflate the $30,000 in current savings by an expected growth rate over a ten-year period—in this case, the 2.9 percent growth rate for the long-term-expenses of suburban office properties, as estimated by Real Estate Research Corporation in winter 2004. We would then capitalize the resulting value at the 8.9 percent exit cap rate for suburban office properties:

$30,000 (year one energy savings) x (1.029)^{10} = $39,828 (year 11 addition to NOI).

$39,828 (year 11 addition to NOI) x 11.24 (multiplier) = $448,786 increase in year ten sales price.

Quantifying the Green Effect

The accompanying feature box offers a conventional real estate investment analysis for a hypothetical, 100,000-square-foot (9,290-square-meter) office building assumed to have been recently constructed in Portland, Oregon. As detailed in the feature box, the green features of the property increase its sales price at the end of a nine-year holding period by approximately 11.7 percent across a range of capitalization rates. The year nine value for an 8.75 percent exit capitalization rate (approximating the Portland-area average for Class A office properties at the time of the analysis) is $2.73 million, for a present value of $1.11 million, or $11.13 per square foot ($119.80 per square meter).

As indicated by this quantitative analysis, building green can enhance the total value of a property during the holding period and at the time of eventual sale, and these changes can be tracked by conventional valuation analysis.

The analytical model can also be used to assess the utility of any additional costs associated with building green. In the model shown in the feature box, for example, additional green construction costs of more than $20.66 per square foot ($222.38 per square meter) would be uneconomic. By contrast, additional costs of $10 per square foot ($107.63 per square meter) would have a good chance of creating value. If the property could be built green for approximately the same amount as the conventional building, the $20.66 increase in present value would go to the bottom line—a clear case for value-engineering green features.

Conclusions and Next Steps

To date, much of the debate about the investment benefits of green real estate has focused on upfront costs, and on whether green properties can be delivered to the market for the same cost as conventional construction. In fact, technology and construction expertise have improved to the point that many properties built to ENERGY STAR, LEED, or

A Ten-Year Discounted Cash Flow Analysis: A Hypothetical Green Office Building versus a Hypothetical Conventional Office Building

Steven A. Zenker and Leanne Tobias

The economic benefits of green buildings under a conventional real estate investment analysis are likely to include the following:

- Energy cost savings;
- Reduction in initial lease-up time;
- Top-tier rents;
- Enhanced tenant retention and reduced turnover;
- The potential for lower discount rate over the holding period, in reflection of lower environmental risks.

At the same time, the economic benefits of green office buildings might be reduced by (1) higher tenant improvement costs, if the owner chooses to provide all-green tenant improvements, and by (2) increased property taxes, as a result of superior market performance.

The following analysis, constructed with conventional commercial real estate modeling software, focuses on a hypothetical 100,000-square-foot (9,290-square-meter) office building assumed to have been constructed in Portland, Oregon, in early 2004. The analysis models the property both as a conventional office building and as a green property. Market conditions reflect those prevailing for Class A buildings in Portland as of the first quarter of 2004. The holding period for the property is modeled at nine years, with an assumed sale in March 2013. (For both properties, the analysis has been shortened to nine years from the typical ten, to avoid distortions resulting from lease terminations in year ten. This is a standard adjustment when five-year average lease terms are assumed, as is the case with these models.)

The assumptions of this analysis suggest that green buildings can achieve slightly enhanced rental rates, absorption schedules, and tenant retention levels relative to conventional buildings, as well as utility cost savings.

Figure 1

Effect of Green Building on Selected Factors

	Green Building	Conventional Building	Effect of Green Features (+ = favorable; − = unfavorable)
Market rent (NNN; per square foot/square meter)	$20/$215	$18/$194	+11.1%
Initial absorption	15 months	18 months	+16.7%
Lease term	5 years	5 years	0
Renewal percentage	75	65	+15%
Downtime between leases	6 months	6 months	0
Tenant improvements, first generation (per square foot/square meter)	$26/$280	$25/$269	-4%
New (per square foot/square meter)	$19/$205	$18/$194	-5.6%
Renewal (per square foot/square meter)	$6/$65	$5/$54	-20%
Utility costs (per square foot/square meter)	$0.90/$9.70	$1.30/$14.00	+31%

The analysis assumes that tenant improvements will average $1 per square foot ($10.75 per square meter) more than conventional improvements over the holding period. (See Figure 1.)

The valuation analysis tracks the differences in total present value between the hypothetical green building and the hypothetical conventional building for a range of discount rates and exit capitalization rates. The assumed discount rates range from 9.5 to 11.5 percent, and the exit capitalization rates from 8 to 10 percent. The analysis considers 25 possible combinations of discount rates and exit capitalization rates.

On average, the green property is valued at approximately $2,088,000 more than the conventional building, an increase of 14.7 percent, or $20.88 per square foot ($117.22

per square meter). Slightly over half of the difference in value—roughly $1,089,000, or $10.89 per square foot ($117.22 per square meter)—represents the present value of an increase in the eventual sale price of the building at the close of the holding period. About 48 percent of the difference—approximately $999,000, or $9.99 per square foot ($107.53 per square meter), is caused by increased revenues and reduced operating expenses over the holding period. (See Figure 2.)

The analysis also demonstrates the future value of the project's green features when the property is sold at the close of the nine-year holding period. The presumed sales price is derived from the year ten NOI, across a range of exit capitalization rates.

As shown in Figure 3, the green features of the property increase its sales price at the

Figure 2

Key Analytical Results

	Amount	Per Square Foot/ Square Meter
Total mean change in value	$2,087,695	$20.88/$117.22
Total mean change in present value, sales price	$1,088,918	$10.89/$117.22
Total mean change attributable to cash flow	$998,776	$9.99/$107.53
Percentage attributable to change in sales price	52%	
Percentage attributable to change in cash flow	48%	

Figure 3

Key Analytical Results

Exit Capitalization Rate (%)	Sales Price				Present Value (at a 10.5% Discount Rate, after Nine Years)
	Standard	Green	Difference	Change in Sales Price	
8	$25,641,492	$28,631,741	$2,990,249	11.7	$1,217,438
8.5	$24,133,169	$26,947,521	$2,814,352	11.7	$1,145,824
8.75	$23,443,649	$26,177,592	$2,733,943	11.7	$1,113,087
9	$22,792,437	$25,450,437	$2,658,000	11.7	$1,082,167
9.5	$21,592,835	$24,110,940	$2,518,105	11.7	$1,025,211
10	$20,513,193	$22,905,393	$2,392,200	11.7	$973,951
Mean change			$2,684,475	11.7	$1,092,946

Of course, the final value of the two hypothetical properties should reflect market conditions as of the valuation date. As of April 1, 2004, Class A properties in Portland commanded a discount rate of 10.5 percent and an exit cap rate of roughly 8.75 percent. Under these market conditions, the hypothetical green property is valued at $16,465,000, approximately $2.1 million (14.7 percent) above the $14,356,000 value of the hypothetical conventional property. A 25-basis-point reduction in end of a nine-year holding period by 11.7 percent across a range of capitalization rates. The average increase in sales price in year nine is roughly $2,684,000, or $26.84 per square foot ($288.90 per square meter). This equates to an enhanced present value for the green property of approximately $1,093,000, assuming a 10.5 percent discount rate.

Finally, the analysis can be further adjusted to consider any impact that might be derived from the reduced long-term environmental risks associated with an environmentally sound building. Over the holding period, a 25-basis-point reduction in the discount rate for the green building would increase its value relative to the conventional property by approximately $300,000, or $3 per square foot ($32.29 per square meter). This adjustment raises the valuation of the green property by approximately $2.39 million, or $23.90 per square foot ($257.25 per square meter), which is 16.8 percent higher than the value of the conventional building.

the discount rate to reflect lessened environmental risk across the holding period would increase the valuation of the green property by an additional $308,000, resulting in a $2.4 million, or 16.8 percent, valuation premium relative to the conventional property.

Steven A. Zenker is senior managing director, Valuation Advisory Services, Cushman & Wakefield, Portland, Oregon. He has been involved in the appraisal industry since 1986.

Silver LEED standards can be delivered for costs equivalent to those for conventional construction. An exclusive focus on upfront costs, moreover, fails to consider the important value-creating characteristics that appear to be associated with sustainable real estate. Perhaps it is time to consider green real estate in the more robust valuation context provided by the conventional real estate financing model.

The Benefits of the Conventional Real Estate Financing Model

The conventional real estate investment model suggests that green projects may represent high-value opportunities by enabling investors to develop or acquire properties with top-tier rents, shorter times for initial lease-up, lower energy costs, and better tenant-retention records. The examples in this chapter suggest that a subset of tenants will seek out a green building and that others will be attracted to the building on the basis of lower utility costs or because green features are perceived as contributing to the building's quality. In addition, green design features are likely to reduce environmental risks over the holding period. These factors should translate into higher investment values and lower risks for potential owners and lenders. These benefits, which are tracked effectively by conventional real estate valuation techniques, continue throughout the initial life cycle of the property, typically assumed to be ten years for underwriting purposes.

The traditional real estate valuation model can also give potential owners, investors, developers, and designers a quantitative means of determining whether the value creation associated with a proposed green project will offset the additional costs associated with green features, either in the base building design or in the tenant improvements.

Finally, the consideration of green real estate projects within the context of the conventional investment model will likely increase interest, on the part of developers,

lenders, and investors, in sustainable design and construction. And these players will, of course, play a key role in mainstreaming sustainable real estate, particularly in the speculative market for commercial real estate.

Investor Expectations

The expectations of investors also make a difference: especially if the project is speculative, institutional owners typically require a market return, which mandates that building costs remain within the envelope established by conventional projects. Noninstitutional owners willing to forgo initial return in order to construct a property to the LEED Gold or Platinum standard may be more tolerant of higher construction costs. Block 2 of the Brewery Blocks, for example, was built to the LEED Silver standard for an institutional owner: costs were held to the market standard, and tenant improvement allowances were strictly market based. Other phases of the Brewery Blocks project are owned by Portland-based private investors who were willing to finance LEED Gold costs, which exceed market standards.

Public Incentives

Public incentives, of course, can play a significant role in offsetting the additional costs associated with building green. The Navy League Building, in Arlington, Virginia, for example, was rendered economically viable because an Arlington County incentive program allowed additional square footage. Tax-credit programs to offset initial development costs have been enacted in a variety of state and local jurisdictions (the New York State and Oregon programs were described earlier in this chapter). To encourage the construction of green buildings, public officials should consider the following:

■ The most effective incentives will improve project financial performance across all or a substantial portion of the property's initial life cycle.

■ Unused incentives should be transferable upon the sale of the property.

■ Tax-credit programs can be used to reduce the upfront development costs of green construction. Such tax credits are the most frequently available source of green building incentives. Local jurisdictions interested in encouraging green development might also wish to consider abatement of local property taxes. It should be noted, however, that the financial benefits associated with tax-credit and property tax abatement programs are reduced over the life of the incentive.

■ Incentives that affect the revenue side of a real estate project are often more potent than expense-side incentives, especially if the benefit continues throughout the project's life cycle. The Arlington County density bonus is a good example of an effective incentive approach.

Build-to-Suit Lease Financing

A tenant interested in developing a new green office building for its own use can help a developer to acquire construction or permanent financing for the project through the mechanism of lease financing. A build-to-suit lease must have the following characteristics:

■ Strong tenant credit.

■ An appropriate lease term. (Seven years is the usual minimum, and ten or more years are preferred.)

■ Rental payments that are sufficient (1) to pay for the construction of the base building and all tenant improvements and (2) to provide investors with an appropriate market return. Lenders typically prefer triple-net leases with rent increases over the lease term.

Lease financing can be used to back a project with more than one credit tenant, although a single-tenant build-to-suit is more common.

Speculative Leasing of Green Properties

The examples considered in this chapter suggest that green real estate projects are greeted positively by tenants as especially high-quality properties that deliver tenant savings on utility costs and enhance tenant well-being over the lease term. Green buildings that are leased on a base-year expense-stop or triple-net basis produce tenant savings on utility expenses. In addition, the examples suggest that green buildings:

■ Lease somewhat faster than competing conventional properties;

■ Command rental rates at the top tier of the market range;

■ May encourage tenant retention and reduce downtime between leases.

At the same time, green tenant improvements may be more expensive than conventional improvements, especially for retail tenants. As a result, it may be necessary to offer a tenant improvement allowance that exceeds market standard, or to take other actions that might help tenants get more for their money on a standard allowance. In conventional real estate projects, the offer of an above-standard tenant improvement allowance is typically used to negotiate a higher rental rate over the lease term. It remains to be seen whether this is possible in the case of green tenant improvements.

Budget-stretching options for green improvements to be built under a standard allowance might include the following:

■ Providing tenants with the services of an environmental consultant, as well as those of an architect or space-planning expert in green building practices. (Space-planning services are typically provided to tenants in institutional properties at the expense of the owner.)

■ Identifying appropriate contractors for tenant spaces and, if possible, negotiating favorable rates for tenant buildouts. (Institutional owners frequently retain their own contractors and manage the construction of tenant improvements in order to reduce buildout costs and ensure quality. These tactics would appear to be especially appropriate in green buildings.)

■ Procuring bulk discounts for green products used in finishing tenant spaces, including paint, carpet, and lighting.

■ Offering tenants information on green specifications and on vendors who are qualified to meet these specifications.

With the possible exception of potentially heightened costs for tenant improvements, the characteristics associated with green buildings would be expected to translate into heightened investment value for developers, owners, and lenders. These attributes can be readily quantified by the conventional real estate investment model. In addition, green buildings are less likely to be sources of environmental risk, a factor that should also be reflected positively under conventional real estate financial models.

While more evidence is needed to build a definitive case, there is good reason to suspect that green real estate is also high-value real estate.

Next Steps

More research is needed to identify and track the effectiveness of public incentives related to sustainable development, especially incentives that enhance project revenues. A key research priority is the development of a database of green building comparables that can be used to track cost and performance relative to conventional Class A projects. A study comparing the lease-up and financial performance of green projects, versus an appropriate control group, would help to document the financial costs and benefits of building green. A study conducted in the context of the conventional real estate valuation model would be particularly helpful in determining more definitively whether the high-performance characteristics of green real estate translate into higher real estate values for developers and investors.

Sustainable-design professionals and public officials engaged in sustainability efforts should be educated in the valuation implications of green design to facilitate more effective and informed conversations with developers and investors about potential projects. At the same time, developers, equity owners, and lenders should be educated more fully about sustainable construction techniques, given information about which techniques can be delivered at competitive costs, and encouraged to think about how the use of green construction techniques can affect the value of a project over its life cycle.

The Plaza at PPL Center achieved LEED Gold certification with a cost premium of less than 1 percent. When the facility opened, in May 2003, 85 percent of the space had already been leased to PPL EnergyPlus, providing an initial development yield of 11 percent on the development cost of $60.68 million. Peter Aaron-Esto/Liberty Property Trust

Notes

1. Donald Moses, telephone interview with author, March 25, 2004.

2. Ibid.

3. Howard Siegel, E-mail to author, March 23, 2004.

4. $30,000 x 12.05 (the national average multiplier for suburban office properties) = $361,500. $361,500/54,500 square feet = $6.63 per square foot.

chapter 8

U.S. Federal Government

Green Policies and Programs of the U.S. Federal Government

Ann Moline

In the 1960s, as part of a larger awakening that inspired activism on a range of fronts, from women's liberation to the antiwar movement, concern about the environment greatly increased in the United States. Environmentally friendly building construction and management became part of the federal mandate in 1969, at the height of this wave. The National Environmental Policy Act of 1969 (NEPA) dictated that federal agencies must consider the environmental impacts of all their activities. Thus, for over 30 years, all federal departments—including those, such as the Department of Justice, with no apparent link to real estate or construction—have faced requirements to "green" their facilities. As agencies translate policy into practice, they have developed programs and initiatives that are applicable not only in the federal realm but in the commercial construction sector as well.

The new California EPA Headquarters, in Sacramento, features innovative air handling, strategic window placement, and recycling systems, resulting in significant energy savings and easily surpassing the state's stringent energy codes. AC Martin Partners, Inc./David C. Martin, FAIA/David Wakely

Commercial developers can learn a great deal from the greening of federal buildings. Because the government has taken a lead role in incorporating sustainable building into the construction of new facilities, and has been at it for some time now, federal agencies have developed a strong understanding of what works and what does *not* work—the result of firsthand and sometimes embarrassing experience.

Today, any new General Services Administration (GSA) facility that is built must obtain LEED certification. As of mid-2004, 50 GSA buildings were in the process of obtaining LEED certification,[1] and five completed federal projects had received a LEED rating:

■ The building renovations at the Social Security Administration complex in Woodlawn, Maryland;

■ The Social Security Administration child care facility in Woodlawn, Maryland;

■ The Nathaniel R. Jones Federal Building and U.S. Courthouse in Youngstown, Ohio;

■ EPA's New England Regional Laboratory in Chelmsford, Massachusetts; and

■ The EPA Science and Technology Center in Kansas City, Kansas.

Guidelines for facilities that are built and operated by commercial developers for federal tenants are not always as stringent. Owners of new buildings that are leased are encouraged, but not required, to have a LEED rating; however, this standard could change soon. According to Donald Horn, of GSA's Public Buildings Service, "We are pushing these projects to be LEED certified as well. As we update our facilities standards, we want to say that all projects

Lessons Learned

Ann Moline

When the flagship headquarters building of EPA, the nation's new environmental watchdog group, was constructed in the 1970s, it was heralded for its innovative approach to energy efficiency and environmentally responsible construction. Unfortunately, the building also made its workers sick.

By 1993, when employees brought a lawsuit against EPA, an estimated 40 percent of the building's staff had suffered from a variety of symptoms ranging from the mild (headaches) to the severe (dizziness, nausea, coughing, fever, chills).[1] Investigators determined that the building itself was the cause of the widespread illness. It was one of the first, and most well publicized, cases of sick building syndrome (SBS).

The designers had planned the building with few windows and little exposure to daylight, which was seen at the time as a means of reducing energy costs and consumption—an environmentally responsive approach. But with poor ventilation, no natural light, and not enough fresh air circulating, people began to complain of flulike symptoms. Dampness set in. Mold grew. Fumes from copiers placed in unventilated areas collected, with no place to go. An extensive renovation in 1987 made the situation worse: workers inhaled chemicals from paint and new carpet, and the overloaded HVAC system could not effectively circulate clean air to replace stale air. The jury awarded $1 million to the plaintiffs in the case; EPA spent approximately $4 million on subsequent renovations to repair the building.[2]

Of course, incorporating sustainability into design is more than just as a means of avoiding legal action. A number of federal buildings now coming online have successfully implemented a holistic approach to sustainability, focusing on reductions in overall life-cycle costs and improved employee productivity. These projects can serve as models for the private commercial sector. In addition, federal research, programs, products, and practical guidelines offer a comprehensive tool kit for developers who want to incorporate green concepts in their own building projects.

The dramatic new 605,000-square-foot (56,200-square-meter) San Francisco Federal Office Building is definitely not a faceless government building. The soaring, 18-story glass-and-perforated-steel tower features innovative energy-efficient design solutions that will save an estimated $500,000 a year—a 45 percent cost reduction. A unique window design allows workers to open and close windows even if they are on the 18th floor, a feature that should help prevent SBS and contribute to increased employee productivity and satisfaction.[3] According to an interview with Nick Nolte, GSA project manager, in *California Construction* magazine, although the installation of alternative cooling systems added 5 percent to the cost of the building, the $11 million in savings achieved by not installing air conditioning in the tower, coupled with anticipated energy savings, should more than make up for the minor cost increase.[4] The building also features an earthquake-resistant design, which was required because of its location. To determine the structural requirements, the engineers used a complex analytical model known as "pushover analysis"—and saved approximately $6 million in construction costs.

Located in a downtown area that had seen its share of deterioration, the building will catalyze redevelopment in the district—another aspect of an integrated approach to sustain-

The GSA expects the San Francisco Federal Office Building's creative energy-efficient design to save 50 percent of the energy used in a traditional office building of similar size and the ample daylight and natural ventilation will promote a healthy, happy, and productive staff. Morphosis

ability. To encourage the use of mass transit, employees will receive commuter subsidies.

Notes

1. David Steinman, "The Architecture of Illness: Millions of Workers are Sick of Work," available at http://www.environmentalhealth.ca/fall93sick.html.
2. California Waste Management Board, training manual, available at http://www.ciwmb.ca.gov/GreenBuilding/Training/StateManual/IAQ.doc.
3. See http://www.arup.com/newsitem.cfm?pageid=970.
4. See http://www.californiaconstruction.com, February 2004.

should be LEED certified." Nevertheless, the process of strengthening requirements for facilities that are leased for use by federal tenants must be balanced by what the market will bear. As Horn notes, "We have heard from some communities that developers don't want to lease to the government because there is so much red tape associated with these federal requirements. We have concerns about this."

Even when a federal agency is leasing a few floors, the government provides guidance for the lessors to ensure that sustainability has been addressed to the extent possible. "We have greened our solicitation for offers when leasing just a couple of floors in a new building," Horn notes. For example, a building owner will have to show a plan for construction-waste management, for recycling, and for the improvement of energy efficiency. In addition, the government encourages the use of environmentally preferable materials, such as ceiling tile that contains recycled content.

Governmentwide Green Building Policies

The U.S. government's commitment to environmentally responsible building and construction precedes the enactment of NEPA 1969 by more than 50 years. President Theodore Roosevelt addressed the American people in 1910: "I recognize the right and duty of this generation to develop and use the natural resources of our land; but I do not recognize the right to waste them, or to rob, by wasteful use, the generations that come after us."[2]

But as the first law enacted, NEPA laid the groundwork for federal agencies to consider the environmental impacts of their actions and decisions. Under the law, federal agencies must systematically assess the environmental impacts of proposed actions and consider alternative ways of accomplishing their missions in ways that are less damaging to the environment. Multidisciplinary identification and analysis of impacts are also required.[3] Other, more specific regulation followed. And as federal agencies began to understand the implications of the law, they began to assign priority to

environmental responsibility and to demand products, programs, guidelines, and standards that would help them direct their efforts.

Much innovation has emerged from the agencies' own needs to be accountable on the environmental front. For example, the ENERGY STAR label, which symbolizes the achievement of energy efficiencies in construction, is widely accepted in the public, commercial, and residential building sectors. More than 116 federal buildings have received this certification.[4]

However, even today, in the absence of a single standard, there are different interpretations of how to apply sustainable design principles to federal projects. But change—in the form of standardization—may be on the horizon. As part of an undertaking called the *Whole Building Design Guide*, a group of agencies have developed the "Federal Guide for Green Construction Specs," which is designed to help building-project managers meet various mandates established by statute and executive order, as well as EPA and Department of Energy (DOE) program recommendations.[5] Organized according to the MasterFormat of the Construction Specifications Institute, the guide will provide users with multiple, performance-based options, allowing for flexibility in the application of requirements.[6] The guide also includes model language to assist federal agencies in using the LEED rating system as a standard of measurement.

GSA plays a hands-on, project-management role in the development and implementation of federal guidelines for green building. The Office of the Federal Environmental Executive (OFEE), which operates independently of GSA, is another resource for federal environmental regulations, and acts as a clearinghouse for agencies attempting to understand the sometimes confusing array of requirements.

As understanding has increased and standards have become more defined, guidance on greening federal facilities has evolved. Whereas earlier legislation mandated a

The Social Security Administration child care center in Woodlawn, Maryland, reclaimed an existing parking lot, restored over 50 percent of the site as vegetated space, and promotes the use of both alternative and public transportation: the center is within a quarter mile (0.4 kilometer) of at least two bus stops, and there are numerous bicycle racks on the campus. GSA

general commitment to environmentally responsible practices, later regulations detailed, in far more specific ways, how this general theory should be put into practice.

The Resource Conservation and Recovery Act (RCRA) was passed in 1976 and amended in 1984. Section 6002 of RCRA requires federal agencies to give preference in their procurement to the purchase of products specially designated by EPA. EPA designates products that are or can be made with recycled materials, and also recommends ranges of recycled-materials content for these products. Designated construction products include building insulation; carpeting; carpet cushions; cement and concrete containing coal fly ash or ground, granulated blast-furnace slag; consolidated and reprocessed latex paint; floor tiles; flowable fill; laminated paperboard; patio blocks; railroad grade crossing surfaces; shower and restroom dividers or partitions; and structural fiberboard.

The Pollution Prevention Act of 1990 established a national policy to prevent pollution whenever feasible. Pollution that cannot be prevented should be recycled; pollution that cannot be prevented or recycled should be treated in an environmentally responsible manner. Disposal should be employed only as a last resort.

The Energy Policy Act (EPAct) of 1992, along with amendments to the National Energy Conservation Policy Act, forms the statutory basis for federal energy and water conservation. Subtitle F of EPAct orders federal agencies to reduce their per-square-foot energy consumption, to install energy- and water-conservation features, to track energy and water consumption, and to institute systems to facilitate the funding of energy-efficiency improvements.

Executive Order 13101 (1998), "Greening the Government through Waste Prevention, Recycling, and Federal Acquisition," strengthens and expands the federal government's commitment to recycling and waste prevention by promoting the increased use of green products, particularly recycled-content, environmentally preferable, and biobased products. The Environmentally Preferable Purchasing (EPP) Program, managed by EPA, promotes federal procurement of products and services that have reduced impacts on human health and the environment over their life cycle. The goal of the program is to make environmental performance—in addition to performance and cost—a factor in federal purchasing decisions.

Executive Order 13123 (1999), "Greening the Government through Efficient Energy Management," increased and broadened energy-efficiency goals by requiring each agency to reduce energy consumption (per square foot, and as compared with 1985 levels) by 30 percent by 2005 and by 35 percent by 2010. It also requires agencies to

■ Reduce greenhouse gas emissions related to energy use at federal facilities by 30 percent by 2010 (from the 1990 baseline);

■ Expand the use of renewable energy;

■ Optimize life-cycle costs, pollution costs, and other environmental and energy costs associated with the construction, life-cycle operation, and decommissioning of facilities;

■ Apply sustainable design principles to the siting, design, and construction of new facilities;

■ Incorporate energy-efficiency criteria consistent with ENERGY STAR and other energy-efficiency levels designated by the Federal Energy Management Program (that is, criteria that correspond to the top 25th percentile of efficiency), into specifications for new construction and renovation; and

■ Consider using energy savings performance contracts (ESPCs) or utility energy-efficiency service contracts (UESCs) to aid in the construction of sustainably designed buildings.[7]

Executive Order 13148 (2000), "Greening the Government through Leadership in Environmental Management," established a framework for integrating environmental considerations into the mission of each federal agency; this goal involves implementing environmental management systems (EMSs), reducing releases of toxic chemicals, and eliminating the procurement of ozone-depleting substances. GSA has taken the lead on developing EMSs, which must be implemented at designated federal facilities by the end of 2005. Designation is based on a facility's size, complexity, and environmental characteristics. Management-system accounting concepts such as life-cycle assessment, environmental cost accounting, and return on investment are also supported by the order. Agencies must have a program in place to periodically audit compliance with environmental regulations.

Executive Order 13134 (1999), "Developing and Promoting Biobased Products and Energy," expands federal procurement requirements related to biobased products and services. Biobased products are made from renewable agricultural, animal, or forestry materials, and include vegetable-based lubricants, biofuels, compost, and biobased construction materials. The executive order set a goal of tripling the U.S. government use of bioenergy and biobased products by 2010.

Title IX of the Farm Security and Rural Investment Act of 2002 (commonly referred to as the 2002 Farm Bill) requires the U.S. Department of Agriculture (USDA) to establish a designation and purchasing program for biobased products much like the one that RCRA established for recycled products. Once the USDA designates a biobased product, federal agencies that purchase the product must give preference to the product that contains the highest level of biobased content practicable, taking into account price, performance, and availability. The USDA is also required to develop a voluntary labeling program for USDA-certified biobased products. Biobased construction products are among those under consideration for designation by the USDA.

Section 55, "Energy and Transportation Efficiency Management," a 2002 revision to the Office of Management and Budget Circular A-11, encourages federal agencies to incorporate ENERGY STAR or LEED standards into initial design concepts for new construction or building renovations. Agencies must file reports if they incur or anticipate incurring additional costs for incorporating these standards.[8]

The General Services Administration

Federal agencies are not always the owners of record of the facilities in which they are housed; GSA builds, owns, and manages most of the civilian federal facilities in operation today. All told, GSA manages 330 million square feet (35 million square meters) of workspace in 2,000 American communities. Approximately 55 percent of the agency's total inventory—1,600 facilities—are government-owned buildings. The remaining 45 percent are privately owned facilities leased by the government, with GSA as the signatory.[9] Thus, GSA has a primary role in implementing environmentally sustainable building practices as it maintains and renovates existing structures and brings new ones online.

For example, the agency played a lead role in an initiative to green the White House, which began during the administration of President Bill Clinton. In announcing the initiative on Earth Day, 1993, President Clinton said,

We're going to identify what it takes to make the White House a model for efficiency and waste reduction, and then we're going to get the job done. I want to make the White House a model for other federal agencies, for state and local governments, for business, and for families in their homes. Before I ask you to do the best you can in your house, I ought to make sure I'm doing the best I can in my house.[10]

A floor-by-floor HVAC system in the California EPA Head-quarters provides at least two air intakes per floor. Fan rooms in the northeast and northwest corners eliminate the possibility of cross-contamination, and the building is flushed with outside air during the night. AC Martin Partners, Inc./David C. Martin, FAIA/David Wakely

Since then, according to a report issued by the DOE, greening measures such as roof and HVAC replacement, pipe insulation, and daylighting have resulted in $1.4 million in total savings at the White House.[11]

In addition to acting as the chief consumer of federal environmental programs and initiatives, GSA establishes green standards for all new federal buildings. Other agencies, though not bound by these standards, make use of GSA guidance. GSA is also the agency that secures contracts with all vendors participating in a construction project. As a result, the agency has become a sort of one-stop shopping source for environmental products and services to be used in construction projects. Through GSA's Real Property Office, a part of the Office of Governmentwide

Policy, several framework documents have been created, most notably the *Real Property Sustainable Development Guide*, which addresses the following topics:

- The business case for sustainability;
- Paying for sustainability;
- Implementing sustainability;
- Design tools;
- Environmental audits; and
- Improving the bottom line.[12]

The Public Buildings Service

GSA's Public Buildings Service (PBS) is the agency that has hands-on responsibility for facilities; in essence, it is the landlord for federal agencies. Once an agency identifies a facilities need, PBS evaluates the various options that any commercial enterprise must consider as well: Expand and renovate in place? Build new? Lease existing space? Lease new space? If a decision to build is made, PBS is a part of the new facility's entire life cycle: it determines the parameters and budget of the project, hires the architect and the general contractor, appoints a GSA project manager, manages the completed facility, and decides on a decommissioning strategy should one be necessary.

In addition to its central responsibility for property management, PBS handles all aspects of environmental management. Its Office of Applied Science undertakes research on sustainability, develops practical applications for the research, creates sustainability standards, and promotes sustainable design principles, including the following: optimizing site potential; minimizing the consumption of nonrenewable energy; using environmentally preferable products; protecting and conserving water; enhancing indoor environmental quality; and optimizing operational and maintenance practices. The goal is to reduce negative impacts on the environment and on the health of occupants without compromising the bottom line.[13]

To help project managers and federal facilities contractors understand the requirements for green design and construction, the office has developed resources on architecture and engineering, design and construction delivery, and greening existing buildings. Through the Office of Applied Science, those involved in the siting, development, and construction of federal facilities have access to a wide range of information and general construction guidelines.

Among the areas of concern of the Office of Applied Science are the following:
■ Workplace initiatives, such as WorkPlace 20•20, a new approach to building design and management that focuses on finding ways to make the facility *work for* an organization, instead of acting only as a physical container. In the WorkPlace 20•20 approach, the full needs of the organization are taken into account, and the workplace is viewed as a means of enabling work to occur.[14]

Organization of the Public Buildings Service

Public Buildings Service

Office of Real Property Asset Management
■ Asset management
■ Build or lease decisions
■ Asset disposal

Office of National Customer Service Management
■ Surveys and analysis
■ Leasing group

Office of the Chief Architect
■ Project management
■ Design
■ Construction
■ Engineering

Office of Organizational Resources
■ Supplier relationships
■ New products and services

Office of the Chief Financial Officer
■ Performance measures

Office of Applied Science
■ Environmental strategy

Note: At the time of publication, PBS was undergoing a reorganization; the reorganization is reflected in the figure.

■ Sustainability standards, such as the Sustainable Design Program, which uses the LEED rating system to ensure that all new federal buildings under GSA purview meet environmental standards.
■ Environmental management, including work on the comprehensive EMS to be rolled out across GSA.
■ Compliance with environmental legislation, such as NEPA.

The EPA Science and Technology Center, Kansas City

The EPA Science and Technology Center, in Kansas City, one of five new federal buildings to achieve a LEED rating, is owned by a private developer, CB Richard Ellis. The commercial developer won the design-build contract on the 72,000-square-foot (6,690-square-meter) build-to-suit facility. The EPA/GSA project management team wrote green language into the specs for the building, which opened in the spring of 2003.

The LEED 2.0 Gold facility, constructed on a brownfield redevelopment site with

Developed on a former brownfield site, the EPA Science and Technology Center, in Kansas City, was constructed to preserve natural resources, protect occupants' health, and serve as a sustainable model for future laboratory design.
Stephen Swalwell, Architectural Fotographics

easy access to public transportation, incorporates daylighting, low-flow plumbing fixtures, and wood products from certified sustainable sources. A unique rooftop rainwater-recovery system captures and filters rainwater for use in flushing toilets; it cuts the use of treated water by approximately 50 percent and reduces site runoff by 40 percent. Since the rainwater-recovery system collects more water than is needed for the toilets, the excess is used in the building's cooling towers. According to LEED docu-

mentation, this unique system saves 735,000 gallons (2.8 million liters) per year.

The solicitation for offers included language to ensure that the facility and all its construction features would promote energy efficiency and environmentally preferable materials and design. The document, called the Kansas City Science and Technology Center Green Lease Rider, encouraged contractors to address energy and water conservation and other environmental factors.

The details of the Kansas City Science and Technology Center Green Lease Rider are as follows:

Energy Efficiency
- Consideration of building siting
- Passive-solar design approaches
- Energy-efficient lighting
- Daylighting
- Energy-efficient building-shell design
- Low-e glass
- Efficient mechanical systems
- Recapture of waste energy streams
- Renewable/innovative energy sources
- Technologically advanced building and mechanical control systems
- Energy modeling conducted upon completion of design to identify additional conservation options

Water Conservation
- Low-flow plumbing fixtures
- Water-efficient mechanical systems
- Landscape design using native species
- Minimal water for irrigation
- Building site that considers water use, retention, and reuse

Resource Conservation
- Use of materials with recycled content at or above average recycled-content percent-

ages according to LEED
- Use of materials that are manufactured, packaged, or transported in a way that reduces energy or material expenditures
- Construction-period recycling and waste minimization
- Designing, building, and operating the building to accommodate EPA's active recycling program

Protection of the Ozone Layer
- Avoidance of chlorofluorocarbons as refrigerants
- Avoidance of blowing agents for insulation

Support of Sustainable Forestry Practices
- No consumptive use of endangered rainforest species
- Wood products from certified sustainable sources

Protection of Human Health
- Use of nonleaded paints
- Provision of plumbing systems that prevent elevated lead levels in water

Indoor Air Quality
- Careful placement of exhaust and air intakes to prevent cross-contamination
- Consideration regarding radon in the building
- Protection of the heating and cooling system during construction
- Use of low-VOC adhesives, paints, sealants, and caulks
- Construction-period installation sequencing
- Sensitive janitorial and cleaning approaches during the building's operating life
- No use of asbestos or materials containing asbestos

Source: Adapted from "A Case Study of the Kansas City Science and Technology Center," http://www.epa.gov/greeningepa/content/kc_brochure.pdf.

■ The development of risk indices.

■ Liability issues associated with toxic substances such as radon, asbestos, and lead.

According to GSA's Donald Horn, who works with GSA's sustainable-design programs in the Office of Applied Science, the agency's goal is to seamlessly incorporate green building principles as it designs, contracts for, and builds new buildings, and maintains older ones. The ideal is to achieve an optimal balance of cost and environmental and human benefits while meeting the mission and function of the intended facility. According to Horn, "GSA aims to incorporate sustainable design across all processes and functions—to build and maintain high-quality workplaces so that federal workers are healthy and productive."

Is the agency willing to sacrifice lowest cost for long-term value? "There is the perception that building green costs more," Horn acknowledges. But that is not necessarily the case, particularly when operating-cost savings, such as lower energy costs brought about by greater efficiency, are factored in. "Of course cost is one of our number-one concerns, but we believe that incorporating sustainable design is important not just to meet required LEED standards, but to enhance the long-term value of the facility," he notes.

Green Tools

GSA produces a number of print publications and Web-based reports that provide practical guidelines for developers who want to be a part of a federal building project. (Additional resources from a number of federal agencies are listed in the resource list at the back of this book.)

Facilities Standards for the Public Buildings Service is PBS's general compendium of rules, requirements, and regulations related to federal building construction. The 2003 edition contains new information on the incorporation of sustainable building practices; for example, the chapter dealing with mechanical engineering now details ways to increase the energy efficiency of a facility.[15] The chapter on site design notes that "the site design . . . should, wherever possible, make a positive contribution to the surrounding urban, suburban or rural landscape in terms of conservation, community design and improvement efforts, local economic development and planning, and environmentally responsible practices."[16]

The *Environmental Products and Services Guide*, an annually updated resource published by GSA's Federal Supply Service, is used by all federal agencies. This publication offers detailed procurement guidelines and lists vendors whose products and services meet federal green guidelines and regulations. The guide includes the following sections: "Comprehensive Procurement Guideline Products and Other Recycled Products"; "ENERGY STAR Products and Other Energy-Efficient Products"; "Safer Paints, Cleaning, and Other Chemical Products"; "Environmental Services"; and "Energy Services." GSA has also begun to introduce biobased products to its offerings.[17]

As noted earlier, GSA is part of a multiagency effort to create the *Whole Building Design Guide*, a comprehensive, Internet-based gateway to a wide range of private sector and federal resources on sustainable development that will include information on design criteria and building types, products, and systems.[18]

The Environmental Protection Agency

EPA's entire mission relates to the preservation of natural resources and the protection of the environment. Congress established the agency in 1970 in response to the growing public demand for cleaner water, air, and land.

The National Computer Center: Transforming Sustainability into Savings

Kimberly T. Nelson

Through its National Computer Center, within EPA's new laboratory complex in Research Triangle Park, North Carolina, EPA recently demonstrated an innovative and cost-effective approach to environmentally friendly design and construction. This project successfully incorporates EPA's green purchasing goals, as established under Executive Order 13101. By incorporating green building construction and landscaping practices, EPA has ensured that its own activities mirror what the agency is encouraging others to do. To obtain official endorsement of its sustainability efforts, EPA has applied for a LEED Silver rating.

The National Computer Center, one component of EPA's new laboratory complex in Research Triangle Park, takes an innovative and cost-effective approach to environmentally friendly design and construction. © Alan Karchmer

The Computer Center is one component of EPA's new campus (the agency's largest construction project to date), a collection of several high-tech research and development facilities totaling approximately 1.2 million square feet (111,500 square meters) and

costing $273 million. In addition to setting a benchmark for green computer facilities, the center also dispels the myth held among those in the design-build community that green buildings are more expensive than traditional buildings.

Building Green without Spending Green

Excluding design, construction management, and energy-grant funds used for the purchase and installation of the facility's photovoltaic roof, the center's construction cost was about $18 million. After deducting the cost of site work and utility infrastructure development, the facility cost approximately $150 per square foot—a typical cost for a comparable supercomputer facility without green features.

Reduced Environmental Footprint

The Computer Center was designed and constructed to use approximately 40 percent less energy than a typical, code-compliant computing and office facility. Atop the center rests a 100-kilowatt photovoltaic roof made up of 2,185 tiles. The solar technology, manufactured by Power Light Corporation, of Berkeley, California, provides enough energy to handle the center's lighting load, while producing zero pollution. The solar roof is one of the largest in the eastern United States, covering more than 15,000 square feet (1,390 square meters). In addition, 70 photovoltaic streetlights line the campus's roads, forming the

longest stretch of solar-energy-powered illuminated roadway in the United States. Combined, these two systems prevent roughly 100 tons of greenhouse gas and air-polluting emissions every year when compared with conventional energy production through the burning of fossil fuels.

To further reduce energy use, the facility incorporates Green Lights practices, which are part of EPA's ENERGY STAR program. High-efficiency fluorescent lighting is used throughout the building, and motion sensors mounted on the ceiling turn lights off when an area is vacant. Sensors automatically dim the lights according to the amount of natural daylight present in a room, and manual switching allows office occupants to override the sensors and select a lower lighting level if desired. These features combined yield a savings of 70 percent on electricity use for lighting, when compared with the energy consumption at a conventional facility.

Much thought went into planning the building's site orientation, a factor that plays a significant role in determining the amount of solar gain that the interior of the building receives. The broadest face of the center lobby faces south, which helps moderate seasonal fluctuations in solar radiation. This orientation, coupled with heat-absorbing floor tiles (which reemit the radiation that is absorbed), enables the facility to harvest "free heating" in the winter. Deep-set windows help to gather and project abundant daylight deep into office areas. No workspace is more than a few steps away from natural daylight, providing a healthy and productive working environment for all employees.

The roof is covered with a highly reflective reinforced thermoplastic polyolefin membrane, which greatly reduces the amount of solar heat absorbed and transmitted into the building—and thus decreases the amount of energy required to maintain the building's temperature. In addition, the windows feature argon-filled low-e glass, which allows beneficial, visible light to pass through the glass while increasing the thermal efficiency of the window. To further reduce the amount of solar heat gain, deep concrete ledges overhang many of the windows. These measures reduce overall cooling costs during the hot summer months.

High-efficiency heating and cooling systems can save a significant amount of energy. At the Computer Center, variable-speed motors, fans, and pumps reduce waste by meeting only the actual energy demands. Outside-air economizers help reduce energy costs by bringing in outside air when the temperature and humidity meet acceptable levels. These systems operate in tandem with a digitally controlled building automation system (BAS). The BAS monitors and controls various aspects of the building, including temperature, pressure, humidity, electrical systems, computer-room cooling units, cooling and heating equipment, maintenance indicators, lighting, and security. To further reduce waste and increase energy efficiency, electronic sensors throughout the facility communicate to the BAS when temperature, humidity, fresh-air ventilation rates, and other environmental conditions need to be adjusted.

Water Conservation and Waste Reduction

The Computer Center and its surrounding landscape were designed to maximize water conservation. Water-efficient features incorporated throughout the facility include flow-restricting nozzles, automated shutoff, and automatic temperature controls. The bath-

rooms are outfitted with sensor-operated, metered faucets, which save water and the energy required to heat it.

In accordance with the green landscaping goals articulated in Executive Order 13101, the landscape incorporates native and adapted species of noninvasive plants. As a result, there are no water sprinklers on the entire campus, as watering is not necessary.

EPA required recycled content in all major building materials. The center's recycled-content carpet is part of a "closed-loop" program in which carpet is designed to be used to manufacture new products at the end of its useful life. Meeting the requirements for the commercially available recycled content specified in the building contract added no extra costs.

Indoor Air

The contractors took measures to ensure safe IAQ, both during construction and once the building was inhabited. Before construction got underway, EPA specified maximum emission levels for VOCs, formaldehyde, and other contaminants in all major building materials. The carpet was installed using low-VOC adhesive. To protect the safety of current and future employees, construction was planned to ensure constant ventilation throughout the construction process. EPA arranged for sequential installation of finish materials, so that off-gassing materials, such as paints and adhesives, could dry before absorbing materials, such as carpet and ceiling tiles, were installed. This approach prevented the absorption of contaminants and the associated risk of subsequent reemission of harmful gases.

The center's printer and copier rooms are equipped with separate exhaust fans to safely discharge toner dust. To further safeguard

against any potential health threats, EPA tested all the building's workstations in special environmental chambers, ensuring compliance with preestablished goals for air quality. As a final evaluation of IAQ, EPA conducted extensive testing throughout the facility.

The computer room is equipped with an environmentally friendly and technologically advanced fire-suppressant system capable of discharging the extinguishing agent within ten seconds of fire detection.

A Unique Approach

By using a design-build approach in which the designer and builder essentially worked under the same contract, the architects and builders were able to effectively communicate project strategies and goals, and to develop new ideas that ultimately enhanced the facility's environmental quality. Chris Long, project manager for EPA's Research Triangle Park campus, confirmed the benefits of a joint design-build contract: "Under a joint contract, architects and builders help each other do a better job and find creative ways to spend less money." Another unique element of EPA's approach to the development of the center was that the contractors interviewed EPA employees in order to ensure optimal functionality and comfort in the building.

Kimberly T. Nelson is assistant administrator and chief information officer, Office of Environmental Information, U.S. Environmental Protection Agency.

Reprinted with permission from Environmental Design+Construction magazine, July 2003.

EPA also serves as a compliance and conformance agency, ensuring that all federal regulations and laws relative to the environment are upheld. In this role, the agency is working to standardize guidelines to help define consistent approaches to sustainability. For example, in a collaborative effort with other federal agencies, EPA developed the *Code of Environmental Management Principles (CEMP)*, a guidance document for the development of an EMS. (As noted earlier, Executive Order 13148 requires all federal agencies to establish EMSs by December 31, 2005.)

The EPA Science and Technology Center in Kansas City achieved LEED Gold certification by including features such as daylighting, low-flow plumbing fixtures, and wood products from certified sustainable sources. Stephen Swalwell, Architectural Fotographics

EPA brings a new building online about once a year, according to Bucky Green, the agency's manager for sustainable building. Current projects include regional offices in Denver and Virginia. Green notes that to ensure sustainability throughout a project, the agency takes the lead in design and in the development of building specifications.

"We are very knowledgeable customers for the GSA, which has ultimate real estate authority over our facilities," Green says. "We tell them what we want, and they partner with us to make it happen." Green adds that as the agency charged with environmental responsibility for the nation, EPA has always been proactive about incorporating sustainable design into its own facilities: "We were asking GSA to do green building before anyone else was."

EPA offers a vast store of information for those who want to incorporate sustainability into their projects and provides specific guidance on environmental requirements for federal construction projects. The agency offers practical information on green building, environmentally preferable purchasing, handling debris from construction and demolition, and indoor environmental quality. Among the EPA resources are the following:

A comprehensive Web site maintained by EPA provides a wide range of information—including procurement standards, technical support, and costing guidelines—logically divided among the five sectors that EPA identifies as contributing to a sustainable building project: energy efficiency and renewable energy, green building materials, indoor environment, water conservation, and waste management.[19]

Environmentally Preferable Purchasing (EPP) is a governmentwide program that encourages and assists executive agencies in the purchasing of environmentally preferable products and services.[20]

EPA provides information on ways to manage and reduce debris, including efficient framing techniques and the reuse of building materials.

EPA is the number-one federal resource on ways to improve IAQ. The agency offers extensive guidance on this subject, including technical tools for use in commercial buildings, modeling analysis for ventilation systems and controls, and comprehensive IAQ data for schools and commercial facilities. The agency has also developed software to evaluate the ventilation and humidity-control performance of energy-recovery systems and to calculate their cost.[21]

The Department of Energy

According to the DOE, the federal government is the largest energy consumer in the United States. So, aside from obligations originating in federal legislation, the DOE has its own impetus to reduce energy costs, to play a lead role in the development of renewable energy sources, and to improve utility management at federal facilities. This department offers a host of programs and resources, many in partnership with other agencies, academic institutions, and the private sector.

Across the country, both public and private sector buildings are incorporating the environmental efficiencies developed and promoted by the DOE, and at costs similar to those for conventional construction. For example, for the Cambria government office building in Ebensburg, Pennsylvania, which houses the state environmental agency, buildout totaled $93 per square foot ($1,000 per square meter) for green construction, a figure that is comparable to standard buildout costs. The facility, built and owned by Miller Brothers Construction, reduces energy consumption through daylight harvesting, passive solar energy, lighting control, glazing, air tightness, on-site renewable electricity, and insulation. The building also contains benign, salvaged, and recycled materials.

A commercial project, the Herman Miller MarketPlace, in Zeeland, Michigan, features (1) creative architectural design with energy-reduction technologies developed by the DOE, (2) the use of recycled and agricultural-fiber waste materials, and (3) a site plan that would withstand a 100-year flood event. Construction costs were comparable to those for a similar facility built to conventional standards. Operational costs have been reduced by increasing the efficiency of heating and cooling systems and by minimizing the energy demands of the lighting system (through

Abundant daylight decreases the amount of energy needed for indoor lighting at Herman Miller MarketPlace; glass accounts for more than 62 percent of the building's exterior walls. The building has earned the ENERGY STAR endorsement. © Jeff Dykehouse Photography

High Performance Buildings Initiative

The DOE's High Performance Buildings Initiative offers how-to information for developers who want to improve the energy performance of buildings. The initiative is also a partnership: DOE staff work with researchers at national laboratories as well as building owners, contractors, private sector engineers, architects, and others involved in commercial building construction to reduce the energy consumption of buildings while improving quality, cost-effectiveness, and the comfort of occupants. To minimize the burden on the environment, researchers use energy-efficient and renewable-energy technologies, recycled and sustainable materials, and site-sensitive design.[1]

The clear, user-friendly Web site includes the following sections:

Design Approach. Frequently asked questions addressing issues such as the following: "Is there a market demand for whole-building design?" "Will I have to come up with more money?"

Toolbox. Includes research, energy-simulation software, design and construction guidelines, weather data, and energy consumption data.

Technologies. Definitions and discussions of energy efficiencies, passive solar energy, solar water heating, and solar electric power; links to specific topics such as photovoltaics for buildings.

High Performance Buildings Database. Case studies on 58 buildings—commercial and public—that have earned the high-performance designation. Among them, the Condé Nast building, the Herman Miller MarketPlace, and EPA's National Computer Center.

Building Industry Roadmap. A study cosponsored by members of the commercial building industry that defines a 20-year technology plan to incorporate energy efficiency into buildings and to align government resources with needs identified by the industry, creating public/private partnerships to deliver high-performance buildings.

Performance Metrics. To benchmark improvements.[2]

Notes

1. See http://www.sustainable.doe/gov/buildings/usgovbe.shtml.
2. See http://www.eere.energy.gov/buildings/highperformance.

daylighting and task lighting). Energy costs are estimated to be 40 percent lower than they would be in a comparable facility without such innovations.[22] The MarketPlace has received EPA/DOE's prestigious ENERGY STAR rating for energy efficiency.

The DOE is one of the government's largest agencies, with a host of offices and subagencies under its management. While all relate to energy, not all deal directly with energy efficiencies related to building construction. The following five sections offer a brief guide to some of DOE's relevant offices and programs.

Office of Energy Efficiency and Renewable Energy

The Office of Energy Efficiency and Renewable Energy (EERE) has set a number of priorities, including efforts to bring new, energy-saving technologies to the marketplace and to reduce dependence on foreign oil through the cultivation of alternative energy sources. The research-driven objectives of the office mean that much of the actual work is done in partnership with private institutions, federal laboratories, and universities.

A number of initiatives related to real estate and construction fall under the umbrella of EERE. Its Web site acts as the DOE's energy-efficiency portal, with connections to numerous efficiency-related sites, research, and information. The office also cosponsors the *Sustainable Building Technical Manual.* A handbook for the private sector, it is published in collaboration with EPA and other federal entities involved in federal real estate and construction projects. The manual is designed as a practical tool to help eliminate waste and to create more productive work environments through the more efficient use of natural resources. Though the manual is a bit outdated—it was published in 1996—it does include good ideas and case studies.[23]

Building Technologies Program

The Building Technologies Program works closely with manufacturers and the building industry to research and develop technologies and practices for energy efficiency; publicizes energy- and money-saving opportunities to builders and consumers; and works with state and local regulatory groups to improve building codes and appliance standards.[24]

Among the key activities this program supports is the High Performance Buildings Initiative, which researches ways to improve the efficiency of commercial buildings. The focus is on whole-building design—that is, a holistic approach to efficient facilities, including energy, materials, and land usage. (See the accompanying feature box for more information.)

Other areas of concern for the Buildings Technologies Program include the following:

Building energy codes. Supporting the development of building energy codes that are more stringent and easier to understand; developing downloadable compliance tools and materials; providing technical and financial assistance to help states adopt, implement, and enforce building energy codes; and working with code officials, builders, designers, and states.

Emerging technologies. Supporting research and development for the next generation of energy-efficient components, materials, and equipment.[25]

Building Toolbox. An electronic resource offering specifics on planning and financing; choosing components; designing, building, and renovating; and operating and maintaining a green commercial building.[26]

The laboratory corridors at the EPA Science and Technology Center are filled with natural daylight and offer views of the landscaped courtyard. Stephen Swalwell, Architectural Fotographics

Federal Energy Management Program

The mission of the Federal Energy Management Program (FEMP) is to reduce the cost of government by promoting energy efficiency, water conservation, and the use of renewable energy sources. FEMP accomplishes its mission by creating partnerships, leveraging resources, transferring technology, and providing training and support.[27] FEMP also offers guidance for reducing energy consumption and meeting regulatory responsibilities for new construction, building retrofits, equipment procurement, O&M, and utility management.[28] FEMP can help obtain project financing through energy savings performance contracts (ESPCs) and utility energy service contracts (UESCs), which leverage private sector capital to finance energy- and water-saving projects at federal buildings.

Through FEMP, the DOE offers managers of federal projects a wide range of assistance in the following areas: energy efficiency, renewable energy, distributed-energy technologies, sustainable design practices, state-of-the-art lighting, and water-saving technologies. Assistance includes technical workshops on project financing, life-cycle costing, O&M, and sustainable design. FEMP also provides technical assistance in the following areas:

■ Energy and water audits for buildings and industrial facilities;

■ Peak-load management;

■ Whole-building design and sustainability;

■ Renewable energy technologies;

■ Distributed-energy resources;

■ Combined heat and power technologies; and

■ Laboratory design.[29]

ENERGY STAR® Labeling

ENERGY STAR is a voluntary labeling program jointly sponsored by the DOE and EPA. Originally begun by the DOE in 1992 as a means of identifying and promoting energy-efficient products, the program has expanded to encompass a broad range of environmentally friendly products and approaches. The ENERGY STAR label helps businesses and consumers easily identify products, homes, and buildings that are highly efficient and that save energy and money while protecting the environment.[30] In addition, ENERGY STAR programs

support the development of unified energy codes for buildings and research on zero-energy buildings.

The DOE works with manufacturers to develop the technical requirements for products, such as windows or lighting fixtures, that are qualified to receive the ENERGY STAR label, which appears on more than 30 categories of products. Guidelines for federal building construction, although they are not uniform across all agencies, do require use, wherever possible, of products that have the ENERGY STAR label. GSA procurement schedules include approved vendors that carry ENERGY STAR–labeled items.

Builders can also access specific information on how to improve the energy performance of buildings. Available tools on the ENERGY STAR Web site include the following:

■ *Guidelines for Energy Management.* A path toward improved financial and energy performance of buildings.

■ *Building-Performance Assessments.* Tools to benchmark energy performance (and savings) on a scale of 1 to 100.

■ *Financial Benefits Calculator.* A free, easy-to-use software tool to calculate the financial viability of potential energy improvements.

■ *Tenant Guide.* A guide to saving energy in an existing lease.

■ *Service and Product Provider Directory.* Information on purchasing energy-efficient products ranging from heat pumps to copiers.

Entire commercial buildings can receive the ENERGY STAR endorsement. To get the endorsement, it is necessary to submit, among other information, data on gross building area, weekly hours of occupancy, number of occupants, and number of personal computers. Facilities managers can find out whether their building qualifies for a rating, calculate the facility's rating, and apply for certification using ENERGY STAR's online "portfolio manager" tool kit.

In general, buildings that achieve a rating of 75 or higher are eligible for the ENERGY STAR label.[31] As of January 2004, close to 1,400 of the nation's most energy-efficient public and commercial buildings, representing about 325 million square feet (30 million square meters), had earned the ENERGY STAR designation for superior energy performance. The following commercial buildings are among those with the ENERGY STAR rating:

- The CalPERS building in Washington, D.C.;
- 100 Pine Street, San Francisco, which is owned and managed by Unico Properties;
- The Hines office tower, 1100 Louisiana Street, Houston;
- The Boston Properties office tower, Prudential Center complex, Boston;
- Eighty-three office buildings owned by Arden Realty (the most in one commercial portfolio); and
- The Herman Miller MarketPlace, Zeeland, Michigan.

The ENERGY STAR Web site offers a complete list of labeled buildings.

National Laboratories

The DOE sponsors a national network of research labs that have been at the cutting edge of developing techniques and products for use in environmentally sustainable construction. For example, at the Oak Ridge National Laboratory, in Oak Ridge, Tennessee, scientists in the Environmental Sciences Division are exploring the biology behind soil contaminants in order to develop ways to more efficiently and effectively remediate brownfield sites.[32] Other environmental research programs are ongoing at Sandia National Laboratory, in Albuquerque, New Mexico, and at Argonne National Laboratory, in Argonne, Illinois, among others. The DOE's own National Renewable Energy Laboratory also conducts research on innovative ways to conserve and renew energy.

The Solar Energy Research Facility, in Golden, Colorado, was designed using a whole-building approach, which considered how the building's site, windows, walls, floors, and electrical and mechanical systems could work together most efficiently. NREL

Solar Energy Research Facility, Golden, Colorado

Laboratory facilities, like the Solar Energy Research Facility of the National Renewable Energy Laboratory, in Golden, Colorado, are energy intensive. So the main challenge for the design team was to find efficient ways to heat, cool, light, and ventilate to meet the exacting requirements of the laboratories while still maintaining comfort in the office spaces.

The designers used a whole-building approach to constructing and operating the $19 million facility—looking at the way the building's site, windows, walls, floors, and electrical and mechanical systems could work together most efficiently. Blending architecture and energy efficiency, the designers took advantage of the south-sloping site by situating the offices to the south, and the partly earth-sheltered labs to the north. A stair-step configuration allows daylight and heat into the office areas. The laboratories, at the back of

the building, are in an environment where tight control over ventilation, humidity, temperature, and light is critical. A unique mechanical system makes the most of the building's design and natural environment; efficient heating and cooling saves nearly $200,000 annually and yields utility costs that are 40 percent lower than those for similar commercial buildings. The Solar Energy Research Facility is not only a laboratory for exploring ways to turn the sun's light into electricity and power, but is also a building that puts the laboratory's research into action.

Energy features of the building include daylighting; siting and orientation; energy-efficient lighting; a heat-recovery system; photo sensor–controlled window shades; direct and indirect evaporative cooling; high-efficiency motors with variable-frequency drives; upsized cooling towers; selective glazing; and a Trombe wall, for passive heating.

NREL's Solar Energy Research Facility is a 115,000-square-foot (10,680-square-meter) research facility for developing technologies that convert sunlight into electricity. Office areas and adjoining corridors are daylit, while laboratories are sited at the back of the building, for a more controlled environment. NREL

Source: National Renewable Energy Laboratory, Office of Energy Efficiency and Renewable Energy, U.S. Department of Energy (http://www.nrel.gov/buildings/highperformance/about.html).

The Department of Defense

The military is governed by the same environmental guidelines as other federal agencies. Each branch of the military handles design, construction, and maintenance for its own installations; offers its own guidance; and has its own systems in place to incorporate sustainable design. The Army looks to the U.S. Army Corps of Engineers, the Army's design and construction branch, for practical guidance on applying policies to the design and construction of facilities. The Navy manages its own construction projects, and those of the Marine Corps, through the Naval Facilities

Engineering Command. The Air Force also has its own green building guidelines.

Within each branch, a facilities-management operation oversees installations. For the Army, that operation is the Housing and Facilities Directorate. Within this directorate, the Department of Sustainable Design and Development guides sustainability efforts, based on the Corps' research. The following memo, directed at Army installation commanders, is an example of policy guidance:

SDD policy memorandum from ASA (I&E) to MACOM Commanders. For FY2006 MILCON projects currently under design, the minimum requirement is a Silver SPiRiT

rating. For all other FY2006 and future-year MILCON projects, the minimum requirement is a Gold SPiRiT rating. This policy applies to vertical construction. Horizontal construction, such as roads and airfield, will continue to incorporate Sustainable Design and Development features to the maximum extent possible. Projects under the Residential Communities Initiative, planned or under design, will meet the Gold SPiRiT rating.[33]

The Army Corps of Engineers

In 2000, the Army Corps of Engineers developed its own sustainability report card—the Sustainable Project Rating Tool, known as SPiRiT—a mandatory self-evaluation tool for assessing the green components of Army facilities. Developed in cooperation with the U.S. Green Building Council, SPiRiT addresses sustainable sites, water efficiency, energy and atmosphere, materials and resources, IAQ, and holistic facility delivery.[34]

According to Harry Goradia, a mechanical engineer with the Army Corps of Engineers, SPiRiT tailors the guidance offered by LEED to the specific needs of Army installations, which can differ from those of commercial buildings. Goradia, who helped develop the SPiRiT rating, also says that SPiRiT evolved as a means of ensuring that the design arm (the Corps), the project managers, and the ultimate users of the facility engaged in a discussion of sustainability earlier in the process. "We wanted to facilitate earlier conversations so that these issues were not an afterthought," he explained. Goradia notes that at the time that the rating tool was developed, LEED placed more emphasis on new construction techniques and less on O&M. "We needed something that would address more of these O&M issues," Goradia added. Already, several Army projects—including Fort Gordon, Georgia, and new construction within the Fort Worth, Texas, military district—have earned a SPIRIT Gold rating.

The new facility for the U.S. Army's Golden Knights Parachute Team has a SPiRiT Gold rating. To help encourage the use of alternative transportation to the facility, the developers added bike racks, showers, changing rooms, and designated carpool areas. GSA

Phoenix Rising: The Pentagon's Green Recovery

When construction began on the Pentagon, September 11, 1940, the notion of environmentally responsible building techniques was not a part of the common imagination. At the height of World War II, following the country's active entrance into the conflict, the massive, five-sided facility was equal parts massive office building and monument to the power of the U.S. military. It was, at the time, a modern facility. Fifty-eight years later, when the renovations began, the Pentagon was in some ways a dinosaur, in need of an internal facelift to suit the purposes of a nation headed into the next century. A $1.2 billion renovation included not only conformance with new environmental guidelines, but leadership in exceeding these guidelines.

Just as contractors completed the renovation of one wedge of the facility, 61 years—to the day—from when Pentagon construction first began, a 747 jet crashed headfirst into the heart of the first newly finished section. The ongoing renovations, coupled with monumental efforts to rebuild the damaged section in time for a commemoration of the disaster one year later, have become part of the country's national lore.

Even before the 9/11 attack, the Pentagon Renovation Program (PenRen) had evolved as the organization to manage, for the Deputy Secretary of Defense, the Pentagon renovation and other construction projects on the Pentagon Reservation.[1] To accomplish these projects in the most efficient and effective manner possible, PenRen created an acquisition process to effectively modernize the facility and build new structures on the sprawling campus, while incorporating environmentally preferable building products and services. This acquisition

---

Pentagon Interior Renovation at a Glance

- 420,000 square feet (39,020 square meters) of gypsum wallboard (drywall)—enough to cover more than nine football fields—containing 100 percent recycled paper on face and 15 percent recycled material by weight.
- 273,200 square feet (25,380 square meters) of recycled acoustical ceiling tiles—enough material to cover more than six football fields.
- 47,200 linear feet (14,390 meters) of wood millwork from sustainably managed forests. Laid end to end, the millwork would be nine miles (14.5 kilometers) long.
- 449 doors from sustainably managed forests.
- 3,279,000 square feet (304,600 square meters) of low-VOC or recycled paint—roughly equivalent to 11,000 gallons (41,600 liters) of paint.
- 59,000 square feet (5,480 square meters) of recycled carpet tile.
- 53,500 linear feet (16,300 meters) of 28 percent recycled-content steel wall studs—over ten miles (16 kilometers) laid end to end.
- 496,000 pounds (224,980 kilograms) of construction debris that was recycled instead of being sent to the landfill.

---

process uses a design-build strategy with performance specifications built into the contract, along with incentives and awards for performance. The process has been hailed by the federal government as leading edge, innovative, and in consonance with sound business practices.

The renovation of the Pentagon is being accomplished in five "wedges." The first renovation efforts in the section, called "Wedge 1," included blast-resistant windows, removal of hazardous debris and materials (such as asbestos), and energy-efficient infrastructure design. Some of Wedge 1 was destroyed on September 11, 2001. Although horrific destruction was endured in the Wedge 1 area, studies have shown that the newly renovated and reinforced materials, including blast-resistant windows and other force protection measures, lessened the damage.

The Pentagon Renovation Office is organized into Integrated Product Teams (IPTs) that implement the various construction and renovation projects. After September 11, 2001, PenRen set up an Integrated Product Team to rebuild and repair the damage caused by the airplane's impact. This Phoenix IPT—justly named after the mythological bird, the Phoenix, symbolizing rebirth and immortality—rose to the challenge to rebuild the damaged Pentagon in one year. Despite the additional renovation challenges, new opportunities surfaced, and the procurement of environmentally preferable products gave hope for the continual success of the Pentagon reconstruction.

Reconstruction Process and Goals

At the onset of the renovation process, PenRen developed prerequisites for environmentally preferable products and services it

Source: "Greening the Pentagon," http://www.epa.gov/oppt/epp/ppg/case/penren.htm.

A performance-based initiative for all acquisition has also been established, which not only specifies the environmentally preferable guidelines for contractors, but also gives them flexibility in following those guidelines to minimize the time and effort needed.

Environmentally Preferable Purchasing: A Summary of the PenRen Team's Accomplishments

The Pentagon Renovation Team worked from guidelines developed and supported by the EPA's EPP Program in creating its green building initiatives. The environmentally preferable products for the interior renovation of Wedge 1 included the use of wood from sustainable managed forests; low-water-use plumbing fixtures; low-VOC paints and sealants; mineral wool insulation; energy-efficient lighting; the use of recycled steel, ceiling tile, ceramic tile, and concrete masonry units; the recycling of construction debris; and the use of packaging, labeling, and instructions made from recycled material. Future applications for incorporating EPP into the Pentagon renovation include the Department of Defense (DOD) custodial, O&M, and recycling programs.

The original coal-fired heating and refrigeration unit, which cost an estimated $200,000 each month, was replaced with state-of-the-art equipment. The new system is approximately 30 percent more efficient, operating with computer controls and with natural gas as its main fuel source. In addition, extensive improvements in energy efficiency ranged from insulation to double-pane windows to lighting.

The project also involved the removal of 25 million pounds (11.3 million kilograms) of

Repairs required after the terrorist attack of September 11, 2001, were made ahead of schedule and under budget—and many safety, health, and environmental features were added to the repaired wedge of the Pentagon. Pentagon Renovation Program

wanted to implement. Additional requirements and methods became more imperative after the terrorist attack, but added more diversity and flexibility to the effort. For example, innovative workspaces, energy-efficient (and blast-resistant) windows, new heating and cooling networks, new energy-management control systems, improved IAQ (such as low-VOC paints), and the massive abatement of hazardous building materials (such as asbestos) became the basis for PenRen's environmentally preferable product procurement.

asbestos, lead paint, mercury, and PCBs. The renovation team recycled 70 percent of construction debris, including, steel, copper wire, aluminum, glass, and concrete.

Cost Considerations

The consideration of cost is very important to the PenRen team because of the allotted quantity of funds already attributed to the project. Congress gave the DOD a $1.2 billion budget, creating the Pentagon Reservation Maintenance Revolving Fund. In order to maximize these funds, cost-effective and sustainable materials were necessary.

With the renovation team's implementation of EPP practices, the Pentagon Renovation project, thus far, has successfully maximized resources. In fact, head Pentagon Building and Management officials first projected the repair costs of September 11 to be $740 million. After the procurement and completion, for most of the project, current estimates place the figure around $501 million. The entire Pentagon Renovation Project is expected to be four years ahead of schedule: 2010 rather than 2014.

In order to attain sustainable construction objectives, the Pentagon Renovation Program has formulated a plan of action to provide clear goal definition and metrics to measure achievement of progress. Earlier efforts to incorporate sustainable design into Pentagon Renovation projects were sporadic, and lacked a clear focus and direction. Although many organizations stated their support for sustainable design and its precepts, PenRen realized that it needed more than mission statements and expressions of support. In August 2001, as a culmination of earlier efforts, the Integrated Sustainable Design and Constructability (ISDC) Team became a viable part of the organization at the Pentagon Renovation Office. Afterward, in the wake of the terrorist attacks of September 11, the Pentagon Renovation Office and its ISDC Team shouldered the additional responsibility of integrating and balancing sustainable design issues with force protection measures necessary to protect the Pentagon.

Lessons Learned

As a result, the ISDC Team is an integral part of all construction projects on the Pentagon

Reservation. The complex nature of the projects implemented by the Pentagon Renovation Program requires that the ISDC Team incorporate sustainable design into the overall acquisition and management strategy of the Pentagon Renovation Program. The acquisition strategy includes two innovative concepts for government contracting, with respect to contract type and method of construction delivery: performance-based contracting, with the delivery method of design-build—not business as usual for the government. In addition, the overall Pentagon Renovation Program management implementation strategy involves IPTs composed of government and contractor personnel from many different organizations and with various duties and responsibilities. Therefore, the Pentagon Renovation Program's ISDC Team is also responsible for integrating the principles and practices of sustainable design with a leading-edge acquisition strategy.

Note

1. See http://renovation.pentagon.mil/sustainabledesign.htm.

The Corps sustainability Web site contains resources and information related to the following topics:

- SPiRiT and how to comply;
- Master planning for installations and communities;
- Water efficiency;
- Energy and atmosphere;
- Materials and resources;
- IAQ;
- Holistic facility-delivery process; and
- Deconstruction and reuse of facilities.[35]

Military Research

In addition to the programs that have been established to assist the military in managing its own vast network of installations, much new technology has emerged from military research. The Internet, which was originally designed by military computer scientists as a secure means of communication during the Cold War era, is one of the most well-known examples of military technology that changed the way the world operates. Military research related to the environment is as important as research related to general technology. For example, the Defense Advanced Research

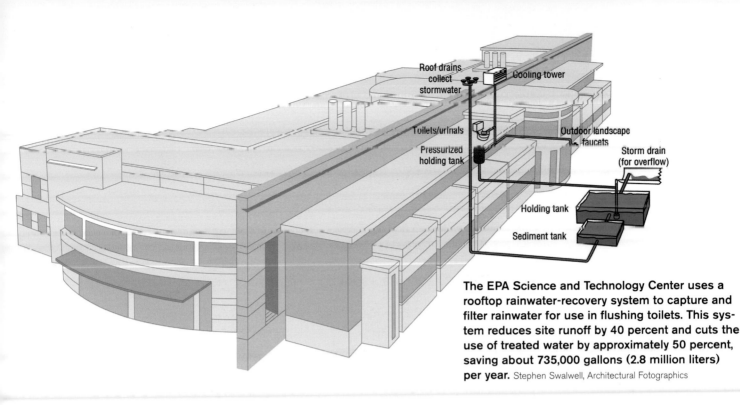

The EPA Science and Technology Center uses a rooftop rainwater-recovery system to capture and filter rainwater for use in flushing toilets. This system reduces site runoff by 40 percent and cuts the use of treated water by approximately 50 percent, saving about 735,000 gallons (2.8 million liters) per year. Stephen Swalwell, Architectural Fotographics

Projects Agency (DARPA) is exploring ways to commercialize the conversion of thermal heat sources to electricity—a notion that has practical uses for soldiers in the field but could also reduce a building's reliance on conventionally generated electrical power.[36]

Another project, the DARPA Titanium Initiative, seeks to establish a U.S.-based, high-volume, low-cost, environmentally benign production capability that would support the widespread use of titanium—a very lightweight material—and its alloys.[37]

DARPA's water purification initiatives, which are of great importance to soldiers in the field, can also have practical uses in wastewater management and in the recycling of industrial liquids.

The Federal Network for Sustainability

According to the mission statement of the Federal Network for Sustainability (FNS), the organization

promotes cost-effective, energy- and resource-efficient operations across all branches of government. Through individual initiatives and joint ventures, we shall strive to better our understanding of the interrelationship between energy use, economics, and environmental impact. We are mindful of our heirs and successors, who will rely on our responsible stewardship today. By leadership and example, we intend to

educate and guide others in reducing federal expenditures, while simultaneously advancing the principles of sustainability throughout the public and the private sectors.[38]

The network, whose offices are on the West Coast, recently adopted a new sustainable buildings initiative to provide increased communication across agencies about progress in greening federal buildings and about emerging technologies that can be applied in the commercial sector.

Other Agencies

Many federal agencies maintain a branch devoted to sustainability. Thus, the guidance that emerges from most agencies is specific to the needs of that agency. For example, the National Park Service, a branch of the Department of the Interior, has developed a handbook on putting sustainability into practice in federal parks. Among other features, the book identifies ways to site a tourist facility so that it blends in well with its surroundings and so that fragile ecosystems are left undisturbed.

Similarly, the sustainability programs of the National Aeronautics and Space Administration (NASA) are directed at ways to reduce the environmental impact of NASA's facilities. And at the U.S. Department of Housing and Urban Development, sustainability guidance focuses on the reclamation of brownfield sites, environmental restoration in decaying urban cores, and the protection of the areas surroundings new housing developments.

The U.S. Postal Service also operates under its own green guidelines, which include increased energy efficiency, improved resource efficiency, and environmental responsiveness in the use of raw materials. A new post office in Fort Worth, Texas—the nation's first green post office—is made of compressed straw panels, an agricultural product, and features, among other innovations, a foundation consisting of 20 percent recycled concrete, and dock bumpers that contain recycled tires. The use of low-VOC materials preserves IAQ at the facility.

A federal facility under construction that has been required to incorporate sustainability across all aspects of design, construction, and operations is the $176.9 million U.S. Census Bureau in Suitland, Maryland. Also in Suitland, the National Oceanic and Atmospheric Administration (NOAA) is constructing a new Satellite Operations Center, under the guidance of GSA and with a design by Morphosis Architects, the same firm that designed the San Francisco Federal Office Building. The NOAA satellite center, carved into a hillside, is essentially an underground facility with satellites perched on its rooftop. Though the building is buried beneath the ground, it features a 146,000-square-foot (13,560-square-meter) green roof.

Notes

1. See http://www.arup.com/newsitem.cfm?pageid=970.

2. GSA, "Real Property Sustainable Development Guide," available at http://www.gsa.gov/gsa/cm_attachments/GSA_DOCUMENT/sus_dev_guide_R2O1X_0Z5RDZ-i34K-pR.pdf.

3. GSA, "NEPA Implementation," available at http://www.gsa.gov/Portal/gsa/ep/contentView.do?contentId=11872&contentType=GSA_OVERVIEW.

4. Ibid.

5. See http://www.wbdg.org/design/index.php?cn=4.3.4&cx=0. *The Whole Building Design Guide* can be downloaded at http://www.wbdg.org/design/greenspec.

6. See http://www.ofee.gov/sb/state_fgb_6.pdf.

7. OFEE, "Sustainable Buildings," updated November 2003, available at http://www.ofee.gov/sb/sb.htm.

8. OFEE, "Federal Governmentwide Green Building Policies," available at http://www.ofeee.gov.

9. See http://www.gsa.gov/Portal/gsa/ep/channelView.do?pageTypeId=8195&channelPage=%2Fep%2Fchannel%2FgsaOverview.jsp&channelId=-12882.

10. DOE, "Greening of the White House," available at http://www.eere.energy.gov/femp/pdfs/gotwh.pdf.

11. Ibid.

12. See http://www.gsa.gov.

13. Ibid.

14. See http://www.gsa.gov/gsa/cm_attachments/GSA_BASIC/WorkPlace2020_DescriptionShortV3_R2G-kB-u_0Z5RDZ-i34K-pR.doc.

15. *Facilities Standards for the Public Buildings Service* can be downloaded from http://www.gsa.gov; a hard-copy version can be purchased from the Government Printing Office web site, http://bookstore.gpo.gov.

16. GSA, "Site, Landscape, and Community Design," in *Facilities Standards for the Public Buildings Service.*

17. GSA, Federal Supply Service, "Overview," in "Environmental Products and Services Guide, 2003–2004," available for download at http://www.gsa.org.

18. *The Whole Building Design Guide* is available online at http://www.wbdg.org.

19. See http://www.epa.gov/greenbuilding.

20. See http://www.epa.gov/oppt/epp/about/about.htm.

21. See http://www.ofee.gov/b/appendix_e.pdf. For more information, see http://www.epa.gov/iaq/largebldgs/ibeam_page.htm, EPA's Indoor Air Quality Building Education and Assessment Model (I-BEAM) Web site.

22. American Institute of Architects, "Earth Day 2003, Environmentally Responsible Architecture and Design," press release.

23. The manual is available for download at http://www.sustainable.doe.gov/pdf/sbt.pdf.

24. See http://www.eere.energy.gov/building.html.

25. See http://www.eere.energy.gov/buildings/programs.cfm.

26. See http://www.eere.energy.gov/buildings/.

27. See http://www.sustainable.doe.gov/buildings/usgovbe.shtml.

28. Federal Energy Management Program, "About the Program," available at http://www.eere.energy.gov/femp/about/about.cfm.

29. Ibid.

30. See http://www.energystar.gov.

31. See http://www.energystar.gov/index.cfm?c=eligibility.bus_portfolio manager _eligibility_offices.

32. Oak Ridge Laboratories, Environmental Sciences Division, "About Us," available at http://www.esd.ornl.gov/images/ESD_brochure_2004.pdf.

33. See http://www.cecer.army.mil/sustdesign/SPiRiT.cfm.

34. U.S. Army Corps of Engineers, Sustainable Project Rating Tool, Version 1.4.1 (June 2002), iii.

35. See http://www.cecer.army.mil/sustdesign.

36. See http://www.darpa.mil/dso/thrust/matdev/dtec.htm.

37. See http://www.darpa.mil/dso/thrust/matdev/titanium.htm.

38. See http://www.federalsustainability.org/about/aboutfns.htm.

Case Studies

Alvento Parque Empresarial
Madrid, Spain

Jenifer Seal

Alvento Parque Empresarial (Alvento) is a spec-built complex of two buildings that stands out in a sea of new office developments in suburban Madrid because of its distinctive design and green features. Very few speculative green office buildings have been developed to date, and this one makes a statement with its innovative design, market-based cost delivery, and extraordinarily fast lease-up. It has the distinction of being the first LEED-certified building in Spain and the entire European Union.

The Site

Alvento is located on an old beverage industry site along the M40 motorway on the northeast side of Madrid. It features excellent access to public transportation. In addition, the building has bicycle storage and changing rooms and alternative fuel refueling stations for electric and hybrid cars. More than 75 percent of the car park capacity is underground.

Alvento, the first LEED-certified building in Spain, is environmentally sensitive and energy efficient. Jenifer Seal

Minimizing the footprint of the buildings means that a minimal amount of the site was disturbed. The project restored indigenous and adapted vegetation to the site and reduced impervious surfaces by 31 percent compared with the previous industrial use. A beautiful xeriscape garden of native vegetation ensures low water consumption.

Development and Planning Process

In 1999, Metrovacesa, a 40-year-old development company and one of Spain's three largest developers, began noticing that green development was coming onto the international radar screen. In studying this emergence of environmental sensitivity and energy efficiency, the com-

Special Features
■ Energy efficiency
■ Green and recycled materials
■ Restored native landscaping
■ Natural stormwater filtration system
■ Extensive natural light in occupied areas
■ Halogen-free cables, switches, plugs, and electric boxes

The speculatively built facility was designed as two oval-shaped buildings connected by a central courtyard. The footprints of the buildings were minimized in order to disturb the site as little as possible. Rachelle Levitt

insurance company) attracted Metrovacesa. As one of the firm's partners, Iñigo Ortiz, noted, "My partner and I have been working on energy-efficient and environmentally responsible architecture since we were in college. This methodology has been a part of our practice all the way through." Ortiz Leon Architects is one of the founding members of the newly established Spain Green Building Council (modeled after the U.S. Green Building Council).

Working with Z3 environmental consultants and the founders of the Spain Green Building Council, the architects collaborated closely with Metrovacesa representatives in thinking through the design. Product differentiation through green buildings, flexibility, and cost-effectiveness were three of the developer's vital concerns. Although the developer greatly admired all the green features of the Sanitas project, Alvento is a speculative building, not owner occupied, and thus the design team had to focus on delivering an efficient core and shell with no frills.

To ensure commitment to the green agenda, Ortiz Léon Architects signed a contract with Metrovacesa that outlined how the building would use the USGBC's LEED rating system. Initially, the developers wanted just a basic LEED certification, but as design progressed, they were intrigued by the challenge of achieving the higher Silver and possibly Gold levels of certification.

Ortiz further noted that they had "no problems at all with regulatory approvals. At this time, the local council is not very interested in green, but this will dramatically change in three to four years, thanks to examples like Alvento and Sanitas."

Design

To achieve the developer's goals for the building, maximize the land plan, and control solar access, the facility includes two oval buildings connected by a central plaza. Architect Ortiz describes his philosophy for the design: "We realize

pany began looking for architects who could assist it in this new way of building. It wanted to develop product that would set it apart in the market. The director of new speculative office buildings predicted that the market in 2003 and 2004 would be very difficult, with short demand and low prices. "Green" was seen as a good option to differentiate product and a way to reach the important northern European market. Moreover, Metrovacesa saw that industrial companies with strong environmental concerns in production were likely to want environmentally friendly headquarters buildings as well. From the outset, one of the company's goals therefore was to create a LEED-certified building.

Ortiz Leon Architects served as project architects. This firm's highly efficient and beautiful solution for the nearby Sanitas headquarters in Madrid (a London-based health how important the architecture in this green building is. We feel that in a sense green is linked more with construction than architecture. Architects have a lot to do in this field with passive solutions, much imagination, and intelligent ideas. I don't believe in intelligent or smart buildings but in buildings smartly designed. We have to spend more time on comfort issues, such as natural light or air quality, but be very rigorous. There is no room here for frivolous design measures."

Starting from the program and summary specifications for the property, the team designed a speculative office building that adjusts itself to the characteristics of the sun, offers an image of high quality, and functions as a sustainable building. The twin buildings are similar in design but are adapted to conform to their terrain. The design is the result of an intermingling of several considerations, including comfort and quality in workstations.

Architect Ortiz notes, "The buildings are designed as capsules with rounded fronts that give an organic form that favors the development of winds without creating brusque changes of orientation." The building's shape provides maximal flexibility for tenants. The design also allows for the creation of garden platforms on each floor. These gardens are designed as "dry-scapes" for plants requiring no maintenance or irrigation, as they are in areas of the building most affected by solar orientation.

Madrid's climate features extreme temperatures in winter and summer, and long periods of moderate temperatures. The buildings are sited to maximize solar gain. Exposure to the sun is controlled by using exterior canopies as shading devices. Each facade, however, is specifically "tuned" for its orientation. Special windows with low-e coatings and light shelves also help control solar gain and daylighting. The buildings enclose a central patio, and two patios on the open ends allow for illumination of the elevator corridors. Daylighting through

these core towers also illuminates the inner office space. Plantings in these cores add to the ambience of the sun-soaked space. The buildings achieve one of their design goals by providing natural light in all common building zones, beginning with the elevator and stair vestibules and ending with the contained smoking rooms. The entire buildings can thus be operated without cost for lighting these spaces.

The building envelope functions as a cross-ventilated facade, where the insulation has been placed on the exterior. The insulation is made much more effective by the Alucubond exterior finish. Architect Ortiz notes that "comfort is much more than temperature and humidity. It is linked to subjectivity; it is personal and psychologically related. In the design, we looked for emotional comfort or emotional architecture linked with 'perma-architecture.' By this I mean architecture in favor of . . . productive systems

Sun exposure is controlled by exterior canopies, shading devices, windows with low-e coating, and interior light shelves. Rachelle Levitt

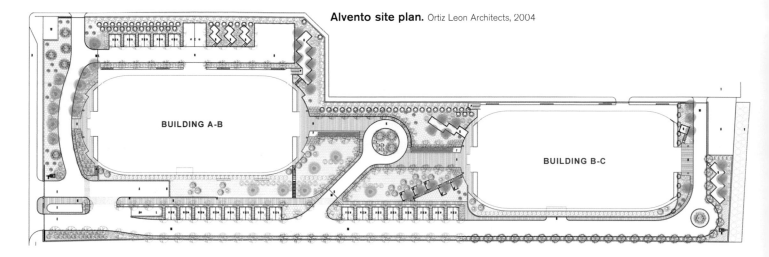

Alvento site plan. Ortiz Leon Architects, 2004

BUILDING A-B

BUILDING B-C

with common sense. This idea combines the application of permaculture to the architecture and biophilia."

A simple palette of materials was chosen. Local materials (glass, granite, concrete, steel, fabrics) and recyclable materials (glass and aluminum in the facade, stainless steel in the interior construction, and natural stone and wood for the interior finishes) were selected for their low maintenance and ease of replacement. Fifty-seven percent of Alvento construction materials were manufactured locally, and 74 percent of them have been harvested, extracted, or recovered locally. To allow for easy recyclability, no materials are mixed.

Indoor air quality was addressed through a variety of techniques: a carbon dioxide monitoring system, use of low-VOC-emitting materials, separate ventilation for cleaning rooms, and individual controls for air flow.

Construction

Fifty-six percent of waste produced was recycled or reused in other locations. During construction, all ductwork and filtering equipment were protected.

Financing and Marketing

Metrovacesa developed a very comprehensive four-color marketing booklet with a bilingual CD to describe the features of the Alvento project. Each page of the brochure

refers to the LEED rating system, and the booklet covers all the project's green features in great detail.

The development company's efforts have paid off. Alvento's occupancy rate is 92 percent, in contrast to many surrounding office buildings, which sit vacant or partially leased.

Alvento was completed in July 2003 at a cost of €11,500 per square foot ($15,240 per square foot).[1] The space is leased to a variety of tenants, with almost 3,000 employees on site. Asking-rents in early 2005 were €192 per square meter ($28 per square foot) per year.

Experience Gained

The development team, having used the LEED rating system to help guide the design process, found it was instrumental in incorporating sustainability in the design.

Careful attention was paid to using energy resources appropriate for the climate of Madrid. A DOE-2 energy model showed an energy savings of 32 percent and a water consumption savings of 56 percent.

Alvento raised the bar for office development in Madrid and throughout Spain. Its quick lease-up and tenant satisfaction alone demonstrate the demand for such high-performance office space.

The building has received LEED certification and is awaiting a Silver rating.

Project Data: Alvento Parque Empresarial

Land Use and Building Information

Site Area 4.13 acres (1.7 hectares)

Gross building area 342,657 square feet (31,845 square meters)

Building height 7 floors

Parking

Total 607 spaces

Surface 149 spaces

Underground 458 spaces

Number of Tenants 22[2]

Development Cost Information

€11,500 per square foot ($15,000 per square foot)

Owner/Developer

Metrovacesa S.A.
7 Plaza Carlos Trías Bertrán
28020 Madrid, Spain
Phone: 34 91 418 41 66
Fax: 34 91 555 83 86
www.metrovacesa.es

Architect

Iñigo Ortiz
Ortiz Leon Architects
263 B Arturo Soria
28033 Madrid, Spain
www.ortizleon.com

Green Building Consultant

Aurelio Ramírez-Zarzosa
Founder and Chair
Consejo Construcción Verde España (Spain Green Building Council)
263-B Arturo Soria
28033 Madrid, Spain
Phone: 34 91 3843946
Fax: 34 91 7660444

Other Consultants

Engineering Consultant: Antonio Carrión ICA
Contractor: FCC
Mechanical Installation: Axima
Electrical Installation: Crespo y Blasco

Development Schedule

1998	Site acquisition
8/2001	Construction began
7/2003	Construction complete
8/2003	Move-in began
9/2004	Move-in complete

Location

Avenida de los Poblados, 3
Madrid, Spain

Notes

1. Currency exchange as of March 2005.
2. Number of tenants as of March 2005.

Bank One Corporate Center
Chicago, Illinois

Jenifer Seal

The Bank One Corporate Center is one of the most technologically advanced office buildings in Chicago. It incorporates cutting-edge technology with under-floor air, cable, and wire management systems. The building is one of the earliest and largest green speculative office projects in the country. Chicago mayor Richard Daley endorsed the project, saying it brought significant revitalization of South State Street, and encouraged the development of green buildings.

The building encompasses 1.77 million square feet (164,500 square meters) of space, with 1.4 million square feet (130,000 square meters) of office space, 100,000 square feet (9,300 square meters) of retail space, and a 210-space parking garage below grade. It is configured in two towers—a 37-story high rise that faces Dearborn Street and an 11-story structure that faces State Street. The site has two distinct faces: Dearborn Street, historically a business street, and State Street, the dominant retail corridor.

The Bank One Corporate Center rises 37 stories in the heart of Chicago's financial district. Endorsed by Mayor Richard Daley, the building sparked significant revitalization and encouraged additional green development.

John Miller© Hedrich Blessing

Site, Development Process, and Planning

The Bank One Corporate Center is located prominently in the heart of the Chicago Loop business district on a site that has been in use for more than 100 years. The first structure on the site was the Fair department store, which was designed and built in 1892 by William LeBaron Jenney, the engineer who invented high-rise construction. In 1896, a single basement was constructed on spread footings, which were designed to sit up high on soft clay, under the building. (All buildings of this height settled significantly; thus, it was designed for 15 inches [38.5 centimeters] of settlement.) The department store was renovated again in 1923. At the location of each column, workers dug holes by hand to cre-

Special Features

- Speculative green development
- Urban infill site
- Tallest building in Chicago with raised floors
- Reuse of historic foundation
- Under-floor air distribution, cable, and wire management systems
- Energy efficiency

ate reinforced concrete caissons that extended all the way to the hardpan clay, adding two additional basements. The structure was sold to Montgomery Ward and survived until 1985, when it was demolished, but the foundations

The 1.8 million-square-foot skyscraper saved both time and money by reusing the existing structure and foundation of the Fair store, built in 1892. John Miller© Hedrich Blessing

Center. Over the past two decades, the Beitler Company has developed more than 10 million square feet (930,000 square meters) of Class A office space in the Chicago area.

A collaboration of companies known as the Meritt Signature Development Alliance laid out the guidelines for building green that influenced this speculative project. In the early 1990s, Kevork Derderian, president of Chicago's Continental Offices Limited and founder of the Meritt Signature Development Alliance, pulled together a collaborative of companies with the aim of making green design and construction more cost-effective and designed for the utmost in employee comfort, flexibility, and energy savings.

In 1998, the Beitler development team commissioned a financial due diligence study and a design due diligence study. Beitler selected the architectural firm DeStefano + Partners of Chicago, which it had worked with on previous projects. Ray Clark, the project's management and technical principal and president of DeStefano + Partners, says that they began with a review of all the old documents on the project, including site conditions, environmental reports, and geotechnical conditions to determine the feasibility of using the old foundations. No serious environmental cleanup was necessary, as only minor environmental hazards were found. Several concepts emerged from the due diligence studies:

■ A mid-rise 15- to 20-story building with "dignified contemporary design";

■ Use of existing infrastructure, including foundations;

■ Maximum building size for the existing infrastructure;

■ High floor-to-ceiling heights;

■ Energy efficiency through raised floors;

■ A fast-track project to increase speed to market.

"A key element of this building is the reuse of the existing foundation infrastructure," says Clark. He sees a viable trend for redevelopment of inner-city sites in the next 20 years as buildings of the 1960s and 1970s become defunct. "There's

remained. The new building now sits on the second wave of foundations.

Various developers considered a series of "Dearborn Centers" and tower schemes on this site through the 1980s. In 1988, a 72-story building was proposed for the site, but with the crash of the real estate market, this scheme never came to fruition. In the mid-1990s, the Beitler Company identified it as a prime location and began looking at different schemes for its own "Dearborn Center" project, which later became known as the Bank One Corporate

July 1998, Prime Group Realty Trust (a real estate investment trust that owns, manages, leases, develops, and redevelops office and industrial properties, principally in the metropolitan Chicago area) became a partner in the project.

Prime brought in designer Ricardo Bofill from Spain. To achieve the tallest and largest building possible on the site, the team looked at all sorts of schemes with Bofill and came up with a tower on the business side and a podium on the State Street side.

The developer did not have an anchor tenant in the first quarter of 1999, and the project was therefore financially questionable. Preparation of construction documents was slowed. Fortunately, however, within weeks the team secured Bank One as the anchor tenant with a 15-year lease for levels 3 through 14. With Bank One on board, the team redesigned the guts of the building in 100 days to meet tenants' needs. They reconfigured core areas and the elevator system, vehicle spaces, and loading docks.

Design and Construction

The team worked closely together during many design charrettes. The environment and energy efficiency were ongoing topics, including air handling and performance characteristics of the walls and glazing. The design that emerged offers among the largest and most sophisticated office floors in Chicago, with superior energy efficiency and temperature controls adjustable by each individual.

a tremendous cost to removing or building around what's there. And there's also a value to the time factor that's involved with abandoning existing infrastructure."

Market research studies and focus groups commissioned by the developer discovered that sophisticated tenants have demanding power supply and technology needs. Very early in the process, raised floor systems, high ceilings, natural light, and comfortable workstations were identified as key elements of the design necessary to meet market demands. The construction manager, Morse Diesel, which later became AMEC Construction Management, was brought on board early in the process to track cost modeling of the development schemes.

In mid-March 1998, the team produced a design concept based on the market research and financial due diligence studies. Beitler decided to move forward with a smaller building than originally envisioned. In July 1998, the architecture team produced a schematic design. Beitler began looking for a development partner, and in

RETURN AIR PLENUM

9'-6" TO 10'-0"
CLEAR CEILING HEIGH

INDIRECT LIGHTING

HIGH PERFORMANCE
LOW "E" INSULATING
GLASS

TYPICAL FLOOR
DIFFUSER

14" RAISED FLOOR

FAN COIL UNIT
FOR PERIMETER
HEATING AND COOLING

The Bank One Corporate Center was the first building in Chicago to use an under-floor air-distribution system, which allows occupants to adjust heat and air conditioning at every workstation. DeStefano + Partners, Ltd.

Design for the operational comfort and efficiency of the building's ventilation had several objectives:

■ Improved indoor air quality, with an increased number of air changes in the workspace for occupants' comfort;

■ Reduced energy consumption through reduced differential in the temperature of the air supply;

■ Superior temperature control and occupancy sensors;

■ Lower initial costs through the use of efficient equipment and less plant area;

■ Integration of building systems;

■ Maximum flexibility for tenants.

Unlike traditional office buildings that incorporate ductwork in the ceilings, the air in Bank One Center is distributed via air columns through the floors. Electricity, heating, and air conditioning are more accessible for modifications than in traditional systems, where they are typically located above the ceilings or in the walls. The system incorporates cutting-edge technology in its under-floor air, cable, and wire management systems. A 14-inch (36-centimeter) pressurized raised floor delivers high-quality conditioned air to every workstation and private office, adjustable by each individual user. This system results in reduced energy use, superior air quality and temperature control, better ventilation, and more comfortable and productive workers. As the air passes up through the space, it pushes heat gain, impurities, and pollutants up and out (referred to as displacement ventilation), improving air quality and ensuring more uniform air distribution.

Fourteen fan-coil units on each of the four sides around the perimeter boost the system. On tenant trading floors with major heat loads resulting from high-density data centers, an extra boost of air is delivered as well. Booster fans, controlled by a variable frequency drive to maintain a constant plenum pressure, are provided at each air column on each floor. An interior zone ventilation system offsets heat gain from building heat sources and maintains constant temperatures inside the perimeter environment.

Throughout the process, the design team met with the city to discuss the benefits of a raised floor system, noting that it is most efficient when line voltage, low-voltage wire management, and air delivery in the plenum are included. Currently, the Chicago building code does not permit this use, so the team sought a variance, which was granted. The raised floor is made of concrete-filled steel panels installed on a pedestal system over the one-hour-rated steel-framed concrete structural floor slab.

The under-floor system is the gem of this office tower. With studies showing an average of 43 percent of occupants changing locations in office space yearly, a primary goal was to make the work environment more flexible for tenants. More flexibility would lower tenants' costs resulting from the inevitable changes in their work environments

as staff members change and corporate needs evolve. Selling the benefits of and savings from the under-floor system was key to the project's success.

With ceilings up to ten feet (three meters) on many floors, the 37-story tower is actually the equivalent of a 50-story building. Daylight penetrates everywhere. Corporate tenants benefit from the floor-to-ceiling windows and extensive glazing in the exterior wall. More natural light reaches not only the perimeters of each floor but also deeper into the interior space.

The Chicago Department of Planning wanted the building to incorporate a green roof as part of its Urban Heat Island green roof pilot program. In the summer, air temperatures in urban areas can be six to ten degrees higher because of higher concentrations of concrete and asphalt.

By offering the city a green roof, three levels of retail space, a covered arcade over Dearborn Street, and improved lighting and landscaping, the developer was given a higher floor/area ratio, allowing a larger building on the site.

The DOE-2 energy computer model was used to guide the project through decisions about energy efficiency and cost-effectiveness. At one point, for example, a double-skin facade was proposed, but the team could not justify it merely on energy savings because energy prices are already low in Chicago.

Experience Gained

Compared with standard Chicago office energy use, the Bank One building achieves a 15 percent reduction in energy use because of the under-floor air delivery system. Typically, under-floor air is delivered at 63 to 65 degrees Fahrenheit (17 to 18 degrees Celsius) from a main air handler, but for a building

Plants for the center's 12th-floor tower garden were selected for their ability to thrive in the heat, wind, and sun of the urban rooftop environment. ©Kildow Photography

Project Data: Bank One Corporate Center

Land Use and Building Information

Site area	66,768 square feet (6,205 square meters)
Gross building area	1,774,242 square feet (165,000 square meters)
Below grade	201,670 square feet (18,742 square meters)
Above grade	1,572,572 square feet (146,150 square meters)
Net rentable area	1,525,536 square feet (141,800 square meters)
Office	1,395,364 square feet (130,000 square meters)
Retail	106,808 square feet (9,925 square meters)
Building height	36 floors above grade plus roof penthouse, 3 below grade
Typical floor size	56,692 square feet (5,270 square meters)
Parking (below grade)	210 spaces

Tenant Information

Office occupancy rate	74%[1]
Office rents	$22–25 per square foot ($237–269 per square meter), triple net
Retail rents	$25–55 per square foot ($269–592 per square meter), triple net
Number of tenants	5
Bank One Corporation	620,000 square feet (57,620 square meters)
Holland & Knight	122,000 square feet (11,340 square meters)
Citadel Investment Group LLC	276,000 square feet (25,650 square meters)
Perkins Coie LLP	56,000 square feet (5,200 square meters)
Beecken Petty O'Keefe	9,000 square feet (835 square meters)

Development Cost Information

Total development cost	$305 million

Original Owner

Prime Group Realty Trust
77 West Wacker Drive, Suite 3900
Chicago, Illinois 60601
Phone: 312-917-4228
www.pgrt.com/

Developer

Prime Beitler Development (a joint venture of the Beitler Company and Prime Group Realty Trust)

The Beitler Company
One North LaSalle, Suite 2850
Chicago, Illinois 60602
Phone: 312-855-0277
www.beitlerco.com

Prime Group Realty Trust

Architect

DeStefano + Partners
445 East Illinois Street, Suite 250
Chicago, Illinois 60611
Phone: 312-836-4321
www.destefanoandpartners.com

Design Architect

Ricardo Bofill Taller de Arquitectura
Avenida Industria, 14
08960 Sant Just Desvern
Barcelona, Spain
Phone: 34-93-499-9900
www.bofill.com

Other Consultants

General Contractor: AMEC (formerly Morse Diesel International), Chicago, Illinois

Structural Engineer: Thornton-Tomasetti Engineers, Chicago, Illinois

Mechanical Engineer: Environmental Systems Design Inc., Chicago, Illinois

Electrical: Gurtz Electric Company, Arlington Heights, Illinois

Fire Protection: Great Lakes Plumbing, Chicago, Illinois

Lighting: Fisher Marantz Stone, Chicago, Illinois

Mechanical: Climatemp, Chicago, Illinois

Structural Steel: Kline Iron and Steel Company, Inc., Columbia, South Carolina

Steel Erector: American Bridge, Downers Grove, Illinois

Development Schedule

1998	Site acquired
1998	Planning started
2000	Construction started
2003	Construction completed
2003	Occupancy

Location

131 South Dearborn Street
Chicago, Illinois

Note

1. As of March 2005.

this size, it would mean a huge handler to serve up to 25 floors. To save space and improve humidity levels, the mechanical engineers developed an innovative scheme using columns of air. The scheme uses air at 47 degrees Fahrenheit (8 degrees Celsius), which requires a small handler because of the cooler temperatures. To raise the temperature at the delivery point, air is blended with some return air to achieve the desired 63 degrees Fahrenheit (17 degrees Celsius). The upper levels of the building use four air columns, the lower level (at the bigger base) eight. The delivery of low-temperature air allowed the design team to eliminate one entire fan room on the top floor, giving the developer more prime leasable space.

Raj Gupta, president of the mechanical engineering firm on the project, stressed that simplicity in high-performance building design is key. The team conducted a debriefing on lessons learned from the project and is compiling a manual with the developer for tenants and their architects to understand the distinctive features of the system and the building.

Capitol Area East End Complex

Block 225 Office Building
Sacramento, California

Jenifer Seal

Located in downtown Sacramento across the street from the state capitol, the program for the Capitol Area East End Complex includes a total of 1.5 million square feet (140,000 square meters) of office space for 1,100 occupants in five buildings. This case study focuses on Block 225, a 479,000-square-foot (44,500-square-meter) building in the complex that houses the California Department of Education. As the first building completed in the complex, it set the standards for sustainability for the rest of the development.

The innovative Capitol Area East End Complex, Block 225, was certified LEED Gold, the second-highest rating of the U.S. Green Building Council's LEED rating system, in January 2003.

The state green building team embraced the whole-building approach from design to construction; the resulting project saved $185,000 for Block 225 and $400,000 for the entire complex. The Capitol Area East End Complex was completed on budget and within the time constraints of an aggressive construction schedule.

Block 225, home to California's Department of Education, was the first building completed at the Capitol Area East End Complex in Sacramento. The building's 110 sustainable design features are expected to save the state an estimated $185,000 annually.
©Erhard Pfeiffer 2003

Site and Development Process

In the early 1990s, the Department of General Services, part of the Consumer Services Agency, decided to consolidate state buildings into the state-owned property near the capitol rather than have them scattered around the perimeter of the city in leased space.

California represents the fifth largest economy in the world and its impact on building is tremendous. By executive order, former California governor Gray Davis required the state to erect buildings that are models of resource efficiency to set the bar high and propel the entire green building industry forward. In early 1999, the California Secretary of State and Consumer Services Agency directed the Department of General Services (the agency that oversees building and construction projects) to engage other state agencies involved in environmental issues to design

Special Features

■ Energy conservation and efficiency, including under-floor air distribution system and high-efficiency glazing

■ [illegible] commissioning and testing throughout the construction process

■ Ninety-five percent (99.67 percent if top soil is included) of construction waste diverted from landfill and recycled

■ Interpretive pocket park with organic pest management

■ Materials include 65 percent local materials

and construct offices buildings unlike any other built in the state of California. The Department of General Services set out to build one of the largest green office complexes and one of the most energy-efficient projects ever built in the country. Through an unprecedented collaborative effort,

Block 225 is 43 percent more efficient than California's Title 24 energy code. To minimize heat gain, the building features high-performance glazing, a white roof, and photo-voltaic cells that provide alternative energy.
©Erhard Pfeiffer 2003

40 government entities came together to participate on the state's Sustainability Task Force, which was in turn instrumental in facilitating the innovative green approach used for this project.

As master architects, Johnson Fain Architects, working with the comprehensive state green team, rendered preliminary design drawings. With a fair and appropriate budget for the project in hand based on the preliminary design, the state asked teams of architects and builders to compete for the design-build construction documents and completion at a fixed cost. The master team, having set high standards, sought teams that could deliver the highest value for the lowest cost. For this project, the state was not just interested in the lowest bidder. The state told the Block 225 team it would pay a fixed cost of $70 million. Also included was the state's aggressive but achievable mandate for 10 to 85 percent recycled content in various materials and the requirement that the project exceed the state's Title 24 energy code by at least 30 percent.

Three design-build teams made the short list for each project (Blocks 171–174 and Block 225). These short-listed teams were given five months to develop their competition entries; teams competed to provide value to the state, set a new benchmark for performance, and attract the rest of the country to these standards. One bidder, Hensel Phelps Construction Company, brought in green consultant Anthony Bernheim, an architect with Simon, Martin-Vegue, Winkelstein and Moris (SMWM) of San Francisco. Their Block 225 team met every two to three weeks for a day each and developed individual and whole-building strategies for energy conservation, indoor environmental and air quality, and resource efficiency and effectiveness. This team drafted 110 additional strategies above and beyond the state's requirements.

The Hensel Phelps team won the design-build contract for the 479,000-square-foot (44,500-square-meter) Department of Education building. With the team selected, partnership sessions and design integration charrettes began. According to Johnson, "We really got up to a 60 percent increase over the energy code (California's Title 24 was in the process of an upgrade), and the design-build team pushed it up 13 percent more." In addition to the energy and environmental elements, art was an important facet of the design. One percent of the project budget, roughly $4 million, was designated for art, with a strong orientation toward energy, human, and spirit themes.

At first, the state government team members were skeptical about how far one could go with green, "but we got through it with creativity," Johnson notes. Everyone came to the table with his own interests and his own agenda. "Some things don't naturally lend themselves to compatibility, so there were some tradeoffs—for example, recycled products and air emissions." Manufacturers were dubious as well about the state's high performance requirements. Some said, "There's no way any company can deliver that." For example, furniture and carpet makers were required to meet strict emission considerations. Even the Business and Institutional Furniture Manufacturers Association said it was "impractical, if not impossible." With a multimillion dollar contract at stake, the manufacturers rolled up their sleeves and got to work. They succeeded in adjusting their products, and now the market has seen a transition. The project is achieving its goal of pushing the mainstream, not only in California but nationwide.

Planning and Design

The design-build team was not allowed to change the exterior design of the building developed by the master architect, so its primary focus was on building systems and the interior. Through the design charrettes, the team stressed to the state that green projects are the result of teamwork, collaboration, consensus, and commitment to improved quality and performance. Further, the design-build process brought the opportunity for a typical builder and its subcontractors to work at the table with the architects, landscape architects, and engineering consultants to identify ways to bring value to the state. Everybody brought ideas

to the table: building-integrated photovoltaics, under-floor air distribution, recycled-content products that only the subcontractor knew about, the cool-roof concept (before code required it). Creative concepts—the result of such a large, integrated team effort—were frequently proposed throughout preparation of the design and construction

Water efficiency is encouraged through the use of plumbing fixtures that conserve water and that restrict the flow. Graywater is used for fountains, and drought-tolerant plants for landscaping. ©Erhard Pfeiffer 2003

documents. For example, the team found a way to reuse 40,000 square feet (3,720 square meters) of marble flooring from the state's renovated library building, which had been in storage and otherwise would have been wasted.

To ensure that their design would be properly implemented, the team developed "Special Environmental Requirements." These specifications were developed at the beginning of the project and included in the project manual so that all materials suppliers would have to abide by them; all specifications were integrated with the special requirements as they were prepared. Thus, fast-track construction packages could be issued when needed, with environmental rules already integrated.

The building envelope was designed for energy efficiency. High-performance glazing and high ceilings were designed to maximize light penetration into the building. The glass reflects heat, and the white roof reflects 70 percent of sunlight, reducing heat gain and air-conditioning and mechanical loads. The photovoltaic panels were installed in the exterior southern face of the mechanical penthouse.

Mechanical and HVAC systems were designed using DOE-2 to maximize energy efficiency. Carrier Evergreen chillers were installed, but even on the hottest day, the building uses only one chiller and never exceeds 76 degrees Fahrenheit (24 degrees Celsius), the set point. The mechanical penthouse on the roof has a wall of mechanical louvers on one side and air filters on the other. Sensors adjust the louvers depending on air temperatures, so less energy is used to cool the building. A built-up under-floor air distribution system uses variable-speed heating fan coils to keep the concrete slab at a constant 64 degrees Fahrenheit (18 degrees Celsius). A 975-ton (885-metric-ton) chilled water plant provides variable-speed chillers and a system-specific pumping system. One master chiller for the water fountains saves money on individual chillers at each fountain.

Energy is provided on site. A 120-foot-long (36.5-meter-long) bank of photovoltaic panels mounted on the southern exterior wall of the mechanical penthouse feeds alternative energy into the main power grid serving the entire building. The Sacramento Municipal Utility District provided the bank of building-integrated photovoltaic modules at no cost to the design-build team, with the stipulation that the contractor install and connect the panels to the electrical system. The contractor provided a two-year energy monitoring program as part of its design-build package to help the state monitor energy use at the beginning of the building's life.

Space planning and materials such as light-colored and reflective walls and ceiling panels help maximize daylight penetration to the interior of the building. The design limits the placement of private offices and other enclosed spaces to the perimeter of the building. Highly reflective ceiling and wall panels allow for multiple bounces of natural and artificial light. T-8 lamps and automated light controls for work areas are part of the lighting strategy. Motion sensors are used in very specific areas.

The building also uses water efficiently with low-water-consumption plumbing fixtures and low-flow restrictors to reduce water consumption and sewage discharge. Graywater is recycled for use in the fountains. The use of predominantly steam-fired chilled water equipment reduces the use of fluorocarbon refrigerants. Recirculation heat tape minimizes the waiting time for hot water. (Heat tape is used to heat all types of fluids in preinsulated pipes.) Environmentally friendly water treatment products in condenser water treatment systems reduce airborne and waterborne pollutants. Drought-tolerant plants are used in the landscaping.

Anthony Bernheim of SMWM and Hal Levin of Building Ecology Research Group Planning guided an extensive chemical analysis of materials to monitor indoor air quality and "develop and implement an effective material source control strategy that could be seamlessly integrated into the overall project schedule." They required that most

About 90 percent of the materials used in Block 225 were recycled, 65 percent were locally sourced, and 97 percent of construction waste was diverted from landfills.
©Erhard Pfeiffer 2003

major building products be tested for emissions of VOCs. Material manufacturers were then required to calculate the predicted indoor VOC concentrations for their products, which were evaluated against a list of "chemicals of concern" (carcinogens, reproductive toxicants, and chemical compounds with long-term heath effects). Data were provided to the architects for evaluation before products were manufactured and delivered. Specifications were developed to prescreen materials and limit concentrations of VOCs. Emission test protocols were developed for the building materials and for the furniture. At least 16 key materials, including insulation, acoustic panels, sealers, carpet tile and other flooring materials, paints, adhesives, and fabric wall covers, were tested.

The building was flushed out for about 30 days at the end of construction and commissioned: the process included building commissioning (including mechanical, electrical, and plumbing systems), indoor air quality commissioning (including testing air quality in the building during construction, before and after the furniture installation, and before and after occupancy), and green building commissioning (including digital documentation of all green materials, with manufacturers' certification to confirm that the products installed met green and testing requirements and that what was installed was the same product tested and submitted as a sample). To maintain the best possible air qual-

ity, monitoring units continually sample the air, and carbon dioxide sensors adjust the fresh air intake. High-pressure air in elevator lobbies ensures that air from parking garages does not enter through the elevator shaft.

Overall, about 90 percent of the materials contain recycled content. Low- and no-VOC materials were used to meet project specifications. Insulation is free of formaldehyde. Ceiling tiles contain 82 percent postindustrial recycled content. Structural steel contains on average 76 percent recycled content. Concrete contains 25 percent fly ash in the floor decks; the mat slab contains 40 percent fly ash. Carpet tiles and roll carpeting meet indoor air quality requirements; they contain 42 percent postindustrial and 10 percent postconsumer recycled content, have no PVC in the backing, and, according to the manufacturer, are 100 percent recyclable at the end of their useful life.

Construction

The project was developed using a modified design-build method known as "bridging," in which the design criteria and related documents describing the state's requirements form the basis of the work when proposals are solicited from teams of contractors and architects. The project's design-build team held meetings regularly to ensure implementation of the green issues and preparation of the LEED doc-

A $2.8 million art program is integrated within the complex, emphasizing California's values and heritage. One percent of Block 225's budget was spent on artistic features, such as the lobby artwork shown here. ©Erhard Pfeiffer 2003

umentation. Anthony Bernheim visited the site regularly to review it for conformance with the green specifications.

The team set a goal of 75 percent of construction and demolition debris to be diverted but came in closer to 97 percent. Five Dumpsters for different materials were set up at the site. All contractors were informed of and educated about the green efforts being made; they eventually started proposing their own innovative ideas.

Financing

From the beginning of this bond-financed project, the Department of Finance and the Office of Management and Budget were on board. The department recognized that some green elements, such as the value of healthy indoor air, do not neatly fit into typical quantitative analysis. Through life-cycle analysis, the team worked with the department to show the cost-effectiveness of other features. The time horizons of these green building investments were considered over the full life of the building to further substantiate cost-

effectiveness. Many commercial buildings last only ten to 15 years, but, the team says, these buildings need to last 100 years and should be an investment.

Master architect Scott Johnson says, "You lease space at $26 per square foot ($280 per square meter), but the cost of people is ten times the cost of the physical plant. Employee costs reach $260 per square foot ($2,800 per square meter). Energy is even less, $2 to $4 per square foot ($21.50 to $43 per square meter). Anything the design can do to improve workers' productivity through better design, good lighting, and healthy indoor air is an investment in human capital. Energy efficiency savings are icing."

Experience Gained

Overall, the Capitol Area East End Complex will save a projected $400,000 annually in energy costs. And more than $200 million will be saved over the cost of leasing comparable office space over the next 30 years. The project serves as a model for more than $500 million in new state projects, according to Aileen Adams, secretary of the State and Consumer Services Agency. With California planning to spend $84.5 billion annually on new construction and facilities maintenance, the potential savings with this green building practice is tremendous. Almost $1 billion could be saved over ten years.

The project brought significant changes in the market toward more environmentally friendly products. Known for its fire-retarding asbestos insulation, Johns Manville, for example, supplies formaldehyde-free insulation. After completion of the project, the company became the first to eliminate formaldehyde from building insulation.

The Center for the Built Environment at the University of California at Berkeley is conducting a study comparing the two projects: Block 171–174 without an under-floor air distribution system and Block 225 with an under-floor air distribution system. It is hoped the study will show the benefits of such a system for energy efficiency and good indoor air quality.

Project Data: Capitol Area East End Complex, Block 225 Office Building

Land Use and Building Information

Gross building area	479,000 square feet (44,500 square meters)
Building height	6 stories
Parking	213 underground spaces

Development Cost Information

Total Development Cost	$392 million

Owner

State of California Department of General Services
1102 Q Street, Suite 1500
Sacramento, California 95814

Occupant

State of California Department of Education

Project Management

State of California Department of General Services
Real Estate Services Division, Project Management Branch
1525 N Street
Sacramento, California 95815
Phone: 916-445-0780
Fax: 916-322-3987

Project Consultant

3D/International
Phone: 916-323-8446
www.3di.com

General Contractor

Hensel Phelps Construction Company
2107 North First Street, Suite 101
San Jose, California 95131
Phone: 916-447-8030
Fax: 916-447-8035
www.henselphelps.com

Architect

Fentress Bradburn Architects
421 Broadway
Denver, Colorado 80203
Phone: 303-722-5000
Fax: 303-722-5080
www.fentressbradburn.com

Associate Architect

Dreyfuss & Blackford Architects
3540 Folsom Boulevard
Sacramento, California 95816
Phone: 916-453-1234
Fax: 916-453-1236
www.dreyfussblackford.com

Green Building Architects and Commissioning Agent

SMWM
989 Market Street, Third Floor
San Francisco, California 94103
Phone: 415-546-0400
Fax: 415-882-7098
www.smwm.com

Indoor Air Quality Consultant

Hal Levin Associates
2548 Empire Grade
Santa Cruz, California 95060
Phone: 831-425-3946
Fax: 831-426-6522

Other Consultants

Mechanical Engineers: Critchfield Mechanical Inc., Menlo Park, California
Plumbing Contractor: J.W. McClenahan Co., Sacramento, California
Energy Efficiency: Taylor Engineering, Alameda, California
Electrical Contractor: Rosendin Electric, San Jose, California
Electrical Engineer: The Engineering Enterprise, Auburn, California
Acoustical Consultant: Acoustics & Vibration Group, Sacramento, California
Air Quality Testing: Indoor Environmental Engineering, San Francisco, California
Office Systems Furniture: HNI Corporation, Muscatine, Iowa

Development Schedule

1960s	Site acquired
1990s	Planning started
2000	Construction started
2002	Construction completed
2002	Occupancy

Location

1430 N Street
Sacramento, California

The Condé Nast Building

Four Times Square
New York, New York

Pamela Lippe

The Condé Nast Building at Four Times Square in New York City is significant as the first environmentally responsible skyscraper in the United States. It marks a commitment to environmentally responsible design and construction on the part of a commercial office developer. The strong focus on air quality and the use of fuel cells and photovoltaics are the most innovative aspects of the project; it was the first time fuel cells were put inside a building and approved in New York City and the first time photovoltaics were integrated into the facade of a skyscraper there.

The Condé Nast Building at Four Times Square in New York was designed with two distinct orientations: to reflect the dynamism of Times Square and to complement the corporate image of midtown Manhattan. Raimondo Di Egidio

The building was constructed by the Durst Organization, a family-run company that owns, builds, and manages premium office buildings. Three generations of the Durst family have focused their considerable energy on Manhattan real estate, mainly in midtown.

Special Features
- Building-integrated photovoltaics
- Two 200-kilowatt phosphoric acid fuel cells
- Indoor air quality monitoring and filtration
- Waste recycling chutes
- Aggressive construction recycling

The Site

The site, in the heart of midtown Manhattan in Times Square, is surrounded by dense urban development that includes office buildings, hotels, theaters, and stores. The original site had no natural features remaining and was completely covered with buildings constructed during the late 19th to mid-20th centuries.

The project sits amid what is probably the largest collection of mass transit in the world, including New York's Grand Central terminal, the Port Authority bus terminal, and connections to the Long Island Rail Road, New Jersey Transit, and innumerable subway and bus lines. The building provides no parking space.

The Development Process

The Durst Organization had been acquiring property on the block for decades. New York State, through its Empire State Development Corporation (ESDC), had acquired through condemnation four sites at 42nd Street and Times

All construction technology and building systems were evaluated for their environmental sensitivity, their effect on the health of occupants, and their ability to reduce energy consumption—making this the first environmentally responsible building of its size. Andrew Gordon

Before Durst's proposal, all the state environmental quality review approvals had been granted for the site. Community reaction at the public hearing related to the new building was very favorable for several reasons: 1) the building's design embraced the character of Times Square; 2) it signaled the end of the real estate recession; and 3) the owner had publicly stated very aggressive environmental goals. The project was exempt from zoning because it was owned by New York State.

Planning

The Condé Nast Building was the first building developed by the third generation of the Durst family, Douglas and Jody Durst. The Dursts had been raised with a strong appreciation of nature and so environmental responsibility in their profession was an instinctive outgrowth of their personal interests and concerns. In addition, Durst properties had for years been taking advantage of utility demand-side reduction programs to increase the efficiency of their existing properties, and they were fully aware of the financial advantages of efficiency. They were also aware of the impact they could have on their industry by making the first building emerging out of the real estate recession in New York City environmentally responsible.

The Dursts hired architects Fox & Fowle, engineers Cosentini Associates, and construction managers Tishman Construction Corporation based on their ability to design and build a high-rise office building in New York City. In the effort to design the first environmentally responsible skyscraper in the United States, the Dursts, Fox & Fowle, and Tishman hired or designated people in their firms to focus on environmental issues and support the project team as needed. This "green team" was responsible for providing support for implementation of the environmental aspects of the process (researching environmental materials and technologies, educating the contractors to ensure construction and demolition [C&D] recycling, reviewing submittals for impact on indoor air quality and recycled content).

Square that had been slated for development in the 1980s. Philip Johnson had designed four monolithic structures for Prudential/Park Tower Realty that engendered considerable public resistance. The timing for that development could not have been worse, as the real estate recession was in full swing. In part because of the public outcry but mostly because of economic realities, the projects were delayed and then canceled. In the mid-1990s, the Durst Organization acquired the ground lease from Prudential, which had leased it from ESDC, and added three other properties to the site by deeding them to ESDC and amending the Prudential ground lease to include the additional properties.

A series of setbacks on the upper floors, combined with a variety of facade treatments, created a design that fits into its diverse urban setting. Andrew Gordon

schemes because the Empire State Development Corporation required 60-foot (18-meter) electric signage on all facades facing Times Square and 42nd Street and seriously considered solar, wind, and fuel cells. Photovoltaics were integrated into the facade, and ultimately two fuel cells were installed.

The building was designed with a strong focus on indoor air quality. Significant time was spent considering how to design the cleanest HVAC system possible in terms of both environmental impact of the systems chosen and indoor air quality. Water-efficient fixtures were used as required by the New York City code.

The New York State Energy Research and Development Authority (NYSERDA) provided financial support through Steven Winter Associates to model and analyze the curtain wall and illustrate the savings that could be provided by several energy-efficiency measures for tenant fitout. The Department of Defense provided $200,000 each to help buy down the cost of the two fuel cells for the building. Rocky Mountain Institute provided support under a grant from the Energy Foundation for strategies related to a performance-based fee experiment in which the design team is financially rewarded for energy-saving design.

The building was designed in 1995–1996, when LEED was in its very early stages and required a smoking ban in any LEED-rated building. At that time, tenants insisted on their right to allow smoking in private offices, and because LEED was unwilling to budge on the requirement, the project team decided not to use the LEED standards for guidance.

The green building objectives were to explore and integrate any environmentally responsible technologies and techniques that made sense for the project. The team was particularly interested in alternative energy-generating

Design

The Condé Nast Building is designed with two distinct orientations; the west and north sides of the building reflect the dynamic environment of Times Square and are clad primarily in metal and glass, while along 42nd Street and the east facade, textured and scaled masonry are more appropriate to the midtown corporate context and the refined style of Bryant Park. The addition of the contiguous property allowed a 30 percent expansion of the original building site and the larger and more efficient floor plates attractive to

The Condé Nast Building was the first skyscraper in New York to integrate photovoltaic panels into its facade. They are incorporated into the spandrel panels of the structure's exterior. Jeff Goldberg

large corporate tenants. It also enabled the architects to employ setback massing. The architects created a varied composition of interlocking setback forms and facade treatments that responded to the diverse scale and character of the neighboring building and suggests a characteristic Times Square layering of buildings that might have evolved over time. The top of the building reflects the principal structural support system and, with its four 70-foot-square (21-meter-square) signs and a communications tower, expresses the project's location at the Crossroads of the World.

Construction

The buildings on the site were salvaged before C&D recycling was aggressively promoted, contractors were extensively educated about the process, and detailed reporting was required. As documented by an EPA case study, the project successfully diverted 67 percent of its construction and demolition waste from the landfill.

Demolition and construction began in early 1996; at that time, no major construction projects had been done in an environmentally responsible manner in the United States. Thus, little direction was available at the time. LEED was in its earliest stages and provided little or no advice for contractors. Each member of the project team had to learn on the job and, in many cases, invent procedures as the job progressed.

Photovoltaics were of interest to the Durst Organization because of their ability to avoid the environmental impact of greenhouse gases and other types of pollution. Incorporating photovoltaic panels into the spandrel panels replaced a nonproductive glass with one that produced clean electricity. Photovoltaics cost less than the roof-mounted system that was originally considered because they required no additional structure and they replaced expensive spandrel glass.

Integrating photovoltaics and fuel cells into the building and negotiating approvals with the utility were extremely time-consuming and difficult. Overcoming jurisdictional issues with respect to the wiring of the photovoltaics was also a major challenge. Originally, the Dursts had hoped to put photovoltaics at the top of the building on all four sides, but ultimately because of the cost and the schedule, they were used only on the south and east facades. They initially had hoped to put eight fuel cells at the top of the building and had strengthened it to accommodate them, but based on the cost and the inability to sell electricity back to the utility at night, the number was decreased to two.

Using waste heat from the fuel cells was more difficult than expected because they provide relatively low-grade heat and were placed in the outside air plenum for the lower half of the building fairly late in the process. The Durst Organization ultimately used the waste heat to deal with a condensation problem created by the fuel cells during cold weather. The fuel cells generate power at 0.10 kilowatt-hour, compared with the ConEdison rate of roughly 0.14 kilowatt-hour. The savings, although they benefit the tenant, have been sufficient to pay back the capital expense of the purchase and installation of the fuel cells one and one-half times.

A free cooling system optimizes the use of secondary water, heat exchangers, and crossover piping. Integrating a massive supplementary air-conditioning system for one tenant and monitoring actual Btu consumption proved complicated but doable. It was achieved through exceptional coordination between the base building and tenant engineers.

The "hat truss" design reduced the amount of steel needed to counter the high wind loads. In addition, heavy equipment placed at the top of the building acts as a damper, reducing the amount of steel needed.

Extensive research conducted by the project team, consultants, tenant teams, contractors, and subcontractors on recycled content and low-VOC materials paid off in finding materials at a no- or low-price premium. Options were much more limited at the time. Every subcontractor was encouraged to find ways to avoid waste and required to report recycled content and recyclability of all materials.

Low-e high-performance glass and extra-large windows maximized the potential for daylighting. The Durst Organization added extra insulation throughout the building. Although the extra insulation has no significant payback, it will decrease the use of fossil fuels over the building's lifetime.

Waste chutes were provided along the full height of the building, with adequate space at the loading dock for proper sorting and storage of recyclables. Overcoming the fire department's opposition to the trash chutes' rising the full height of the building was another unexpected challenge. Nevertheless, the waste chutes paid for themselves quickly because of the high cost of labor and carting in New York City.

The Durst Organization developed tenant guidelines and provided a green library for tenants and their architects and engineers to assist in tenant fitout.

Extensive use of sustainable features and equipment is expected to result in operational costs that are 10 to 15 percent lower than such costs in a comparable building. Andrew Gordon

Financing

The owner funded the purchase of the land and a portion of the initial construction costs for approximately 25 percent of total project costs. The owner and development entity were both wholly owned Durst Organization affiliates.

A syndicate led by Bank of New York provided the construction financing. At the time of closing, the building was 90 percent preleased. UBS provided long-term financing through the issuance of commercial mortgage–backed securities. No public financing was used.

Marketing

Many different members of the project team have conducted hundreds of tours of the building. Visitors have come from all over the world—Japan, China, Korea, Australia, Great Britain, France, Germany, Italy, and many other countries.

Project Data: The Condé Nast Building

Land Use and Building Information

Site area	1.2 acres (0.5 hectare)
Gross building area	1.7 million square feet (158,000 square meters)
Net rentable area	1.7 million square feet (158,000 square meters)
Building height	48 floors; 866 feet (264 meters) to top of spire
Typical floor size	34,000–54,000 square feet (3,160–5,020 square meters)

Tenant Information

Office occupancy rate	100%
Office rents	$60–75 per square foot per month ($645–810 per square meter)
Retail rents	$250 per square foot per month ($2,700 per square meter)
Average lease length	15–20 years
Lease terms	6–8 months rent free; electricity submetered

Development Cost Information

Site Acquisition	$100,000,000
Construction Cost	$250,000,000
Soft Costs	$80,000,000
Green Building Costs[1]	
Fuel cells	$1,400,000
Photovoltaics	650,000
Recycling chutes	165,000
Total Development Cost	$432,215,000

Annual Operating Expenses

Taxes	$3.68 per square foot[2] ($39.60 per square meter)
Annual operating costs	$8.78 per square foot ($94.50 per square meter)

Owner/Developer

The Durst Organization
1155 Avenue of the Americas, Ninth Floor
New York, New York 10038
Phone: 212-789-1155
Fax: 212-789-1199
www.durst.org

Architect

Fox & Fowle
22 West 19th Street, 11th Floor
New York, New York 10011
Phone: 212-627-1700
Fax: 212-463-8716
www.foxfowle.com

Construction Manager

Tishman Construction Company
666 Fifth Avenue
New York, New York 10103
Phone: 212-399-3600
Fax: 212-489-9694
www.tishmanconstruction.com

The building has been featured in numerous television and radio documentaries and news reports. Four Times Square was the site of the U.S. EPA ENERGY STAR awards in 2001; numerous other organizations have used it for many other events highlighting environmental responsibility.

The building has received a number of awards: National Honor Award from the American Institute of Architects in 2001; Excellence in Design from the American Institute of Architects of New York State in 2000; Major Achievement from the New York City Audubon Society in 2000; New Construction Building of the Year for 1999–2000 from Building Owners and Managers Association; and the Star of Efficiency from the Alliance to Save Energy in 1999. The building has also qualified for ENERGY STAR status.

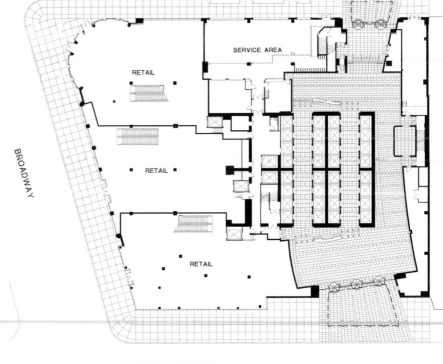

WEST 43RD STREET

SERVICE AREA

RETAIL

BROADWAY

RETAIL

RETAIL

WEST 42ND STREET

Site plan. Fox + Fowle Architects

Mechanical Engineer

Cosentini Associates
Two Penn Plaza
New York, New York 10121
Phone: 212-615-3600
Fax: 212-615-3700
www.cosentini.com

Structural Engineer

Cantor Seinuk Group
228 East 45th Street
Third Floor
New York, New York 10017
Phone: 212-687-9888
Fax: 646-487-5501
www.cantorseinuk.com

Development Schedule

5/1995	Planning started
5/1996	Construction started
7/1996	Site purchased
9/1996	Sales/leasing started
6/1999	Construction completed
12/1999	Move-in completed

Location

Four Times Square (Broadway between 42nd and 43rd streets)
New York, New York

Notes

1. Includes full installation costs.
2. Pilot payments for 20 years to the Empire State Development Corporation.

Management

The building was extensively commissioned by the Durst Organization staff and is regularly recommissioned. Building personnel constantly monitor and manage 10,000 data points. A Web-enabled metering system allows tracking of energy consumption for both tenants and the building. Green cleaning agents are used. The trash chute facilitates pickup and recycling of office paper.

Extensive filtration of outside air removes 85 percent of particulate matter. Filters are changed every two weeks. Permanent carbon dioxide monitors are placed in return air ducts, and carbon monoxide monitors near loading docks are tied into the building management system. Permanent tubing in the floor facilitates quarterly monitoring for VOCs and other indoor contaminants. The HVAC system allows three floors at a time to be flushed with 100 percent outside air should any contaminants be identified.

Experience Gained

The building was rented primarily to two major tenants for 20-year leases. Therefore, it has been 100 percent rented from the beginning and has consistently outperformed the market in terms of vacancy rate and absorption.

The goal of the Durst Organization is to continue to set new standards in environmentally responsible design and construction and to provide the most efficient and environmentally beneficial buildings possible for their tenants. The Durst Organization continues to learn and apply the knowledge gained, currently in two residential high rises, one commercial office tower, and one new weekend home community.

Eastgate

Harare, Zimbabwe

Alexis Karolides

Eastgate is the largest commercial office/shopping building in Zimbabwe. The development occupies two city blocks and consists of two narrow nine-story towers linked by a 52-foot-wide (16-meter-wide) glazed atrium. The first and second floors contain retail uses, the upper floors offices. Parking is provided on two levels below ground and at ground level on the north side of the complex.

The complex is ventilated with a combination of natural and mechanical systems. Cooling strategies modeled after those of termites on the local savannah maintain comfortable temperatures without a conventional air-conditioning plant. These regional termite mounds maintain a constant temperature of 87 degrees Fahrenheit (30.5 degrees Celsius) despite extreme outdoor temperature fluctuations from night to day of 35 to 104 degrees Fahrenheit (1.7 to 40 degrees Celsius). Eastgate consumes 35 percent less energy than comparable conventional buildings with full air conditioning in Harare.

The Eastgate building in Harare, Zimbabwe, uses dramatically less energy by copying the successful strategies of an indigenous natural system—a termite mound. Mick Pearce, Pearce McComish Architects

The Site

Rather than locate this office/shopping complex in the suburbs—the trend in the region—Old Mutual Properties, which has a history of ecologically and socially sensitive development, chose an inner-city site. The building blocks are oriented with the long sides facing north and south, and they were designed to enhance natural ventilation and daylighting. Because Eastgate is located in the heart of Harare rather than in the low-density suburbs, it is accessible to commuters, who typically walk or travel by public transportation.

Development Process and Planning

Harare, the capital of Zimbabwe, is located at 18°5' latitude at an altitude of 4,930 feet (1,503 meters). It enjoys a tropical high-altitude climate that is warm and dry with

Special Features

■ Ventilation system combining natural and mechanical systems, including chimneys for air extraction
■ Solar panels for water heating
■ Precast concrete sun screens
■ Double-thick brick exterior walls
■ Atrium with open, louvered sides for ventilation
■ Extensive use of local materials
■ Urban infill location

clear skies for much of the year. With warm, sunny days and cool nights, it has the ideal climate for natural ventilation combined with night cooling.

During the day, the sun warms the roof. At night, the warm roof draws cool air into the building, which in turn chills the concrete slabs under the office floors and keeps the interior comfortable for the following day. Mick Pearce, Pearce McComish Architects

Old Mutual Properties, an insurance and real estate conglomerate, required the project architect and engineers to design a building that would take advantage of local climate and materials to eliminate the need for an air-conditioning plant. Architect Mick Pearce realized that he needed to assemble a multidisciplinary design team to come up with an integrated solution that would meet the client's environmental requirements. After an intensive two-day design session involving the collaborative architecture/engineering design team, the basic scheme that emerged remained the basic concept throughout the design process.

During the concept stage, Arup Engineers modeled the building extensively, using dynamic thermal analysis to ascertain the optimal daytime and nighttime flows. The study predicted that the building could stay 5.4 degrees Fahrenheit (3 degrees Celsius) cooler inside than outside at the hottest time of day, which has been proved by building monitoring. This performance was remarkable, because until the mid-1990s, the benchmark performance for passively treated offices was to achieve inside temperatures no hotter than outside temperatures. Eastgate is able to harvest 7 degrees Fahrenheit (4 degrees Celsius) of cooling from a diurnal shift of 21.5 degrees Fahrenheit (12 degrees Celsius).

Design

African termites build their mounds so that inside the temperature is a constant 87 degrees Fahrenheit (30.5 degrees Celsius) despite extreme outdoor temperature fluctuations of 35 to 104 degrees Fahrenheit (1.7 to 40 degrees Celsius). They can do so by taking full advantage of three environmental conditions: a stable ground temperature (thermal mass), diurnal external temperature shift, and water from the water table. The termites dig chambers in the earth below their structures, which are cooled by water in the water table. During the day, cool air is drawn into the base of the mound to replace hot air sucked out through sunbaked flues on the top of the mound. The termites constantly dig new tunnels and block others to fine-tune the temperature and humidity of the interior.

This design was the inspiration for providing indoor comfort in Eastgate. Before considering ventilation and cooling, the design team minimized the building's potential solar gain by reducing the internal heat gain of lighting and equipment, orienting the building east-west, providing extensive shading, restricting glazing to only 25 percent of the north and south facades, and shading all those windows with precast concrete sun screens, intricately patterned after traditional designs. Double-thick brick in the exterior walls moderates the temperature swings (while also keeping out the bustling noise of the city), and light-colored finishes reduce heat absorption.

The building was initially designed to use its natural "stack effect" to draw nighttime air over the massive floor slabs. (The stack effect in buildings is the same as stack effect in a chimney. The draft produced in a chimney depends on the difference between the temperatures of the flue gas and the outside air as well as on the chimney's height. During cold weather, similar action occurs in buildings, although the difference between inside and outside air temperature is much less.) When Arup's computer simulations showed that it would be hard to balance temperature throughout the building year round, however, the design team decided to use locally made fans to ensure that cool air is distributed evenly to all floors.

Eastgate exploits the diurnal shift (the difference between daytime and nighttime air temperatures), which is available almost year-round in this medium altitude climatic zone. The average temperature shift is about 12 degrees; by mechanically driving air through the structure at night at a rate of ten air changes per hour, the concrete structure is cooled down as the heat accumulated during the previous day is flushed out through the vertical ducts and chimneys.

The first two floors and the underground garage use conventional mechanical ventilation. Hollow floor slabs on the upper seven office levels allow nighttime cooling by outside air. Fresh air intakes and filters are located between the first and second floors. The atrium also serves as a fresh air intake. Air is distributed vertically through ducts along the central spine of each office block. From the vertical risers, air flows through a double slab in the central corridor that runs the length of each wing and then through transverse channels in the floor slabs out to the edge of the building. (Electrical service also runs through these voids in the floor.) The floor slabs are specially designed to increase surface area and turbulence of the air as it flows past. From the floor slab, air flows into the offices through grilles below each window.

Warm air exits through 48 round brick chimneys on Eastgate's roof.
Mick Pearce, Pearce McComish Architects

Some of these supply grilles contain low-capacity electric heaters (250 to 500 watts) for winter heating. Return air is vented through ports in the vaulted ceiling into a ceiling plenum in the corridor. It then flows into exhaust shafts connected to 32 brick chimneys. During the day, the chimneys heat up in the sun, creating a stack effect that assists air movement. Sixteen additional chimneys provide mechanical exhaust from the four nonoffice levels.

Ventilation rates are increased significantly at night (on the order of four times) to ensure that an optimal amount of cool nighttime air flows through the massive structure, which can then soak up heat the next day. The ventilation rate is reduced during the day to provide enough fresh air without raising the building's temperature greatly.

Eastgate's external structural frame and central structural corridor are made of cast-in-place concrete, with precast concrete floors spanning the frame. The floors were made hollow by placing precast stools on the cast-in-place slab and then topping them with a leveling screed. The stools have protrusions that increase the air turbulence and surface area in the hollow slab, thus increasing heat transfer to and from the mass (for summer cooling and winter heating). The structural slab also forms the ceiling for the floor below. Its underside is vaulted to increase the surface area available for heat transfer to and from the office below. A jagged facade reflects heat during the day and provides increased surface area to emit what it did absorb during the night.

The seven-story atrium provides natural light to interior spaces. Light-colored finishes in the atrium reflect light into the adjoining spaces, while light-colored office interiors enhance the effectiveness of both natural and artificial light sources. Because every other window is operable, building users also have a good amount of personal control over their environment.

The atrium serves as the fresh-air intake for the building's ventilation systems. Its ends are fitted with ventilation louvers and are open to breezes and stack pressures, but it still provides protection from rain and blown sand. The atrium also accommodates all the vertical circulation.

Eastgate juxtaposes steel and glass architecture reminiscent of early settlers' mining towns with detailing such as lattice steelwork, hanging elevators, glass and steel suspension bridges, and the glass roof. Precast concrete was made

The Eastgate complex actually is two buildings linked by sky bridges across an open-air, glass-roofed atrium. Fans move fresh air from the atrium into the office space. Mick Pearce, Pearce McComish Architects

to look like stone by adding granite aggregate and granite sand to the concrete and brushing it before it set to achieve a stone-like finish. Layered atop these manmade materials are green vines attached to the building's facade to bring nature back into the city.

Construction and Performance

Construction of the building began in 1993 and was completed in 1996. The owner required that local artisans and local materials be used in construction of the building; as a result, only 12 percent of the total project cost was spent on imported materials or processes.

The building is designed for small or large tenants; the smallest space with its own front door is 2,700 square feet (250 square meters). This design fits the tendency in Zimbabwe for the growth of small enterprises. The building is also very easy to convert into residential units, as the band of services runs down the center of the blocks. Convertibility is a very important qualification for a sustainable building.

Eastgate's use of natural ventilation was financially motivated. The owner/developer insisted that air-conditioning systems not be designed into the project, at the same time comfort was not to be sacrificed. Such air-conditioning systems are expensive in both upfront and operational costs; they have to be imported, making them sensitive to fluctuations in currency, they require expensive foreign parts when they break—especially without guaranteed skilled labor to service them—and they are subject to the debilitating effects of Harare's frequent power outages. Arup's engineers, by using the natural system instead of an

air-conditioning plant, saved $3.5 million on a $36 million building. The cost of the heat-exchange floor was recouped by eliminating the cost of the suspended ceiling that normally covers air-conditioning ducts.

Eastgate's operational costs are appealing as well. Compared with the energy bills of five conventional air-conditioned buildings in Harare of similar quality and status, Eastgate's operational energy costs are 17 to 52 percent lower (36 percent lower than the average).

Marketing

Eastgate's chimneys have established the building's image—it is often referred to as the Queen Mary or the Titanic—but as smokeless chimneys, they symbolize the building's green character.

Some of the building's operational cost savings are passed on to tenants, who pay 20 percent less for rent than the market rate. Obviously lower rents are a strong marketing point. The only notable marketing challenge has been the perception that a building without conventional air conditioning is a substandard building. According to architect Pearce, "The biggest barrier we have found is the social acceptance of passive cooling in an environment where air conditioning has all the glamour and prestige of the western lifestyle."

Experience Gained

Arup has carefully monitored the building's performance over several years. Except for three weeks during Zimbabwe's hot, dry season (just before the October summer rains), the building fluctuates between 73 and 77 degrees Fahrenheit (23 and 25 degrees Celsius). Tenants confirm that the building is comfortable except during three summer weeks,

Vegetated screens naturally filter air on Eastgate's east end. Mick Pearce, Pearce McComish Architects

when several days of cloud buildup prevent effective night cooling. The success of the nighttime ventilation was particularly evident when the fans were accidentally left off one night, causing temperatures to rise.

One disadvantage of the ventilation system's low air speeds is the lack of white noise; combined with predominantly hard interior surfaces, it makes for reverberant acoustics.

With such stellar performance and savings, why has Eastgate not been extensively copied since its completion in 1996? Pearce suggests several "perverse incentives" are at work. First, speculative developers do not typically pay for operational costs and are therefore uninterested in energy savings provided by efficient designs. Second, architects and engineers are typically paid a percentage of the building cost, thus the elimination of an expensive air-conditioning plant actually reduces their fees. The Eastgate project succeeded because of an enlightened and sophisticated developer. Old Mutual recognized the benefits of sustainable design and made adjustments as necessary to provide incentives to produce an efficient green system. For example, the design team was paid the amount it would have earned on a conventional project. Savings from the elimination of air-conditioning equipment were spent on additional research and modeling.

Eastgate taught the engineering team much about passive design, performance, and operation, lessons that have already influenced other projects. For instance, at a subsequent Pearce/Arup project, Harare International School, the ventilated floor slabs used at Eastgate were replaced with buried rock chambers, and the chimneys were replaced with other forms of wind-assisted ventilation.

Although the elimination of air conditioning represented a savings of 10 percent of the total investment, the complexity of construction for the building and the higher-than-expected commissioning costs reduced the overall savings. Total rents at a fully air-conditioned neighboring building built at the same time are 20 percent higher because the savings in electricity are passed on to tenants at Eastgate. Pearce is convinced that the experience gained from Eastgate will help reduce costs for future buildings as the construction type is refined.

An important lesson learned was that tenants should have been better educated from the start about the principles of the building's design and operation. When they did finally understand the building's unconventional comfort control systems, tenants were much happier to accept a wider range of indoor temperature. It also helped them take potential heat gains (from office equipment, lighting, and high occupancy) into account when designing their internal spaces. Finally, they learned that they could use desk fans or open windows (when temperatures outside were cool) and not upset the system.

Project Data: Eastgate

Land Use and Building Information

Site area	100,200 square feet (9,313 square meters)
Building footprint	2.42 acres (1 hectare)
Gross building area	324,000 square feet (30,000 square meters)
Retail	60,278 square feet (5,600 square meters)
Office	279,862 square feet (26,000 square meters)
Underground and surface parking	433 spaces

Development Cost Information

Total Development Cost   US$36 million

Owner/Developer

Old Mutual Properties
The Property Factory
Howard Drive and Gardiner Way
Pinelands, Cape Town, South Africa
Phone: 27 21 530 458
www.oldmutual.co.za

Architect

Pearce McComish Architects (formerly Pearce Partnership)
Box 138
Eastgate
Harare, Zimbabwe
Phone: 263 4 751271
Fax: 263 4 751273
www.pearcemccomish.com

Engineer

Ove Arup
Astra Park
Ridgeway North and Northend Roads
Highlands, Harare, Zimbabwe
Phone: 263 4 882250
Fax: 263 4 882698
www.arup.com

Development Schedule

1991	Planning started
1993	Construction started
1996	Construction completed
1996	Occupancy

Location

Eastgate
Harare, Zimbabwe

Ford Motor Company PAG
North American Headquarters
Irvine, California

Dan Heinfeld

The 253,606-square-foot (23,570-square-meter) North American Headquarters for the Ford Motor Company's Premier Automotive Group (PAG) in the Irvine Spectrum Center, 40 miles (65 kilometers) south of downtown Los Angeles, is the first privately developed facility in California—and one of the largest private facilities in the United States—to receive LEED certification from the U.S. Green Building Council. Ford chose to meet the stringent LEED requirements with a facility that lowers the company's long-term operating costs and also meets its strategic business needs.

The North American Headquarters of the Ford Motor Company's Premier Automotive Group brings together the company's five luxury brands under one green roof—illustrating the company's commitment to the environment and providing a superior work environment for employees. LPA, Inc./Adrian Velicescu

This five-story green headquarters accommodates each luxury brand of Ford's Premier Automotive Group—Aston Martin, Jaguar, Land Rover, Lincoln, and Volvo—and approximately 800 people on one site to create a synergistic relationship of design, marketing, and distribution and to increase Ford's luxury car business.

The headquarters building was designed by LPA, Inc., and developed by Ford Motor Land Services Corporation, the worldwide strategic and operational real estate arm of Ford Motor Company. Construction on the headquarters began in May 2000, employees moved into the facility in November 2001, and the complex was completed in January 2002.

The Site and Planning Process

In 1998, the Ford Motor Company decided to bring together for the first time all five of its luxury brands under one umbrella, the Premier Automotive Group, to create an identi-

Special Features

- 200-kilowatt natural gas fuel cell system
- Raised-floor air-distribution system
- ENERGY STAR roof
- Outdoor views and natural daylighting for 90 percent of employees
- Automatic perimeter light dimming system
- Green screens and shading devices on the facade
- Landscaped roof and bird sanctuary
- Drought-tolerant landscaping
- 30 percent recycled content of building and furnishing materials and finishes
- 60 percent of construction waste recycled
- 35 electric vehicle charging stations

fiable and united entity in the marketplace and to create synergies in investment, engineering, marketing, and distribution.

Ford also wanted to bring the national headquarters for its luxury brands together under one roof. So in 1999, it decided to construct a North American headquarters for its Premier Automotive Group in the world's largest luxury market—southern California—to mount a stronger challenge to rival brands. Ford chose the 11.9-acre (4.8-hectare) site because of its centralized location in southern California. The property is in the vast Irvine Spectrum Center business and retail park (home to corporate headquarters and office, retail, restaurant, and entertainment tenants) near the I-405/I-5 interchange in the city of Irvine in Orange County. The west side of the headquarters site also faces Gateway Boulevard, which connects directly to the region's largest entertainment center.

From the beginning, the headquarters was planned as a green facility. Building design that supports the conservation of resources and development of natural habitats was essential to Ford's corporate mission and global future. The green orientation was also championed by William Clay Ford, Jr., a committed environmentalist, who was elected chair of Ford Motor Company in September 1998 and named chief executive officer in October 2001.

Design

The Ford Motor Company had several objectives for the new North American headquarters of the Premier Automotive Group that it wanted incorporated into the facility's design:

■ Demonstrate Ford Motor Company's commitment to the environment by showcasing intelligent, sustainable building design;

■ Provide a superior work environment for all employees that also immerses them in the competitive southern California luxury automobile market;

■ Create a design that consolidates the luxury subsidiaries under one roof, builds synergies among the brands, maximizes efficiencies, and maintains and strengthens the individual brand identities.

The headquarters site includes a 176,484-square-foot (16,400-square-meter) five-story office building with an additional one-story 77,122-square-foot (7,170-square-meter) wing for product development, a four-story parking structure, 268 surface parking spaces, and three acres (1.2 hectares) or 25 percent of the site of usable open space, including a 30,000-square-foot (2,790-square-meter) landscaped garden on the majority of the roof of the product development wing.

Ford's commitment to fuel cell technology led to the inclusion of a 200-kilowatt natural gas fuel cell system that provides 25 percent of the building's power and hot water, reducing the campus's reliance on outside energy sources. A raised-floor air distribution system delivers conditioned air to the buildings more efficiently by allowing natural stratification to occur. Under-floor air distribution can deliver air at higher and lower temperatures and at lower velocity than the traditional system of forcing air down from the ceiling plenum. This system is also 30 percent more efficient than a typical top-down forced-air system.

Restrooms are equipped with low-flow toilets and sinks with infrared sensors. Reclaimed water is provided by a municipal recycling system for all irrigation and for flushing toilets on the headquarters site.

The open-office floor plan and glass-enclosed perimeter offices give more than 90 percent of the 800 employees outdoor views and natural daylighting. The artificial lighting system includes indirect lighting in office areas, energy-efficient light bulbs, and energy-saving high-intensity T-5 fluorescent lamps with high-efficiency reflectors that direct most light output downward. A control system automatically dims perimeter lights when daylighting is adequate to properly illuminate the space, saving energy and operating costs.

The light, reflective color of the ENERGY STAR roof on the office building reduces heat island effects on the site and the heat absorption of a darker roof surface, which in turn lowers air-conditioning needs and costs. The majority of the product development wing's roof has been landscaped with more than 30 different native plant species, significantly reducing heat island effects on the site. The rooftop landscaping uses rainwater for drip irrigation, requires 67 percent less water than standard campus landscaping, helps insulate the upper floors of the wing, saves on future roofing costs, and increases energy efficiency. The rooftop landscaping also serves as a bird sanctuary.

The landscaping uses drought-tolerant plants and trees that are easy to maintain. "Green" screens on the exterior of the product development wing, the freeway side of the office building, and the freeway side of the parking structure shade the walls and top floors, providing insulation for the interior spaces. Together, the green screens and the rooftop garden add approximately 70,000 square feet (6,505 square meters) of additional landscaping to the campus, reducing heat islands and water runoff and improving air quality.

Materials and finishes incorporated into the facility use 30 percent recycled content; for example, fly ash (a byproduct of steel manufacturing) was recycled and used in the concrete building components. Various furnishings, furniture systems, fabrics, and carpeting throughout the office building are made of recycled materials.

The building supports employees' use of alternative transportation by providing 35 charging stations for electric vehicles, bicycle storage, showers, and direct connections to local bus lines and the commuter rail system.

By going green, the headquarters exceeds California's Title 24 energy requirements—the strictest in the nation—by more than 25 percent. That fact, coupled with the fuel

cell system, which provides approximately 25 percent of the buildings' overall power, creates a much more efficient environment than a standard office campus, reduces reliance on the local power grid by 50 percent, and therefore reduces the costs of operation.

The project architect had to overcome several challenges in designing the new headquarters as a green facility with a

A landscaped roof on the product development wing reduces the heat island effect on the site, helps insulate the upper floors of the building, provides increased energy efficiency, and also serves as a bird sanctuary. LPA, Inc./Adrian Velicescu

striking corporate presence. The long, linear, narrow site, for example, did not provide the optimal sustainable building orientation or configuration for a facility of this size and magnitude. In addition, the Irvine Spectrum area's specific design guidelines permitted little variation from an accepted standard, and they do not allow an aggressive, environmentally sensitive approach to building design.

Different sides of the property border very different developments. The east side of the site faces a freeway and the Irvine Spectrum Center office and retail developments. The west side of the site faces Gateway Boulevard, which connects directly to the region's largest entertainment center. The biggest challenge, however, was not green design but consolidating five very distinct brands in a unified group framework while using design to express each brand's individual identity. The architect responded to these challenges in several ways.

The main office tower, the product development wing, and the parking structure, for example, have two different facades. The freeway-facing building facades were designed to fit within design requirements for the Irvine Spectrum and the overall aesthetic through the use of precast con-

Green screens, such as this one on the freeway side of the parking structure, soften facades, provide shading, and insulate exterior building surfaces.
LPA, Inc./Adrian Velicescu

crete, punched openings, and an orthogonal frame. Metal fins create a 30-foot (nine-meter) rhythm along the freeway and are used to attach a series of accessories, including shading devices and green screens, that soften the facades.

The building facades facing Gateway Boulevard provide the formal entries into the buildings. The architect selected materials for the facade of the main office building that are used in the automotive industry: glass and recycled aluminum panels in the branded group color, a dark champagne metallic. The exterior design is also based on the automobile. The striking curved metal and glass facade borrows its soft form and shape from elements found in each of the five premier brands. The pattern of the glass, metal, and concrete facade, for example, mimics Lincoln's vertical front grill design and Land Rover's horizontal grill.

The Gateway facade of the product development wing does not include the broad glass bands of the main office tower for security reasons. Instead, high clerestory glass protected by a metal louver system runs in a broad horizontal strip along the top of the facade, providing both security and natural light for the interior.

A green screen surrounds both the four-story, 633-stall parking structure and the product development wing, shading them and blending them into the headquarters landscape. That screening in turn enables the main office building to become the dominant feature on the site.

The headquarters has 268 surface parking spaces. Surface lots were kept to a minimum to lessen the amount of hard surfaces and heat islands on campus and to maximize open space and landscaping. At the back of the main office building are 35 universal charging stations for electric vehicles.

The interior was designed to showcase the vehicles on display and to support the identity of the different brands. Thus, the common areas of the building use the group's dark champagne metallic color palette, which provides a neutral backdrop for each of the five distinct brands. The 37,000-square-foot (3,440-square-meter) floors for each premier brand, however, were designed to reflect the individual style, personality, operations, and people of each brand while also incorporating features that refer to the overall group identity. Glass-enclosed perimeter offices in the office tower maximize interior daylighting and provide outdoor views for 90 percent of the occupants.

On the first floor, a two-story, 13,000-square-foot (1,210-square-meter-long) lobby spans the entire front of the building. The inverted curve of the 250-foot-long (76-meter-long) lobby, which is used as an exhibition area for the different automotive brands, plays off the facade's clear glass. The lobby provides a neutral background for the display vehicles. A floating mural depicts the history and future of each of the five automotive brands.

The first floor also has a 4,400-square-foot (410-square-meter) full-service conference center that can hold up to 250 people and can also be divided into four separate meeting rooms. A separate multimedia room provides state-of-the-art conferencing services, including videoconferencing. The first floor also has four additional breakout meeting rooms with a neutral design that all the brands can use.

Employee amenities on this floor include a 3,500-square-foot (325-square-meter) state-of-the-art fitness center, a 105-seat café with two executive dining rooms, a multicultural room celebrating employees' heritages, and an auto concierge (a valet service for employees' vehicles).

The second floor is devoted to Aston Martin and Jaguar. The curves of the sea-green glass walls, reception desk, and coffee bar reflect the sensual lines of these British-born automobiles. Colors, materials, furnishings, and form used throughout the floor were selected to reflect the curvilinear character of the Jaguar brand and the handcrafted detailing of the Aston Martin brand.

The third floor houses the Volvo group. The spacious lobby of light wood and Volvo's signature blue reflects the brand's Scandinavian heritage. The lobby's open design and unobstructed views through the exterior glass walls reflect Volvo's corporate culture, and the crisp, clean contemporary style throughout the third floor represents Volvo's dis-

tinct design philosophy. This floor has photographic displays, a coffee bar, and a main conference room accessed through a series of graphic pivoting doors.

The fourth floor houses Lincoln/Mercury. The architect designed a split configuration of rich earth tones with dramatic splashes of color that allows both brands to make a distinctive statement within a singular environment. In the lobby, for example, limestone on a "runway" and the reception desk reflects Lincoln's "American luxury" character, while the detailing and choice of color and materials complement the Mercury palette. An interstitial staircase connects the fourth floor to the fifth-floor conference center.

The fifth floor is devoted to Land Rover and the premier automotive group. The lobby's wood floor, sisal rugs, and stone reception desk reflect the cross-country orientation and sophistication of Land Rover. The floor also has a seating area around a large plasma screen, a large retail display wall, and a conference center.

The interior of the one-story, 77,000-square-foot (7,155-square-meter) design studio for the product development wing has a mezzanine, an exposed ceiling, and a more high-tech design than the main office building. The interior focus is on flexible, movable spaces that support the different and changeable project teams and work groups.

The wing has a 10,000-square-foot (930-square-meter) product showroom with three vehicle display turntables, six projectors, audiovisual systems, and an elaborate lighting system that mimics dawn-to-dusk lighting. The showroom displays prototypes and new models from each brand, allowing designers to study vehicle models more closely.

A clay model studio for designers opens into a working courtyard with a turntable where clay models can be studied in the sunlight. The wing also has office space for 85 design employees, a paint booth, wood and metal fabricating areas, and a vehicle teardown area.

Sixty percent of construction waste is recycled, and 30 percent of new materials and finishes—such as furniture, fabrics, and carpeting—contain recycled material. LPA, Inc./ Adrian Velicescu

The Premier Automotive Group wanted an architectural design for this wing that brought in considerable natural sunlight while providing security. A 25-foot (7.6-meter) wall prevents views into the courtyard. Solid walls with clerestory windows at the top also mitigate views, provide privacy, and admit abundant sunlight.

Landscaping

Open space takes up 25 percent of the headquarters site. The landscape architect created a plan that maximizes the amount of open space and landscape, minimizes water consumption, and relates to the structural building module used throughout the campus. The green rooftop garden on the product development wing and the green screens, for example, play an important role in the insulation of exterior building surfaces and interior building spaces. The green screens also provide privacy for the outdoor meeting and gathering spaces off the conferencing center on the first floor.

The landscaped portion of the roof of the product development wing, while not open to employees, provides a visual amenity—30,000 square feet (2,790 square meters) of landscaping rather than 30,000 square feet of rooftop—for workers in the main office building.

Construction and Financing

Construction of the headquarters began in May 2000, and employees moved in in November 2001. Construction was completed in January 2002.

The curved metal and glass facade mimics elements found in each of the five premier brands and provides more than 90 percent of Ford's employees with outdoor views and natural daylighting.

LPA, Inc./Adrian Velicescu

Sixty percent of the construction waste was recycled. Construction operations were completed before major portions of the building were enclosed and the HVAC systems started to minimize off-gassing from building materials.

With all the many green features and design components incorporated into the new headquarters, the project still met Ford's budget of less than $100 per square foot ($1,080 per square meter), and Ford will enjoy reduced operating costs every year over the life of the buildings.

By going green, for example, the Premier Automotive Group headquarters exceeds California's Title 24 energy requirements for office buildings, which are the strictest in the nation, by more than 25 percent. That, coupled with the fuel cell system, which provides approximately 25 percent of the buildings' overall power, creates a much more efficient environment then a standard office campus, reduces reliance on the local power grid by 50 percent, and therefore reduces operation costs.

Ford financed the Premier Automotive Group headquarters through its Ford Motor Land Services Corporation, the worldwide strategic and operational real estate arm of Ford Motor Company. Ford purchased the 11.9-acre (4.8-hectare) Irvine site for $35 million.

Experience Gained

As the first privately developed facility in California to receive LEED certification, the Premier Automotive Group headquarters proves that it is possible to design and construct a green building even within the strict nongreen design guidelines of an existing office park and to do so on a mainstream budget.

Project Data: Ford Motor Company PAG: North American Headquarters

Land Use and Building Information

Site area	11.9 acres (4.8 hectares)
Gross building area	253,606 square feet (23,570 square meters)
Typical floor area	37,000 square feet (3,440 square meters)

Parking

Surface	268 spaces
Structured	633 spaces

Land Use Plan

Use	Acres/Hectares	Percentage of Site
Buildings	2.98/1.2	25
Paved areas	5.00/2.0	42
Landscaped areas	3.92/1.6	33
Total	11.9/4.8	100

Development Cost Information

Site acquisition[1]	
Site improvement	$5.2 million

Construction Costs

Buildings/shell	$100 per square foot ($1,080 per square meter)
Buildings/interior	$35 per square foot ($375 per square meter)
Total Project Cost	$100 million

Owner/Developer

Ford Motor Company Premier Automotive Group
One Premier Place
Irvine, California
Phone: 949-341-6100
Toll free: 1-800-452-4827
Fax: 949-341-6152
www.ford.com

Architect

LPA, Inc.
17848 Sky Park Circle
Irvine, California 92614
Phone: 949-261-1001
Fax: 949-260-1190
www.lpairvine.com

Landscape Architect

The SWA Group
580 Broadway
Suite 200
Laguna Beach, California 92651
Phone: 949-497-5471
Fax: 949-494-7861
www.swagroup.com

Structural Engineers

Brandon & Johnson
20301 SW Birch Street
Suite 100
Newport Beach, California 92660
Phone: 949-476-8319
Fax: 949-955-0794
www.bjase.com

Mechanical Engineers

Tsuchiyama, Kaino, Sun & Carter
17911 Von Karman Avenue
Suite 250
Irvine, California 92614
Phone: 949-756-0565
Fax: 949-756-0927
www.tkscengineering.com

Electrical Engineers

Konsortum 1
1532 Brookhollow Drive
Santa Ana, California 92705
Phone: 714-668-4200
Fax: 714-668-4215
www.konsortum1.com

General Contractor

Koll Construction LP
4343 Von Karman Avenue
Newport Beach, California 92660
Phone: 949-833-3030
Fax: 949-250-4344
www.koll.com

Development Schedule

1999	Site acquired
1/1999	Planning started
5/2000	Construction started
1/2002	Construction completed
11/2001	First phase of occupancy

Location

1 Premier Place
Irvine Spectrum Center
Irvine, California

Note:
1. Not applicable. Part of existing campus.

Gewerbehof Prisma
Nuremberg, Germany

Alexis Karolides

Gewerbehof Prisma is a green, high-density, mixed-use urban infill development. Located in downtown Nuremberg, it contains 61 flats, 32 office units, nine shops, a café, a kindergarten, and a 10,800-square-foot (1,000-square-meter) public atrium that moderates internal temperatures.

Commissioned by the Nuremberg City Council as a catalyst for revitalization in the heart of the city, Prisma is a hub for living, working, shopping, and recreation. Its large public atrium is a green sanctuary filled with plants and water features, natural daylight, and fresh air. Through solar gain and the use of circulating water, the atrium creates a pleasant microclimate for the building year-round. These features, combined with other low-tech energy-efficient measures such as passive solar design, thermal heat storage, super-insulation, good solar orientation, shading, and natural ventilation, helped

The Prisma building, in Nuremberg, Germany, is focused around an internal biophilic greenhouse that regulates humidity and indoor air quality. Atelier Dreiseitl

reduce building costs by 30 percent compared with conventional construction while decreasing heating costs to less than half those of a conventional building. The building leased up quickly in a tight real estate market.

The Site

Prisma was built on one of the last available inner-city sites in Nuremberg with the intention of reinvigorating the downtown area by including a mixture of functions. Rather than choosing a greenfield site outside the city, the city council decided to add density to the city core. The site is located at an important traffic junction, close to shops, restaurants, and public transportation (bus and underground rail).

Special Features

- Urban infill site
- Passive solar design, including a large atrium greenhouse
- Innovative ventilation and cooling strategies
- Monolithic brick walls that store thermal energy and regulate temperatures
- Ecological building materials and finishes
- Reusable materials
- Rainwater management system

Instead of a mechanical air-conditioning system, the building uses operable windows and night flush cooling, which can open and close 80 percent of the glass roof.
Atelier Dreiseitl

Planning and Development Process

The idea for this building dates back to 1987. Project investors and the architect firm were chosen by competition, and the first concept drawings were produced in 1988 and 1989. Long negotiations between the city of Nuremberg and the investor, and between the investor and architects followed, and it was not until 1991 that the planning started. Construction began in December 1994, and in 1996–1997 tenants moved in.

Joachim Eble, head architect and project mastermind, decided to make the building green. He worked with lead project architect Gordon Richter and with water feature designer Herbert Dreiseitl to develop the natural climatic concept.

Design

The project consists of three buildings arranged around a courtyard. Two of them are connected by a greenhouse atrium. Prisma is inwardly focused; masonry sheer walls face the exterior, and walls of glass and timber cladding face the greenhouse atrium.

One of the primary design concepts was to create a large, protected atrium that would temper the environment in several innovative ways for all building occupants and create a sense of outdoor living year-round. The design team was able to eliminate the need for a conventional air-conditioning system; rather, the buildings rely on the huge greenhouse atrium—filled with waterfalls and plants—to moderate the indoor climate. Although the Moguls in India and Arabic cultures traditionally used water features for indoor climate regulation (in the Alhambra, for example), this concept of heating and cooling with the help of a greenhouse and water features is new to contemporary western buildings.

Prisma is successful because of its integrated system of smart design features. The architects optimized the building materials, massing, and envelope using appropriate facade materials for each orientation. Heavily insulated 19-inch-thick (483-millimeter-thick) masonry walls store thermal energy and help regulate building temperature. The atrium plants help clean, oxygenate, and humidify the air. When solar gain is not required to increase the temperature, hydraulic controls activate blinds to shade southern greenhouse windows and open panels in the glass roof for ventilation.

Water is the building's lifeblood. Rainwater that falls on Prisma's roofs flows into a garden pond in the outdoor courtyard. From there, it flows through cleansing biotopes and filters and then into collection cisterns in the underground parking garage. Any overflow seeps into the ground. A 60,760-gallon (230,000-liter) cistern serves a complex watering system for the plants in the passive solar greenhouse. A 39,600-gallon (150,000-liter) cistern serves the six water walls and the interior streams and ponds that help heat and cool the building. In the summer, water flowing through the water walls pulls air in and down and forces it—cleaner and cooler—out at the bottom. In winter, water in the water walls warms the cool outside air before it enters the building. Besides cleaning and tempering air, these water walls provide soothing background sound and visual excitement as the water splashes behind colored and lighted glass panels. Graywater is not used in the buildings, which are served by city water. A 6,100-gallon (23,000-liter) cistern in the basement is available for fire suppression.

The greenhouse atrium and the office require approximately the same air volume (130,700 cubic yards [100,000 cubic meters]). The ventilation rate is about one air change per hour. Air is exhausted through the basement of the buildings, causing a latent negative pressure in the greenhouse, which in turn causes air to be pulled in over slots in the water walls. The water, which comes from the cisterns at about 50 degrees Fahrenheit (10 degrees Celsius), cools the air and flows freely in the greenhouse. The offices that do not open into the greenhouse have an outside air supply that is heated in the winter. For offices facing the greenhouse, air is exhausted but fresh air comes from the greenhouse only and there is no ducted outside air supply. The businesses on the ground floor are directly connected to the greenhouse and have no other source of supply air or exhaust.

Financing

Prisma was built during slow economic times in Germany. Calculated not to turn a profit for several years, the project was seen as a risky investment and therefore its budget tightly controlled. After value engineering, photovoltaic

Rainwater collected in a courtyard flows into a basement cistern that feeds the greenhouse pond, six water walls in the foyer, and the landscape irrigation system on the roof, balconies, and terraces. Brightly colored artwork (shown here) disguises the water walls, or "flow forms." Atelier Dreiseitl

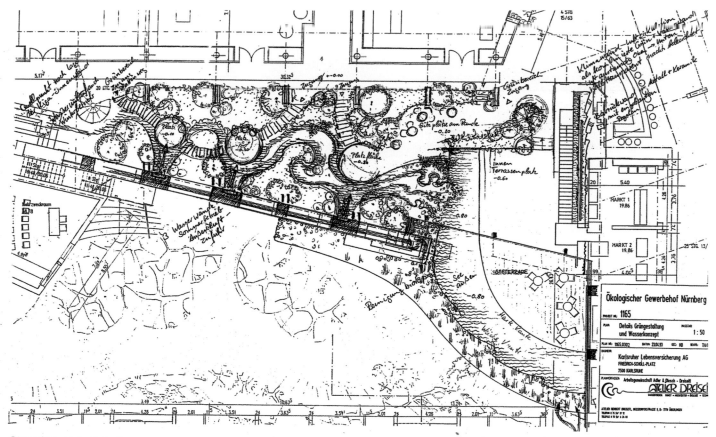

Site plan. Atelier Dreiseitl

panels and rainwater flushing of bathroom fixtures were eliminated. Even the glazed atrium was at risk of deletion until cost estimators calculated that weatherproofing the building facades facing the atrium would be more costly than the glass atrium.

Experience Gained

In its first years of operation, Prisma has performed remarkably well. The building has been completely leased since it opened. The ground-floor shops are well frequented. The climate control system keeps the building comfortable, and the indoor landscaping is thriving.

Prisma is supplied by district heating and power from the local utility. The building saves more than 2,000 gallons (8,000 liters) of fuel oil per heating period and is expected to reduce carbon dioxide emissions by 27,500 tons (25,000 metric tons) within a decade.

At first, the client did not believe the building's unusual heating and cooling system would work, so the architects asked him to hire a physicist to run simulation calculations with various parameters. The results convinced the client to keep the innovative systems in the program. The fact that Prisma's climate control systems have proved successful should make it easier for other investors and designers to follow suit.

Project Data: Gewerbehof Prisma

Land Use and Building Data

Site area	64,583 square feet (6,000 square meters)
Office/retail	7 stories
Apartments	5 stories
Kindergarten	2 stories
Parking	19,400 square feet (1,800 square meters)
Underground parking	110 auto spaces 200 bicycle spaces
Gross building area	193,750 square feet (18,000 square meters)

	Square Feet/Square Meters
Net Rentable Area	142,310/13,225
Office/retail	81,775/7,600
Apartments	48,420/4,500
Kindergarten	5,380/500

Development Cost Information

Building construction	$28.5 million (€21.3 million)
Total Development Cost	$51.2 million (€38.3 million)

Developer

Karlsruher Insurance Company
Rothenburgerstrasse 9
90443 Nuremberg
Germany

Architect

Joachim Eble Architects
Berliner Ring 47a
72076 Tübingen
Germany
Phone: 49 7071 96940
Fax: 49 7071 600912

Architect/Project Manager

Gordon Richter
Immentalstrasse 4
72406 Bisingen-Zimmern
Germany
Phone: 49 0 7471-91953
Fax: 49 0 7471-91955
arch_richter.hechingen@t-online.de

Landscape Architect

Adler & Olesch
Marienstrasse 8
90402 Nuremberg
Germany

Water Features and Systems

Atelier Dreiseitl
Nussdorfer Strasse 9
88662 Ueberlingen
Germany
Phone: 49 7551 9288 41
Fax: 49 7551 9288 88
www.dreiseitl.de

Other Consultants

Construction Manager: Haushoch Architects, Nuremberg, Germany
Construction Supervisor: Bauingenieure Harms und Partner, Hanover, Germany
Structural Engineer: Schneck & Schaal, Germany

Development Schedule

Late 1980s	Project commissioned by city
1991	Planning
12/1994	Construction started
1996–1997	Occupancy
1997	Project completed

Location

Nuremberg, Germany

Jean Vollum Natural Capital Center

Portland, Oregon

Jenifer Seal

The Jean Vollum Natural Capital Center is a 70,000-square-foot (6,505-square-meter) historic structure that serves as the headquarters for Ecotrust and also houses a mix of various environmentally focused businesses and nonprofit organizations. Ecotrust is a Portland-based nonprofit that promotes compatibility of economic development and environmental protection. The organization was created in 1991 to help focus attention and resources on the ecologically significant and highly threatened coastal temperate rain forests in coastal communities from northern California to Alaska. Ecotrust helped to found ShoreBank Pacific, a bank that promotes environmental conservation and economic development in the Pacific Northwest. With a mission to help support "the emergence of a conservation economy in the region—an economy that makes money and creates value, but does so by explicitly considering the long-term vitality of communities"—the organization seeks to be a model of sustainable development in the region.

The Jean Vollum Natural Capital Center in Portland was one of the first renovated historic structures to earn LEED Gold rating in the United States. This former warehouse building now houses businesses and nonprofit organizations with an environmental focus. Ecotrust

As one of the first elements in the redevelopment of Portland's Pearl River District, the Jean Vollum Natural Capital Center demonstrates how sustainability can work in an urban setting. It also proves that older historic buildings can effectively be redeveloped as green buildings: it was the first renovated historic structure to earn the LEED Gold rating in the United States. It is also a Portland General Electric (PGE) Earth Advantage (a green building certification program) building.

The Site

At the urging of Ecotrust board member Jane Jacobs, author of the acclaimed *The Death and Life of Great American Cities*, the organization began looking for an urban location with a mixed-use program. According to Bettina von Hagen, managing director of Ecotrust, the concept developed into

Special Features

- Redevelopment of urban historic structure
- Energy-efficient features and environmentally sensitive design
- Tenant involvement in design process
- Recycled and local materials
- Natural stormwater filtration system
- Construction waste management
- Environmentally sensitive janitorial and maintenance program
- First historic structure to earn LEED Gold rating certification.

the "idea of creating a marketplace for the conservation economy—a place where the emerging ideas, products, and services of the conservation economy could find a home and a growing audience." The program developed to include space needs for retail and office space for for-profit and non-profit organizations, and for Ecotrust headquarters.

Criteria for site selection to meet these needs included a historic building anchored in the rich western history of Portland—a place where Ecotrust could build on the idea of "conservation economy." Proximity to mass transit and a central location were also important. As von Hagen explained, such a site would "reduce transportation infrastructure and energy use, reduce urban sprawl, support the vitality of the city center, and maximize the flow of people to the building."

In February 1998, the team found that building in the Pearl River District, a historic area northwest of downtown with old industrial warehouse buildings and 34 acres (13.8

hectares) of vacant rail yards. In the early 1990s, a loosely knit group of business leaders spent half a year developing a vision for the River District that called for a high-density urban residential neighborhood housing a resident population of 15,000 and providing jobs, services, and recreation for Portland's central city. This vision has guided substantial public and private investment in the area. Ecotrust felt this revitalized area was an ideal location for the project.

Located on a full city block, the 1895 J. McCraken Company warehouse featured a loading and parking area. Although the exterior needed restoration, the building was structurally sound. The building features Richardson Romanesque architectural style with a flat roof and parapet, a recessed round-arch entrance, arched window openings, stucco and brick facing, and a massive appearance. The building was divided down the center by a load-bearing brick wall with a 200-foot (61-meter) span of old-growth Douglas fir post-and-beam structure. Original Douglas fir plank floors are another distinctive feature of the building. Later during the development process, the building was placed on the National Register of Historic Places so that federal historic preservation tax credits could be used.

The site offers many opportunities to use mass transit, including a streetcar and seven bus stops within a quarter mile (0.4 kilometer) of the building. Fifty bicycle parking spaces are available, and showers and lockers are provided. Two Toyota Prius vehicles for employee car sharing and a refueling station are also available.

Over 75 percent of the exterior shell and interior elements of the original 1985 structure were reused. On the ground floor, the original wood plank floor was retained and restored. New materials were selected based on environmental and health impacts. Ecotrust

Development Process

The team held two charrettes to aid in developing the building design and program objectives. Several program objectives emerged in the first charrette:

■ Retain the building's historic character "to maintain the openness and views, to minimize the use of floor-to-ceiling walls, and to maintain as much of the original brick and timbers as possible."

■ Develop generous and inviting public spaces "to create a center for the growing conservation economy."

■ Invite collaboration and community among tenants "to create a cluster of organizations [that are] different and diverse, but clustered around similar themes."

■ Incorporate green building "to achieve practical and appropriate green building strategies, minimizing the use of materials and energy and maximizing natural light and fresh air."

The second building charrette focused on tenants' needs and on interior design and the creation of workspaces that would invite interaction and partnerships. Shared space and flexible workplace design to encourage innovation and collaboration were key objectives. The tenants were invited to participate in this step of the design process.

Ecotrust selected Robert Naito of Heritage Consulting Group to help bring its vision to life. Heritage Consulting Group was involved in many historic rehabilitation projects in Portland, and the team believed that this developer understood the "complexity and magic of combining historic and green redevelopment objectives." In addition, Naito's partner, John Tess, is one of the nation's leading consultants on historic rehabilitation. Naito commented, "What made this project unique was the mantra of Ecotrust founder Spencer Beebe: 'Let's keep this simple: make it green but not just for the sake of being green—economically viable as well.'"

As a developer, Naito found this process unusual in that tenants were brought into the design. Normally, a developer as landlord does not want tenants involved so closely, but in the end, including them yielded impressive results. For example, a representative from Progressive Investment, a prospective tenant, came up with the idea of increasing allowable temperature ranges. With the agreement of other tenants in the building, the design team was able to down-

In an effort to create a cost-effective and replicable project, the design team favored practical, low-tech and no-tech solutions. The building's conference room is open to all those who occupy the building as well as to community events. Ecotrust

size systems (based on the agreement to increase allowable temperature ranges) and save money. The tenant charrette also produced the idea of a "permeable walls" open-office scheme. According to Naito, "Normally, you would never do this in an office building." The team talked about the concept as "building a kitchen/hearth of the home." Coffee bars are located in elevator lobbies. The idea, generated by users, has proved to be a successful model for a mix of tenants with common environmental and socially conscious goals. Some on the team were skeptical about the openness of the interior design and feared street people would migrate into the building, attracted by all the public space, but it has proved to not be a problem. Individual tenant spaces have no real doors, but roll-up crates define tenant spaces.

The landscape design reduced impervious surfaces by 26 percent through the use of planters, landscape islands, vegetated swales, and a roof garden. Ecotrust

Heritage looked at several development scenarios, from a low-cost, minimalist scheme to one that realized the maximal development potential of the block. Existing zoning allowed for a maximum 160,000-square-foot (14,900-square-meter), 75-foot-tall (23-meter-tall) building on the block with office, retail, and residential uses. Portland code states that if more than 10,000 square feet (930 square meters) of new construction is added to the site, at least 14 housing units must be built. Although full development would have resulted in the greatest net present value, it also would have required substantially more equity, complicated the program by adding a housing component, and presented significantly more risk, according to von Hagen. Ecotrust selected a strategy that saved the historic warehouse building and added a 10,000-square-foot (930-square-meter) penthouse to the roof.

Holst Architecture, with a history of successful warehouse conversion projects in the Pearl River District, was selected to design the project. In addition, the team engaged green building consultants early in the process: Greg Acker, a local architect specializing in sustainable design, and PGE's Green Building Services, which coordinated LEED certification.

The Ecotrust team decided to use a negotiated bid process for the project, so the contractor, Walsh Construction, participated in the design from the beginning to keep costs in line all the way through the process. This approach was essential in providing feedback to both the architect and to Ecotrust on construction costs and feasibility throughout the design process.

Planning and Design

Ecotrust directed the architects to stick with practical, low-tech and no-tech solutions. It was looking for a replicable demonstration project. "Sometimes," von Hagen noted, "we found ourselves trading off one goal against another. For example, we could have been even more energy efficient if we had replaced the old single-glazed windows with new double-glazed low-e windows and insulated and drywalled the interior side of the exterior brick walls. Instead, we chose to rebuild the original wood windows and keep the brick walls exposed." Initially a great deal of time was spent looking at photovoltaics and fuel cells, but they just did not make economic sense at the time.

Even during the earliest stages of the design process, the Natural Capital Center's building team was interested in creating a space that encouraged energy and productivity. Just as the designers valued the health and integrity of the greater urban ecosystem within which the building stood, they also considered the building itself an ecosystem, one that required the same attention to balance, diversity, and healthy inputs and outputs and one that ultimately felt alive, according to von Hagen.

In its design, the team emphasized the requirements of the information age, flexible space in an open, simple, industrial warehouse, an air-conditioning system that could bring 100 percent outside air into the building, reuse of existing materials, optimal use of ambient light, and natural ways to manage rainwater. The Portland Development Commission was so excited about the project that it approved the design in two meetings. The team submitted a special green building section on project specifications along with the construction documents.

The design optimizes energy performance. A new skylight was installed in the roof to bring daylight into the center of the building and the open staircase between the first and second floors. Daylighting bathes the interior and reaches 75 percent of occupied spaces. More than 90 percent of spaces have access to outside views. Icynene—a polyicynene insulation expanding spray foam that does not contain ozone-destroying gases or formaldehyde and is one of the few market-certified insulations for healthy indoor air quality—was used to insulate the building. The HVAC system allows percentages of fresh and recycled air to vary depending on existing conditions. The system is equipped with carbon dioxide sensors that trigger a flush of fresh air when air grows stale.

For energy performance, the building exceeds ASHRAE standards by more than 20 percent, and water use is reduced by 33 percent compared with a conventional office building. In addition, the center purchases Clean Wind and Salmon Friendly power each month through PGE's renewable power program, supporting environmental stewardship and supporting additional renewable resources in the Northwest.

Stormwater runoff is diverted from city's already overloaded combined stormwater-sewer system. The design reduced impervious surfaces by 26 percent through the incorporation of planters, landscape islands, vegetated swales, and a roof garden accessible by the public. The Portland Bureau of Environmental Services offered a grant to pay the incremental cost increases of the green roof because it wanted to include it in three demonstration projects to illustrate a filtering system that recycles all a building's rainwater. The bureau chose Natural Capital Center because it was a renovation project. Infiltration swales recharge groundwater while removing all suspended solids and phosphorous, semipermeable asphalt was used in parking lots, and rainwater from downspouts filters through vegetation and soil. These efforts, plus the use of native trees, light-colored

paving, and shade on impervious surfaces, also reduce potential heat island effect.

Today, the ground floor of the building houses retail uses; the second floor houses office tenants, a public mezzanine, and a conference center for business and community events; and the third-floor rooftop addition includes two offices overlooking a terrace and surrounded by an "ecoroof" planted with vegetation to absorb and filter stormwater. One of these offices is the Portland Office of Sustainable Development.

Construction

Materials used were selected with their environmental and health impacts in mind; for example, carpets are made from recycled fibers and paints have low levels of toxicity. More than 75 percent of the 1895 exterior structure and shell and interior nonshell elements of the historic building were reused. In addition, the original wood plank floor that 100 years ago supported horse-drawn freight wagons was refinished on the ground floor. About 66 percent of new wood, including lumber, plywood, decking, and windows, is from certified forests. All structural steel contains roughly 97 percent recycled steel scrap. Thirty-four percent of the materials were produced locally, including salvaged materials, lumber, concrete, structural steel, and doors. Environmentally innovative interior materials were used, including rubber flooring from recycled tires and wheatboard cabinets. Ninety-eight percent of construction materials were recycled or salvaged, and the HVAC system was protected during construction and flushed after construction.

Financing

A total of $6 million in grants and contributions was raised toward the purchase and construction of the Natural Capital Center. Ecotrust used a $2.5 million gift from Jean Vollum, founding board member, and a $2 million low-interest loan from the Ford Foundation to help finance the project.

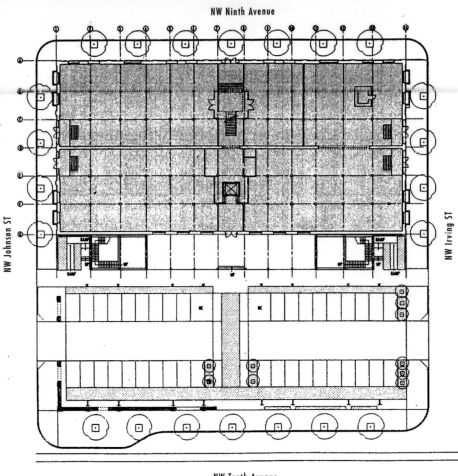

NW Ninth Avenue

NW Johnson ST

NW Irving ST

NW Tenth Avenue

Site plan. Ecotrust

Additional equity was provided by Guilford Capital, which purchased rehabilitation tax credits. Construction financing was provided through Bank of America, and permanent financing came from Bank of the West, the Ford Foundation, and the Portland Development Commission.

At each stage in the design, Walsh Construction prepared a new cost estimate. According to von Hagen, "As the estimates went up, we met with Bob Naito, the architect, and the contractor to go through a painful process of value engineering. Sometimes we stayed with the more expensive alternative, as was the case of the penthouse." At one point, the team considered a less expensive structural system using new lumber and lightweight trusses but chose to keep the salvaged 100-year-old Douglas fir post-and-beam construction. In addition, windows made from certified wood that opened were selected instead of less expensive ones. The final construction contract price was $6,672,216, and the total project cost was $12.83 million.

Experience Gained

In addition to the green building itself, Ecotrust and the team wove many other elements into the project that would ensure the project's long-term sustainable operation. For example, tenant leases mandate green building practices, and a green building tenant improvement guideline is incorporated into each lease. The maintenance company, Corporate Building Maintenance, Inc., has eliminated the use of environmentally hazardous products and chemicals. Cleaning materials are biodegradable, all natural, phosphate free, and without animal products. For the 125 individuals working in the building, von Hagen notes that the Natural Capital Center Building Council was established soon after the building opened. With representatives from most of the building's tenants, the council meets every other month in a casual environment to discuss and plan a variety of buildingwide activities that fall under the categories of both work and play. Topics include energy purchasing and conservation, purchasing practices (seeking opportunities for green office supplies, for example), and upcoming events, and subcommittees report on their progress at the beginning of each meeting.

The project overflows with life and activity. Fifteen months after it opened, more than 230,000 curious visitors had come to see the rehabilitated warehouse, and they continue to come in droves. Each tenant becomes an active participant in the conservation economy through support of a community that includes government, business, and nonprofit groups gathered around themes of sustainable forestry, farming, fishing, green construction, community building, and socially responsible investing and financial services.

The building is fully leased, with a waiting list of prospective tenants. About the success of the open-office layout and the project's environmental sensitivity, Naito notes, "The proof is in the pudding." The businesses are doing well, and there is a buzz around town about the building's success.

Project Data: Jean Vollum Natural Capital Center

Land Use and Building Information

Site area	0.92 acre (0.4 hectare)
Gross building area	70,000 square feet (6,505 square meters)
Typical floor area	20,000 square feet (1,860 square meters)
Building height	2 stories plus 9,900-square-foot (920-square-meter) rooftop addition
Total net rentable area	35,480 rentable square feet (3,300 square meters)/34,556 rented square feet (3,210 square meters)
Parking	38 surface spaces
	50 bicycle spaces

Tenant Information

Total number of tenants	19
Office occupancy rate	97%

Total Development Cost

$12,830,000

Owner

Ecotrust
721 NW Ninth Avenue
Suite 200
Portland, Oregon 97209
Phone: 503-467-075
www.ecotrust.org

Developer

Heritage Consulting Group
721 NW Ninth Avenue
Portland, Oregon 97209
Phone: 503-228-0272
www.heritage-consulting.com

Architect

Holst Architecture
537 SE Ash Street
Portland, Oregon 97214
Phone: 503-233-9854
www.holstarc.com

Contractor

Walsh Construction Company
2905 SW First Avenue
Portland, Oregon 97201
Phone: 503-222-4375
www.walshconstructionco.com

Other Consultants

Interior Design: Edelman Soljaga Watson
LEED: PGE Green Building Services
Structural and Civil: KPFF Engineers
Mechanical: Interface Engineering
Consulting Engineers: Flack & Kurtz Engineers
Design Concepts: Greg Acker Architecture
Green Design Consultation: Rocky Mountain Institute
Daylighting: ENSAR Group
Lighting: Clanton Engineering
Green Design: Sustainable Development Group

Development Schedule

1998	Site acquired
1999	Planning started
2000	Construction started
2001	Construction completed

Location

721 NW Ninth Avenue
Portland, Oregon

JohnsonDiversey Worldwide Headquarters

Sturtevant, Wisconsin

Jenifer Seal

The global headquarters for JohnsonDiversey Inc. is a 250,000-square-foot (23,235-square-meter) office and laboratory facility that also includes a cafeteria, a conference center, and a fitness center. It is the first building to earn LEED certification for a structure that contains a global company headquarters and a comprehensive chemical research and development laboratory.

JohnsonDiversey is a leading worldwide provider of commercial cleaning, sanitation, and hygiene products, serving customers in the lodging, food service, retail, health care, and food and beverage sectors as well as service contractors. The company is a member of the SC Johnson family of businesses headquartered in Racine, Wisconsin.

The JohnsonDiversey site in Sturtevant, Wisconsin, was once a field with no landscaping. Today, it is a restored prairie with native landscaping, holding ponds, and wetlands to contain water runoff—as well as fruit orchards and gardens that supply the company cafeteria. Jenifer Seal

The corporate vision for SC Johnson, which was founded in 1886, is to be a world-recognized leader in providing demonstrably superior products and services for the home and workplace to make them clean, healthy, and pleasant while respecting and protecting the environment. In the early 1990s, SC Johnson was preparing to divide into separate corporate entities for commercial products and consumer products. The organization wanted to bring all people associated with JohnsonDiversey (the new commercial entity), including research and development, finance, marketing, and administration, under one roof.

The mandate to create a green project came from the top of the corporation. As a member of the U.S. President's Council on Sustainable Development, Samuel Johnson, chair of SC Johnson, directed the green thinking for the building. The company's corporate environmental mission statement helped put into perspective its commitment to green design. That mission statement covers environmental protection, marketing products and services, reducing disposal and waste, sustainable use of natural resources, compliance, risk reduction, protection of the biosphere, public policy and education, and internal policy and assessment.

Special Features

- ■ Energy management systems
- ■ Under-floor air distribution
- ■ Personal environmental controls
- ■ Extensive interior daylighting
- ■ Restored native prairie landscaping and wetlands
- ■ Natural stormwater collection and filtration system
- ■ Significant solid waste reduction during construction
- ■ LEED Gold certification

The JohnsonDiversey Worldwide Headquarters was one of four projects to receive the first LEED certification for existing buildings. The project realized an annual return on investment of $137,000 in operational cost savings.

JohnsonDiversey

The Site

Located less than eight miles (13 kilometers) from Racine, the 57-acre (23-hectare) site is adjacent to the old SC Johnson headquarters and was once a farmer's field with virtually no landscaping. With nothing to preserve, the team worked instead to develop a restoration plan. Today, the building is nestled in a restored native prairie landscape. Compared with a conventional Kentucky bluegrass corporate-style landscape, the prairie plan saves thousands of dollars annually in mowing, fertilizer, herbicide, insecticide, and irrigation costs. A series of holding ponds and constructed wetlands were constructed to clean contaminated upstream runoff before it is released downstream. New apple, plum, and pear orchards provide fruit for the cafeteria.

Planning and Development Process

When planning for the building began in 1994, the green building industry was still in its infancy, but this project was to set a course that helped educate its team and play an influential role in the creation of the U.S. Green Building Council's LEED rating system. Scott Weas, SC Johnson manager of corporate facilities, construction, and property, headed up the project. No one on the project was an expert on green building when the project began, but team members educated themselves systematically throughout the process. In the end, many involved in the design and construction went on to create their own niche in the green building industry. Both Weas and HOK lead architect Bill O'Dell stressed that the message for this project was "all about the process" and a thoroughly involved and engaged integrated planning team. Key objectives included sustainability, enhanced communication, a safe working environment, flexibility, and adherence to the budget. Weas notes with firm conviction that if you set out the right goals, 99 percent of the people get behind you.

"We realized we had to involve everybody and educate ourselves if we wanted to become experts in sustainability," says Weas. O'Dell describes the process as developing a "positive tension" among the team members, aligning theory and practice, determining what feasible solutions and cost-effective solutions looked like. They knew the conventional linear team organization would not work to achieve their energy-saving and environmental goals. The creation of an inclusive, integrated design team (18 disciplines involved) was key to the project's success. The architects, interior designers, laboratory designers, engineers, daylighting consultants, construction manager, major subcontractors, key suppliers, and the eventual building manager worked together with SC Johnson's project manager, user representatives, and chief financial officer throughout the design process. According to O'Dell, "Many of the ultimate successes of the project came from often unexpected interactions between team members who would traditionally never have gotten to know each other. For example, the piping subcontractor was able to make recommendations about the plumbing design to the structural engineers that made it easier to use standard-length material and thus eliminate a large percentage of the usual waste."

With Weas at the helm, the team spent eight hours a day twice a week in meetings from the concept through the construction documentation phases on the project. These meetings were mandatory for the whole team. Weas says he was very guarded about "closet engineering" (having participants do it on their own) and encouraged full participation in group meetings.

With a charge from the chair, the integrated design team ensured that sustainability was part of its conceptual thinking from the outset of the design. "Mr. Johnson communicated to us that our goal was to do whatever we could to make the design and construction of the building environmentally responsible without adding to the cost," according to O'Dell. They focused on "state-of-the-art market solutions rather than state of the art."

David Hempel, vice president of the company's Global Workplace Services, played a crucial role in bringing together the employees in the design process as well. Surveys, newsletters, a mock-up project room, employee process groups on furniture, customers and marketing, fun, and a wellness center provided input and feedback to the project's development.

In 1994, the team held a charrette with many of the foremost authorities on sustainability to kick off the project and to stimulate the team's thinking: Amory Lovins, founder of the Colorado think tank Rocky Mountain Institute; Terry Minger and Meredith Miller from the Center for Resource Management; William McDonough, renowned green architect; Hal Levin, research architect and indoor air quality expert; and Jim Rogers, an energy consultant. The charrette framed schematic perspectives and defined the project's outer limits and constraints. Through this process, the mission for the facility, design principles, and decision matrix were derived. The decision matrix addressed cost, environmental impact, quality, and schedule. It was used to evaluate the impact of every material, system, and process in terms of environment, budget, schedule, and risk.

Goals for energy efficiency stretched the creative limits of systems that were available at that time. A gain-avoidance strategy was used to design for least energy use, which meant a tight building envelope, efficient lighting, daylighting/shading techniques, and the use of renewable energy sources.

The building was completed under a tight schedule. Programming began in June 1995, the design concept was initiated in July, construction began in late August, and final move-in was in summer 1997.

The final project was ahead of schedule, $4 million under budget, and 10 to 15 percent below the cost per square foot for similar conventional buildings, according to Weas. The building was intended to bring a competitive advantage for the business and to help retain and attract new employees. And it has been proved to work: the company went from a $700 million business in 1997 to a $3 billion business in 2004.

Design

The building is a three-story masonry, poured-in-place concrete structure with an open office plan to encourage communication and collaboration. Two sides of the building are devoted to laboratory space (116,000 square feet [10,780 square meters]), and the rest is office space (72,000 square feet [6,700 square meters]) and common space (62,000 square feet [5,760 square meters]) consisting of a cafeteria and fitness center. It is a compact, almost square building.

Hempel notes that the last portion of the building designed was the exterior; that is, the building was designed from the inside out. Everything is designed to make employees more efficient and able to change faster than the com-

Superior daylighting in the building is achieved by high floor-to-floor heights and large windows, exterior light shelves, and a central atrium topped by a skylight. JohnsonDiversey

The design achieves some of the most exquisite daylighting in office space today. It features a floor-to-floor height of 14 feet (4.3 meters) to optimize daylighting while reducing energy consumption from electric light. A 10,000-square-foot (930-square-meter) atrium rises through the core, bringing in natural light through a skylight and vertical glass. The atrium is located in the center of the building, so light is distributed uniformly over the open floor plan. Light shelves on the west and south facades bounce light off the ceiling throughout the office space. Wherever one is in the building, daylight bathes the space. Although it is gray outside 80 percent of the time in Racine, the building is active and alive with natural light.

To achieve the superior daylighting made possible by the design, the team carefully analyzed schemes using computer modeling and physical models. LAM Lighting

petition. The concept underlying the design is "the whole building is your office and a living laboratory." The project incorporates many of the company's own products, allowing staff and visitors to "kick the tires."

The resulting design includes daylighting, a tight building envelope, a heat-recovery system, efficient mechanical systems, energy management systems, and personal environmental controls. Considerable attention was also paid to the durability, waste generation, and contribution to indoor air quality of materials chosen. The waste strategy resulted in recycling 86 tons (95 metric tons) of material and requiring suppliers to take back pallets and packaging.

Sitework included wetlands restoration, habitat restoration, and the creation of orchards and food gardens for the SC Johnson dining facilities.

Environmentally responsible workstations allow individuals to control temperature, lighting, and air flow, and they are equipped with occupancy sensors that automatically turn off the environmental controls when an office is unoccupied. Jenifer Seal

Design used its own software and large-scale physical models (the size of a Volkswagen) fitted with daylighting sensors. A University of Wisconsin team used Lumen Micro software to look at each design proposal. The ultimate design solution was reached by comparing results and reaching a consensus. The team compared the results of physical modeling with the computer model to optimize design. Daylighting models helped convince the client to incorporate higher-than-average ceilings. In addition, each office has task lights and occupancy sensors for light control. Overhead lights are dimmed as daylight intensifies.

Analysis from the daylighting studies was also incorporated into the HVAC analysis and system design. Mechanical engineers Ring & DuChateau reduced the cooling load requirements because designers assumed 40 percent of the lighting would not be turned on. Multiple benefits resulted: smaller chillers, less ductwork, and lower energy costs. A variable–air volume system was selected for its flexibility in changing loads resulting from fluctuations in lighting. The system also uses an innovative boiler scheme. Instead of specifying two large boilers typical for a building of this size, 12 smaller boilers are used to better address variations in load, yielding 90 percent efficiency. Similarly, the team selected two smaller chillers rather than one large one.

Variable–air volume fume hoods and heat recovery wheels are used in the laboratories. Heatwheel air-handling units provide total energy recovery for the outside air before any mechanical heating or cooling is performed and provide up to 88 percent total (sensible plus latent) energy recovery. In the summer, the wheel precools and dehumidifies the air, and in the winter, it preheats and humidifies the air with no cross-contamination of the outside and exhaust airstreams. The atrium is conditioned with air pulled from the open offices.

Under-floor air distribution is a main feature of the green design. This system results in reduced energy use, superior air quality and temperature control, better ventilation, and more comfortable workers. In addition, future relocation of personnel can be accomplished in a fraction of the time and at a fraction of the cost.

Each employee workstation is equipped with a Johnson Controls personal environmental module, allowing the employee to control air velocity, temperature, direction, light, and noise. By allowing each employee to control his or her own heating and cooling, ambient temperatures can be raised or lowered by three degrees, producing significant long-term energy savings. It also is equipped with an occupancy sensor that automatically turns off the fan, lighting, and equipment when the employee leaves the office for 15 minutes.

Energy modeling guided the team in the search for optimal design solutions: lighting systems, exterior form and massing, integrated internal equipment loads, window and skylight detailing, and landscaping with mechanical and electrical systems. Energy consumption is 73,000 Btu per square foot (785,500 Btu per square meter), 60 percent less than the average for a typical building.

Because no LEED system existed during the design process, the team used HOK's own "Healthy and Sustainable Materials" database for selecting the most appropriate local environmentally sensitive materials.

In November 2003, the project was submitted for the U.S. Green Building Council's LEED certification. It earned a Gold certification for existing buildings for its exceptional performance.

Construction

An impressive 86 tons (95 metric tons) of cardboard, concrete, metal, glass, wood, and drywall were recycled during the construction process. During the process, subcontractors were educated about green procedures related to the entire process, not just recycling. To convey project goals and challenges and help them understand that what they were doing made a difference, contractors were included in the design

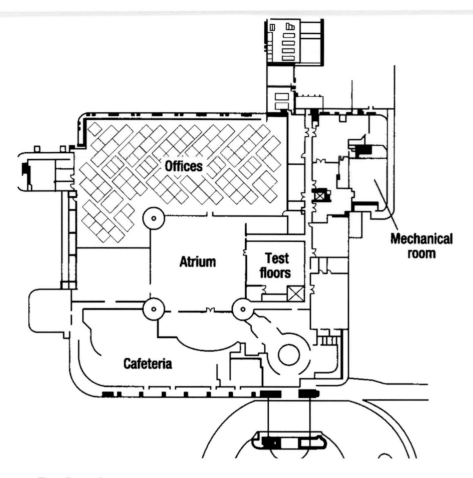

First-floor plan. HOK Architects

Impressive energy savings of $0.46 per square foot ($4.95 per square meter), compared with the old $1.51 per square foot ($16.25 per square meter) and national average of $2.20 per square foot ($23.65 per square meter), were achieved. Lower energy consumption saves more than $100,000 year. The indigenous low-maintenance landscaping saves more than $3,000 per acre ($7,400 per hectare) in annual maintenance costs.

Experience Gained

The process for this project helped tremendously in drafting the U.S. Green Building Council's LEED rating system and HOK's *Guidebook to Sustainable Design*. The team used drafts of the LEED system to gauge the project. O'Dell notes that it became a game: everyone on the team jumped in to see how he or she could make the building better and get more points.

Many lessons were learned throughout the process. Because the building manager, David Hempel, was part of the team from early on, he knew what to expect of the energy performance. Although overall energy use was very good, he noted that electricity used was greater than the team's projections. Upon investigation, he discovered that the blind system that was designed to lower glare on the lower vision glass had also been placed above the upper daylighting glass above the lightshelf. Monitors detected that glare was a problem and the shades were lowered, blocking not only the glare but also the light that was supposed to provide natural daylighting for the building. More electric lighting was being turned on than necessary, affecting the resulting cooling loads. Had Hempel not been part of the team, he would not have known to look beyond the general low energy figures.

Weas notes, "My favorite part of the project is that under the umbrella of sustainable design we met the company's business objectives and employees love the building. We succeeded."

phase. Calls or substitutions were reduced because contractors better understood the overall design concept and could offer innovative, creative solutions that would limit environmental impacts during construction.

The weekly safety meetings at the jobsite for contractors began to incorporate environmental issues as well. Contractors started coming up with creative environmental ideas of their own. For example, they arranged with suppliers that no bubble wrap be included in packages—just blankets, which were returned.

Initial goal-setting sessions and the upfront interdisciplinary team approach were key to the project's success in delivering the building on a fast track at 15 percent less than the average cost for U.S. office and lab buildings and a savings of $4 million in capital costs.

Project Data: JohnsonDiversey Worldwide Headquarters

Land Use and Building Information

Site area	52 acres (21 hectares)
Gross building area	250,000 square feet (23,235 square meters)
Building height	3 stories
Parking	287 surface spaces

Development Cost Information

Excavation and foundation	$1,740,000
Structure	4,787,000
Building envelope	3,332,000
Roof	552,500
Interior construction	6,965,000
Furnishings and equipment	2,690,000
Elevator	197,500
Mechanical systems	7,160,000
Electrical systems	5,317,000
Sitework	2,185,000
Total Development Cost	**$34,926,000**

Developer/Owner

JohnsonDiversey
1525 Howe Street
Racine, Wisconsin 53403-5011
Phone: 800-494-4855 (switchboard)
Headquarters: 262-260-2000
www.johnsondiversey.com

Architects

Hellmuth, Obata + Kassabaum (HOK)
211 North Broadway
Suite 700
St. Louis, Missouri 63102
Phone: 314-421-2000
Fax: 314-421-6073
www.hok.com

Zimmerman Design Group
7707 Harwood Avenue
Milwaukee, Wisconsin 53213
Phone: 414-476-9500

General Contractor

Riley Construction Company (in a joint venture with MA Mortenson Company)
5614 52nd Street
Kenosha, Wisconsin 53144
Phone: 262-658-4381
Fax: 262-658-0312

Structural Engineer

Harwood Engineering Company, Inc.
455 South Street
Walpole, Massachusetts 02081
Phone: 508-668-3600
Fax: 508-660-2276

Mechanical Engineer

Ring & DuChateau
10101 Innovation Drive
Suite 200
Milwaukee, Wisconsin 53226
Phone: 414-778-1700
Fax: 414-778-2360

Consultant

R. Scott Weas (former manager of corporate facilities, construction, and property management for SC Johnson)
Weas Development
3505 Bay Highlands Drive
Green Bay, Wisconsin 54311
Phone: 920-468-5948
Fax: 920-468-5947
www.weasdevelopment.com

Development Schedule

1994	Planning started
7/1995	Design concept
8/1995	Construction started
Summer 1997	Construction completed

Location

8310 16th Street
Sturtevant, Wisconsin

Philip Merrill Environmental Center

Annapolis, Maryland

Victoria Wilbur The 32,000-square-foot (2,975-square-meter) resource- and energy-efficient headquarters of the Chesapeake Bay Foundation (CBF) was built in 2000 to consolidate the foundation's operations. The 93,000-member environmental education and advocacy organization set out to establish the model for green building. Its "cradle-to-cradle" building design uses recycled materials, energy-efficient ventilation and lighting, low-VOC-emitting materials, and water conservation equipment.

The Chesapeake Bay Foundation embraced the concept of sustainable design for its headquarters in Annapolis, Maryland. It uses recycled materials, energy-efficient ventilation and lighting, low-VOC-emitting materials, and water conservation equipment. ©PrakashPatel.com

The Site

For its new headquarters, the CBF wanted a building that would embody its mission and history to save the (Chesapeake) Bay. The 30-year-old organization had been using four separate buildings in Annapolis; in the mid 1990s, it began its search for a new, consolidated headquarters site.

In 1997, the owner of a bay-front inn and pool announced the sale of her property. Worried that the large-scale 60-home development proposed for the property would destroy the natural features of the site as well as the community, the neighborhood civic association in Bay Ridge quickly approached CBF in an attempt to control the fate of the land. This secluded residential community of Annapolis offered CBF a location on the bay that had on-site natural wetlands to protect, the adjacent Black Walnut Creek to restore, and support of the surrounding commu-

Special Features

- "Cradle-to-cradle" building design
- Passive and active solar energy
- Recycled materials, low- or non-VOC materials used throughout
- Indoor air quality monitoring system
- Potential for natural ventilation when conditions are favorable
- Native landscaping using native genetic stock
- Natural stormwater filtration and collection systems
- Composting toilets
- Total traffic management
- LEED Platinum rating

nity. In return, CBF donated two acres (0.8 hectare) of the property to the community for a new pool facility to replace the one that would be deconstructed.

Rain falling on the building's roof is filtered for leaves and other debris before being collected in three 7,000-gallon cisterns. Water from the cisterns is used in suppressing fires and in landscaping or is filtered for hand-washing and laundry. ©PrakashPatel.com

The nearly 31-acre (12.5-hectare) site located four miles (6.5 kilometers) from Annapolis appealed to CBF for several reasons. Its location 100 yards (91 meters) from the bay related directly to the foundation's mission, but CBF also wanted a place where the building would have the least impact on the bay. It was challenging to design a building that would require minimal land area and be low enough

that the view of the bay would not be compromised. The site was constrained by on-site wetlands, its location in a 100-year floodplain, the adjacent creek, unstable soils, and steep slopes. In the end, only 4.9 acres (two hectares) was developed, leaving 84 percent as open space. Through thoughtful design, the total area of impervious surface on the site was actually reduced from what had existed before construction. During construction, eight trees were removed to extend the existing driveway, but 132 new ones were planted.

Except for the south side, which faces the bay, the property is surrounded by single-family detached homes. Throughout the development process, neighbors were given tours of the site, and input into its design was incorporated into the final product.

Development Process and Planning

CBF wanted a building that was resource- and energy-efficient and of a design that would blend naturally into the surrounding landscape. Four overall planning concepts guided the site's design—to disturb as little of the site as possible, to build an energy-efficient structure, to use ecologically responsible materials, and to place little stress on water resources.

CBF set a goal of not obtaining any variances or waivers for its building, a challenge that would require strong coordination and discussion between the development team and county officials. Early in the design process, these parties met to discuss any controversial design issues, to answer questions, and to foster dialogue. These meetings also introduced the construction team to various green materials including unfinished products, the toilet systems, and the stormwater conveyance system. The team architect, who was already familiar with the design and project goals, handled construction administration, which helped ensure that the intent of the original design was carried through construction. The team dealt with and overcame many concerns about construction materials and designs. For example, toward the end of the project, the team realized that county inspectors had not understood the design intent and were questioning things that they had never seen before, such as using filtered rainwater for washing hands. Both the inspectors and the fire marshal had to be educated but eventually came on board, with the fire marshal even bringing his entire staff to see this unusual building. In the end, the CBF staff, the development team, and county officials shared a sense of pride in the building.

The project was completed with only one variance from local codes. That environmentally positive variance allowed for a reduction in the required number of parking spaces. The facility is located in a smart growth priority funding area, and many staff walk, bike, or paddle to work. A transportation management strategy and on-site dining further reduce single-occupant vehicle trips.

Design and Construction

CBF approached SmithGroup and several experts in sustainability to design its headquarters. Clark Construction subsequently was retained as the contractor. Because "green construction can take many shapes and forms," explains Chuck Foster, the foundation's director of fleet and facilities, the first step of the development process involved the development team's boarding a boat and touring CBF's three existing "green" buildings—Fox Island, Port Isobel Island, and the Karen Noonan Environmental Education Center.

CBF also hired Janet Harrison, an architect who specializes in the U.S. Green Building Council's LEED certification program. CBF sought the nationally recognized LEED certification because it is the most holistic, credible green construction recognition program with a methodology that is quantifiable and defendable. Unlike other programs based on local environments, LEED allows projects to be compared across the country and throughout environments. The building was awarded the LEED Platinum rating and has won several design awards, including the

2001 Associated General Contractors' Build America Merit Award, New Building Category, and has been recognized by the American Institute of Architects as one of the 2001 top ten green projects.

During design, a peer review of the concept design was organized by the Sustainable Building Industries Council (funded by the U.S. Department of Energy); it included reviewers from the Maryland Energy Administration, Maryland Department of Natural Resources, World Wildlife Fund, and National Renewable Energy Laboratory.

Starting in spring 1997, CBF conducted a series of feasibility studies before purchasing the land. CBF, SmithGroup, and several other experts spent 14 months creating the master plan and identifying requirements before construction. It took 14 months to build the building, which was completed in November 2000. Future plans include the construction of a habitat restoration center, bunk and meeting houses for the foundation's education programs, and a boathouse. CBF sold its excess development rights to the Maryland Land Trust.

In keeping with the bay's traditional uses, CBF's building was designed like the shed-roof buildings used by watermen in the area for storage and shelter. It consists of two structures that occupy the footprint of the former swim center and the century-old Bay Ridge Inn. Both structures are built on seven- to ten-foot (two- to three-meter) pilings and are connected by a ten-foot (three-meter) deck. The building's interior was designed to allow for a healthful work environment and is organized into quadrants, two on each floor, each separated by the central lobby and exhibit space.

SmithGroup's integrated approach to design, where in-house engineers work closely with architects, facilitated a holistic approach to the building and the way its mechanical and electrical systems work together with the architectural design to enhance its overall sustainability.

The Philip Merrill Environmental Center accomplishes energy efficiency by maximizing natural light and by using both passive and active solar energy, geothermal heating and cooling, and timers. One-third of the energy is generated from renewable resources, and the facility uses two-thirds less energy than a conventional office building.

By reducing energy consumption, the facility contributes to a reduction in air pollution from power plants (one of the most significant pollution sources on the bay). Reducing water consumption allows the local wastewater plant to more efficiently remove pollutants. A permeable gravel driveway, biofiltration system (including natural wetlands), and rainwater-catchment system improve water clarity and thus help restore natural water filters and habitat like oysters and underwater grasses.

One of the most obvious energy efficiencies is the use of natural light and the deliberate orientation of the building. Large southern windows, the open loft interior, and the narrow width (50 feet [15 meters]) of the building allow plenty of sunlight to filter through it. Dormers add light at the midsection of the building's width, while the north facade has a continuous clerestory window and smaller window area. The building's east/west axis is elongated to allow light to infiltrate, to retain views to the south, and to protect against northern winter winds. The continuous trellis on the south end of the building prevents summer solar heat gain without compromising the building's daylighting. On the south side of the building, the angle of the louvers, made from barrels recycled from a former Eastern Shore pickle plant, baffles the hot summer sun but allows the winter sun to penetrate. To increase the efficiency of the daylighting system, photo cell sensors on the ceiling detect when supplemental light is necessary and automatically supplement ambient light. The chlorofluorocarbon-free heating and cooling system, which consists of 48 geothermal wells extended 300 feet (91 meters) into the ground, extracts heat from the 50-degree thermal gradient. A heat pump circulates the water to cool the building in the summer and warm it in the winter. Before the air is cooled, a desiccant system removes 70 percent of the humidity from outside air to improve efficiency. The entire ventilation system operates on a timer, and a backup boiler system is available. To control unnecessary use of heating and cooling, "open windows" lights illuminate, alerting employees that outside conditions are favorable for natural ventilation and automatically opening nonaccessible windows. Given the climate of this region, it is expected that employees will use natural ventilation only about 10 percent of the year. All windows in the building have high-efficiency glazing and are made of low-e coated insulated glass filled with argon between the lights.

On the exterior, the silver galvanized roof and siding reflect light and keep the roof cool. Photovoltaic solar panels on the south wall generate supplemental electricity for the center, and a roof-mounted evacuated heat pipe solar collector system, which is 20 percent more efficient than flat plates, heats water for showers and laundry. An energy monitor maintains a uniform temperature (+ 2 degrees) throughout the building. When not in use, the conference center, which has a separate entrance, is "turned down."

To protect indoor air quality, CBF relies on a ventilation system that monitors VOCs and carbon dioxide levels and automatically adjusts ventilation to retain acceptable levels. Two monitors for VOC levels, one indoors and the other outdoors, and a carbon dioxide monitor in the main conference room automatically adjust ventilation during higher occupancy levels. In the conference room, this system allows for the default setting to be lower, thus saving energy. Moreover, doormats retard dust and dirt from being tracked into the building.

CBF was also concerned about outdoor air quality. A total traffic management plan reduces the need for employees to make single-occupancy vehicle trips as well as the number of trips. To encourage employees to bike, walk, or kayak to work, the foundation provides bicycle racks, showers, and changing rooms. Because the building is located a ten-minute drive from area restaurants, vendors bring breakfast and lunch to the building's kitchen. Bicycles are provided for employees to run errands. CBF also offers a free battery-charging station for employees' electric cars, and the staff car is a low-emission hybrid. Videoconferencing and telecommuting connections are available on site to reduce travel to meetings.

Although CBF employs nearly 100 people at its headquarters, the facility provides only 45 employee parking spaces, all of which are located beneath the building. Because this number is 25 percent less than the county requires, the visitors' lot accommodates overflow parking. The loose gravel used on the visitors' lot retains water until it is absorbed. All stormwater from this area and the up-slope portion of the site is diverted through a bioretention swale that removes pollutants from the runoff before it is released (piped) to on-site wetlands through two outfalls.

Another unusual aspect of the building is the amount of construction material obtained from vendors located within a 300-mile (484-kilometer) radius of the building, which resulted in fewer emissions to transport materials. Even with the exceptions made for the Swedish toilets and the Portuguese cork flooring, 51 percent of the materials came from within the desired distance.

To reduce the amount of construction materials and waste, to take advantage of natural light, and to allow all employees a view of the bay, offices are located in an open loft. The simple plywood walls that separate individual workspaces use fewer materials and create less waste. Fears that the open-loft concept would be too noisy were eliminated by the implementation of a white-noise system, which improves the building's acoustics. Throughout the building, materials such as fasteners, pipes, and ductwork were left exposed, and most walls were left unpainted. Where ceiling tiles do exist, as in some of the meeting rooms, they are constructed from cardboard.

The philosophy of construction for the building is "cradle to cradle" rather than "cradle to grave." This philosophy requires consideration of all materials not only for what they are made of but for what they can be made into at the end

The building's beams are parallel strand lumber constructed from new-growth, regenerable wood. All beams were sized and cut at the lumber-yard and scrap materials from the cuts were recycled into the next beam. From a distance, these beams look like regular wood. They are manufactured by pressing and gluing together strips of wood. Cutting strips of wood reduces the amount of scrap normally generated by carving beams out of logs. ©PrakashPatel.com

All wood either was certified by the U.S. Forestry Stewardship Council as coming from sustainably harvested forests or was from renewable resources.

Sustainable wood products were key to the building's construction. The flooring of the atrium is made from 3/4-inch (1.9-centimeter) boards of bamboo, a natural renewable resource that automatically replenishes itself by its strong root system and can be reharvested in three to five years. Upstairs, light-colored floor tiles are made from cork, which can be harvested without killing the tree and regenerates in seven to nine years. The cork tiles absorb sound and provide a cushion. To add to the contrast from the light-colored unfinished walls and cork tiles and to make the rooms more attractive, the floor design incorporates a tile trim made from dark cork, the color of which is the result of a cork processing byproduct.

The timber framing the building is microlam-extruded beams or Parallam Strand Lumber beams made from compressed scrap wood. Structurally engineered Parallam is stronger than conventional wood beams and is treated with pesticides to be termite resistant. Instead of plywood in the building's millwork, medium-density fiberboard made of sawdust and formaldehyde-free resins was used. All interior finishes, paints, sealants, and adhesives emit low levels of VOCs. A ten-foot (three-meter-long) deck connecting the building to the conference center is made of nonarsenic, pressure-treated wood. Ceilings and walls made of structural insulated panels, two 20-foot-long (six-meter-long) panels of oriented strand board with six- to eight-inch-thick (15.4- to 20.5-centimeter-thick) layers of insulation in between them. The insulation is free of compounds containing carbon, hydrogen, chlorine, or fluorine. The panels are twice as long as the standard eight to ten feet (2.4 to three meters), are a sustainable construction material because they require less wood, contain no finishes, have high strength, can breathe and therefore last longer than conventional materials, and have a higher R-value. The panels create an insulation value of R-25 for the walls and R-32

The open loft design maximizes natural light, gives all employees a view of the bay, and requires fewer building materials. ©PrakashPatel.com

of their useful lives. All existing structures on the construction site were recycled (concrete from original foundations is now being used as the roadbed, for example). Materials were selected for recycled content (galvanized siding made from cans, cars, and guns, for example). Likewise, materials from renewable or regenerable resources were incorporated.

for the roof. They are so easy to use that the entire building was enclosed within two weeks. Their seams and joints are made tight with smooth saw cuts to improve efficiency and make them aesthetically pleasing.

Water use at CBF's headquarters is an impressive 90 percent lower than for the average office building of its size, which typically uses 2,500 gallons (9,460 liters) of water per day. CBF is able to use fewer than 200 gallons (755 liters) per day by reusing rainwater and installing flushless toilets. The Clivus Multrum toilet system is an aerobic, odorless compost method of converting human waste into landscaping fertilizer within three years. Toilets empty into three holding tanks until compost is removed. According to SmithGroup architect Greg Mella, the composting toilets raised some initial concerns, but the architect's working with the county enabled them to be included in the design. Clivus toilets are available only from Sweden and cost $50,000 each, but the amount of savings in water use is substantial.

In a typical office building development, the goal of stormwater management is to remove runoff from the site as quickly as possible. Not so at CBF, where stormwater is diverted into cisterns, a gravel parking lot, a bioretention filter, or the landscape. As rain falls onto the building's roof, it is filtered for leaves and other debris before being collected into three 7,000-gallon (26,490-liter) cisterns. Water from the cisterns is reused for fire suppression and landscaping or is filtered for hand washing and laundry. During heavy storms, rainwater that exceeds the collection system's capacity is diverted into three overflow tanks that release water into on-site wetlands.

The landscaping is one of the most noteworthy features of the center. It uses only native genetic stock. Since CBF has moved to its new building, it has begun restoring Walnut Creek and will continue restoring vegetation. Summer grasses cover most of the nonwooded area. Although they take several years to mature, they are self-sufficient, require minimal maintenance, and stabilize the ground.

Financing

As a nonprofit organization, CBF purchased the land for $3.5 million—below market value—and was able to secure a low-interest loan. Total construction costs reached $8.2 million, and Clark Construction completed the project at cost. Although the building did not make money for Clark Construction, whose average project ranges from $30 million to $50 million, Tom French, the construction supervisor, says, "It felt good to do what we were doing."

All costs of development were covered by private donations, including $7.5 million from Philip Merrill, publisher of *Washingtonian* magazine and *The Capital* (an Annapolis newspaper), for whom the building is named.

Experience Gained

Although the sustainable design added an extra $46 per square foot ($495 per square meter), the building uses two-thirds less energy and 90 percent less water than typical office buildings of its size. CBF officials believe that these cumulative savings will more than adequately cover the difference in the upfront construction costs.

Through a combination of leading-edge technology (geothermal wells, photovoltaic panels, natural daylighting and cooling) and age-old techniques (privies and rain barrels), the center's environmental footprint was drastically reduced. More than one-third of the energy used comes from renewable resources.

For SmithGroup, CBF provided many lessons and affirmed some long-held philosophies. Mella, the project's architect, is surprised by the amount of interest the project continues to generate, several years after completion. He notes some key factors critical to successful projects and essential to this one:

Project Data: Philip Merrill Environmental Center

Land Use and Building Information

Site area	31 acres (12.5 hectares)
Gross building area	32,000 square feet (2,975 square meters)
Typical floor area	15,000 square feet (1,395 square meters)
Building height	3 stories
Parking	117 spaces (45 underground, 72 surface)

Land Use Plan

Use	Acres/ Hectares	Percentage of Site
Buildings	0.46/0.18	9.5
Paved areas (surface parking/roads)	0.58/0.23	12.0
Gravel surface parking	0.78/0.31	16.2
Landscaped areas	3.00/1.21	62.2
Total	4.82/1.95	100.0

Development Cost Information

Site Costs

Site acquisition	$3,500,000

Site Improvements

Excavation	$222,000
Sewer/water/drainage	54,000
Paving	20,000
Curbs/sidewalks	16,000
Landscaping/irrigation	49,500
Fees/general conditions	555,000
Other	120,700
Total	$1,037,200

Construction Costs

Superstructure	$3,165,000
HVAC/electric/plumbing	1,669,000
Sprinklers	110,000
Elevators	53,200
Finishes	1,265,000
Graphics/specialties	27,000
Other	838,700
Total	$7,127,900
Soft Costs	$2,800,000
Total Development Cost	$14,500,000

Owner/Developer

Chesapeake Bay Foundation
6 Herndon Avenue
Annapolis, Maryland 21403
Phone: 410-268-8816
Fax: 410-269-0481
www.cbf.org

Architects

SmithGroup
1825 I Street, N.W.
Suite 250
Washington, D.C. 20006
Phone: 202-842-2100
Fax: 202-974-4500
www.smithgroup.com

J. Harrison Architect
1867 Lindamoor Drive
Annapolis, Maryland 21401
Phone: 410-266-0987
Fax: 410-266-0987

Engineer

SmithGroup
1825 I Street, N.W.
Suite 250
Washington, D.C. 20006
Phone: 202-842-2100
Fax: 202-974-4500
www.smithgroup.com

Environmental Consultant, Restoration Landscape Design

Karene Motivans
211 West High Street
Shepherdstown, West Virginia 25443
Phone: 304-876-0580

Project Manager

Synthesis Inc.
9175 Guilford Road
Columbia, Maryland 21046
Phone: 410-792-4447
Fax: 410-792-4458

General Contractor

Clark Construction
7500 Old Georgetown Road
Bethesda, Maryland 20814
Phone: 301-272-8100
Fax: 301-272-1928
www.clarkus.com

Development Schedule

7/1998	Site purchased
7/1998	Planning started
9/1999	Construction started
11/2000	Occupancy
12/2001	Project completed

Location

6 Herndon Avenue
Annapolis, Maryland

■ Establishing goals at the beginning of the project against a clear benchmarking system so that the entire team—client, architect/engineer, and contractor—can retain the focus on the project's objectives and intent. For example, although the sustainable design was not cost prohibitive, it was substantially higher than the average office rate for this area. A significant portion of the additional cost was the building's mechanical systems; however, subsequent studies have proved that these first-cost items will more than pay for themselves—and more quickly than originally anticipated.

■ Designing integrated systems and measuring them against the established benchmarks at every step of the process.

■ Using a thorough commissioning period to balance the technology's and systems' real use and users. This period is key to ensuring that the systems provide the energy efficiency for which they were designed.

■ To French, one of the greatest outcomes of this project has been the amount of press coverage it has received. Since the completion of the building, Clark Construction also has seen interest increase in sustainable design and construction.

CBF also has also enjoyed the successes of its headquarters. Not only is the foundation practicing what it advocates, but ever since it moved into its new building, employee productivity has increased too. It also has learned several lessons:

■ Throughout construction of the center, CBF allowed no substitutions of materials, which presented some difficulties, especially when supplies were unavailable or when problems existed with particular vendors.

■ All landscaping was required to use native genetic stock vegetation, which meant some species were harder to obtain, especially those available only from a limited number of providers. Absolutely no plant substitutions were allowed.

■ The most challenging materials to obtain were the cork flooring and the composting toilets because they had to be shipped from overseas.

■ During construction, the use of low-VOC products eliminated the need for special breathing apparatus.

PNC *Firstside Center*

Pittsburgh, Pennsylvania

Anne B. Frej

PNC Firstside Center is a large-scale environmentally sustainable facility that serves PNC Financial Services Group in Pittsburgh, Pennsylvania, for operations, processing, and many other traditional back-office functions. The building, completed in September 2000, was awarded LEED Silver certification. At the time of construction, the PNC Firstside Center was one of only 12 buildings to achieve LEED-certified green building status. In addition, Firstside Center was determined to be the largest certified green building in the world.

Located on a former brownfield site in downtown Pittsburgh, the building offers an employee-friendly environment with plenty of natural light, fresh air, and sustainable building systems. As a benefit to the city of Pittsburgh, the redevelopment of this formerly idle site brought new life and activity to this underused section of downtown.

Located on a former brownfield site, the PNC Firstside Center has brought new life to the historic Firstside area in downtown Pittsburgh.
Astorino & Ed Massery

The Site

PNC's Realty Services Group, the in-house team responsible for all aspects of PNC's real estate needs, undertook an extensive site selection process, reviewing 17 sites throughout the entire metropolitan area. PNC ultimately chose the site of the former B&O Railway terminal at the corner of First Avenue and Grant Street. The 4.9-acre (two-hectare) site is located in the historic Firstside area at the southern edge of Pittsburgh's central business district. The property was previously a parking lot recognized by the Pennsylvania Department of Environmental Protection as a brownfield that had remained relatively undeveloped because of concerns regarding its past use.

Special Features

■ Large-scale, environmentally sustainable office building
■ First structure in the nation to earn LEED Silver certification
■ Urban infill/brownfield redevelopment site
■ Natural lighting for large floor plates
■ Hybrid air distribution system

PNC's decision to locate the new operations center in downtown Pittsburgh was influenced by an in-house survey indicating that the majority of employees to be housed in the new facility use public transportation to get to and from work. The city's public transit lines radiate outward from the city center, so a central location would provide the easiest access and lowest number of transfers for the majority of employees.

No employee parking is located on site, but a new structured parking garage for 1,200 cars built by the Pittsburgh Parking Authority at PNC's request is located nearby. A large number of bus lines serve the area, and a new light-rail station was built next to the building after extensive discussions with the port authority and a contribution from PNC to the project. In fact, all of PNC's downtown office facilities sit next to light-rail stations, and the company considers the system its corporate transit system.

According to Gary Jay Saulson, senior vice president and director of corporate real estate, it was the best infill site in downtown Pittsburgh. The company estimates that,

if the same facility were built in the suburbs, not only would commuting be more difficult for employees but also a 20-acre (eight-hectare) site rather than a 4.9-acre (two-hectare) site would be necessary to meet parking and stormwater management needs.

Two-thirds of the site is developed, with one-third devoted to open space. An extension of the Eliza Furnace cycling and running trail runs along the southern, riverfront edge of the site, and on the north side of the building, an urban plaza provides an attractive outdoor setting with water elements such as falls, cascades, and streams.

Development Process

PNC Financial Services Group has been experiencing excellent growth. This fact, coupled with the sale of the PNC Fort Duquesne building to the Sports and Exhibition Authority

The southern facade of the building reflects the curve of the river and the adjacent elevated highway. Astorino & Ed Mass

Inserting a large-scale, five-story building into an urban infill site required a sensitive design approach. To reduce its overall visual impact, the building's mass is broken into smaller components and each of its exterior facades is designed to complement its immediate surroundings. Astorino & Ed Massery

to the project's architect, the L.D. Astorino Companies, considerable effort was spent researching sustainable design and construction throughout the design process. The decision to make Firstside Center a USGBC-certified green building, however, was not made until the design was approximately 80 percent complete. Achieving the LEED Silver rating was therefore all the more significant, because some retrofitting was necessary.

The Carnegie Mellon University Center for Building Performance and Diagnostics assisted by developing computer models to analyze daylighting alternatives.

Planning and Design

The project team from PNC Realty Services, which served as developer, plus the project's architects, engineers, and construction managers met weekly to address design and construction issues. Literally hundreds of different planning, design, and development criteria and decisions had to be made to complete the project. The USGBC LEED standards provided a checklist for actions to be taken to achieve high performance goals.

PNC began the planning and design process with the primary goal of creating an employee-friendly building. Natural light, fresh air, and pleasant surroundings were important considerations. Because of the growth that PNC has experienced in recent years, space planning and flexibility also were key design issues.

The final steel-frame structure is five stories high with a total area of 648,833 square feet (60,300 square meters). Inserting a building of this scale in a downtown grid required sensitive planning and design. To reduce its overall visual impact, the building is tucked in the sloping contour of the site that angles downward toward the

to make way for the expansion of the David L. Lawrence Convention Center, made it necessary for PNC either to purchase or build a new facility. The decision was made to build a new regional operations center to house more than 1,500 employees from more than 20 departments. The search led to the consideration of 17 different sites, each of which possessed its own qualities and benefits. Ultimately, PNC chose to locate the facility on the edge of downtown Pittsburgh along the Monongahela River.

The decision to locate the new facility on an urban brownfield site ultimately influenced design by emphasizing the creation of an environmentally sustainable building. Pittsburgh's Green Building Alliance and Paladino Associates, a green building consultant from Seattle, Washington, also were strong advocates in convincing PNC to adopt a sustainable development and green building design. According

Skylights, lightwells, tall windows, low workstations, and open floor plates all help introduce natural light into the interior of the building. Astorino & Ed Massery

Monongahela River. The lower level on the riverfront side houses service areas and loading docks. The main entrance to the building is at the main level on First Avenue.

The building's exterior facades complement the diverse features that make up its surrounding environment, from low-scale historic buildings to the north to an elevated highway at the southern edge of the site. To do so, the building mass was articulated into three smaller components, each with distinctive forms, window treatments, and materials. The western and northern facades align with the historic riverfront warehouses along Fort Pitt Boulevard and the nearby Allegheny County warehouse, designed by H.H. Richardson. The southern facade reflects the curve of the river and the elevated highway.

Landscaping, paving, and roof materials used in the building were designed to reduce the heat island effect created by common paving materials. Lighting systems are intended to minimize sky glow and off-site illumination.

Major entrances to the building respect urban circulation patterns, both new and old. The primary employee entrance on First Avenue is placed at the terminus of Ross Street, an important visual and functional connection to downtown. The other major entrance at the corner of Grant Street and First Avenue is located for convenience of employees entering the building from PNC's other downtown offices.

The building was designed with the goal of providing a flexible and functional workspace for a high-tech workforce. A horizontal design and expansive floor plates measuring 125,000 square feet (11,620 square meters) allow the clustering of large work groups. The elimination of walled offices also contributes to greater interaction and communication among employees. Wide corridors with skylights and light wells provide abundant daylight and facilitate circulation. All workstations are made up of stackable lower furniture systems. Indirect lighting is provided from pendant fixtures.

The introduction of natural light into the deep floor plates of the building is maximized by 11-foot-high (3.3-meter-high) window walls. A generous skylight known as "the slice" runs along the entire roof elevation and allows light to filter down through the fifth, fourth, and third floors. Exterior sun screening devices and motorized interior shades are used to reduce glare and heat gain. HVAC systems use natural gas to conserve energy and ensure lower costs. A hybrid air distribution system provides improved control and comfort while providing maximum flexibility. It distributes fresh air through the raised floor as well as through overhead units that recirculate conditioned air. Vertical shafts servicing each floor saved money by eliminating the need for horizontal ductwork. A hybrid chiller plant can use natural gas or electricity to take advantage of the lowest utility price available.

An estimated third of the 1,500 employees at Firstside Center are relocated over a five-year period as a result of shifting market trends and changing business practices. To allow maximal flexibility for future changes in technology and the work environment, 95 percent of the floor area has accessible raised floors topped with carpet tiles that allow easy reconfiguration of workstations. The under-floor space is used for communication wiring and modular power wiring.

Recyclable materials are used extensively. Carpet is made of 72 percent recycled material, and hard floor surfaces in the cafeteria and restrooms are made of 100 percent recycled materials, including plastic soda bottles and sawdust. Hogs-hair carpeting used in entry areas not only is durable but also grips dirt and therefore helps reduce cleaning costs. Some materials can be returned to the manufac-

The main employee entrance on First Avenue is functionally and visually connected to downtown Pittsburgh and includes a security clearance area.
Astorino & Ed Massery

turer at the end of their useful life for another round of recycling. The location where materials were produced was also considered; 61 percent of the materials were manufactured within 500 miles (805 kilometers), thus allowing for easier delivery and service.

Water-conserving plumbing fixtures are used throughout the building. A purification system for drinking water eliminates the need for the delivery of bottled water. Even the decorative water features in the building were designed to use recirculated water that is purified without chemicals. The HVAC system relies on an electromagnetic system rather than chemicals for water treatment.

Art is integral to the design of the building. A long gallery space on the main level features revolving art displays. Major permanent works of art evoke the themes of water by Koryn Rolstad of Seattle and Reiner John of Germany. The terrace holds eight boldly colored whimsical aluminum sculptures by Pam Castano of Phoenix that double as benches.

Amenities for employees include a 24-hour full-service cafeteria with a rooftop terrace overlooking the river. Each floor has two employee break rooms with kitchen areas. The O'Brien Family Center is the first corporate-operated child care program in downtown Pittsburgh. This on-site facility provides backup child-care services for all employees in PNC's downtown facilities. The building also provides showers for bicycle commuters and a recharging station for electric vehicles.

The building has made a positive contribution to the lives of workers and visitors alike, with its aesthetic significance on a former brownfield site. Not only is the building pleasant to look at, but it also is pleasant to work in and look out of.

Management of the building is outsourced to Oxford Realty Services, a professional management company. To ensure that sustainability is a component of ongoing operations, employees of the management company have undergone training programs. Environmentally friendly cleaning products are used.

The design and construction process for PNC Firstside took three years. An excellent relationship with the city ensured that the approval process went smoothly. The architects and PNC Realty Services note that the key to this success was to initiate contact with appropriate city officials and staff early in the process and update them regularly on progress. To speed up the process, a fast-track construction management system was used. Excavation of the site began before interior plans were completed. During construction, erosion and sediment control systems were used to ensure sustainability. Total construction cost for the project was $114 million, $5 million under budget.

Experience Gained

PNC Realty Services found that most sustainable development concepts are actually good business practices. Creating an environment where workers can thrive creates the potential for greater productivity and less employee turnover. The project team found that, in general, the costs incurred for sustainable features tend to average out over the total project. In many cases, the upfront cost increase in one material or system was offset by the upfront savings in another.

Documenting and meeting LEED requirements can take extra effort and time, but the standards provide an excellent checklist for the project team to follow.

Developers of large-scale projects have clout with manufacturers. PNC Realty Services actively worked with manufacturers to create customized environmentally sustainable products such as floor coverings, light fixtures, and accessible floors.

At the time it was LEED certified in 2000, the PNC Firstside Center was one of the largest certified green buildings in the world.

Astorino & Ed Massery

Technology and building systems change rapidly, and building designs must be flexible enough to undergo future innovations. By using the LEED system as a design guideline and third-party certification tool, PNC Firstside Center allows for enhanced comfort for workers, environmental performance, and economic return on investment.

By promoting sustainable development and green building principles throughout planning, design, and development, substantial quantities of natural resources and raw building materials were conserved during construction, and the ongoing reliance on energy supplies and additional building materials has been greatly reduced compared with standard office buildings.

Project Data: PNC Firstside Center

Land Use and Building Information

Site area	4.9 acres (2 hectares)
Gross building area	648,833 square feet (60,300 square meters)
Net rentable area	592,016 square feet (55,020 square meters)
Typical floor area	125,000 square feet (11,620 square meters)

Land Use Plan

Use	Square Feet/ Square Meters	Percentage of Site
Buildings	129,000/12,000	62
Hardscape	60,002/5,575	29
Landscaping/open space	18,202/1,690	8
Total	207,204/19,255	100
Parking	0	

Development Cost Information

Site Costs

Site acquisition[1]

Construction Costs

Shell and core	$70,451,830
Tenant fitout	29,833,170
Security	735,815
Signage	164,477
Utilities and miscellaneous expenses	579,156
Furniture systems	5,949,571
Total	$107,714,019

Soft Costs

Architecture/engineering	$5,298,253
Project management[2]	
Legal/accounting[2]	
Relocation costs	1,223,742
Title fees[1]	
Construction interest and fees[3]	
Total	$6,521,995
Additional costs[4]	$95,244
Total Development Cost	**$114,331,258**

Annual Operating Expenses

Taxes	$2,636,542
Insurance	434,616
Security	680,100
Repairs and maintenance	1,885,524
Janitorial	1,288,130
Utilities	1,520,466
Legal	0
Management	266,441
Miscellaneous	44,658
Tenant improvements	0
Total	$8,756,477
Operating Costs	$13.43 per square foot ($144.50 per square meter)

Owner/Developer

PNC Financial Services Group
Realty Services Group
Two PNC Plaza
620 Liberty Avenue
Pittsburgh, Pennsylvania 15222
Phone: 412-762-5544
Fax: 412-768-2078
www.pncbank.com

Architect

L.D. Astorino Companies
227 Fort Pitt Boulevard
Pittsburgh, Pennsylvania 15222
Phone: 412-765-1700
Fax: 412-765-1711
www.ldastorino.com

Structural, Mechanical, and Electrical Engineer

Astorino/Branch Engineering
227 Fort Pitt Boulevard
Pittsburgh, Pennsylvania 15222
Phone: 412-765-1700
Fax: 412-765-1711
www.ldastorino.com

General Contractor

Dick Corporation
1900 State Route 51
Large, Pennsylvania 15025
Phone: 412-384-1000
Fax: 412-384-1150
www.dickcorp.com

Development Schedule

10/1998	Construction started
9/2000	Construction completed
10/2000	Occupancy

Location

500 First Avenue
Pittsburgh, Pennsylvania

Notes

1. Land lease.
2. In house.
3. Self-financed.
4. Costs associated with green buildings such as LEED certification and downtown location.

30 St. Mary Axe

Swiss Reinsurance Company Headquarters

London, England

Jenifer Seal

Known widely as "the gherkin," the gleaming 40-story 30 St. Mary Axe (the official name) is the London headquarters for the Swiss Reinsurance Company (Swiss Re, the well-known informal name). The distinctive tower, located in the heart of London's financial district, provides 360-degree panoramic views. It features Class A office space, public spaces, and retail amenities. In guiding the design of this first tall green building in London, Swiss Re set a high standard for office towers and building performance around the world.

Swiss Re reinsures life, health, property, motor, and liability insurance. Established more than 140 years ago, the company has 8,000 employees worldwide and is one of the world's largest reinsurers. An integral part of Swiss

London's first sustainable skyrise, located at 30 St. Mary Axe, is an instantly recognizable addition to the city's skyline. The distinctive form, often called a "gherkin," was designed using parametric modeling common to the aerospace and automotive industries. Grant Smith 2004

Re's ethos and management practices is sustainable development. It is known as a socially responsible company and works to raise awareness of sustainability. This environmental ethic is reflected not only in its reinsurance products and investments, but also in its buildings and operations. Because green standards are a part of doing business, the company wanted a stately building as well as a superior example of green design for its headquarters building.

Site Design and Development Process

The project sits on the 1.4-acre (0.6-hectare) former site of the Baltic Exchange. Historic remnants of the exchange, including the stained glass from the main hall, were donated to the National Maritime Museum. An agreement to purchase the land was obtained in 1997 contingent upon planning and design approval. The development received full planning permission three years later—a great testament to

Special Features

■ Unusual form and small footprint
■ Sky gardens to regulate internal climate
■ Double-skin facade
■ Floor-by-floor mechanical plant
■ Building management system, wind velocity unit, pyranometer, and photo cell sensors
■ Use of green and recycled materials
■ Stormwater filtration system
■ Wind-reduced ground-level design

the project in that for the first time in 30 years, permission was granted for a new tall building in the heart of the City of London's financial district, known as the Square Mile. Construction began in January 2001, and a topping-out ceremony was held in late November 2002 to mark the completion of the steel structure.

Wind pressure differentials generated by the building's aerodynamic form assist natural ventilation and reduce the need for conventional air conditioning. A computerized system monitors critical data to determine when to open and close windows and even when to raise and change the tilt on interior blinds.

Graham Harle 2004

The building's shape responds well to its tight, urban infill site. Its small circular footprint provides room for pleasant public spaces at the ground level, a bulge in the middle allows for larger office floor plates, and the tapering top of the building minimizes the impact on the city skyline.

Grant Smith 2004

The building encompasses a small circular footprint, leaving the remaining area for public enjoyment. With the site's limitations, there would have been room for only very narrow streets at the edges had the building design occupied the entire area. Instead, the creativity of this site design allows the provision of landscaped public space with mature trees and a new plaza that features low stone walls defining the historical site boundary and serving as street furniture.

The lack of private car parking in the development required creative planning to reduce dependence on private automobiles. Several modes of public transportation surround the site, and three times the minimum standard of bicycle spaces is provided in the basement. Shower and changing facilities are also provided to further encourage alternative modes of transportation.

The building was intended to serve primarily as the headquarters for Swiss Re, but the company has not required as much space as previously envisioned. Swiss Re occupies floors 2 through 15; floors 16 to 34 are leased to other companies. The ground-floor plaza is open to the public. It features a variety of shops and restaurants.

Planning and Design

Swiss Re selected world-renowned architects Foster and Partners for its headquarters. Weaving together 11,000 tons (10,000 metric tons) of steel, the futuristic and curvaceous tower has already become an iconic landmark.

Conceptually, the project builds on ideas first explored in Buckminster Fuller's design of Climatroffice in the 1970s. At the time, Fuller's complex, double-curved geometry would have been difficult to build. Thirty years later, parametric modeling and other digital tools facilitated the design and construction of 30 St. Mary Axe in a fraction of the time.

Use of parametric modeling, originally developed in the aerospace and automotive industries for designing complex curved forms, helped the team design the building's egg-shaped geometry. Excellence in engineering design helped to make this building one of the most efficient and elegant green projects in the world.

The circular plan of the egg-shaped structure responds to the specific demands of the small site. Its appearance is less bulky than a conventional rectangular block of equivalent floor area. This slim profile improves transparency and increases daylighting at ground level. The floor plates at the middle of the structure offer larger areas for office space, while the tapering apex minimizes the extent of reflected sky.

Two of the most striking elements of the building's green design are its natural ventilation and daylighting. Light wells, configured between the "six fingers" of office space on each floor and spanning between two and six stories, maximize daylight penetration and reduce artificial lighting requirements. For up to 40 percent of the year, much of the mechanical cooling and ventilation supply systems can be turned off because of this innovative design, resulting in dramatically reduced energy consumption and carbon dioxide emissions. Sky gardens regulate the internal climate and essentially serve as the building's lungs. Slots lining the outer edges of each floor plate draw in fresh air for mechanical ventilation at each floor and expel it into the gardens. The garden plants oxygenate the air, creating a healthy and vibrant indoor environment.

The aerodynamic shape creates pressure differentials in the ventilated double skin that move air up the 590-foot (180-meter) building. This innovative design allows the use of this space to maximize benefits of the prevailing internal and external environment. Blinds in the cavity of the double skin intercept solar gain before it enters the office space. Heat captured there can then be reclaimed or rejected, depending on heating or cooling requirements. A computerized building management system monitors the critical data to determine when to open and close the windows and when to change the tilt on the blinds. A decentralized plant offers the flexibility to supply and control mechanical ventilation for each floor. By closely matching supply with demand, energy consumption is reduced compared with a central system for the whole building.

The United Kingdom's leading center of expertise on buildings, construction, energy, environment, fire, and risk, the Building Research Establishment, lists the annual energy consumption guidelines for low-energy, mixed-mode offices. By this standard, the Swiss Re building will use seven times less energy than a standard office building.

Construction

Construction began on the development in the first quarter of 2001. Skanska Construction worked within the confined site to construct more than 360 new permanent piles. Arup engineered the building's curvaceous form by designing the efficient external system of intersecting steel sections around the perimeter of the tower. By providing this vertical support system, large internal column-free office spaces are available. This highly efficient system also aptly resists wind forces while internally framing the light wells, enabling occupants to enjoy natural light deep within the floor plates.

Working within such a tight site required rigorous planning to best coordinate the construction, and absolute precision was required to create the vertical support system. As a result, all the contractors were required to participate in special training. In addition to creating a superb building, these efforts also resulted in an accident frequency well below the norm.

Project Data: 30 St. Mary Axe (Swiss Reinsurance Company Headquarters)

Land Use and Building Information

Site area	1.4 acres (0.5 hectare)
Typical floor size	6,500–19,500 square feet (605–1,810 square meters)
Building height	40 stories: 590 feet (180 meters)

Net Rentable Area

Office	500,000 square feet (46,500 square meters)
Retail	15,000 square feet (1,400 square meters)

Parking

No employee or visitor parking
5 parking spaces for the handicapped
52 motorcycle spaces
118 bicycle spaces

Developer/Owner

Swiss Reinsurance Company
30 St. Mary Axe
London EC3A 8EP
England
www.swissre.com
www.30stmaryaxe.com

Development Manager

RWG Associates
311 Butlers Wharf Building
36 Shad Thames
London SE1 2YE
England

Architect

Foster and Partners
Riverside Three
22 Hester Road
London SW11 4AN
England
Phone: 44 20 773 80455
Fax: 44 20 7738 1107
www.fosterandpartners.com

Structural Engineer

Arup
13 Fitzroy Street
London W1T 4BQ
England
Phone: 44 20 7636 1531
www.arup.com/london

Preliminary Cost Estimator

Gleeds
95 New Cavandish Street
London W1W6XF
England
Phone: 44 20 7631 7000
Fax: 44 20 7631 7001
www.gleeds.co.uk

Cost Manager

Gardiner & Theobald
32 Bedford Square
London WC1B 3JT
England
Phone: 44 20 7209 3000
Fax: 44 20 7209 1840
www.gardiner.com

General Contractor

Skanska Construction UK Ltd.
Maple Cross House
Denham Way
Maple Cross Rickmansworth
Hertfordshire WD3 2SW
England
Phone: 44 22 7294 2918

Building Service

Moran Partnership Limited
16 Armstrong Mall
Southwood
Farnborough
Hampshire GU14 0NR
England

Lift Engineer

Van Deusen & Associates
5 Regent Street
Suite 524
Livingston, New Jersey 07039

Other Consultants

Fire Engineering: Arup Fire, London, England
Mechanical and Electrical Engineers: Hilson Moran Partnership,
South Farnborough, Hampshire, England
Interior Architects: Bennett Interior Design/Foster and Partners,
London, England
Lighting Architects: Speirs and Major Associates, London, England

Development Schedule

1997	Planning started
2001	Construction started
2003	Construction completed
2004	Building opened

Location

30 St. Mary Axe
London, England

The tower's diagonally braced shape allows column-free floor space. This club room sits atop 41 floors, making it London's highest occupied floor and providing a 360-degree panorama across the city. Grant Smith 2004

Experience Gained

The iconic project has received much recognition. It was chosen for the 2003 Emporis Skyscraper Award by an unusually clear consensus of the jury—the first time this award was presented in a European country. The jury selected the project not only for its shape but also for its spiraling chain of atriums. The project also won the 2003 European award for Steel Structures and was awarded the prestigious 2004 RIBA Stirling prize.

John Fitzpatrick, member of the executive board and head of Swiss Re's Life & Health Business Group, says that the company's objectives for the building have been met: "London seems to have taken this building to its heart, our employees are enthusiastic and proud to work here, clients are now visiting us in large numbers, and now that we're up and running, interest from potential tenants in the available space is high. Swiss Re has the asset it always envisioned."

Toyota Motor Sales
North American Headquarters

South Campus Office Development
Torrance, California

Dan Heinfeld

The new 624,000-square-foot (58,000-square-meter) South Campus office development on the 135-acre (55-hectare) U.S. headquarters of Toyota Motor Sales in Torrance, California, is the first privately developed office campus in California—and the largest facility in the country—to receive the U.S. Green Building Council's LEED Gold award, which only 11 other buildings in the United States had attained by late 2003.

The project brings together Toyota's Customer Services Division and the Toyota Financial Services main office on one site in two buildings that can accommodate approximately 2,500 employees.

Toyota Motor Sales designed its new South Campus Headquarters in Torrance, California, to meet transportation needs in an environmentally and socially responsible manner. LPA, Inc./Adrian Velicescu, Standard

The South Campus expansion was developed by Toyota Motor Sales, the U.S. sales and marketing arm of Toyota Motor Corporation. South Campus construction began in September 2001 and was completed in April 2003. Irvine, California–based LPA provided master planning, building, interior, and landscape architecture design for the green South Campus expansion.

Site

The project site is a previously vacant 40-acre (16-hectare) parcel at the southern portion of the 135-acre (55-hectare) Toyota Motor Sales U.S. headquarters campus 16 miles (26 kilometers) south of downtown Los Angeles.

Special Features

■ Largest single rooftop installation of photovoltaic panels in California
■ Natural daylight and outdoor views for 90 percent of employees
■ On-site recycled water system used for irrigation, mechanical systems, and plumbing
■ Landscape water use reduced by more than 50 percent
■ More than 50 percent (by value) of building materials contain recycled content
■ Highly efficient air-handling units and chillers
■ 64 charging stations for electric vehicles
■ Nearly 90 percent of construction waste recycled

Toyota's South Campus Headquarters building has the largest single rooftop installation of photovoltaic panels in California. The 536-kilowatt system provides up to 20 percent of the building's electricity.
LPA, Inc./Adrian Velicescu, Standard

■ Earn at least LEED Silver certification.

■ Design and develop the green project at a cost no greater than for speculative low-rise office development in Torrance.

■ Bring together all Toyota Motor Sales's associates on one campus.

■ Integrate Toyota's corporate philosophy—an emphasis on workers' comfort, efficiency, and larger social and environmental values such as earth-friendly products and processes—into a high-quality office facility.

The project architect faced the challenge of master planning and designing the South Campus according to LEED guidelines when the LEED program was still in its infancy—planning, testing, and implementing new,

Planning

Toyota's Customer Services Division and Toyota Financial Services occupied several leased buildings off campus in Torrance, California. Toyota wanted to bring them together on its headquarters campus to save money, and also believed that having its employees on one site would promote greater team spirit and productivity. The company would also have greater control over owned rather than leased buildings.

Toyota chose to build green because of its corporate commitment to the environment—the company, for example, makes the Prius hybrid electric-/gas-powered car—and its belief that an automaker going green would make an important statement to other companies around the world.

Toyota Motor Sales had several objectives for the design of the South Campus office development:

The landscape design encourages outdoor meetings and functions with tables and seating set amid shade trees, flowering shrubs, and native grasses. LPA, Inc./ Adrian Velicescu, Standard

innovative technology and strategies that had never been tried before and meeting Toyota's schedule for occupancy and the rigorous LEED requirements.

Design

The South Campus office development has 624,000 gross square feet (58,000 square meters) of office space in two three-story office buildings with a total of five "pods," or sections. The two main buildings are connected by a long common lobby. The financial services building has three distinct sections connected by smaller lobbies. The Customer Services Division building—parallel to the Toyota Financial Services building—has two distinct sections that are also connected by lobbies. Each floor of the multisection buildings averages 119,428 gross square feet (11,100 square meters), excluding lobbies.

The South Campus also has 2,339 surface parking spaces, a pedestrian circulation loop, and more than eight acres (3.2 hectares) of landscaped open space, including an outdoor seating area for the employee dining center, break rooms, a jogging trail, and an outdoor stage. Two undeveloped lots have been set aside for future growth.

Dozens of design features were integrated into the South Campus site and buildings that helped Toyota earn LEED Gold certification:

■ Both South Campus buildings use photovoltaic panels, a source of renewable energy, which provide 20 percent of the buildings' energy requirements. The South Campus has the single largest rooftop installation of photovoltaic panels in California.

■ The South Campus's energy performance exceeds both the California Title 24 energy code, which is the strictest in the nation, and the minimum LEED requirements by more than 42 percent annually.

■ Both buildings maximize natural lighting through the extensive use of exterior glazing, an interior open-space plan, and open furniture systems. The artificial lighting system includes task lighting and overhead indirect lighting.

■ The open office floor plan and glass-enclosed perimeter offices in both buildings give more than 90 percent of the Toyota employees natural daylight and outdoor views.

■ None of the HVAC, fire suppression, and refrigeration equipment uses ozone-depleting HCFC, Halon, or CFC-based refrigerants.

■ The ductwork has a special Mylar lining that is easy to clean and does not release fibers into the indoor environment.

■ Each building on the South Campus was designed to connect flushing plumbing fixtures and cooling towers in the central plants to a recycled water system that Toyota extended more than a half mile (0.8 kilometer) to serve the South Campus as well as the entire 135-acre (55-hectare) headquarters campus. Toyota's use of recycled water for irrigation, mechanical systems, and plumbing fixtures saves 11,000 gallons (41,600 liters) of potable water a year.

■ The drip irrigation system uses recycled rather than potable water and that, coupled with drought-tolerant plantings, reduces water use for landscaping by more than 50 percent.

■ More than 50 percent (by value) of building materials have recycled content. The gypsum board walls, for example, have 15 percent recycled content, and the structural steel system has 100 percent recycled content.

■ A pedestrian circulation system integrated into the landscape design of the South Campus provides an alternative to short car trips between different campus buildings.

■ The South Campus reduces the use of fossil fuels and supports employees' use of alternative transportation by providing 64 charging stations for electric vehicles, preferred parking for those who carpool, bicycle storage for more than 100 bikes, showers, and an on-campus electric vehicle shuttle system to local bus lines.

The design of the South Campus also employs a variety of cost-saving strategies, including highly efficient air-handling units and gas-fired chillers to optimize the performance of the HVAC system well beyond California's Title 24 energy requirements. Photovoltaic panels on the buildings provide a renewable energy source for the South Campus and greatly reduce costs of electricity. Together, these two systems alone will generate annual energy savings of more than 40 percent for Toyota over the life of the project.

These green features not only help the environment but also provide a safe, attractive, and healthy workplace for 2,500 Toyota associates, meet Toyota's environmental goals, and demonstrate to other companies that they too can build green on a budget. For example, design and development of the shells and interiors of South Campus buildings cost $90 per square foot ($970 per square meter), comparable to a typical low-rise speculative office development in that market.

To minimize construction costs and free up additional money for green features, concrete tilt-up walls were used for all the buildings. Concrete was poured over a steel deck to strengthen the roofs and floors and to improve acoustics. A steel frame was used in the main lobby to support the open floor plan. The building mass was shaped in response to the site's solar orientation to maximize interior daylighting and reduce heat gain.

The windows on the south side of the buildings are glazed with low-e glass and slightly inset into the concrete wall to provide greater interior shade and lessen heat buildup in the interior. The windows on the other three sides of the buildings are flush with the concrete walls.

The South Campus's 2,339 surface parking spaces are located around the perimeter of the site; they are heavily landscaped with trees to provide shade for pedestrians and building facades, to minimize the heat island effect of buildings and parking lots, and to help clean the air.

Each floor of the two multisection buildings averages 119,428 gross square feet (11,100 square meters), excluding the connecting lobbies. The floor plan for each of the five building sections was designed around a central core that has restrooms, business centers, file/storage rooms, copy rooms, break rooms, and designated recycling areas.

Beyond the central core of each building section are open floor plan office areas with open workstations that can easily be moved or reconfigured to meet the changing needs of each business unit. The perimeter of each floor plate is ringed with glass-enclosed

private offices, allowing daylight to pass from the exterior to the interior of the floors. Offices have 9.5-foot (2.9-meter) ceilings to provide greater openness and better natural lighting. Each building was designed to provide natural daylighting and outdoor views to more than 90 percent of the occupants.

The two three-story main buildings and the five separate sections in those buildings are connected by 28,629 gross square feet (2,660 square meters) of common lobbies. A two-story light-filled common lobby with a limestone floor connects the two main buildings. The north wall of the lobby is glass and overlooks an entry garden. A series of smaller, horizontal ground-floor lobbies connect the five different sections to each other in the main buildings and all floors of the five building sections to each other with horizontal circulation, elevators (which are lubricated with recycled vegetable oil), and stairs.

At $90 per square foot, the design and development costs were comparable to surrounding nongreen, low-rise office campuses in southern California. LPA, Inc./Adrian Velicescu, Standard

In addition to elevators, lobby-based glass stairwells provide vertical circulation and act as extensions of the office floor plates, encouraging floor-to-floor interaction.

Installation of a special pipeline supplies recycled water to the complex for cooling, landscaping, and restroom flushing. Along with other conservation efforts, this reduces potable water demand by 84 percent. LPA, Inc /
Adrian Velicescu, Standard

A 350-seat multipurpose dining center on the ground floor of the Customer Service building has an outdoor seating area with an international food court. It can easily be reconfigured into a meeting area if necessary.

Landscape Architecture

Landscaping for the South Campus was one of the most important features of the site plan. The abundant landscape, and particularly the many trees, represent Toyota's commitment to the environment and to its future in Torrance.

The landscape design incorporates a variety of usable outdoor spaces, enabling Toyota associates to take typical indoor functions outside and helping unite the northern and southern portions of the headquarters campus into a whole. The landscape was designed to promote socialization and informal interactions and information sharing, to reduce heat

islands, and to encourage pedestrian activity rather than vehicular use on short trips. Toyota Court on the west side of the South Campus buildings, for example, has informal conference and break areas with tables, seating, and bike racks amid grass, shade trees, and a variety of flowering shrubs. The promenade, lined by flowering plum trees, reinforces the east-west axis of the South Campus and enables way-finding by terminating at "portals" in the parking lots.

The perimeter landscaping was designed to provide Toyota with a secure edge, blend with the surrounding environment, and present a friendly face to the community. A hedge was used rather than a fence on the site's most public side. The southernmost surface parking lots are lined with rows of carrotwood trees as a metaphor for California's agricultural past and to help prevent heat islands. The surface parking lots are actually land banks. Eventually, structured parking will be constructed and the surface lots redeveloped with green buildings.

The circulation system for the South Campus was designed to separate pedestrian and vehicular paths. Vehicular circulation also separates deliveries and recycling pickup routes from the rest of the on-campus traffic. The circulation system is also intended to strengthen the South Campus's direct relationship with the rest of the Toyota campus. An existing jogging trail, for example, was extended to the South Campus to create a campuswide loop. A combination of landscaped pedestrian routes and campus electric shuttles was designed to encourage Toyota associates to use the pedestrian systems.

Construction

Toyota's waste management program recycled close to 90 percent of construction waste from the South Campus. The buildings' concrete tilt-up wall molds, for example, were reused in hardscape features such as sidewalks. To prevent

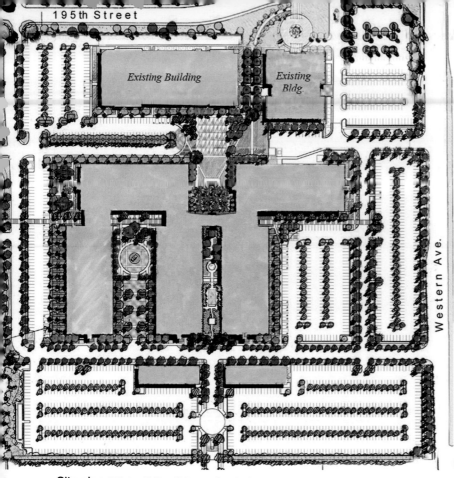

195th Street

Existing Building

Existing
Bldg.

Western Ave.

Site plan. LPA, Inc./Adrian Velicescu, Standard

construction from creating air quality problems in the surrounding area, pollutant sources were controlled by, for example, sealing mechanical ductwork in the shop before installing it and keeping the ducts sealed until they were connected. Coordinated construction sequencing of wet and dry activities avoided contaminating dry materials that would otherwise absorb moisture and become a breeding ground for mold or bacteria.

To safeguard indoor air quality, the HVAC systems were protected from contamination during construction, and proper housekeeping schedules were enforced. The HVAC systems and ductwork were also flushed to remove construction dust and debris left over from the original manufacturing process before the buildings were occupied.

Ground was broken in September 2001. Toyota employees began moving into the new buildings in March 2003, and the move-in was completed in August that year. On April 22, 2003—Earth Day—the South Campus received its LEED Gold certification from the USGBC.

Financing

Toyota financed the South Campus Expansion project in house through Toyota Motor Sales, the U.S. sales and marketing arm of Toyota Motor Corporation.

Toyota already owned the 40-acre (16-hectare) South Campus site. Design and development of the South Campus buildings' shell and interiors cost $90 per square foot ($970 per square meter), which is comparable to a typical low-rise speculative office development in that market. Green planning and design features will save Toyota money over the long term. The South Campus's energy performance, for example, exceeds both the California Title 24 energy code and the minimum LEED requirements by more than 42 percent annually.

Experience Gained

This project demonstrates that green design can surmount any of the usual challenges found in the real estate industry, from relocating electrical transmission lines to seamlessly integrating a new office development into an existing campus.

LPA had to master plan and design the South Campus according to LEED guidelines when the LEED program was just in its infancy, which meant dealing with planning and design areas that were unknown; implementing new, innovative technology and strategies that had never been tried before; and meeting both Toyota's schedule for occupancy and the rigorous LEED requirements. On Earth Day, April 22, 2003, the South Campus received its LEED Gold certification from the USGBC.

LPA was able to apply its experience on this project to the firm's later green projects, including schools and civic institutions.

Toyota has clearly demonstrated to other companies that it is possible to build green on a budget.

Project Data: Toyota Motor Sales North American Headquarters

Land Use and Building Information

Site area	40 acres (16 hectares)
Gross building area	624,000 square feet (58,000 square meters)
Typical floor area	119,428 square feet (11,100 square meters)
Surface parking	2,339 spaces

Development Cost Information

Site Costs

Site acquisition N/A (Toyota had long owned the site as part of its larger headquarters campus)

Construction Costs and Soft Costs $90 per square foot ($970 per square meter)

Total Development Cost $87 million

Owner/Developer

Toyota Motor Sales
19001 South Western Avenue
Torrance, California 90509
Phone: 310-468-4000
Fax: 310-468-7800
www.toyota.com

Architect and Landscape Architect

LPA
17848 Sky Park Circle
Irvine, California 92614
Phone: 949-261-1001
Fax: 949-260-1190
www.lpairvine.com

General Contractor

Turner Construction Company
2484 Natomas Park Drive
Suite 101
Sacramento, California 95833
Phone: 916-614-9311
Fax: 916-614-9345
www.turnerconstruction.com

Structural Engineer

Culp & Tanner
23686 Birtcher
Lake Forest, California 92630
Phone: 949-951-1171
Fax: 949-951-0902
www.culp-tanner.com

Mechanical Engineer

Glumac International, Inc.
16735 Von Karman Avenue
Suite 250
Irvine, California 92614
Phone: 949-833-8910
Fax: 949-833-0252
www.glumac-la.com

Electrical Engineer

Konsortum 1
1632 Brookhollow Drive
Santa Ana, California 92705
Phone: 714-668-4200
Fax: 714-668-4215
www.konsortum1.com

Development Schedule

9/2001	Construction started
4/2002	Construction completed
8/2003	Occupancy

Location

19001 South Western Avenue
Torrance, California

Tuthill Corporate Center

Burr Ridge, Illinois

Jenifer Seal

Tuthill Corporate Center is a 53,000-square-foot (4,925-square-meter) building located on a 20-acre (eight-hectare) tract of land, a portion of which is designated as "critical wetland." The facility, the first of three phases, uses state-of-the-art energy-efficient mechanical and lighting systems and natural daylight. In 2002, the project won the AIA Northern Illinois Award and the Association of Licensed Architects Award.

The building was built by the Tuthill Corporation, a company established in 1892 to meet the city of Chicago's growing needs for construction materials. Today, the company encompasses nine divisions supplying engineered industrial products worldwide.

The Tuthill
Corporate Center
in Burr Ridge,
Illinois, is designed
to be at least 40
percent more
efficient than
similar buildings
in the region.
Jenifer Seal

According to its CEO, Jay Tuthill, "In everything, we are committed to the community and environment." This fourth-generation company's core values include valuing people, performance, and progress; setting goals that are ambitious, creative, and reasoned; and understanding that the company's culture is open, collaborative, and results oriented.

The Site, Development Process, and Planning

Tuthill's team created a state-of-the-art sustainable corporate headquarters that has been called "aggressive" and "forward thinking." According to Jay Tuthill, "The project came at a time when the company was in transition. The goal was to develop an inspiring space that supported collaboration, technological advances, and international connections while maintaining a flexible, amenable atmosphere."

Special Features

■ Environmentally sensitive building configuration and placement
■ Tight building shell construction
■ Natural light throughout and high-performance supplemental lighting
■ Efficient HVAC system
■ Raised floors
■ Restoration of on-site wetlands and native prairie landscape
■ Natural stormwater drainage
■ Modeled to use 4 percent less energy than similar facilities

The company started work on the project in 1994. Working with Stephen Baird, Peter Maggos, and Brian Hayes of Baird & Warner Commercial Real Estate in Chicago, the team began site selection and interviewing architects to select

The building sits amid a restored native prairie landscape. Site amenities include walking trails, boardwalk terraces, a patio, a pond, and a waterfall. Jenifer Seal

a short list of three firms. At the interview with Prisco Serena Sturm, principal Bill Sturm presented a cartoonlike drawing with a progressive sustainable design complete with green roofs, good orientation, gardens, and no parking. Tuthill said they were "so far off the wall I kind of liked them."

During the long 18-month search for a suitable site, the project team played with several design concepts. Initially, Sturm described basic green concepts and educated Tuthill and the team on the approach. Tuthill became more engaged in the discussion when it turned to materials. To fit in the context of the company, Sturm suggested using a combination of raw concrete and wood. Tuthill was not sure about this suggestion at first, but as they discussed the tension between manmade and natural materials, the conversation grew to include the careful stewardship of nature and how it can coexist with the built environment. This concept resonated with Tuthill and he later commissioned a sculpture of stainless steel cradling a two-ton (955-kilogram) hunk of granite to further this concept. This combination of innovation and tradition was the foundation for the project's environmentally focused, synergistic design.

The team selected a 20-acre (eight-hectare) site with designated critical wetlands 20 miles (32 kilometers) outside Chicago. In addition to the wetlands, the property contained one dwelling. The northern border was zoned for light manufacturing, the east and west borders for residential. Forty acres (16 hectares) at the southern edge of the property was slated for high-end residential. The surrounding area is high-end residential, so the project had community and neighborhood support from a village whose tax revenue is basically from such real estate developments.

Site design went through several iterations of development ideas. The chosen concept was for the office to "float in the prairie," creating a parklike setting, in contrast to the one- and two-acre (0.4- and 0.8-hectare) homesites. Neighbors were included in discussions throughout the process. Tuthill hosted review meetings at the local Holiday Inn and walked people through the site. When the team applied for rezoning of the site, the neighbors felt comfortable with the project and supported it. The only complaints were about lighting the building, which was easily corrected with shielding around the lights.

Tuthill wanted a headquarters for the international company and needed more space. The plan was to consolidate, moving information technology, computer applications, finance, and human resources employees from three locations to the new location. With an interest in employee productivity and health, Tuthill envisioned office space where people could function at their peak. Sturm tied this desire into the design with good lighting and acoustics for the space. The organization functions as a type of holding company owner of nearly 20 light-manufacturing companies. Training for staff from around the world is a large part of the facility's function, and the training area features a central café, a court area, open office, breakout rooms, a training room for 60, and a workout room. A caretaker unit, where the building facility manager lives, is also located on site. Tuthill believes that buildings, like people, need someone to watch them.

Tuthill was intimately involved throughout the whole process. He wanted to create a building to exemplify the company's mission and to serve as a recruiting tool for Tuthill. The building was intended to help convey the company's values to the many new employees coming on board and to the general public.

The building program includes three phases. The first phase includes the 53,000-square-foot (4,925-square-meter) main headquarters building, with offices, a conference center, and a training facility. (This portion is completed today.) Total buildout is planned for 100,000 square feet (9,300 square meters). The company currently has no plans to develop the next phases, but, based on the positive experience with the first phase, when it does expand, Tuthill hopes to make future phases as green or greener than the first.

Design

Designing the office space involved considerable research, including a review of *Harvard Business Review*'s "Office of Tomorrow" study and visits to model offices such as Herman Miller and Steelcase. The building form that emerged is like a caterpillar that curves gently around the site. The 180-by-60-square-foot (17-by-5.5-square-meter) two-story building houses up to 90 people in an open office plan. Workspaces are designed to promote teamwork, infor-

mal communication, and efficiency. Tuthill moved from a 300-square-foot (28-square-meter) private office to, in this building, a cubicle to make himself accessible to employees and to share in the environment created for them.

The building is oriented to bring in daylight and reduce solar gain. A 14-foot (4.3-meter) overhang ensures no glare in office interiors. Window blinds are operated by automatic sun sensors. The building shell is coated with a barrier to protect against air and moisture penetration and thermal transfer. The site slopes from high on the north to low on the south. By using the existing sloping terrain, a buffer is provided against winter winds and allows for optimal southern exposure.

The envelope is a spray-on combined insulation and vapor barrier covering intersections of the panels (which typically have large gaps). Unlike many conventional office buildings, perimeter spaces are very comfortable as a result of high-performance glazing and insulated walls.

Inside, displacement air ventilation and wiring through a raised floor are central features of the energy-efficient and flexible design concept. The system results in reduced energy use, superior air quality and temperature control, better ventilation, and more comfortable workers. Relocating personnel in the future can be accomplished in a fraction of the time and at a fraction of the cost normally required because workstations can be unplugged from services below the raised floor, broken down to be relocated, and reassembled and plugged in by maintenance staff at a new location overnight.

At the time the building was designed, raised floors were a new concept, and Sturm had not yet used the system on other projects because of costs. Tuthill saw the concept as flexible and thought it would work well in a training and office center. The team successfully incorporated the strategy into the office space; it was one of the first installations of a raised floor in the Chicago area.

The facility's building materials were chosen for their durability, lack of volatile organic compounds, local availability, and recyclability. Jenifer Seal

Deep overhangs on the exterior minimize glare while allowing in daylight. Window blinds, operated by automatic sun sensors and high-performance lighting, are used in the interior. Jenifer Seal

Through the 18-inch (46-centimeter) raised access floor, low-velocity fresh air is distributed directly to users at their desks through floor diffusers, allowing the employee to control air velocity, temperature, and direction, and light. The system cleanses air of indoor pollutants. For increased energy efficiency, the return air goes through a heat wheel to exchange air with incoming 100 percent fresh outside air. Air-handling units with heat wheels provide total energy recovery of up to 88 percent from the out-

side air before any mechanical heating or cooling is performed. In the summer, the wheel precools and dehumidifies outside air, and in the winter, it preheats and humidifies it; no cross contamination of the outside and exhaust airstreams occurs. Seventeen fan coil units were installed around the interior perimeter boost to the system.

The team wanted to capitalize on the facility's view of the prairie and incorporate significant natural light in the space. Kristine Anstead of Anstead Group analyzed proposed daylighting strategies. Using the modeling tool Lightscape, she optimized exterior overhang lengths and glazing specifi-

cations for efficiency, in the process reducing glare and allowing more light to penetrate.

High-performance indirect fluorescent pendant fixtures are controlled by photosensors, which can be adjusted according to the amount of daylight entering the building. All indirect lighting uses efficient T-8 lamps. The photosensors also control the blinds. Light-colored perforated blinds prismatically illuminate the room when light comes through, absorbing light and helping to control glare. As part of the strategy, each employee was allotted $800 to buy his or her own task lamp, but the lighting is so good that only a few have purchased one.

The team selected Boulder Energy Associates to look at energy performance, simulated by detailed geometrically accurate computer models. Fifteen measures of energy efficiency were considered using the DOE-2.1 model: daylighting, electric lighting, glazing, infiltration, insulation, and high-efficiency office equipment (because plug loads are a high user of electricity), among others. An eight-year payback was selected.

To reduce construction costs, the original six-bay building design was reduced to five bays. The model analyzed and optimized raised-floor air distribution, a variable-air-volume fan system, and daylighting. Six glazing types, three window sizes, and three light shelf configurations were selected for analysis, totaling 48 combinations. During this process, the light shelf was eliminated because it did not provide enough value for its cost, but the large exterior overhang was retained. The design did not consider operable windows because of concerns of how draft turbulence might affect the low-velocity air distribution of the raised floor system.

Both electric and gas chillers are used to maximize cost efficiencies. Gas chillers are used during peak periods, electric at night.

Material selection was another important facet of the green measures. Materials had to contribute to a healthy environment, be durable, require minimal maintenance and energy use, and be available locally. Sturm used the Environmental Building News conceptual criteria matrix in considering materials. Most materials selected were from local and recyclable sources, reducing the facility's impact on the surrounding environment. Precast metal, concrete, and wood were selected to enhance energy efficiency, durability, maintenance, and employees' health. Exterior materials are light in color to reduce heat absorption.

In September 1999, the facilities manager started using Siebe Environmental Controls computer controls to carefully monitor 36 points, including water, electrical, heat recovery, and mechanical. The system is adjusted as needed.

The design features "service triangles" that house much of the mechanical and support functions such as stairways. This scheme also easily allows for expansion, as the building can grow in increments of three. This inspiration grew from the *Harvard Business Review* article on expansion and change. Parking and the open office plan can grow incrementally as well.

Landscape Design

When the site was acquired, the wetlands were functioning as a catch basin for residential runoff, so they contained a major algae bloom. The team worked with the Du Page County Department of Environment and consultants from the Conservation Design Forum to develop a plan to restore the prairie and the wetlands. At present, the wetlands are a clear body of water. A wetlands wastewater treatment plant whose economics were largely the same as a conventional system was designed for the project; the county approved it, but in the end the city did not for fear that it would smell.

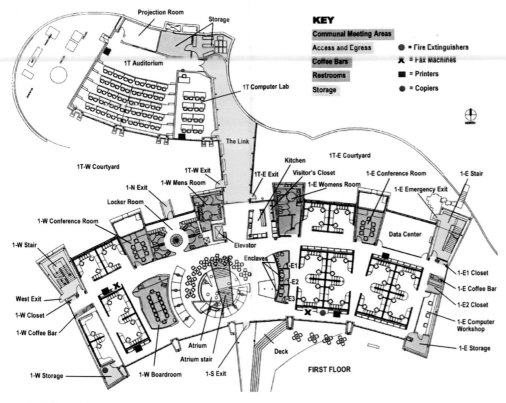

KEY

Communal Meeting Areas
Access and Egress
Coffee Bars
Restrooms
Storage

● = Fire Extinguishers
✕ = Fax Machines
■ = Printers
● = Copiers

First floor plan. Tuthill

A restored native prairie was designed for the project. When compared with a conventional Kentucky Bluegrass corporate landscape, the prairie plan saves $1,500 per acre ($3,705 per hectare) per year in mowing, fertilizer, herbicides, insecticides, and irrigation—and is beautiful besides. Gus Groeber, the facilities manager, notes that the prairie has been burned off four times so far as part of natural maintenance.

Native plants with expansive root systems were planted in combination with level spreaders and buried perforated pipe. As part of the plan, stormwater is sent through perforated piping to recharge the groundwater. Pervious pedestrian paths, made of flagstone, continue inside the building areas and are lined with permeable blue stone. Amenities include walking trails through the prairie landscape, boardwalk terraces, a patio, a pond, and a waterfall.

Financing and Construction

Because Tuthill Corporate Center was one of the first installations of raised floors in the region, some issues arose with regard to construction. The contractor ensured good indoor air quality by keeping the raised floor plenums clean during construction and vacuumed when construction was complete. In retrospect, Sturm says that specifications needed to be tighter to disallow substitutions related to the raised floor.

During construction of the building, staff from a nearby existing building brought lunches with them to learn about the new green building.

Total project cost, financed privately, was $14.79 million.

Experience Gained

"The building represents a vehicle to express the company's mission," Jay Tuthill states. "This is a building that respects peoples' needs. This is a building that is sensitive to habitat and resources. This is a building about excellence and the owner's charge 'to see that we achieve nothing less.' "

A small office guide was put together for each employee summarizing the new building and grounds and their green characteristics. According to the booklet, "From the strength of the steel to the warmth of the atrium to the respect that we pay our beautiful grounds, this is a building designed to [promote] excellence."

Both the architect and the facilities manager say that construction of the raised floor could have been better handled today with current knowledge of these systems. A third-party engineer was hired later to look at the raised floor and fine-tune the system. Sturm notes that the lighting could have benefited from a simpler design to minimize the number of fixtures and to reduce maintenance.

Project Data: Tuthill Corporate Center

Land Use and Building Information

Site Area

	20 acres (8 hectares)
Under water	5 acres (2 hectares)
Protected wetland	50 feet (15 meters)
Protected native prairie	Roughly 1 acre (0.4 hectare)

Parking

Surface	59 spaces
Below grade	32 spaces

	Square Feet/Square Meters
Gross Building Area	50,827/4,725
Basement garage/mechanical	17,142/1,593
First-floor office/atrium lobby	19,700/1,830
Second-floor office/ entrance atrium	13,985/1,300
Caretaker house	2,775/258

Development Cost Information

Building construction cost	$11,600,000
Caretaker unit	400,000
Site improvements	1,000,000
Design fees	990,000
Furniture and fitout	800,000
Total	$14,790,000

Developer/Owner

Tuthill Corporation
8500 South Madison
Burr Ridge, Illinois 60521
Phone: 630-382-4900
www.tuthill.com

Architect

Serena Sturm Architects, Ltd.
3351 Commercial Avenue
Northbrook, Illinois 60062
Phone: 847-564-0307
www.serenasturm.com

Contractor

Pepper Construction
643 North Orleans Street
Chicago, Illinois 60610
Phone: 312-266-4700
www.pepperconstruction.com

Engineer

B+A Engineers
156 North Jefferson Street
Chicago, Illinois 60661
Phone: 312-699-0609

Other Consultants

Real Estate: Baird & Warner Commercial Real Estate, Chicago, Illinois
Engineering: Larson Engineering, Naperville, Illinois
Ecological Restoration: Conservation Design Forum, Elmhurst, Illinois
Lighting: Luminous Design, Longmont, Colorado
Acoustics: Yerges Acoustics, Downers Grove, Illinois

Development Schedule

1994	Planning started
1996	Site acquired
1999	Construction completed

Location

8500 South Madison Street
Burr Ridge, Illinois

University of Texas

School of Nursing and Student Community Center
Houston, Texas

Jenifer Seal

Established in 1972, the University of Texas School of Nursing and Student Community Center (SONSCC) in Houston is ranked in the top 10 percent of nursing schools in the country. The School of Nursing is one of six schools that belong to the University of Texas Health Science Center at Houston, which is located in the world-renowned Texas Medical Center (TMC). The SONSCC building is designed to accommodate 1,200 people (278 faculty, 774 students, and 148 visitors). It houses the School of Nursing and facilities, including classrooms, an auditorium accommodating 200 people, student lounges and break areas, a café, a bookstore, faculty offices, an entire floor devoted to nursing research, a skills lab with 32 beds, and 12 individual patient rooms. The building design incorporates best practices for sustainability, durability, and maintainability over its functional life.

The University of Texas School of Nursing and Student Community Center in Houston is a stacked community center, with six floors of offices, classrooms, and research laboratories above two floors of student facilities, including a large lounge, a cafeteria, an auditorium, and a bookstore. The 200,000-square-foot (18,580-square-meter) facility, referred to as the "100-Year Building," achieved a LEED Gold rating. BNIM Architects, 2004

Many of the materials used in the building's construction—including recycled brick from a 19th-century warehouse and wood siding from reclaimed cypress logs— originated from sources within a 500-mile (805-kilometer) radius of the construction site.

The concept for the SONSCC began in 1984 with a mandate for a new school from the former executive vice president for administration and finance, John Porretto. As the university made a commitment to be the model health sciences university for the 21st century, it set goals to provide a healthier, cleaner, and more environmentally friendly campus. The university has initiated a number of sustainability measures in its comprehensive effort to reduce use of natural resources and dependence on persistent manmade compounds. M. David Low, former president of the university, says, "With our commitment, we must respect the biosphere

Special Features

■ Blend of passive and mechanical strategies
■ Cutting-edge under-floor air, cable, and wire management systems
■ High-performance glazing
■ Innovative use of natural lighting
■ Dramatically downsized chiller capacity
■ Rainwater collection and natural stormwater filtration system
■ Sophisticated measurement and verification systems to monitor mechanical systems
■ Designed for a future sizable photovoltaic installation
■ LEED Gold certification

and biodiversity in our decision making as well as become more open, fair, and inclusive with regard to the surrounding Houston community." At the urging of Brian Yeoman, former chief facilities officer and assistant vice president for facility operation and planning, the university chose the Natural Step framework as its educational tool regarding sustainability and offered free training to faculty and staff. (Natural Step provides a visionary blueprint for a sustainable world, addressing problems at the source and turning them into opportunities for innovation. See www.naturalstep.org.) Shell Energy gave the university a grant to teach the Natural Step to vendors and the city of Houston.

The Site

Located south of downtown Houston, the half-acre (0.2-hectare) site on which the project sits was previously occupied by a 46,000-square-foot (4,275-square-meter) laboratory building. The new building is located on roughly the same footprint as the previous structure but at a higher density and height. At least 77 percent of the older building was reused or recycled.

The Development Process

With inspiration from the Natural Step commitment, the SONSCC design team set out to craft its own green goals and principles to help guide the development of its new facility. Lessons learned from older inherited building problems such as deferred maintenance and indoor air quality further influenced the team to build a high-performance project. The team articulated several goals early in the process:

The school makes use of many recycled materials including fly ash in place of Portland cement, aluminum panels made from 92 percent recycled material, wood siding made of Sinker Cypress hauled from the bottom of the Mississippi River, and red bricks reclaimed from a 19th-century warehouse in San Antonio. BNIM Architects, Lake/Flato Architects, Hesler + Hardaway Photography

■ To endure for more than 100 years and facilitate adapted use.

■ To uplift the spirit of occupants with interior spaces that capitalize on daylighting, radiate simple elegance, reflect timeless design, and are welcoming and comfortable.

■ To respect its surroundings and thus create an academic climate that inspires creativity, collaboration, collegiality, and learning.

■ To minimize the negative effect of the structure on its natural site.

The east facade incorporates Birdair fabric wings (shown here) to modulate light while the west elevation uses perforated metal panels as a second skin for sun protection. BNIM Architects, 2004

■ To extol the indigenous environment by landscaping exterior spaces with plants and trees that are natural to the Houston area and that take minimal care, chemicals, and water.

■ To focus on nontoxic materials and take advantage of renewable energy sources wherever health and economy are issues. To arrive at these decisions, end-use least-cost assumptions will be applied.

■ To use natural, recycled, and reclaimed materials from sources and manufacturers in Texas to the fullest extent possible.

■ To incorporate systems into the infrastructure that ensure efficient use of resources and drive recycling.

As a gateway to the university campus and bridge to the Texas Medical Center, the SONSCC's integration with the site and creation of a sense of place were crucial for the establishment of a new campus heart. The team wanted to create a landmark learning environment that would promote health, wellness, and community, and would serve as a prototype for the design and construction of future university buildings and ultimately all buildings. Despite the many iterations of the project, the team adhered to these goals and principles all the way through the process, continually refining them. The result is an exemplary building. The project is distinguished by the extent of the client's involvement in the specifications and design requirements.

■ To contain the best workmanship by partnering with companies that use only proven state-of-the-art equipment and materials.

■ To sustain economic efficiencies by mandating that utility costs be 70 percent less than for the University of Texas School of Public Health, and to target actual construction costs not to exceed 105 percent of the cost of a conventionally constructed building.

■ To incorporate all natural opportunities presented by the physical site and to design economy into long-term maintenance and operational costs.

As a state agency, the university did not have to undergo a formal local permitting process, although the project team worked extensively with other TMC institutions and university regents, students, faculty, and staff. The team also communicated its project goals to the larger Houston and Harris County communities.

To the east is the deed-restricted Grant Fay Park. The 234,000-square-foot (21,750-square-meter) School of Public Health building lies to the southeast, and immediately to the south is the TMC central chilled water and steam plant. The site is served by light rail and buses and is located near a new transit hub providing transportation to the entire Houston area. Bike storage and shower facilities for building occupants are provided.

The university transplanted 17 trees from the site so they would not be disturbed during construction. Twenty-one native Texan trees were planted to replace those trees that could not be moved or transplanted as a result of age, size, or other conditions.

Planning and Design

With strong goals and design principles in place, the university sent out a request for qualifications to attract the best design team. It contained several requirements:

■ That utility costs be 70 percent less than for the University of Texas School of Public Health, a comparable building.

■ That actual construction costs not exceed 105 percent of the cost of a conventionally constructed building.

■ That the LEED Green Building Rating System be used as the basis of measuring sustainability.

Berkebile Nelson Immenschuh McDowell (BNIM) architects in collaboration with Lake/Flato Architects were selected for the design. Championed by the enthusiasm and tenacity of campus architect Rives Taylor, the entire design team—including experts from Rocky Mountain Institute, the Center for Maximum Building Potential, and Supersymmetry—held a charrette to think collaboratively about the project. The team concentrated on an integrated design, materials selection, energy conservation, and quality of life to ensure high indoor air quality and long-range sustainability. The resulting 194,000-square-foot (18,000-

Natural light floods the building through two large atriums, walls of windows, three massive skylights, and stairwells open to the glass exterior. BNIM Architects, Lake/Flato Architects, Hesler + Hardaway Photography

square-meter) building reflects the newest thinking about human health and a healthy environment.

The building has five different facades that reflect the environmental conditions of each exposure and respond to orientation, views, and internal organization. As part of TMC's campus, this building attempts to convey human scale and a special sense of place through internal and external orientation to nearby Fay Park. The sawtooth roof, where photovoltaic cells can be mounted in the future, creates a distinctive profile in the Texas landscape.

Design of the sophisticated building envelope responds to climatic conditions in Houston, from the percentage and type of glazing used on each facade to the design of shading devices. The lower two floors are clad in brick, granite, and sinker cypress, and the upper six floors feature an aluminum curtain wall of 92 percent recycled content.

This panel system creates a rain screen with water barriers behind a three-inch (eight-centimeter) air space behind the aluminum panels. It acts essentially as a double skin, which is important in the hot Texas climate. This system is now being used on a new university building, the Institute of Molecular Medicine.

Operable windows were installed throughout the buildings for the comfort of occupants and to bring in natural cooling breezes. (Given the climate in Houston, windows can be open approximately 134 days—or more than one-third of the year.) The super-efficient windows are capable of harvesting daylight through the use of frosted glass louvers and translucent sailcloth.

The building's blend of passive and efficient mechanical systems is estimated to result in 41 percent less energy consumption than such energy performance indicators as ASHRAE 90.1. Results indicate that the building will use 80 percent less energy per square foot than the adjacent School of Public Health, built in 1977.

In three places in the building, daylighting is maximized through light control/reflecting devices and three three-story skylit atrium spaces. Lighting controls include a combination of controls users can adjust for lighting, heat, and cooling on nonperimeter areas and daylighting controls on the perimeter of floor plates. Targeted task lighting reduces the overall ambient light levels required in the building, thereby reducing lighting loads. High-performance double low-e glazing is used throughout. The south facade has light shelves, and the east facade uses Teflon-coated sunshades. Reduction of heat islands on the site is achieved through a green roof on the eighth floor and shade trees planted on the north and south sides of the building.

The building incorporates cutting-edge technology with its under-floor air, cable, and wire management systems. This raised-floor, low-air-velocity system reduces fan power required and provides a stratified air system. Electrical and air-conditioning installations are more readily accessible for modifications under raised floors than in traditional systems, where they are typically located above the ceilings or in the walls. Sophisticated measurement and verification systems for continuous metering and optimization of mechanical systems over time are part of the design. The building was commissioned to ensure high performance.

Efficient plumbing fixtures—waterless urinals and low-flow lavatories and showerheads—are used throughout the buildings. A nonpotable water system is used for a large percentage of the building's sewerage conveyance. (Rainwater storage tanks capture approximately 826,140 gallons [3.1 million liters] of rainwater and graywater from an average rainfall of 50 inches [130 centimeters] per year, providing the estimated 42,000 gallons [159,000 liters] needed each month for flushing toilets and irrigation.) Initial planning for a future biological wastewater treatment system is part of the design; in the future, this system will treat all black- and graywater through a closed-loop water system in the building. The building also collects its rainwater and graywater to use for the irrigation system, so the landscape does not require potable water for a majority of the time. As a result of the capture of rainwater on the roof, stormwater runoff leaving the site has been reduced by more than 63 percent.

Project consultants from the Center for Maximum Building Potential designed the Baseline Green Analysis Program to use in selecting materials. Use of rapidly renewable materials such as cotton insulation, linoleum, and agri-fiber boards is a strong component of materials selection. An estimated 75 percent of the building's materials have recycled content, including concrete with an average of 48 percent fly ash (a waste byproduct of coal-burning plants) as a replacement for Portland cement. This substitution saves

Except for the first level, the floors of the entire building sit on pedestals that are 18 inches (45.7 centimeters) off the ground. This design, known as access flooring, allows most ductwork to be placed underneath the floor. BNIM Architects, 2004

approximately 1,808 tons (1,640 metric tons) of carbon dioxide that would have been released into the atmosphere.

Human health and productivity are considered through a variety of design techniques. Carbon monoxide is monitored throughout the building. Chemical pollutant areas such as janitor closets and copy/print rooms incorporate ventilation systems minimizing cross contamination. Construction management plans called for changing all air filters and flushing out the building two weeks before building occupancy. The design team selected products that would be safer for installers, such as cotton insulation and low-VOC adhesives and sealants. A permanent temperature and humidity monitoring system incorporated into the building is part of the building management system.

Construction

The project began with deconstruction of the existing Graduate School of Biomedical Sciences building; of a potential total of 6,162 tons (5,590 metric tons) of construction waste (concrete, wood, site debris, masonry, scrap metal), 4,753 tons (4,315 metric tons) was salvaged. One thousand square yards (1,200 square meters) of carpet was returned to DuPont, 14.3 tons (13 metric tons) of ceiling tile was returned to Armstrong, and 50,000 bricks were stockpiled for later use.

Seventy-five percent of total construction waste was recycled or salvaged. To achieve this goal, a very detailed construction waste management plan for the project was prepared. Construction Materials Management Guidelines from AIA Houston was an important guide to the team with its waste recycling economics worksheets, recycling market information, and other related information for estimating quantities of construction waste and recycling costs. The construction waste management plan identified each type of demolished and waste material produced, each type and quantities of demolished waste material intended to be recycled or reused, separation requirements, on-site storage, and other specifications.

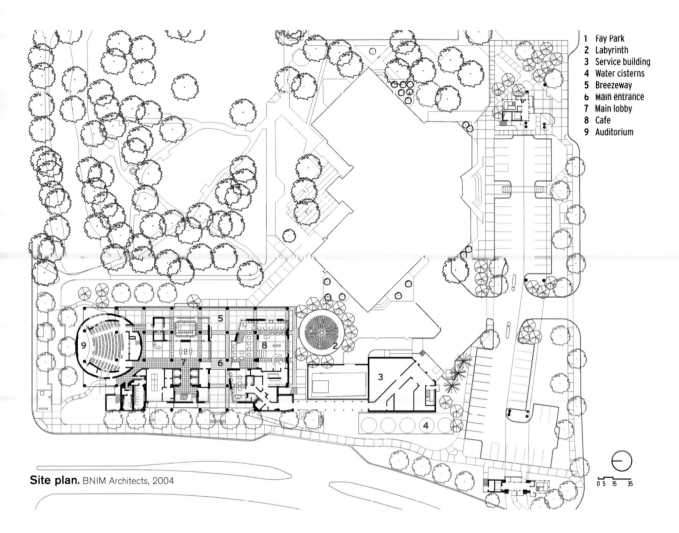

Site plan. BNIM Architects, 2004

1 Fay Park
2 Labyrinth
3 Service building
4 Water cisterns
5 Breezeway
6 Main entrance
7 Main lobby
8 Cafe
9 Auditorium

Financing

The $57 million project is 50 percent financed through student fees and a $17 million revenue bond (from the Texas Legislature). The remainder comes from local fundraising by the university. The school was renamed "School of Nursing and Student Community Center" because of the high percentage of student funds used.

Experience Gained

According to campus architect Rives Taylor, the team realized early that education would be key to making this far-reaching building project a success. To publicize the lessons learned from the project and to track energy use, the building features an informative video wall in the lobby area to educate people about the building's aspects.

Energy performance is estimated to equal an impressive annual savings of $76,838 in energy costs based on current energy prices.

The team found that conventional rules of thumb for cost estimating were not appropriate for a project with a whole-systems approach: the first cost estimates incorrectly double counted many expenses.

The team had difficulty bringing all systems in through the floors, in part because the design is not solely open office. The mechanical engineers were concerned that people would close office doors and inhibit proper air flow. As a solution, fairly small and quiet exhaust fans were added around the perimeter to keep the air flowing. Issues also arose with the demountable partitions and floor air diffuser locations. Some systems are dropped from the ceiling (emergency power and lights), limiting the problem from floor air diffusers and demountable partitions.

Steve McDowell, principal with BNIM Architects, summed up the elegance of the building, "This project is truly the result of collaboration at each level. The building's structural design tested the fundamental beliefs of many involved and directly involved almost every design discipline well beyond the normal cast of design characters. The School of Nursing is much more than a traditional teaching or academic environment. It will be the community center for University of Texas students and many others who have not found the fundamental attributes that define our collective understanding of what collegiate life is expected to provide. It will fulfill the meaning of the words alma mater, or nurturing mother."

The building has received LEED Gold certification. It may receive Platinum certification if the university is able to secure funding for the planned roof-mounted photovoltaic system. The project also received a Citation of Honor from the AIA Houston (Sustainability Award) for its environmentally responsible features. BNIM Architects received the AIA Kansas City Chapter's Honor Award, the 2004 AIA Kansas City Committee on the Environment Award, the 2004 AIA Kansas Honor Award, the 2004 AIA Central States Merit Award, the 2004 AIA San Antonio Honor Award, a 2005 AIA Houston Chapter Honor Award, and the 2005 AIA Committee on the Environment, Top Ten Green Projects Award.

Project Data: University of Texas School of Nursing and Student Community Center

Land Use and Information

Site area	0.5 acre (0.2 hectare)
Gross building area	194,000 square feet (18,000 square meters)
Building height	8 stories; 130 feet, 7 inches (40 meters) at highest elevation
Parking	None on site (general university parking facilities used)

Development Cost Information

Site cost	$211 per square foot ($2,270 per square meter)
Construction budget	$41 million
Total cost	$57 million

Owner

University of Texas
7000 Fannin
Suite 1720
Houston, Texas 77030
Phone: 713-500-4766
www.utexas.edu/sonscc

Architect

Berkebile Nelson Immenschuh McDowell Architects
106 West 14th Street
Suite 200
Kansas City, Kansas 64105
Phone: 816-783-1500
www.bnim.com

Associate Architect

Lake/Flato Architects
311 Third Street
Suite 200
San Antonio, Texas 78205
Phone: 210-227-3335
Fax: 210-224-9575
www.lakeflato.com

Construction Managers

Jacobs/Vaughn, Inc.
5995 Rogerdale Road
Houston, Texas 77072
Phone: 832-351-6000
Fax: 832-351-7700
www.jacobs.com

Vaughn Construction
10355 Westpark Drive
Houston, Texas 77042
Phone: 713-243-8300
Fax: 713-243-8350
www.vaughnconstruction.com

Other Consultants

Engineer: Ove Arup, San Francisco, California
Structural Engineer: Jaster-Quintanilla & Associates, Houston, Texas
MEP Engineer: Carter & Burgess, Inc., Houston, Texas
Energy Strategies: Supersymmetry, Houston, Texas
Civil Engineering: Epsilon Engineering, Houston, Texas
Landscape Architect: Coleman & Associates, Austin, Texas
Cost Consultant: Apex/Busby, Dallas/Houston, Texas
Code Consultant: Rolf Jensen & Associates, Houston, Texas
Lighting Designer: Clanton Associates, Boulder, Colorado
Interior Designer: BNIM Architects, Houston, Texas
Vertical Transportation: Lerch Bates & Associates, Houston, Texas
Sustainable Strategies: Center for Maximum Potential Building Systems, Austin, Texas; Rocky Mountain Institute, Snowmass, Colorado; Elements, a division of BNIM Architects, Houston, Texas

Development Schedule

5/2000	Planning started, request for quotations issued
2/2002	Construction started
8/2004	Construction completed
8/2004	Occupancy

Location

6901 Bertner Avenue
Houston, Texas

chapter 10

Outlook
Trends

Outlook and Trends

Jenifer Seal and William D. Browning

The trend toward green development is growing in the real estate industry. More than a fad, it is a movement toward higher-performance buildings that are better for the bottom line *and* for communities and the environment.

Awareness of green building has increased rapidly in recent years. Groups such as the U.S. Green Building Council have grown in size, and their membership now includes representation from a broad cross-section of organizations and industries, including product manufacturers, developers, engineers, architects, building owners, all levels of government, international real estate interests, and even doctors and lawyers. Green certification or benchmarking systems—such as LEED, in the United States, and BREEAM, in the United Kingdom—continue to grow in use and influence around the world. In places

Green features and a design that responds to the environment help differentiate Alvento from the rest of the buildings in the Madrid office market. The rapid lease-up and high level of tenant satisfaction point to the potential demand for high-performance office space.
Ortiz Léon Architects

like India and Spain, new green building councils have been formed, and more buildings are being certified as green. In fact, the Confederation of Indian Industry–Godrej Green Building Center, one of the world's most environmentally advanced buildings, is located in Hyderabad, India.

This chapter explores emerging trends related to green buildings. As background, it begins with a look at the lessons learned from Europe, where the green building movement is older and in some ways more advanced than in North America. The chapter also looks at changes in the perception and implementation of green development and design. It then offers an overview of some of the challenges and barriers facing the widespread adoption of green development. The chapter concludes by investigating two interesting new concepts, biomimetic and biophilic design, which could lead to healthier and more sustainable developments.

Lessons from Europe

Much of Europe's green building practice is driven by regulations and mandates, whereas in the United States, building green is generally a voluntary decision involving the collaboration of designers, developers, product manufac-

At the Thames Court office building, in London, operable windows, and extensive daylighting enhance the work environment. Automatic solar panels modulate the natural light. H.G. Esch

more in buildings and to ensure that they are properly engineered. Although most green projects around the world are owner occupied or institutional, the number of speculative projects is growing.

Europeans have intriguing approaches to reducing energy use in buildings: for example, structures that are daylit and large passively ventilated can be seen across the continent. Few buildings of this type and scale are located in the United States. In Germany, the Netherlands, and Switzerland, new approaches to capturing urban stormwater are leading to the restoration of natural waterways, and to the creation of water parks and urban water features. Leading stormwater experts are even using biologically treated stormwater to create urban art. Considering that more than 1,500 American communities are out of compliance with EPA's stormwater regulations, these European approaches should be of significant interest in the United States.

In many European cities, sewer systems reached capacity before those in the United States, leading to the extensive use of green, or vegetated, roofs. Various green roof technologies are now debuting in projects in the United States, including the Chicago City Hall; several projects in the San Francisco Bay Area; and the Ford Motor Company's $2 billion renewal of its 90-year-old Rouge manufacturing complex, in Dearborn, Michigan. The benefits can go beyond stormwater management. Architect William McDonough says that for the Rouge plant, "We found a contingent liability for stormwater that was $35 million more than the $13 million invested in the green roof."

Several countries in Europe have set 23 feet (seven meters) as the maximum distance that an office worker can be located from a window, a requirement that results in daylit buildings with narrow floor plates that can be entirely naturally ventilated. Energy use in some of these buildings can be quite high, however, because of very high surface-to-

turers, environmental groups, and government agencies. In addition, Europeans historically have spent more on buildings, in part because lease terms are longer: longer leases give real estate developers a greater incentive both to invest volume ratios, which may require substantial additional heating capacity around the perimeter. This arrangement generates large heating bills because the air passes once through the building and the heat is not recaptured before the air is exhausted. In comparison, American office buildings tend to have very wide floor plates, which has led to interesting innovations such as light shelves and other devices that bounce light deep into the center of buildings.

The perception that European buildings are significantly more energy efficient than American buildings is not necessarily correct. Comparisons of energy-performance targets under BREEAM and LEED show that the energy-efficiency targets in the United Kingdom are lower than in the United States. Moreover, some European countries do not include lighting and plug loads in their energy estimates. Sweden, for example, counts only heating energy to determine the energy consumed in a building.

Advanced glass coatings, low-e coatings in particular, first became available in the United States in the early 1980s. Because these technologies became available in Europe much later, European buildings use double-skin, or "climate wall" buildings instead. These systems use two layers of widely spaced glazing and allow a column of semiconditioned exhaust air to move between them. The radiant surface temperature of the inner pane of glass is thus brought closer to the target temperature for the occupied space. The result is an insulation effect equivalent to the use of high-performance low-e glazing. Double-skin buildings will not likely catch on in the United States, however, because of a much higher initial cost and the loss of net leasable space at the interior. The same thermal performance can be achieved with less costly and readily available glazing systems.

Substantially more attention is paid to natural ventilation in the United Kingdom than in the United States. One reason is that per-project mechanical engineering fees in the United Kingdom are almost double those in the United States. Climate also plays a role. Many European locations have mild climates and rarely have to deal with huge latent loads in the air (humidity). The U.S. response to these conditions has been to create mixed-mode buildings, which can be naturally ventilated, sealed and fully air conditioned, or a combination of the two.

It is clear that countries around the world can learn much from each other as more green buildings are built, as technologies evolve, and as the potential to improve the environmental performance of buildings grows.

Trends

Greater Integration in Green Design

A green building cannot be created through a series of add-ons or plug-ins; to achieve the optimal synergistic benefits and performance, the green features must be integrated into the overall design. The best way to achieve this kind of thoughtful integration is through a charrette in which participants collaborate, share ideas, and devise recommendations that can later be refined into specific design directives.

Both the exhibits and the sustainable features of the California Academy of Science, in San Francisco's Golden Gate Park, are designed to inspire concern about the natural environment. © Renzo Piano Building Workshop

Bocas Del Toro Station is the Smithsonian Institution's new research campus in Panama. Located on a sensitive coastal site next to a mangrove swamp, the facility approaches the goal of having zero impact on the environment. Kiss + Cathcart Architects

Charrettes for green development typically address economic, social, and environmental considerations, then use this information to plan the type, mix, and location of buildings and other project elements. This particular approach began in 1993, with the landmark "greening of the White House" charrette, and today it is rare to see a green building project that begins without a charrette.

In a conventional design process, the design is passed from one party to another like a baton in a relay race. The developer defines the parameters; the architect designs the project; and the engineers each add their respective systems. A successful green real estate development, in contrast, results from whole-system, end-use thinking that is possible only when all team members work together from the outset to capture the interconnections between the disciplines. With this approach, developers consistently reduce their energy-use assumptions by 30 to 40 percent—in some cases up to 70 or 80 percent—over code, saving tens of thousands of dollars in energy costs per year.

Commissioning, the process of ensuring that a building and its systems are functioning as designed, is another facet of green development that yields more integrated design. Over the last several years, commissioning has been increasingly accepted in the marketplace. (See Chapter 5, "Sustainable Construction.")

An Interview with Douglas Durst, Copresident, The Durst Organization

Rocky Mountain Institute
August 2004

RMI: What is your most exciting project?
DD: One Bryant Park, in midtown Manhattan.
RMI: What do you like about it?
DD: The opportunity to try out very innovative approaches to green development in an urban setting. I am excited by incorporating the water-saving features, which we didn't do in Four Times Square [the Condé Nast Building].
RMI: What do you see for the future of green building?
DD: For many years after we built Four Times Square, we didn't see much following. Now, with what is happening downtown, where green principles are being incorporated into designs, I believe that green development will become the standard.

Fully integrated building designs are now being realized, many by internationally renowned architectural firms. These are not projects with tacked-on green features or technologies. Several projects that are underway will achieve excellent environmental performance largely as a result of core design decisions. In each of these projects, the form, skin, and systems of the buildings are inseparable from the environmental performance goals. When you walk into these buildings, you realize that they are fundamentally different. Take the David L. Lawrence Convention Center, a 1.2 million-square-foot (111,500-square-meter) project with a LEED Gold rating, an outstanding example of the full integration of green design principles: estimates of energy savings are in the 30 to 50 percent range and worth hundreds of thousands of dollars annually.

The California Academy of Science is another prime example of the core approach to green building. The academy's design weaves natural stormwater management, biological wastewater, and energy production throughout the structure *and* the exhibits, which include a planetarium, an aquarium, and a rainforest. One of the ten largest natural history museums in the world, the academy makes ecological research come alive for nearly 1.5 million visitors each year.

One Bryant Park, the 2.2 million-square-foot (204,400-square-meter) Manhattan skyscraper designed by architects Cook + Fox and developed by the Durst Organization, is another striking example. The developer is exploring a partial double-skin building design for the sky garden. Raised floors, daylighting, on-site energy generation, sophisticated water conservation strategies, and highly efficient mechanical systems are also important components under consideration.

The Durst Organization also created the well-known Condé Nast building at Four Times Square (see Chapter 9), one of the first big signature speculative buildings created using green design principles. The use of green design for speculative projects, instead of just for owner-occupied or build-to-suit buildings, marks a significant shift.

An Interview with Robert Fox, Principal, Cook + Fox

Rocky Mountain Institute
August 2004

RMI: What current project are you most excited about?

RF: One Bryant Park. At over 2.2 million square feet [204,400 square meters], it's big enough to be three buildings and has enough of a budget to let us explore issues. It will be one of the biggest buildings that will ever be built in Manhattan, and it will be the second-tallest building in the city [only the Empire State Building is taller].

The team [owners, engineers, tenant, and consultants] is committed to making it the greenest building possible. No one has said we can't afford it. But that doesn't mean that we aren't asking "Does this make sense?" or "Is this appropriate?"

We have an anemometer, or wind meter, on top of Four Times Square [the nearby Condé Nast headquarters building], and it shows there is a lot of wind up there, so we are considering a wind turbine on top of One Bryant Park.

We are looking at an anaerobic digester for turning food waste from restaurants and cafeterias into gas to run a microturbine that will provide electricity for the Bank of America branch [anchor tenant]. A liquid fertilizer will be produced by the digester and used across the street in Bryant Park.

Other features include a deep, ground-source geothermal well to produce all the heating and cooling for the branch bank. In the bank lobby, we have a diagram for visitors that displays all the systems. There will be photovoltaic [panels] in the glass in the urban garden room [a 3,000-square-foot (280-square-meter) atrium on Sixth Avenue]. We are also looking into integrating photovoltaics into the skin of the upper portion of the building.

These, of course, are just interesting features. The really exciting elements are in the fundamental design. The building has nine-foot-six-inch [three-meter] ceilings, floor-to-ceiling glass, and we are looking for light shelves to bounce light deep into the spaces. The bank has agreed to install glass doors on the perimeter offices. This building will have great daylight and air. We will have 95 percent air filtration. We will have three megawatts of cogeneration, and an ice-storage system allowing us to downsize mechanicals. Energy issues are important, but the real focus is on health and productivity.

RMI: What do you see for the future of green building?

RF: I see more and more laypeople understanding the issues we face with the planet, and the changes will come from them. The tenants will demand it, once the benefits of green building are understood. It won't be the owners and building managers driving this. I'm eager for the time when LEED Gold is the norm.

More Green Speculative and Large-Scale Development

Any trend in real estate development usually starts with institutional, owner-occupied, or build-to-suit projects. When the idea is adopted for speculative projects, you know that an important change is underway. Real estate

The Plaza at PPL Center, the first new downtown office development in Allentown, Pennsylvania, in more than 25 years, has received LEED Gold certification. Peter Aaron-Esto/Liberty Property Trust

investment trusts (REITs) are typically the most risk averse of commercial property owners because they are publicly traded and driven by quarterly financial results. But these are exciting times in the green building field: REITs are starting to do speculative green projects. Michael Reschke, former chair of Prime Group Realty Trust, describes the 1.5 million-square-foot (138,900-square-meter) Bank One Corporate Center on Chicago's Dearborn Street: "The building creates a workplace for the new millennium, featuring numerous innovations in design and system technologies that will enhance the productivity and efficiency of any workforce located within." (See Chapter 9.)

John Gattuso, senior vice president of Liberty Property Trust and head of its Urban National Development group, had four LEED projects underway in 2004, even though at that time, only one potential tenant—the PPL Corporation—had made green features a criterion in selecting its office space. Construction of the 280,000-square-foot (26,000-square-meter) Plaza at PPL Center, for the PPL Corporation, gave Gattuso's development team the opportunity to practice green design, something that Liberty Property Trust had been considering. The team ended up with an impressive project that was awarded LEED Gold certification. Still, Gattuso comments that this project is a small fraction of the 13 million square feet (1.21 million square meters) the company leases annually. His group continues to test the waters with green design and is helping to educate the rest of the company.

Others in the industry are realizing the importance of getting beyond the pure commoditization of space and rent. High-performance green building can be seen as a measure of quality and as a way to lead the market. Gattuso says that *not* to engage in the emerging field of green building is a risk to companies because the market is becoming more cognizant of the full benefits of green development: lower operating costs; higher worker productivity, attraction, and reten-

The 54-story One Bryant Park office building, in New York City, will incorporate innovative, high-performance environmental technologies to enhance the health and productivity of tenants, ensure the highest levels of environmental sustainability, and reduce waste. © dbox studio for Cook + Fox Architects

tion; lower employee-turnover costs; lower capital costs; and benefits to the overall community.

Large buildings, both speculative and build-to-suit, have big budgets—and big budgets allow developers, architects, and engineers to push their creativity and try things that would not be considered for smaller projects with smaller budgets. These big buildings serve as important economic engines because they can increase demand for green products and technologies, thereby expanding production capabilities and lowering the price of items such as photovoltaics, turbines, and special glazings.

More Advocates for Green Building

From industry professionals to the general public, people are hearing more and more about green building, and there is a groundswell of interest in this topic. Mainstream newspapers are beginning to feature major stories on green building, and advertisements for LEED-certified office space are starting to appear. Even in the real estate brokerage community, which has been slow to recognize green design, the National Association of Realtors devoted the winter 2004 issue of its trade magazine, *On Common Ground,* to "Building Green: Designs that Work with Nature and for People."

The Development Community. Somewhat surprisingly, some members of the development community have been at the forefront of the transition to high-performance green buildings. Industry stalwarts such as Hines, Equity Office Properties, and Arden Realty have been aggressively pursuing the EPA's ENERGY STAR certification to show existing and prospective tenants that their buildings are more energy efficient than competing properties, and thus have significantly lower operating costs. This provides a competitive advantage in terms of retaining existing tenants, attracting new ones, and raising rents in accordance with the occupants' savings on operating costs.

In 1996, the Rocky Mountain Institute (RMI) began working with Hines on a comprehensive green development strategy that would guide the creation of a prototype for future Hines office projects. Hines wants to provide the most competitive buildings in the marketplace. Ken Hubbard, vice president of the company, says, "For us it's a given. It really is a best-practice approach." He notes that while "green is not foremost in the minds of most customers yet, at Hines we want to be ahead of the curve."

An Interview with Kevork Derderian, Founder, Meritt Signature Development Alliance, and Owner, Continental Offices Limited

**Rocky Mountain Institute
August 2004**

RMI: What is the most exciting development you have underway?

KD: The redevelopment of the Columbus Hospital site in Chicago, a 770,000-square-foot [71,540-square-meter] residential project on Lake Michigan.

RMI: What can you tell us about the project?

KD: There is a parking deck under the three-acre [1.2-hectare] site, and all the landscaping is on top of the deck. Working with Conservation Design Forum, a local ecological restoration and landscape architecture firm, we were able to craft a design that will capture all of the potential runoff and use it on site. There will be no stormwater runoff generated by this project.

RMI: What do you see for the future of green building?

KD: With Dearborn Center [Bank One Corporate Center, in Chicago], we learned you can't do everything. It has great daylighting and a great under-floor HVAC system, with the exhaust being taken out at the top of the space. Now everyone is doing it in Chicago. So we helped open the door. You don't call it green building; you call it a better environment.

I see greening happening gradually. Fuel cells aren't there yet, but other things have been adopted. Look at how compact fluorescent lamps and electronic ballasts have become standard. Energy costs are weighing more on design choices. As younger engineers are entering practice, we are achieving an acceptance of new ideas and whole-system design.

At least in the Midwest, developers are doing it [green buildings] in advance of public demand. In the Bank One building, we did set ourselves apart in the marketplace. The U.S. Green Building Council's LEED certification is going to have more value over time. It is creating a marketing advantage.

Pension fund managers and investors are also becoming advocates for green building. The largest pension fund in the United States, the California Public Employees' Retirement System (CalPERS), selected Hines Interests Limited Partnership and Commonwealth Pacific to manage its largest real estate portfolio: $1.3 billion in office properties, including both existing offices and future office investments.[1] Hines is investing up to $50 million in CalPERS's office portfolio. CalPERS has also made a commitment to distributed energy. As Michael Flaherman, of CalPERS, notes, "We hope distributed generation will be a win-win [prospect] because it can potentially enhance [a] property's investment potential. It is also environmentally friendly."[2]

The Public Sector. As described in Chapter 8, the greening of U.S. federal facilities and programs has been ongo-

ENERGY STAR has recognized the 25-story California EPA Headquarters, in Sacramento, as one of the most energy-efficient high rises in the United States. It is estimated that the building's green features will save approximately $1 million per year compared with other buildings in the downtown area. AC Martin Partners, Inc./David C. Martin, FAIA/David Wakely

ing for a number of years, the public sector's understanding of green design has increased, and standards are being defined. DOE, EPA, GSA, DoD, and other agencies have all played a role. GSA, the government's biggest landlord, requires that all new federal building projects meet the criteria for basic LEED certification. By incorporating green building principles into its requirements for big signature buildings, such as federal courthouses, GSA has introduced designers and a host of other consultants to this approach.

In collaboration with Arup Engineers, Kiss + Cathcart Architects designed the 2020 Tower, a model speculative building that is expected to be practical and economical by 2020. Solar and wind power are planned to meet 100 percent of the energy needs of this tall building. Kiss + Cathcart Architects

Federal and state incentives for renewable energy and energy efficiency are helping bring more developers to the table and are facilitating their adoption of high-performance building practices. Major incentives include accelerated depreciation, tax deductions, renewable-energy credits, real estate tax incentives, and utility incentives. At the local government level, communities across the country are embracing green design and sustainability, and creating programs that raise awareness of and encourage—and in some cases require—such development.

Mary Tucker, who is with the Sustainable City Project, in San Jose, and is a member of the board of directors of the USGBC, designed and implemented an energy-management program designed to reduce San Jose's energy use by 10 percent. This goal was achieved through requirements (1) to incorporate resource-efficient technologies (including solar design features) into new construction and (2) to install high-efficiency lighting in existing fixtures. San Jose has also expanded its programs in water conservation, waste management and recycling, and pollution prevention.

Barriers and Opportunities

Barriers

There are a number of barriers to green development, including market research, financing, the attitudes of intermediaries, and media coverage.

Conventional market research asks questions only about the past market performance of comparable products. Because such comparisons may not accurately portray the benefits of the new, greener product, this practice can create a barrier to green development by inhibiting innovation and encouraging risk-averse developers and financiers to shy away. This "rear-view mirror" approach to market research, which assesses the feasibility of proposed projects by extrapolating from the past, often portrays innovative green projects as inherently less feasible simply because they cannot be evaluated through traditional methodology.

Some say the financial community itself is a barrier—that it is difficult to finance green projects. Green projects need to stand on their own merits and be financially viable. To understand the benefits of resource efficiency, lenders need to see how it will reduce operating costs and affect NOI, cash flow, and debt service. Most lenders and investors are unfamiliar with green building practices, and there is skepticism from financial institutions. Until more comparable projects exist—and their numbers are growing rapidly—conservative

A Conversation with Dan Emmett, President and CEO, Douglas Emmett and Company

Rocky Mountain Institute
August 2004

Dan Emmett, president and CEO of Douglas Emmett and Company, in southern California, has worked diligently for years to weave green building into his development projects and to educate the market. He expresses concern about the adoption of green practices: "It is disturbing how few building owners have done what they should have done. Sadly, it continues to be a foot-dragging process. Even when paybacks are under three years!" Emmett says that the market penetration of green design into Class A office space in California has been mixed, and that only around half of those implementing green design have done a reasonably thorough job. These efficiency measures have largely been for lighting. In Class B buildings, about a quarter have had lighting retrofits.

Emmett stresses the need for more education: "Typical space planners aren't pushing the envelope at all; [neither are] the leasing brokers and property managers." For the most part, the information is available, Emmett says: "People need to stop, read, and do it!" Currently, Emmett is working with BOMA on a resource seminar to help educate those in the industry. "We need more educational incentives, and regulation could be pushed harder," he notes. "The development community needs incentives that aren't questionable—such as a guaranteed break on utility bills."

Emmett commends companies—like Equity Office Properties and Arden Realty—that are making green building a priority. In the Sherman Oaks Galleria, a Douglas Emmett and Company project, the design team looked at greening the envelope, efficient mechanical systems, and the use of daylighting to convert a failed mall into a mixed office and retail project. Douglas Emmett and Company just finished audits on all its existing buildings: the whole portfolio is ENERGY STAR compatible. Emmett concludes, "Peer pressure is helpful."

lenders and "path-of-least-resistance" developers are naturally reluctant to enter into the unknown. (See Chapter 7, "Financing, Leasing, and Investment Considerations.")

Intermediaries such as appraisers and brokers have been slow to embrace and promote green buildings, and often act as a firewall between developers and potential users. One solution is for developers to market directly to chief executive officers (CEOs) and other corporate decision makers, but this is not always possible. Jerry Lea, senior vice president of Hines, says, "In the 150 million square feet [14 million square meters] of projects built, I can only think of five projects where the CEOs were directly involved."

Joe van Bellegham, of BuildGreen Developments, notes that the brokerage community tends to focus on net rents, not gross rents. "So what's happening is that tenants are becoming more aware of total costs of occupancy, but the brokerage community has not caught up to that. At the Vancouver Tech Park, the majority of the leasing was done by us, not by brokers. We were able to sell the benefits of green buildings."

Many developers consider only first costs, without considering the reductions in postoccupancy operating costs that are associated with building green, so there is no obvious incentive for them to build green. The typical triple-net lease structure further inhibits investment in green measures because the owner is responsible for financing the efficiency improvements but is unable to profit from them; instead, tenants benefit directly from the lower operating costs.

In some areas, code issues have been a barrier for certain technologies, such as green roofs and under-floor air distribution. Often, local officials are unaware of new technologies and hesitant to approve their use without more information on their track records.

Nor has media coverage of green building always been rosy. A summer 2003 *Wall Street Journal* article described green high-performance building as "a developer's marketing gimmick." Communicating the true benefits of green building and documenting the achievements of the many successful projects will help clarify the genuine benefits of the approach.

Opportunities

Conversations with developers, REIT executives, real estate investors, and others in the industry reveal a variety of reasons to promote and sell green buildings: higher asset value; reduced energy costs, resulting in higher NOI; quicker

An Interview with Joe van Bellegham, BuildGreen Developments, Inc.

Rocky Mountain Institute
August 2004

RMI: What are your most exciting projects, and what details can you share?

JVB: I'm working on several mixed-use projects, but in terms of office developments, the Vancouver Tech Park is an exciting one. This project changed people's minds that green is more than the building. There were spin-off results—a landfill-gas company that created a market for addressing the Kyoto Treaty at a profit. The restaurant/cafeteria in the Tech Park is promoting organic food, and it is even growing some things on site.

Also at the Tech Park, we used grass-paving and gravel-paving techniques. To make it economical, we introduced the U.S. manufacturer to a local Canadian company, and now the Canadian company makes the products. Linking to local economics is important. Stormwater measures like grass- and gravel-paving, along with bioswales, are now becoming common practice.

The thing that really surprised me was the reaction of the tenants in the Tech Park. A reporter went in and interviewed several, and three tenants' comments really stand out. Etraffic Solutions, Inc., an educational software company, had been interested in the benefits of the green measures while negotiating the lease, but uncertain of the real value. Well into the interview, Etraffic staffers told the reporter their productivity and sales went up 30 percent. But what was really impressive was how proud they have become of their space. They are really happy to give tours of their space to visitors and other potential tenants of the Tech Park. Another tenant, Stressgen, a biotech company, said that one of the major reasons they chose to lease in the Tech Park was to enhance the company's ability to attract and retain new people. The third tenant, Omega Biotech, said that the environmental theme behind the buildings was important to their marketing efforts. The most exciting thing is to see the increasing environmental awareness of the companies within the Vancouver Tech Park.

RMI: What do you see for the future of green building?

JVB: As people see more of them [green buildings], there will be more and more demand. If I were a developer or a pension manager, I would be very nervous if I weren't building green. One reason to be nervous is that North America is about to move into a long-term labor shortage, so attracting and retaining employees is more important than ever. Developers and institutional owners not doing green buildings are just making themselves less competitive. The risk to developers comes not just in the private real estate market: government entities are increasingly demanding green buildings.

As the development community becomes more enlightened, we will change the way we finance buildings to incorporate more green features. Measures that might increase the first cost, but lower the cost of occupancy, will be built in. There is a huge opportunity on the utilities side, particularly with microutilities [self-generation of power within a project]. The savings for tenants will be significant. Even if energy costs were to increase 10 percent, a tenant would see only a 5 percent increase if the basic energy use is half that of a conventional building. The whole financing model will change.

lease-up and lower turnover; and more desirable properties. Douglas Durst, of the Durst Organization, has said, "I believe that green development will become the standard."

By taking advantage of sophisticated design tools like computational fluid dynamics (CFD), green designers are finding elegant solutions to perennial problems. For example, the Bluewater shopping mall, in Kent, England, which was developed by Lend Lease, is completely naturally ventilated. Using CFD modeling, the engineering firm Battle McCarthy developed a natural ventilation system that introduces a fresh, natural breeze along the concourse and eliminates the need for air conditioning. Wind scoops on the roof rotate on a vertical axis, ensuring a continuous air supply and allowing cooler air to drop and mix within the space. The scoops also double as exhaust outlets in case of fire. Such simple systems require rigorous design.

New technologies, products, and techniques will continue to create opportunities and make it even easier to develop green buildings in the future. When asked at a

Commentary from Alex Wilson, President, BuildingGreen, Inc., and Executive Editor, *Environmental Building News*

Rocky Mountain Institute
August 2004

"Dozens of green technologies have made their way into commercial office buildings over the past ten years," notes Alex Wilson. "From natural daylighting systems to green roofs to building-integrated photovoltaics. Even the most unusual technologies and practices, such as green roofs, are beginning to appear on more conventional office buildings.

"Photovoltaic panels began appearing in buildings back in the 1970s, but did not really find their way onto commercial buildings until the late 1990s. While still far from widespread, PV panels are being integrated into commercial building facades as spandrel panels and rooftop arrays. When used as spandrel panels, they may not even be noticed, except for the bluish tint.

"Water efficiency is another green building issue that deserves attention. While there has been a great deal of focus on saving energy since the early 1970s, there is still relatively little attention paid to water conservation. Yet some experts suggest that water may actually be a more limited resource over the coming decades than energy. Among the water-efficiency measures finding their way into commercial office buildings are low-flow, sensor-activated faucets; non-water-using urinals; and water-efficient outdoor irrigation systems. In some buildings, rainwater is being captured on roofs and used for flushing toilets or irrigation. In a few buildings, black water [sewage] is being treated on site and used for toilet flushing."

2003 ULI forum on sustainable development what opportunities are now available for a conventional suburban office designer, architect William McDonough referred to Buckminster Fuller's *Anticipatory Design Science* and suggested that development teams plan for a time when green is more mainstream, so that today's buildings can be easily transformed into sustainable facilities in the future. "Anticipate a delightful future," he commented.

Future opportunities will also lie in the transition from high-tech green practices to less complex solutions. Before the invention of big-building mechanical systems, access to light and air was one of the most important design considerations for large structures. While the big buildings of the late 19th and early 20th centuries were often heated with steam, they were just as often passively cooled and illuminated, using deep-set windows; retractable canvas awnings; thermally absorbent stone; and other, now-forgotten passive air-conditioning tricks. After World War II, however, as building mechanical systems evolved and the International Style came to dominate architecture, access to light and air became end-of-design-process considerations. With unlimited ducts, fans, pumps, and electricity, the light, temperature, and humidity of any building could be brought into a habitable range.

New Horizons: Bringing Buildings to Life

Research underway at RMI is exploring ways to take green building to a new horizon. Efforts are beginning to investigate the fundamental relationship of humans to their environments, and the relevance of this relationship to building design and construction. The question is, how do we create buildings and places that are well adapted to nurture human development? Visionaries like E.O. Wilson, of Harvard, and Stephen Kellert, of Yale University, working in conjunction with RMI, are exploring the expanding field of inquiry known as *biophilia*.

Biophilia

Biophilic design acknowledges the human need for experiential connection with natural systems as a necessary condition for childhood development, human well-being, and worker productivity. Such contact can occur through the direct, indirect, or symbolic experience of nature in buildings and landscapes, and can be achieved through design features such as natural lighting, natural ventilation, natural materials, shapes and forms that mimic natural systems and processes, certain qualities of light and space, and views and prospects of nature. Successful biophilic design also includes buildings and landscapes that are connected to the distinctive culture and ecology of their locations. As Grant Hildebrand, a professor of architectural history at the University of Washington, notes,

> *We are biologically predisposed to liking buildings and landscapes with prominent natural elements. When we cannot actually place ourselves in a natural setting, we make some effort to provide ourselves with substitutes. There is evidence that we like to have natural archetypes or simulations of them around us. The point is not that a building or landscape resembles nature but that some architectural scenes accord (e.g., in form and space, in light and darkness) with an archetypal image of the natural world.*[3]

Biophilic design has a simple underlying assumption, but one with profound implications. Architect James Wines explains:

> *There is much talk of sustainable architecture as an alternative to industrialized societies' wasteful legacy of short-term construction. People will, however, never want to keep an aesthetically inferior building around no matter how well stocked . . . with cutting-edge thermal glass, photovoltaic cells, recycled materials, and zero-emissions carpeting. The mission of sustainable design is to recover those fragile threads of connectedness with nature.*[4]

If biophilic design is intentionally incorporated into our developments, human health and well-being can be enhanced—and in ways that are of particular relevance to both public and private organizations, such as improved productivity, reduced absenteeism, the ability to attract and retain workers and residents, and improved quality of life. Though early research on biophilic design offers tantalizing evidence to suggest potential links between building design and positive human experience, the data have not been well tested or integrated in a way that would make them readily accessible and practicable.

At Gewerbehof Prisma, in Nuremberg, Germany, a greenhouse atrium with circulating water features and lush landscaping moderates the indoor climate and creates a sense of outdoor living year-round. RMI

Biomimicry

As more and more companies realize the consumptive and destructive impacts of the building industry, they are beginning to look for a new model: not one that produces toxic or useless waste, but one that can reuse and reclaim once-used products. This new model mimics natural principles and sees nature as the cornerstone of an exciting, emerging field called *biomimicry*.

Imagine if, instead of using concrete, we could create much stronger and more resilient structures by mimicking the self-assembling properties of abalone shells. Imagine a self-cleaning skyscraper. This may seem farfetched, but a new exterior paint, Lotusan, was developed to imitate the

Modeled on the movement of seaweed in the ocean, the PAX impeller moves water far more efficiently than conventional propellers—and illustrates a practical application of biomimicry. © PAX Scientific

self-cleaning properties of the lotus leaf. Available in any color, this silicon-based paint is also water and dirt repellent. It owes its name to the "lotus effect," discovered in the 1970s by Dr. Wilhelm Barthlott, a biologist at the University of Bonn, Germany, and his associates. Barthlott and his group found that the lotus leaf, instead of having a slick, smooth surface, has billions of nanosized bumps—each smaller than a dirt particle—on its petals. These bumps keep virtually anything (even honey) from sticking, and allow falling raindrops to carry away microbes and other organic contaminants.

Biomimicry is contagious. The product development world (particularly the chemical industry) has taken strongly to the concept, and the number of companies researching or creating biomimetic products is increasing rapidly. The shift toward efficient, nontoxic solutions that do not create waste has been made possible because of our technology. The implications for the real estate industry are profound.

The Choice: Not Whether, but When

Smart development companies are benefiting from embracing green development. The elements that today define a development as green are beginning to be conventional practice. In the first half of 2004, approximately 5 percent of all commercial and institutional building projects were pursuing LEED ratings. In the future, standard development will exceed even the green features described in this book and will embrace strategies such as biophilia and biomimicry.

As the industry grows, more developers will say what Jonathan Rose says: "If you hire us, you get a green building." Jonathan Rose and Companies recently launched a real estate fund focused on properties located near transit. "It's not just the green building that matters," Rose comments. "It's the building's location and access to mass transit. More energy is consumed getting there than in operating the building."

Architect William McDonough notes, "Twenty years ago, there was very little research on the impact of building design on users. Today, the contingent liability is front and center." Green buildings don't reduce liability just by affording protection from the problems associated with conventional construction: green buildings reduce the risk that a developer will be left behind by the market.

Green building is spotlighted in the media almost daily. Feature stories in leading news outlets such as the *New York Times,* the *Wall Street Journal,* the *Washington Post, USA Today,* and on CNN, are educating the general market. A March 2004 article in *USA Today* reported, "Profit-driven developers and builders are going green because today's sustainable buildings are price-competitive with conventional ones." The general public's concern with health (particularly asthma) and with other environmental issues is on the rise. Green building is now on the radar of every building-industry trade group, and has commanded serious attention and program development within the government.

As developer Douglas Durst so aptly states, the choice is not whether, but when—when each developer will weave green into his or her own set of skills. Developers can offer the kind of places Jim Rouse described—places that are "productive for business and for the people, places that are infused with nature and stimulating to man's creative sense of beauty."

Notes

1. See http://www.calpers.com/whatsnew/press/1998/0413a.htm.

2. Ron Heckmann, "Real Estate Industry Switches On On-site Power as Hedge to California's Power Crisis," *Business Wire* press release, December 6, 2000.

3. Grant Hildebrand, *Origins of Architectural Pleasure* (Berkeley: University of California Press, 1999), pp. 10–11.

4. James Wines, *Green Architecture: The Art of Architecture in the Age of Ecology* (Los Angeles: Taschen, 2000), p. 16.

Green Building Resources

Rocky Mountain Institute

Books

Alexander, Christopher, et al. *A Pattern Language: Towns, Buildings, Construction.* Oxford, UK: Oxford University Press, 1997.
Illustrates a new approach to architecture, building, and planning that reflects the traditional ways in which people created their living environment.

Bachman, Leonard R. *Integrated Buildings: The Systems Basis of Architecture.* New York: Wiley, 2002.
Thirty in-depth case studies with explanation and analysis. Provides technical data as well as the architectural and cultural context of each building. A good text for advanced A&E courses.

Barnett, Dianna Lopez, with William D. Browning. *A Primer on Sustainable Building.* Snowmass, CO: Rocky Mountain Institute, 2004.
An overview for architects, builders, developers, students, and others interested in environmentally responsive homebuilding and small commercial development. Topics include site and habitat restoration, transportation integration, food-producing landscapes, energy-efficient design, materials selection, indoor air quality, and cost implications.

Barnett, Jonathan. *Redesigning Cities.* Chicago: APA Planners Press, 2004.
With a focus on redesigning existing cities, explains how design can reshape suburban growth patterns, revitalize older cities, and retrofit metropolitan areas where earlier development went wrong.

Battle, Guy, and Christopher McCarthy. *Sustainable Ecosystems and the Built Environment.* Indianapolis: Wiley Academy Press, 2001.
Offers guidelines for professional practice and highlights the potential of radical new technologies to increase and maintain the quality of life on this planet. Uses a compilation of published articles documenting projects from the authors' sustainable engineering firm to examine topics related to the effect of buildings on their immediate environment and on the global ecosystem.

Benyus, Janine M. *Biomimicry: Innovation Inspired by Nature.* New York: William Morrow & Company, Quill, 1997.
Countless examples from nature of how to design our products, our processes, and our lives. Benyus, a noted science writer, explains how this new science is transforming everything from harnessing energy to feeding the world.

Brand, Stewart. *How Buildings Learn.* New York: Viking Penguin, 1995.
How buildings adapt over time. Photos in case studies show the before and after condition of buildings. Describes design principles for creating an adaptable and flexible building.

Crosbie, Michael J. *Green Architecture: A Guide to Sustainable Design.* Washington, DC: American Institute of Architects Press, 1993.
The first comprehensive guide to the work of architects and designers representing the cutting edge of sustainable architecture, including a collection of environmentally sensitive buildings. Design strategies include building siting, daylighting, use of wastewater, energy-saving lighting and HVAC controls, indoor air, and thermally insulated building envelopes. Includes a list of resources for sustainable design.

Edwards, Brian. *Green Buildings Pay.* New York: E & FN Spon Press, 2003.
Now in its second printing, this book uses case studies of commercial and educational buildings to examine how different approaches to green design can produce more sustainable patterns of development.

Eley, Joanna, and Alexi Marmot. *Office Space Planning: Designs for Tomorrow's Workplace.* London: McGraw-Hill Professional, 2000.
A one-stop, on-the-job resource for modern office space planning and design. Considers optimal use of space; employee and task space needs; enclosed versus open-plan offices; furniture, fixtures, and lighting; climate and comfort; and much more. Includes case studies from major international companies. Covers topical issues such as design for productivity and technology, on-site parking, daycare centers, and gym facilities.

Eley, Joanna, and Alexi Marmot. *Understanding Offices: What Every Manager Needs to Know about Office Buildings.* London: Penguin Books, 1999.

Ewing, Reed. *Best Development Practices.* Chicago: APA Planners Press, 1996.
Through lessons learned from the "best" developments in Florida, this book compiles a set of guidelines for best development that focus on land use, transportation, environmental, and housing issues.

Farmer, John. *Green Shift: Changing Attitudes in Architecture to the Natural World, Second Edition.* Oxford, UK: Architectural Press, 1999.
An alternative reading of the development of modern architecture as seen from a green standpoint. Emphasizes changing attitudes toward nature and the emergence of green thinking.

Gissen, David, ed. *Big & Green: Toward Sustainable Architecture in the 21st Century.* Princeton, NJ: Princeton Architectural Press, 2002.
A hardbound version of the National Building Museum's exhibition catalog for *Big & Green,* this publication documents recent large-scale green developments such as skyscrapers, shopping complexes, and convention centers. Highlights 50 projects.

Gottfried, David. *Greed to Green: The Transformation of an Industry and a Life.* San Francisco: WorldBuild Publishing, 2004.
An intimate personal account of David Gottfried's transition from "greed" to "green," with an insider's look into the formation of USGBC and the development of the LEED rating system.

Hawken, Paul, Amory Lovins, and Hunter Lovins. *Natural Capitalism: Creating the Next Industrial Revolution.* New York: Little, Brown, 1999.
Citing hundreds of compelling stories from a wide array of sectors, shows how to realize benefits for today's shareholders and for future generations—and how, by firing the "unproductive tons, gallons, and kilowatt-hours," it is possible to keep the people who will foster the innovation that drives future improvement. Available from Rocky Mountain Institute (www.rmi.org, a Web site created by RMI as part of the book's release).

Hersey, George. *The Monumental Impulse: Architecture's Biological Roots.* Cambridge, MA: Massachusetts Institute of Technology, 1999.
Uses several juxtaposed examples to make the point that many structures are modeled after natural phenomenon.

Jones, David L. *Architecture and the Environment: Bioclimatic Building Design.* New York: Overlook Press, 1998.
A compilation of 44 case studies of architecture throughout the world built according to bioclimatic—or green—guidelines. Puts the green building movement into a historical context. Past, present, and future examples are accompanied by charts of building energy features, energy performance, and environmental health features.

Kibert, Charles J. *Sustainable Construction: Green Building Design and Delivery.* New York: Wiley, 2005.
A complete introduction to the design and construction of high-performance green buildings.

Langston, Craig. *Sustainable Practices in the Built Environment.* Newbury, UK: Butterworth Heinemann, 2001.
Deals with sustainability as it affects the construction industry, looking at the techniques and issues that designers, engineers, planners, and construction managers need to deal with in their day-to-day activities. Covers environmental impact assessment, cost-benefit analysis, design, energy regulation, and conservation.

McDonough, William, and Michael Braungart. *Cradle to Cradle: Remaking the Way We Make Things.* New York: North Point Press, 2002.
Argues that when making environmental decisions, we often settle for the lesser of two evils, although we should really demand a true solution that is better for the environment and the bottom line.

McHarg, Ian L. *Design with Nature.* New York: Wiley, 1992.
A thorough analysis of the relationship between the built environment and nature. One of the first books to advance planning concepts in environmental sensitivity.

McLennan, Jason. *The Philosophy of Sustainable Design.* Kansas City, MO: Ecotone Publishing LLC, 2004.
Intended as a starting point for anyone involved in the building industry to learn how he or she can build more responsibly.

Mendler, Sandra F., and William Odell, eds. *HOK Guidebook to Sustainable Design.* New York: Wiley, 2000.
Overview of sustainable design for commercial buildings, including detailed checklists for each stage of the design and construction process and case studies drawn from HOK's recent work.

Orr, David. *The Nature of Design: Ecology, Culture, and Human Intention.* Oxford, UK: Oxford University Press, 2002.
Although the environmental movement has often been accused of being overly negative and trying to stop "progress," this book is about starting things, specifically an ecological design revolution that changes how we provide food, shelter, energy, materials, and livelihood and how we deal with waste.

Rocky Mountain Institute. *Green Development: Integrating Ecology and Real Estate.* New York: Wiley, 1998.
A book that speaks your language if you are a developer, architect, planner, contractor, lender, or city official. Examines every stage of the development process in detail: market research, site planning, design, approvals, financing, construction, marketing, and occupancy. Based on 80 case studies drawn from Rocky Mountain Institute's worldwide research and consulting.

Romm, Joseph, and William D. Browning. *Greening the Building and the Bottom Line: Increasing Productivity through Energy-Efficient Design.* Snowmass, CO: Rocky Mountain Institute, 1994.
A succinct report that sends a powerful message to corporate managers: although energy-efficient design can pay for itself in reduced energy costs alone, it may also produce vastly greater benefits in higher productivity for workers, lower absenteeism, fewer errors, better quality, and increased retail sales. Eight documented case studies show that productivity gains from green design can be as high as 16 percent.

Rosenthal, Ed Cohen. *Eco-Industrial Strategies.* Ithaca, NY: Cornell University Publishing, 2003.
Focusing on ecoindustrial development, this book contains process analysis, a breakdown of responsibilities for stakeholders, and case studies. Pools resources and knowledge from a wide array of sources in the ecoindustrial field and the framing of the concept from multiple angles.

Smith, Peter F. *Architecture in a Climate of Change.* Oxford, UK: Architectural Press, 2001.
A primer focusing on sustainability. Provides students with a good grounding in the basic principles of sustainability and the future of sustainable technology. Also provides valuable insight into the relationship between the physical and cultural context of architecture. An argument for a new approach to architecture and for the profession to make minimum environmental demands.

Spiegel, Ross. *Green Building Materials.* New York: Wiley, 1999.
Helps guide architects and planners in selecting and specifying green building materials. Provides insight into both rudimentary environmental design guidelines and more involved methods such as life-cycle analysis.

Thompson, J. William, Kim Sorvig, and Craig D. Farnsworth. *Sustainable Landscape Construction.* Washington, DC: Island Press, 2000.
A reevaluation of the assumption that all built landscapes are environmentally sound, offering practical, professional alternatives for more sustainable landscape construction, design, and maintenance. An inspiring overview of important practices and concerns and packed with clear concepts and never-before-compiled resources on "green" landscape work.

Vale, Brenda, and Robert Vale. *Green Architecture: Design for an Energy-Conscious Future.* New York: Bulfinch Press & Little, Brown, 1991.
An overview of resource-conscious building and an exploration of the relationship between the built environment and such critical problems as power supply, waste and recycling, food production, and transportation.

Van der Ryn, Sim, and Stuart Cowan. *Ecological Design.* Washington, DC: Island Press, 1995.
A discussion of how making ecology the basis for design can reunite the living world and humanity. Ecological design, the marriage of nature and technology, can be applied at all levels of scale to create revolutionary forms of buildings, landscapes, cities, and technologies. Design principles are presented that can help build a more efficient, less toxic, healthier, and more sustainable world.

Wilson, Edward O. *Biophilia: The Human Bond with Other Species.* Cambridge, MA: Harvard University Press, 1984.
Wilson proposes a compelling idea that, although we have surrounded ourselves with a made environment intended to serve our uniquely human needs, "we are, in the fullest sense a biological species and will find little ultimate meaning apart from the remainder of life."

Wines, James. *Green Architecture.* Los Angeles: Taschen, 2000.
A collection of photos that highlight some of the most impressive ecodesigns of the past 30 years.

Wolley, Tom, and Sam Kimmins. *Green Building Handbook: A Companion Guide to Building Products and Their Impact on the Environment.* London: Spon Press, 2000.
A detailed reference for environmentally concerned purchasers of building products. Introduction outlines the case for sustainable building techniques; content addresses a comprehensive list of material choices for builders or owners.

Yeang, Ken. *The Green Skyscraper: The Basis for Designing Sustainable Intensive Buildings.* New York: Prestel Publishing, 2000.
Presents the idea that skyscrapers can be part of the solution to environmental problems rather than a source of the problem.

Yudelson, Jerry. *The Insider's Guide to Marketing Green Buildings.* Portland, OR: Green Building Marketing, 2004.
The strategies, data, tools, and techniques needed to succeed at marketing green buildings, products, and design and construction services.

Periodicals

Buildings—a monthly magazine for facilities decision makers. Its online newsletter, buildings.com, includes a special section on "greener facilities." Stamats Business Media, 615 Fifth Street, Cedar Rapids, IA 52401.

Environmental Building News—a monthly newsletter full of clear, concise information about environmental design and construction. Also offers the *GreenSpec® Directory,* the *EBN Archives,* a CD-ROM of back issue contents, and the online *BuildingGreen Suite,* which includes the entire archives of *EBN,* the *GreenSpec®* database (updated weekly), and a case study of high-performance buildings. BuildingGreen, Inc., 122 Birge Street, Suite 30, Brattleboro, VT 05301. Phone: 802-257-7300; fax: 802-257-7304; E-mail: info@buildinggreen.com; Web site: www.buildinggreen.com.

Environmental Design + Construction—A magazine that covers all aspects of environmentally sound building design and construction, including recycled building products, energy efficiency, alternative building sources, indoor air quality, and more. Business News Publishing, 2401 West Big Beaver Road, Suite 700, Troy, MI 48084. Phone: 248-244-1280; fax: 248-362-5103; E-mail: EnvDC@aol.com; Web site: www.edcmag.com.

Indoor Air Bulletin—A monthly publication focusing on indoor air quality but considering all aspects of indoor environment important to occupants' health, comfort, and productivity. Indoor Air Information Service, Inc., P.O. Box 8446, Santa Cruz, CA 95061-8446. Phone: 408-426-6522.

The Urban Ecologist—Quarterly newsletter published by an Oakland-based organization that focuses on sustainability and resource efficiency in urban areas. A compendium of actions undertaken by national and worldwide municipalities, institutions, and community groups. Urban Ecology, 405 14th Street, Suite 900, Oakland, CA 94612. Phone: 510-251-6330; fax: 510-251-2117; E-mail: urbanecology@urbanecology.com; Web site: www.urbanecology.org.

Urban Land. A monthly magazine distributed to ULI members that often includes articles on green buildings and sustainable development. ULI—the Urban Land Institute, 1025 Thomas Jefferson Street, N.W., Suite 500 West, Washington, D.C. 20007. Phone: 202-624-7000. Web site: www.uli.org.

Web Sites

Note: Many of these addresses are linked to other informative resource sites.

Advanced Building Technologies and Practices (www.advancedbuildings.org)—A building professional's guide to more than 90 environmentally appropriate technologies and practices. The site offers links to case studies and information sources with a helpful search function.

Big Green Discussion Group (www.biggreen.org)—An online E-mail forum focusing on implementing sustainable design and construction principles on large-scale projects.

BetterBricks.com (www.betterbricks.com)—A project of the Northwest Energy Efficiency Alliance, a nonprofit organization supported by electric utilities. Web site provides case studies, news, and other information.

Brownfieldnews (www.brownfield.com)—The official publication of the National Brownfield Association.

BuildingGreen Suite (www.buildinggreen.com)—A comprehensive online resource that includes up-to-date information on green building. Some information available free. Full access to *Environmental Building News* archives and the *GreenSpec* database of green building products requires a subscription.

Building Science Corporation (www.buildingscience.com)—Articles, technical reports, and other materials on moisture control, mold, durability, and energy-efficient construction.

Center for the Built Environment (www.cbe.berkeley.edu)—A collaborative of industry, government, and the University of California at Berkeley to create a dynamic place where people can share ideas for improving the design and operation of commercial buildings. Known for its extensive work on under-floor distribution systems for heating and cooling.

Center for Energy Efficiency and Renewable Technologies (www.cnt.org/)—A collaborative nonprofit organization that advocates power from sustainable sources. Has links to government agencies, nonprofit organizations, and industry.

Center for Resourceful Building Technology (www.crbt.org)—Lists resource-efficient building materials in a free, searchable database. Links to manufacturers' sites and related links.

Database of State Incentives for Renewable Energy (www.dsireusa.org)—Comprehensive source of information on state, local, utility, and selected federal incentives promoting renewable energy.

Ecosystem Valuation (www.ecosystemvaluation.org)—A Web site describing how economists value the beneficial ways that ecosystems affect people. Designed for noneconomists who need answers to questions about the benefits of ecosystem conservation, preservation, or restoration. Provides a clear, nontechnical explanation of ecosystem valuation concepts, methods, and applications.

E Design Online (sustainable.state.fl.us/fdi/edesign/index.html)—An electronic journal published by the Florida Design Initiative to promote best practices in building design, construction, operation, and delivery. Florida Design Initiative is also managing the Built Environment Center on the Florida Communities Network, which was originally designed to be a hub for all state agencies involved with the built environment.

EnviroLink Network (www.envirolink.org/)—A nonprofit organization that provides access to thousands of online environmental sources.

Environmental News Network (www.enn.com)—Through its Web site, helps to educate the public on major environmental issues and provides tools to help individuals take action in their own communities. The e-newsletters provide a free summary of environmental news articles. Stories updated throughout each day.

E Source (www.esource.com)—Provides member organizations with unbiased, independent analysis of retail energy markets, services, and technologies. Although the majority of the information is for members only, contains several overviews of recent articles and an upcoming energy events list.

Geothermal Heat Pump Consortium (www.geoexchange.org/index.htm)—Basic information about this method of heating and cooling as well as several geothermal heat pump success stories.

Greenbiz.com—Environmental practices for businesses. The toolbox for businesses offers checklists, assessments, and action plans for greening facilities: www.greenbiz.com/toolbox/.

Greenerbuildings—A resource for environmentally responsible building development, jointly sponsored by the U.S. Green Building Council and Greenbiz: www.greenerbuildings.com/index.cfm.

Green Building Pages (www.greenbuildingpages.com)—A sustainable building materials database and design tool for environmentally and socially responsible designers, builders, and clients.

Greening the Building Lifecycle (buildlca.rmit.edu.au)—A Web page with extensive links to other sites, programs, and relevant information.

Green Roofs (peck.ca/grhcc/)—The latest information about green roofs. See also www.roofmeadow.com; www.roofscapes.com, a commercial site; www.greengridroofs.com, another commercial site with good pictures; and www.greenroofs.com/, a good source for recent buildings and projects.

Green Seal (www.greenseal.org)—an independent, nonprofit organization that provides information on environmentally responsible products and services.

iGreenBuild.com (www.igreenbuild.com)—Provides articles about sustainable building design for commercial and residential buildings, news on upcoming events, and information about green products.

Institute for Market Transformation (www.imt.org)—Promotes energy efficiency and environmental protection in the United Sates and abroad. Considers both the technical and market-driven aspects of energy efficiency and lays out their findings in a link, Resources for Real Estate Professionals.

Natural Capitalism (www.naturalcapitalism.org)—A Web site created by RMI that allows one to read the book, buy the book, participate in online discussions, find out about the authors and where they are speaking, see what companies are doing to create natural capitalism, and more.

New Buildings Institute (www.newbuildings.org)—A 501(c)(3) not for profit public benefits corporation dedicated to making buildings better for people and the environment whose mission is to promote energy efficiency in buildings through policy development, research, guidelines, and codes.

Oikos (www.oikos.com)—A Web site devoted to serving professionals whose work promotes sustainable design and construction. Frequently updated, with many useful links to products, books, and information about green building.

Rocky Mountain Institute (www.rmi.org)—Includes answers to frequently asked questions, recent issues of RMI's newsletter, consulting services, "What's New" at RMI, and lists of RMI publications and how to order.

SD-ONLINE (sd-online.ewindows.eu.org/)—A comprehensive Web site provided by the European Foundation for the Improvement of Living and Working Conditions (a publicly funded autonomous agency of the European Union). Aimed at policy makers, employers, researchers, and trade union representatives interested in sustainable development. Contains more than 600 links and a set of tools available to subscribers.

Sustainable Sources (www.greenbuilder.com)—A comprehensive search engine that contains sections for sustainable building, green real estate, and a list of green building professionals. Fast and comprehensive search, drawing from hundreds of sources.

Whole Building Design Guide (www.wbdg.org)—A Web site sponsored by several government organizations that is dedicated to explaining the whole systems design approach on large projects. Especially helpful for work on federal facilities.

Windows—Web sites with information about windows: www.efficient-windows.org (Efficient Windows Collaborative); www.pge.com/window/what.html (what to look for in windows); windows.lbl.gov/technology/highly_insulating.htm (Window Technology); and windows.lbl.gov/pub/selectingwindows/window.pdf (Selecting Windows for Energy Efficiency).

Manuals

American Institute of Architects. *Environmental Resource Guide.* New York: Wiley.
A comprehensive guide to resources for environmental building that is updated three times a year. *Project reports* present case studies incorporating environmental concepts and technologies. *Material reports* detail the environmental aspects and life cycle of building materials.

E Source. *Technology Atlas* Series. Boulder, CO: Author.
Comprehensive technical documents from the premier source for up-to-date information about retail energy market trends, products, services, and technologies. Individual books in the series can be purchased from E Source, 1-800-376-8723 or www.esource.com, or as a set through the Iris Catalog at shop.oikos.com/catalog/.

Greening Federal Facilities. Information for those working on commercial and institutional projects. Organized into two-page sections about specific technologies. Available free on request from EREC at 1 800 363-3732 (ask for FEMP Document No. FE320). Also available online at www.eere.energy.gov/femp/ordermaterials.html or download it from www.eere.energy.gov/femp/techassist/green_fed_facilities.htmlGrowing.

Grumman, David L., ed. *ASHRAE GreenGuide.* Atlanta: ASHRAE, 2004.
Provides direction to designers of HVAC and refrigeration systems about how to participate effectively on design teams charged with producing green buildings. Contains green design techniques applicable to related technical disciplines, including plumbing and electrical and mechanical engineering.

Public Technology, Inc. *Sustainable Building Technical Manual.* Washington, DC: Public Technology, Inc., U.S. Green Building Council, and U.S. Department of Energy, 1996.
Addresses green building practices from predesign and site planning through operations and maintenance. Fifteen practitioners have provided sections of the book pertaining to their area of expertise. Includes checklists and a list of resources.

RSMeans. *Green Building: Project Planning and Cost Estimating.* Kingston, MA: Author, 2002.
A practical guide and helpful resource about green building for all members of the design team, including building owners, architects, engineers, contractors, and facility managers. Covers the gamut from green building concepts and material selection to cost estimating.

U.S. Green Building Council. *LEED Green Building Rating System.* Washington, DC: Author.
Extensive background information and guidance for meeting the requirements of USGBC's rating systems for new commercial buildings, existing building operations, commercial interiors, core and shell projects, homes, and neighborhood development. Reference Packages available for purchase online at www.usgbc.org.

Wilson, Alex, Nadav Malin, Tori Wiechers, and Larry Strain. *The GreenSpec Directory: Product Directory with Guideline Specifications,* Fifth Edition. Brattleboro, VT: BuildingGreen, 2005.
Information on more than 1,850 green building products in more than 250 categories, carefully screened by the editors of *Environmental Building News*, combined with guideline specification language and organized according to the 16-division CSI *MasterFormat* system. Includes product descriptions, environmental characteristics and considerations, and contact information with Internet addresses for manufacturers. Also provides information on selecting and installing environmentally preferable products. The directory can also be accessed as part of a subscription to BuildingGreen.com online tools. Available from 800-861-0954 or www.BuildingGreen.com.

Woolley, Tom, Sam Kimmins, Paul Harrison, and Rob Harrison, eds. *Green Building Handbook. Vols. 1 and 2: A Guide to Building Products and Their Impact on the Environment.* London: SPON Press, Taylor & Francis Group Press, 1997.
Compilation of the first 20 reports from the *Green Building Digest*, a British periodical that compares various products and materials for various applications. Available from +44 0 207 583 9855.

Yudelson, Jerry, and Alan Whitson. *365 Important Questions to Ask about Green Buildings.* Portland, OR: Corporate Realty Design and Management Institute, 2004.
A compilation of the most important questions for architects, designers, and building owners to ask and when to ask them. Questions presented chronologically based on the project timeline and cross referenced to their environmental significance.

CD-ROMs

ASTM International Standards on Sustainability in Buildings. A collection of 127 ASTM standards running the gamut from soil testing to plastic lumber to solar collection systems to indoor air quality. ASTM International, 610-832-9585; fax: 610-832-9555; www.astm.org.

EBN Archives, 8th Edition. This CD-ROM includes back issues of *Environmental Building News*, with full text-search capabilities as well as searching by relevance to LEED credits, and detailed bibliography of green building resources. Updated annually. BuildingGreen, Inc., 1-800-861-0954, ext.191; E-mail: info@buildinggreen.com; Web site: www.buildinggreen.com/ecommerce/index.jsp.

E Source Atlas Series CD-ROM. A comprehensive set of technical documents from the premier source for up-to-date information on retail energy market trends, products, services, and technologies. Updated annually. The Atlas series can be purchased individually from E Source, 1-800-376-8723, www.esource.com, or as a set through the Iris Catalog at shop.oikos.com/catalog/.

Green Building Advisor CD-ROM. An interactive CD-ROM featuring specific design strategies that can improve the environmental performance, cost-effectiveness, and healthiness of a building and its site, from predesign through occupancy. Draws from a database of more than 700 green building checklists. Each strategy linked to a detailed explanation, in-depth case studies, and sources of further information. Updated in 2002. 1-800-861-0954; www.BuildingGreen.com.

Green Developments CD-ROM. Researched and written by Rocky Mountain Institute with funding, contributions, and review from the U.S. Department of Energy's Office of Energy Efficiency and Renewable Energy, EPA, and the Florida House Foundation; programmed and produced by the Center for Renewable Energy and Sustainable Technology. Enables viewers to explore 100 individual green real estate development case studies and presents information rich in detail. Features photographs, plans, and drawings as well as video and audio clips of projects and their resources, Web links, financing, marketing, and approvals, and an introduction to green development and sustainable building.

Green Developments 2.0 CD-ROM. Version 2.0, a companion to *Green Developments,* features expanded information on each project as well as a larger screen display, added images, updated resources, and Web links. This new version contains more than 200 case studies of green buildings and projects from around the world. Developed in cooperation with and funded by the U.S. Department of Energy and the Kettering Family Foundation, with additional funding provided by the U.S. EPA. Produced for the Rocky Mountain Institute by Sunnywood Designs.

Tools

ArcGIS—A set of geographical and mapping software that can be scaled to the user's requirements. Package includes ArcInfo, ArcEditor, ArcView, and ArcReader. The combined GIS data supply an update, query, mapping, and analysis system that provides data management, analysis, data conversion, generalization, aggregation, overlays, buffer creation, and statistical calculation tools. Product information available from www.esri.com or 1-800-447-9778.

Community Viz—A tool designed for planning consultants and municipal planners to simulate development decisions, create the predicted long-term affects of each, and take a virtual walk through the resulting development. Outputs include solutions for land use and zoning, parks and recreation management, neighborhood planning, redevelopment strategies, wildfire risk assessment, forest management plans, habitat fragmentation evaluation, land evaluation and suitability analysis, and environmental visioning. Information available from info@communityviz.com or 303-442-8800.

Computational Fluid Dynamics—A computational modeling analysis for fluid flow problems. Models air movement, pressure gradients, and heat transfers while showing particulate movement in a space. Typically used for numerical analysis of laboratory spaces to develop strategies to improve laboratory safety, comfort, and efficiency to support scientific research. Also used extensively to prove the ability of natural ventilation strategies. Particularly useful for buoyancy-driven building designs where stack effects or airflows are important in the ventilation design. Program starts with a 3-D CAD model of the building and performs a system of equations that allows each specific cell of the volume to be determined based on the adjacent cells. See *Flovent* and *Phoenics* below for specific software packages.

Energy 10—A relatively user-friendly energy simulation package created by several of the United States's top national labs. Helps architects and building designers identify the key energy saving features of small commercial and residential projects. The software package has two distinct features: autobuild and rank. Autobuild uses the known information (location, square footage, number of stories, HVAC system, and building type) to create a baseline model with the corresponding energy use. It then displays the result of adding selected energy saving features as a comparison. The program's simple design allows for quick and accurate results that are ideal for smaller projects. Available from NREL's Web page at www.nrel.gov/buildings/energy10/.

EQUEST (DOE-2)—An unbiased computer program for determining building energy consumption. This modeling software has become the industry standard by allowing a design team to quickly determine building parameters that can improve energy performance while maintaining thermal comfort. Combines a user-friendly front end program called "eQUEST" with DOE-2, the sophisticated energy simulation package developed by the U.S. Department of Energy. Allows a designer or an architect to modify certain aspects of a building (design, HVAC components, insulation, for example) and compare the results through daily, monthly, and yearly charts. From the DOE-2 results, one can accurately estimate a building's energy consumption, interior conditions, and long-term operations cost, all of which can determine alternative options. The preferred choice for accurate energy calculations in large projects. Free and downloadable from www.doe2.com/equest/.

Flovent—A computational fluid dynamics package designed to calculate airflow, heat transfer, and contamination distribution for built environments. Uses techniques of computational fluid dynamics packaged in a form that addresses the needs of mechanical engineers involved in the design and optimization of ventilation systems. Information and ordering information available at www.flovent.com/.

Green Map Atlas—A free Web-based community tool that provides inspirational stories from around the world that promote sustainable communities. Includes a combination of 88 locally authored pages and 350 illustrated maps. Available from www.greenatlas.com.

The Green Pages, a 350-page interior specifier's guide to environmental products. Cross references interior design products (energy-efficient lighting fixtures with energy-efficient lamps, for example) and lists special environmental consultants, contractors, advocacy groups, books, and related services. Compares sustainable interior products with conventional counterparts and quantifies their impact on the environment. Identifies nontoxic products and lists nonoffgassing chemicals used in them. Backing up *Green Pages* are a product literature library, material safety data sheets, and research reports from the U.S. Department of Energy and EPA, among others. For more information, see greenpgs@idt.net.

LCADesign (Life Cycle Analysis of Design)—A "green calculator" for architects, who often have little idea of the environmental and health impacts of the materials they have chosen for their designs. Software plugs into many of the CAD programs commonly used by architects. Calculator uses information from online databases to calculate the amount of energy and water consumed in the production of these materials and estimates the quantities of chemicals emitted in their manufacture and the impact it will have on the ozone layer. Information available at www.cfd.rmit.edu.au/life_cycle_assessment/lcadesign.

LoopDA 1.0 (Loop Design and Analysis)—A simulation tool that enables building designers and engineers to determine the size of natural ventilation openings needed to provide desired airflow by allowing users to sketch rooms and vertical sections of a building, the location of natural ventilation openings (such as windows, doors, and ducts), and the paths the air should take through the building (for example, pressure loops). Designers can then estimate the size of the natural ventilation openings needed to control indoor air quality and thermal comfort using an engineering-based design process. More information available at www.bfrl.nist.gov/IAQanalysis/LOOPDAdesc.htm or 301-975-5860.

Lumen Micro—A PC-based simulation package with features to handle most building lighting needs. Combines electricity and daylighting with orientation and furniture placement to calculate the lighting predictions for all times and dates. Also includes tools for calculating the exterior lighting configuration that automatically changes with building design changes. Available from 720-891-0330.

Occupant Indoor Environmental Quality Survey—Postoccupancy evaluations of buildings can offer valuable lessons about how well the building serves occupants' needs. The Center for the Built Environment at the University of California at Berkeley has created a survey tool intended to facilitate this feedback. Currently in testing to create benchmarks, but a sample is available at www.cbe.berkeley.edu/RESEARCH/survey.htm.

PHOENICS—A computational fluid dynamics program that incorporates an easy-to-use, interactive, 3-D graphic user interface for both pre- and postprocessing, making computational fluid dynamics accessible for design and research engineers, regardless of their background and experience. Ordering information and free demo available from www.cham.co.uk/.

Radiance—A UNIX-based program widely acclaimed as the most accurate lighting design software. Contains many of the same features of other lighting packages but allows for greater flexibility in geometry and material simulation. Used by architects and engineers to determine the quality and quantity of light in the development of new lighting and daylighting technologies. Available from radsite.lbl.gov/radiance/HOME.html and for PC users under the name Adeline (www.ibp.fhg.de/wt/adeline/).

TAS—A suite of software products that simulate the dynamic thermal performance of buildings and their systems. A complete solution for the thermal simulation of new or existing buildings, allowing design professionals to compare alternative heating and cooling strategies and facade designs for comfort, equipment sizing, and energy demand. Further product information and ordering information available from www.edsl.net/.

WAVE—A water management software package that can be used to help reduce water consumption in a variety of settings in commercial offices, hotels, and schools. Free download available from www.epa.gov/owm/water-efficiency.

Other Resources

Business Guide to Waste Reduction and Recycling, Xerox Corporation: www.getf.org/file/toolmanager/O16F7319.pdf.

The Energy Source Directory. Lorane, OR: Iris Communications. Provides access to more than 500 products that help make homes energy efficient. Information about air barriers, heat recovery ventilators, sealants, heating and cooling equipment, solar water heaters, insulation materials, and more. Indexed by manufacturer, product name, and product category.

Facility Manager's Guide to Water Management. Practical advice and step-by-step implementation plans, plus tips on how workers can help conserve water: www.getf.org/file/toolmanager/O16F8609.pdf.

The Fifteen Best O&M Practices for Energy-Efficient Buildings, U.S. DOE: www.rebuild.org/attachments/solutioncenter/15bestOM.pdf.

GREENGUARD Environmental Institute's Greenguard certification program—A guide to third-party certified low emitting interior products and building materials: www.greenguard.org.

Kats, Greg, Leon Alevantis, Adam Berman, Evan Mills, and Jeff Perlman. *The Costs and Financial Benefits of Green Building.* Report to California's Sustainable Building Task Force, October 2003. A comprehensive report outlining the financial benefits related to green buildings, including lower O&M costs increases in workers' productivity and health.

Lovins, Amory B., Kyle Datta, Thomas Feiler, Karl R. Rábago, Joel N. Swisher PE, André Lehmann, and Ken Wicker *Small Is Profitable. The Hidden Economic Benefits of Making Electrical Resources the Right Size*. Snowmass, CO: Rocky Mountain Institute, 2002.
Describes 207 ways in which the size of devices that make, save, or store electricity affects their economic value. Finds that properly considering the economic benefits of "distributed" (decentralized) electrical resources typically raises their value by a large factor, often approximately tenfold, by improving system planning, utility construction and operation, and service quality, and avoiding societal costs.

Making the Business Case for High-Performance Buildings. Washington, DC: U.S. Green Building Council, with ULI—the Urban Land Institute and the Real Estate Roundtable.
Ten compelling reasons to "go green."

Thompson, George F., and Frederick R. Steiner, eds. *Ecological Design and Planning*. New York: Wiley, 1997.
Papers from an international symposium, "Landscape Architecture: Ecology and Design and Planning," Tempe, AZ, April 1993.

Watson, Donald. *Environmental Design Charrette Workbook*. Washington, DC: American Institute of Architects, 1996.
Highlights intensive design workshops dealing with energy efficiency, building technology, environmental approaches to landscaping, waste prevention and resource reclamation, and planning and cultural issues. Also contains guidelines for organizers and facilitators and a sample briefing booklet, plus advice from expert practitioners pondering the art of community dialogue.

ULI—the Urban Land Institute. Policy papers available from www.uli.org summarizing recent ULI forums on sustainable development and green buildings:
■ Corporate Location and Smart Growth. Washington, DC, April 8–9, 2002.
■ Green Buildings and Sustainable Development: Making the Business Case. Aspen, CO, August 24–25, 2003.
■ Sustainable Development and Green Building. Washington, DC, March 30, 2004.
■ Moving from Obstacles to Opportunities: Sustainable Buildings and Development. Madrid, Spain, June 11–12, 2004.

Organizations

American Council for an Energy-Efficient Economy (ACEEE)
1001 Connecticut Avenue, NW
Suite 801
Washington, DC 20036
Publications: 202-429-0063
Research and conferences: 202-429-8873
Fax: 202-429-2248
info@aceee.org; www.aceee.org
Publishes books and papers on industrial, commercial, and residential energy-efficiency.

American Institute of Architects
Committee on the Environment (COTE)
1735 New York Avenue, NW
Washington, DC 20006-5292
COTE Phone: 202-626-7482
COTE Fax: 202-626-7518
aiaonline@aiamail.aia.org or pia@aiamail.aia.org
www.aiaonline.com or e-architect.com/pia/cote/home.asp
The Committee on the Environment is a professional interest area of the AIA. COTE works to create sustainable buildings and communities by advancing, disseminating, and advocating environmental knowledge and values to the profession, industry, and the public.

American Society of Heating, Refrigerating and Air-Conditioning Engineers (ASHRAE)
1791 Tullie Circle, NE
Atlanta, Georgia 30329
Phone: 404-636-8400
Fax: 404-321-5478
ashrae@ashrae.org; www.ashrae.org
The preeminent professional organization for HVAC and refrigeration professionals. Its mission is to advance the arts and sciences of heating, ventilation, air conditioning, refrigeration and related human factors to solve the evolving needs of the public. Responsible for publishing numerous books and publications, including the monthly *ASHRAE Journal*. The "Green Guide" is intended to help HVAC and refrigeration designers in producing green buildings.

American Society of Interior Designers (ASID)
608 Massachusetts Avenue, NE
Washington, DC 20002-6006
Phone: 202-546-3480
www.asid.org
A nonprofit professional society representing the interests of interior designers and the interior design community. The organization's Sustainable Design Council oversees ASID's sustainable design strategic initiative and supervises its online Sustainable Design Information Center.

American Solar Energy Society, Inc. (ASES)
2400 Central Avenue
Suite G-1
Boulder, Colorado 80301
Phone: 303-443-3130
Fax: 303-443-3212
ases@ases.org; www.ases.org/
Disseminates and transfers research on practical uses of solar energy, wind power, and photovoltaics.

Building Environment and Thermal Envelope Council (BETEC)
National Institute of Building Sciences
1090 Vermont Avenue, NW
Suite 700
Washington, DC 20005
Phone: 202-289-7800
Fax: 202-289-1092
www.nibs.org/projbetec.html
Identifies and coordinates research and other programs on building envelope energy and the indoor environment.

Building Owners and Managers Association (BOMA) International
1201 New York Avenue, NW
Suite 300
Washington, DC 20005
Phone: 202-408-2662
Fax: 202-371-0181
The mission of BOMA International is to enhance the human, intellectual, and physical assets of the commercial real estate industry through advocacy, education, research, standards, and information.

Building Research Establishment (BRE)
Garston, Watford
WD25 9XX
England
Phone: 01923 664000
www.bre.co.uk
With a wide range of research focused on the built environment, BRE offers research-based consultancy, testing, and certification services to customers worldwide. The BRE environmental assessment method is a widely accepted measurement of the best practices in environmental design and management of offices, retail developments, industrial buildings, and homes.

Center for Green Building Research
Electric Power Research Institute/Lawrence Berkeley National
Laboratory
3412 Hillview Avenue
Palo Alto, California 94304
Phone: 800-313-3774 or 650-855-2121
askepri@epri.com
www.epri.com
The goals of the center are to advance understanding of the impacts
of green building specifications on energy use, internal environmental
quality, and occupants' health, comfort, and productivity, and to use
this advanced understanding to motivate improvements in the specifications for green buildings.

Center for Maximum Potential Building Systems, Inc.
8604 FM 969
Austin, Texas 78724
Phone: 512-928-4786
Fax: 512-926-4418
center@cmpbs.org
www.cmpbs.org
The center is a nonprofit ecological planning and design firm that works
with public entities, professional organizations, community groups, universities, and individuals in pursuit of sustainable development policies
and practices, ranging from individual buildings to entire regions.

Construction Materials Recycling Association (CMRA)
P.O. Box 122
Eola, Illinois 60519
Phone: 630-585-7530
Fax: 630-585-7593
CMRA provides information on new technologies and campaigns to
promote the acceptance and use of recycled construction materials,
including concrete, asphalt, wood, and gypsum.

Construction Specifications Institute
99 Canal Center Plaza
Suite 300
Alexandria, Virginia 22314
Phone: 800-689-2900 or 703-684-8436
This 17,000-member organization seeks to improve the process of
creating and sustaining the built environment through engaging all
disciplines of the building design and construction process.

CoreNet Global
260 Peachtree Street, NW
Suite 1500
Atlanta, Georgia 30303
Phone: 800-726-8111
www.corenetglobal.org
CoreNet Global is a 7,500-member professional association of corporate real estate executives that stresses sustainable design and
development in the organization's research and education efforts.

Green Building Initiative (GBI)
222 SW Columbia Street
Suite 1800
Portland, Oregon 97201
Phone: 877-GBI-GBI1
Fax: 503-961-8991
www.thegbi.org
GBI is a national organization to promote green building for builders,
architects, and others who want practical and affordable options for
creating environmentally friendly structures. Works closely with the
National Association of Homebuilders and local homebuilder associa-
tions; also addresses commercial buildings.

Green Roofs for Healthy Cities (GRHC)
177 Danforth Avenue
Suite 304
Toronto, Ontario M4K 1N2
Canada
Phone: 416-971-4494
Fax: 416-971-9844
www.greenroofs.org
GRHC North America is a nonprofit industry association consisting of
public and private organizations and individuals. The organization's
mission is to develop a market for green roof infrastructure products
and services in cities across North America.

Healthy Building Network (HBN)
Institute for Local Self-Reliance
927 15th Street, NW
Fourth Floor
Washington, DC 20005
Phone: 202-898-1610
Fax: 202-898-1612
www.healthybuilding.net
HBN is a national network of green building professionals, environmen-
tal and health activists, socially responsible investment advocates, and
others interested in promoting healthier building materials as a means
of improving public health and preserving the global environment.

Institute for Sustainable Futures (ISF)
National Innovation Centre
Australian Technology Park
Eveleigh NSW, Australia
Phone: +61 2 9209 4350
Fax: +61 2 9209 4351
isf@uts.edu.au
ISF was established by the University of Technology, Sydney in 1996
to work with industry, government, and the community to develop sus-
tainable futures through research, consultancy, and training.

International Facility Management Association (IFMA)
1 East Greenway Plaza
Suite 1100
Houston, Texas 77046
Phone: 713-623-4362
Fax: 713-623-6124
IFMA certifies facility managers, conducts research, provides educa-
tional programs, recognizes facility management degree and certificate
programs, and produces World Workplace, a facility management-
related conference and exposition.

International Interior Design Association (IIDA)
13-500 Merchandise Mart
Chicago, Illinois 60654
Phone: 312-467-1950 or 888-799-IIDA (4432) (continental United
States only)
Fax: 312-467-0779
IIDA is a professional networking and educational association com-
mitted to enhancing the quality of life through excellence in interior
design and advancing interior design through knowledge. The IIDA
Foundation is a not-for-profit philanthropic organization that works in
collaboration with IIDA. It offers the Sustainable Design Education
Fund to advance awareness and knowledge of sustainable design.

NATIONAL ASSOCIATION OF REALTORS® (NAR)
430 North Michigan Avenue
Chicago, Illinois 60611
Phone: 800-874-6500
NAR strives to be the collective force influencing and shaping the real estate industry. It seeks to be the leading advocate of the right to own, use, and transfer real property; the acknowledged leader in developing standards for efficient, effective, and ethical real estate business practices; and valued by highly skilled real estate professionals and viewed by them as crucial to their success.

National Resources Defense Council (NRDC)
40 West 20th Street
New York, New York 10011
Phone: 212-727-2700
Fax: 212-727-1773
nrdcinfor@nrdc.org
www.nrdc.org
A nonprofit organization dedicated to the defense of all Earth's natural resources, NRDC is a source for current news and information relating to environmental issues.

Rocky Mountain Institute (RMI)
1739 Snowmass Creek Road
Snowmass, Colorado 81654
Phone: 970-927-3851
outreach@rmi.org
www.rmi.org
A nonprofit organization that fosters the efficient and restorative use of natural, human, and other capital to make the world more secure, just, prosperous, and life sustaining by inspiring business, civil society, and government to design integrative solutions that create true wealth.

Royal Institute of Chartered Surveyors (RICS)
12 Great George Street
Parliament Square
London SW1P 3AD
England
Phone: +44 0870 333 1600
A worldwide property organization with more than 110,000 members, RICS is dedicated to promoting excellence and safeguarding public interest in all property-related matters.

Sustainable Buildings Industry Council
1112 16th Street, NW
Suite 240
Washington, DC 20036
Phone: 202-628-7400
Fax: 202-393-5043
SBIC@SBICouncil.org
www.sbicouncil.org
An organization committed to the design and construction of high-performance buildings through a systems approach.

Urban Ecology, Inc.
405 14th Street
Suite 900
Oakland, California 94612
Phone: 510-251-6330
Fax: 510-251-2117
urbanecology@urbanecology.org
www.urbanecology.org
Urban Ecology believes that vibrant, successful cities are not only possible but also necessary for the health of society and the planet. The organization plans and designs cities that sustain the people, natural resources, and economy necessary for everyone to thrive.

ULI the Urban Land Institute
1025 Thomas Jefferson Street, NW
Suite 500 West
Washington, DC 20007
Phone: 202-624-7000
Fax: 202-624-7140
www.uli.org
ULI–the Urban Land Institute is a nonprofit education and research institute supported by its members. Its mission is to provide responsible leadership in the use of land to enhance the total environment.

U.S. Green Building Council (USGBC)
1015 18th Street, NW
Suite 805
Washington, DC 20036
Phone: 202-828-7422
Fax: 202-828-5110
info@usgbc.org
www.usgbc.org
USGBC is a nonprofit trade association whose primary purpose is to promote green building policies, programs, and technologies. Membership is offered to manufacturers, utilities, building owners, real estate advisers, scientific and technical organizations, and nonprofit trade associations that support green building.

World Business Council for Sustainable Development (WBCSD)
4, Chemin de Conches
1231 Conches-Geneva
Switzerland
Phone: +41 (22) 839 3100
Fax: +41 (22) 839 3131
WBCSD is a coalition of 170 international companies united by a shared commitment to sustainable development through economic growth, ecological balance, and social progress. Members are drawn from more than 35 countries and 20 major industrial sectors. WBCSD's activities reflect the belief that the pursuit of sustainable development is good for business and business is good for sustainable development.

World Green Building Council (WGBC)
P.O. Box 6245
North Sydney, NSW 2060
Australia
Phone: +61 2 8907 0926
Fax: +61 2 9957 4016
che@worldgbc.org
worldgc.org
WGBC was formed in 1999 with the goal of coordinating and advancing the work of national green building organizations that support the development of standards, technologies, products, and projects.

U.S. Agencies and Organizations

Federal Network for Sustainability (FNS)
www.federalsustainability.org
FNS promotes cost-effective, energy- and resource-efficient operations across all branches of government. See http://www.federalsustainability.org/about/aboutfns.htm.

National Institute of Standards and Technologies (NIST)
Building for Environmental and Economic Sustainability (BEES)—green buildings decision support software developed by NIST to help select cost-effective, environmentally preferable building products: http://www.bfrl.nist.gov/oae/software/bees.html.

Office of the Federal Environmental Executive (OFEE)
www.ofee.gov.

U.S. Air Force
Sustainability Guide:
http://www.afcee.brooks.af.mil/dc/dcd/arch/rfg/index.html.

U.S. Army Corps of Engineers
Sustainability Web site: www.cecer.army.mil/sustdesign.

U.S. Department of Energy (DOE)
www.doe.gov
Greening federal facilities Web site: www.eere.energy.gov/femp.

■ The Building Technologies Program works closely with manufacturers and the building industry to research and develop technologies and practices for energy efficiency, publicizes energy- and money-saving opportunities to builders and consumers, and works with state and local regulatory groups to improve building codes and appliance standards. See http://www.eere.energy.gov/buildings.

■ The Building Toolbox (part of the Building Technologies Program) is an electronic resource offering specifics on planning and financing; choosing components; designing, building, and renovating; and operating and maintaining a green commercial building. See http://www.eere.energy.gov/buildings.

■ Commercial Buildings Energy Consumption Survey—Every four years, the U.S. DOE collects an array of data, from building size, location, and occupancy to the buildings' energy sources, consumption, and expenditures. Includes tables, reports on a variety of topics, and PDF downloads of individual responses to survey questions. See www.eia.doe.gov/emeu/cbecs/contents.html.

■ ENERGY STAR®—A government site offering a wide range of resources, from purchasing to do-it-yourself energy audits to ways to improve energy efficiency in buildings: www.energystar.gov.

■ ENERGY STAR's Delta estimator®—Tracks the progress of energy improvements: www.energystar.gov/index.cfm?c=delta.index.

■ Guidelines on Integrating Sustainable Design into Site Level Operations—includes information on how to receive Environmental Design Guide for Engineers (EDGE) software (http://www.pnl.gov/doesustainabledesign/index.html) and suggested green language for contractor letters of intent.

■ High-Performance Buildings Web site—an initiative of the DOE, this rich site provides a wide range of practical, hands-on information for those in the building and real estate industries, including a database of high-performance building projects and ongoing research: http://www.eere.energy.gov/buildings/highperformance/.

■ Office of Energy Efficiency and Renewable Energy (EERE): www.eere.energy.gov/building.html.

■ Smart Communities Network (www.sustainable.doe.gov)—A Web site offering information and services about how communities can adopt sustainable development as a strategy for well-being. Allows the user to read about other communities that have discovered the benefits of sustainable development, and locate technical and financial resources for planning and carrying out sustainable development. Conferences section provides a monthly calendar of events.

■ Sustainable Building Technical Manual—a technical guide for builders about sustainable building techniques. Published in 1996, the information could be a bit dated, but the manual offers good overall guidance. Cosponsored by U.S. DOE and EPA, the manual was written by numerous experts in the field. See http://www.sustainable.doe.gov/pdf/sbt.pdf.

U.S. Environmental Protection Agency
www.epa.gov
Green building Web site: www.epa.gov/greenbuilding.

■ EPA offers extensive guidance on this subject, including technical tools for use in commercial buildings, modeling analysis for ventilation systems and controls, and comprehensive IAQ data for schools and commercial facilities. The agency has also developed software to evaluate the ventilation and humidity control performance of energy recovery systems and to calculate their cost. See http://www.ofee.gov/b/appendix_e.pdf. For more information, see http://www.epa.gov/iaq/largebldgs/ibeam_page.htm, EPA's Indoor Air Quality Building Education and Assessment Model (I-BEAM) Web site.

■ Brownfields redevelopment—how to apply for a brownfields grant application and other redevelopment-related information: http://www.epa.gov/brownfields/.

■ Cleaning Products Pilot Project Web site identifies environmentally preferable cleaning products: www.epa.gov/opptintr/epp/cleaners/select/.

■ Comprehensive Procurement Guidelines—information on requirements related to federal purchasing of recycled products: www.epa/cpg.

■ Construction and Demolition Debris—what to do with construction debris in an environmentally responsible way: www.epa.gov/epaoswer/non-hw/debris.

■ Environmentally Preferable Purchasing (EPP) program: www.epa.gov/oppt/epp/index.htm.

■ National Environmental Compliance Assistance Clearinghouse—resources for the construction industry on compliance with various environmental regulations such as waste water management and stormwater pollution prevention management: http://cfpub.epa.gov/clearinghouse/index.cfm?TopicID=C:10:900:23:

■ WAVE water management software—free, downloadable software that can be used to help reduce water consumption in a variety of settings, including commercial offices, hotels, and schools: www.epa.gov/owm/water-efficiency.

U.S. General Services Administration
www.gsa.gov

Sustainability Web site: www.gsa.gov/sustainabledesign.

■ Environmental Products and Services Guide—published by the Federal Supply Service (FSS) of GSA and updated annually for use by all federal agencies. See http://www.gsa.gov/Portal/gsa/ep/contentView.do?P=FCOEE&contentId=9845&contentType=GSA_OVERVIEW.

■ Facilities Standards for the Public Buildings Service (P100)—published by GSA's Office of the Chief Architect: http://www.gsa.gov/Portal/gsa/ep/channelView.do?pageTypeId=8195&channelPage

■ Real Property Sustainable Development Guide—http://www.gsa.gov/gsa/cm_attachments/GSA_DOCUMENT/sus_dev_guide_R2O1X_0Z5RDZ-i34K-pR.pdf.

U.S. National Park Service
Sustainability Web site: www.nps.gov/dsc/dsngncnstr/gpsd/toc.html.

Index

Italic page numbers indicate figures, photos, and illustrations. **Bold** page numbers indicate feature boxes and case studies.